LIST THE BUGLE

Reminiscences of an Irish Soldier

LIST THE BUGLE

Reminiscences of an Irish Soldier

CORRAN PURDON

"And you will list the bugle
That blows in lands of morn"

A Shropshire Lad

A.E. Housman

GREYSTONE BOOKS
1993

To Patricia, my wife.

First published by
Greystone Books, Antrim, Northern Ireland, 1993

ISBN 1 870157 19 2

Cover: Rodney Miller Associates

Printed by W & G Baird Ltd., Antrim, Northern Ireland

CONTENTS

FOREWORD

By Field Marshal Sir Roland Gibbs, GCB, CBE, DSO, MC, HML.

'I am certainly not one of those who need to be prodded
In fact, if anything, I am a prod.'
Winston Churchill in the House of Commons, 11th November 1942.

I write this brief foreword as an old friend of Corran Purdon from Sandhurst Days.

With so many forebears, who had served others, as soldiers, and doctors in particular, it was foreseeable that Corran would follow suit. From the time he inherited and added to a formidable collection of lead soldiers it was inevitable that it was the Army that claimed him. The infantry and the Irish infantry at that was his choice.

This autobiography is an epic, particularly for those who believe in taking advantage of opportunities whenever they present themselves. Denied by his age active service with his Regiment in the early years of the war, Corran immediately saw how to shortcircuit this by joining the Commandos. And his story of the raid on St. Nazaire is gripping and a tribute to those élite troops.

That it should end in imprisonment for one so young and active could have been disastrous. His years as a POW, ending with two years in Colditz, must have eaten into his soul. But he survived unscathed: a credit to his innermost beliefs and the energy he put into his own escape attempts and the help he gave to those of others.

It was typical that before being sent home he joined the American troops who liberated Colditz in their subsequent actions. And he continued to pursue such enterprise after the war to make himself an expert in the small wars and internal security situations which faced the British Army, Palestine, the Canal Zone Egypt, Malaya, Cyprus, Borneo, Aden, the Radfan and the Oman - the list is long, and in several instances he sought active experience from his office chair whereas others would have been happy to have kept it warm.

The chapters on his command of his Regiment and of the Sultan's Armed Forces in Oman are the longest and the most fascinating. Corran is, after all, the born leader. The lessons for aspiring commanders are to be found in abundance - the iron hand in getting rid of the troublemakers in his Regiment and in a battalion of the Sultan's Armed Forces, followed by the kid glove of enthusiasm and humour which cemented the rest to him for evermore: his attention to detail: his ability to do everything asked of his juniors: his honesty and directness: his deep interest in the welfare of those under him: his wistful humour and his dynamic energy. The examples go on and on.

Perhaps the most remarkable theme which reappears endlessly through this book is his appreciation of his fellow men. Corran does not make enemies. It is not in his nature to do so. He does not hesitate to correct faults but he is really always looking for the best in the characters of others. And this is why they have always been happy to serve him to the best of their ability. 'You always feel braver after the Chief has been to see you,' wrote General O'Connor of General Wavell in the Desert War. And that is what officers and soldiers felt when Corran visited.

ACKNOWLEDGEMENTS

My grateful thanks are due to the following:

That distinguished soldier Field Marshal Sir Roland Gibbs, GCB, CBE, DSO, MC, who has remained my friend since we were Gentlemen Cadets together at pre-war Sandhurst, and who has written such a kind and generous Foreword. Major Frederick Myatt, MC, the military historian, who read the original manuscript and gave me much sound advice, as did Leo Marks. The late Brigadier Peter Thwaites, who read and commented on the chapters on Oman, and the late Sir Torquhil Matheson of Matheson Bt who gave me valuable advice as to content and layout, as did David Picton-Phillips. My deep thanks also to James Ruston, who read my book, made many helpful comments, had the manuscript re-typed and bound, and advised as to content and photographs. I am most grateful to Bryan McCabe, Marketing Director of Greystone Press for his encouragement, and his kindness in publishing this book, and to Richard Doherty, the well known Irish military historian, for reading and commenting on it, and for his valuable advice and edit. I thank Colonel Fergus MacKain-Bremner, OBE, for permission to reproduce the map of Dhofar, showing the operational layout when I left in April 1970.

I am grateful to my three children Patrick, Timothy and Angela for their never failing interest, and finally, my special thanks to Patricia my wife, for her patience and forbearance, unfailing and sustaining support, advice and encouragement, and for her belief in this book.

Corran Purdon

15 July 1993

Devizes Wiltshire

AUTHOR'S NOTE

Throughout my Army service I never kept a diary until my last appointment – GOC Near East Land Forces, from January 1975 to April 1976. I have had to rely on my memory, so I hope that the reader will bear with me if an event I say took place on 1 August 1967, for example, occurred on 31 July 1967. Similarly, my descriptions of actions, skirmishes and battles are as I personally saw and experienced them. Other participants who were perhaps a hundred yards away, may well have seen them from a slightly different angle.

Anything I have achieved has largely been made possible by those with whom I served, most of whom were mentioned in my original manuscript. However, some may have been edited out to keep this book to a reasonable size. I wish to pay tribute to all my comrades in arms, named or otherwise, whose friendship, help and support made my Army life so happy and fulfilled.

CHAPTER ONE

EARLY DAYS

My first memories are of glaring Indian sunlight on the whitewashed walls of my parents' bungalow at Wellington in the Nilghiri Hills, and of the silvery notes of the bugles of the Royal Irish Rifles from their nearby barracks.

My father, Major General W. Brooke Purdon, was at that time serving as a major on the staff of Major General Sir John Ponsonby, the General Officer Commanding Madras District.

I have the happiest memories of my Indian childhood; the kindness of the Indian servants, of my pony 'Papyrus' on which I would ride before breakfast accompanying my father around the polo ground of the Gymkhana Club close by. Events that could have been frightening were not, because my mother and father made them seem commonplace, such as the weird calling of jackals, hyenas and screech owls at night, and the time my father killed a cobra that had come into their bedroom while my mother was dressing for dinner. How calm she was, and how quick and decisive was my father. I felt no fear because of their behaviour.

We had various pets; dogs, a cheatle deer and, for a short time, a tiger cub who ended his days in Regent's Park Zoo.

I remember one evening being brought back in my push chair from a children's party by my father's bearer. We passed a shrine, and I still recall the great brazen face of some god that seemed to be alive, shimmering in flames, and how the bearer broke into a frightened run for the rest of the way home, and of a jackal slinking across our path.

The garden in our bungalow had three earthen tennis courts, and I remember the blaze of blossoms in the flower beds; vivid scarlets, yellows and purples in particular.

I had two friends of my own age, Bobby Smith, who was later to command the Gordon Highlanders in the Borneo Campaign, and Bill Bradley, who was to be commissioned into the Royal Inniskilling Fusiliers, and to join the Army Commandos, as I did, on their formation. He and I were both to take part in the Saint Nazaire Raid.

My father and mother had a dreadful tragedy while in India as my brother Pat, who was ten years older than me and at preparatory school in England, died of meningitis. There were no modern drugs in those days which could have saved him, no jet aircraft in which my parents could have flown to be at his bedside. Pat was so full of promise at work and at games and so greatly loved, not only by his family but by his teachers and school fellows. He is buried in Donaghadee Churchyard, Co. Down, and beside him lie my Aunt Gwen, who adored him, members of my mother's family, the Coates's; here also are interred my mother's ashes.

On a happier note, my sister Biddy was born in Wellington and I remember my father coming into where I was sleeping on a camp bed in his dressing room to waken me with the news of my sister's arrival.

I always wanted to be a soldier and one of my earliest photographs is of me seated on a camel, held by a stalwart sowar of the Royal Deccan Horse.

We went back to England by troopship, and then on to Ireland to live with my maternal grandfather William Coates in his house in Belfast while my father returned to India.

My father was a tremendously extrovert character, very good looking and an outstanding sportsman. His father, Richard Purdon, and his grandfather, were Belfast doctors. My father had been to school both at the Royal Belfast Academical Institute ('Inst') and at its rival school, the Methodist College Belfast, ('Methody'). He studied medicine at Queen's University, Belfast, played for them at rugby football, and in 1906, his last year there, he captained the first XV and won three caps for Ireland as a half-back against England, Scotland and Wales. He scored the winning try against England at Leicester. Against Wales he had his leg so badly broken that he was never able to play for Ireland again, although he did represent both the Army and Blackheath in 1907 before going out to Maymyo in Burma to be Regimental Medical Officer to the Royal Irish Rifles, who changed their name to the Royal Ulster Rifles in 1921.

He had won one of the first Military Crosses to be awarded in the Great War, as Regimental Medical Officer to the 2nd Bn. The York and Lancaster Regiment. An officer of that battalion told me that my father was fearless and that he used to go 'over the top' with our attacking infantry so that he could tend the wounded as they fell. Apart from the usual leaves to Britain, my father served on the Western Front throughout the entire war, taking part in many major battles; the Retreat from Mons, the Aisne,

Ypres, Passchendaele and the Somme. By the end of the war he was a temporary Lieutenant Colonel with, in addition to his Military Cross, the Distinguished Service Order and three Mentions in Despatches, having commanded a Field Ambulance, and later, in the Army of Occupation, a convalescent depot.

I reproduce from one of his obituaries:

'He was completely fearless, and I cannot forbear to quote from a letter lately received from Colonel Rutherford who describes how he (Purdon) although a medical officer, was selected as being the most suitable to perform one of the most hazardous duties in the Second Battle of Ypres. He writes, 'In all his career I remember him best as Town Major of Ypres in 1915. The General Officer Commanding, Sir John Weir, told his Deputy Director of Medical Services, Harry Thompson, that he could not find an officer to stick out that arduous job for more than a few weeks. Thompson said at once, 'I think I have an officer who can stick anything, Brooke Purdon.' And so Purdon assumed duty in the ruins of Ypres and controlled all traffic through the shell-torn city by night and walked about dodging shells by day. There is no doubt that in any branch of the Army he would have risen to the very top.'

After the war my father served in the south of Ireland in Co. Cork during the Sinn Fein 'Troubles', and was awarded the OBE. Whether it was because he was a well-known Irish rugby international or because his driver was a 'Sinn Feiner', or both, my father established a rapport that resulted in sanity and saving of life on both sides when other British officers were being murdered. It was during this time, on 4 May 1921, that I was born at Rushbrooke, Co. Cork.

My father told me of several experiences he had during the 'Troubles'. On one occasion, after dining in Mess, he came out on to the road with several other officers, en route for their quarters. Seeing it was a new moon that night, my father stopped to follow an old Irish tradition and bow to the new moon three times, turning round after each bow. 'Come on, you superstitious Irishman,' cried out one of them as they continued on their way to their sleeping quarters, leaving my father to carry out his obeisances. My father hurried after them, when there was a sudden burst of fire and they were shot down ahead of him.

On another occasion a friend came to my father's quarters to say his wife was in labour and was there a midwife? My father, who was in bed with a severe go of 'flu and a high temperature, got out of bed, put on a great-coat and scarf over his pyjamas, and a pair of Wellington boots, and set off to look for one in Queenstown. On the way he was halted by a patrol of Cameronians. 'Halt! Who goes there?' 'Major Brooke Purdon, RAMC, looking for a midwife.' On he went and was halted again, this time by a patrol of Sinn Feiners, 'Who are you? What is your business?' 'Major Brooke Purdon, RAMC. I'm looking for a midwife for an officer's wife.' 'Try Mrs O'Carroll at number 10, Major.' 'Many thanks, I will,' and on my father went, and knocked at the door.

The midwife said she was too scared to venture out and despite my father's cajolings refused to leave her home. My father retraced his steps and was stopped by the same Sinn Fein patrol. 'Is the midwife coming, Major?' 'No, she is too frightened.' So my father went into his quarters to look at a list of other possible midwives. While he was upstairs doing this he heard a commotion outside his house, followed by knocking at the door. Looking from an upper floor window he could see a group of people. 'Is that Major Purdon?' 'It is.' 'We've brought you a midwife, Major.' My mother went downstairs to find it was the Sinn Fein patrol, and on being joined by my father, both thanked the midwife for coming after all. 'I had no choice,' snorted the midwife, 'sure these fellas came for me and said I had to come and deliver the baby the British officer's wife was going to have!'

After Ireland he served in Madras District, where I began this story.

His service over in India, my father became Assistant Director of Hygiene at the War Office in London from 1930 to 1934, when he was awarded the brevet rank of Colonel. He and my mother spent the next two years in Egypt where they were stationed in Cairo, after which they returned to London, as my father had been appointed Professor of Hygiene at the Royal Army Medical College, Millbank. In 1938 he was promoted Major General and appointed Commandant and Director of Studies there.

Shortly before Dunkirk he was made Director of Medical Services, Lines of Communication of the British Expeditionary Force, and given the task of getting the Medical Services back to the United Kingdom. He got a large part out through Saint Nazaire, where he missed sailing home in the ill-fated *Lancastria* and returned to England with his staff in a ship packed with troops, who included my future brother-in-law, Colán MacArthur. When the vessel reached Portsmouth, the authorities refused to disembark the soldiers and said that only my father and his staff could land. He refused to leave the men and went with them to Tilbury, the voyage lasting nineteen days! He then went up to London with them all; where the entire body of soldiers lined up on Vauxhall station platform and cheered him. For his exploits the French government decorated him with the Legion of Honour and the Medaille Militaire en Vermeil du Service de Santé Militaire.

After serving as Director of Medical Services in Western Command my father reached retiring age. He then ran a hospital in Liverpool during the city's blitz, after which he took over Queen Mary's Hospital for the limbless in Roehampton. Here he was blown off his feet and injured during an air raid, but believing that his place was with limbless patients in time of danger, even when he was incapacitated by his injuries, he would go around the wards in an electric wheelchair during the bombing and the V1 and V2 raids.

'It was in the spring of 1946,' I quote from his obituary in *The Times*, 'that he accepted the urgent representations of Sir Basil Brooke, the Ulster Premier, to succeed to the post of Northern Ireland Government Agent in London on the retirement of Sir Ernest Cooper as honorary director of Ulster Information Services in the capital. His intense loyalty to his native province, his knowledge of its people, its industries and their problems, all combined to make him the ideal representative. He was as successful in his administrative as in his social duties, assiduous, accessible, a great friend of the Ulster Association and Club and as a former international, President of the London Irish Rugby Football Club. In London, Brooke Purdon served Ulster people regardless of religion and politics.'

My father died in my mother's arms whilst in this appointment, during which time my family, my sister and I were in Egypt. My mother died in 1978. I adored my parents and still miss them. After my father died, my sister, Biddy, married Colán MacArthur, son of Lieutenant General Sir William MacArthur, a close friend of my father. Colán, having soldiered in France in 1940, served in the 1st Airborne Division at Nijmegen, ending a distinguished business career as a director of the Rank Organisation. They now live in Marble Hill in lovely Co. Donegal.

My grandfather, Dr Richard Purdon, was one of a family of seventeen children so, as can be imagined, I am related to a lot of people in my native land! My grandmother was a Miss Corran from Liverpool, hence my Christian name - in Gaelic 'Corran' means a *sickle*. She was half-Welsh and I imagine this is why I feel such an affinity for both Welsh people and 'Scouses'! Her father was a sea captain who traded on the West Coast of Africa and I have a silver salver presented to him by King Pepple of Bonny River.

My family had a house in Donaghadee, the delightful little seaside town in Co. Down in whose development my de Lacherois ancestors played a major part. My uncle, Charlie Purdon, later to be lost in the S.S. *Downshire*, climbed to the top of the lighthouse up the outside, and my father rode a bicycle off the end of the pier nearby, both for bets!

As children they used to go to Donaghadee by themselves on occasions, and my father told me that they would use every plate and saucer in the house, then turn them upside down and use them again rather than wash up! When my grandparents were due to descend on them all the household crockery was washed up in the bath! My father's younger brother, Uncle Dick, had poor health and emigrated to Vancouver in Canada. He had served in the North Irish Horse. His son, Flight Lieutenant Richard Purdon, a gallant Typhoon pilot in the Royal Canadian Air Force, was killed in action during the Normandy Campaign. One daughter, Mary Siddall, lives in California, and the other, Mrs Felicite shannon, in Comber, Co. Down.

My father had two sisters; Aunt Nell, who married Captain Alexander Campbell CIE, DSO, Royal Indian Marine, and Aunt Gwen, who married Joe Shannon whom she met when she was a VAD and had nursed him, a badly wounded Royal Inniskilling Fusilier Subaltern, on his return from the War. My father always used to say that Uncle Joe had tried to take on the entire German Army singlehanded! Aunt Nell had two sons and a daughter. The eldest son, Alec, is the well-known Vice President of the Kennel Club, Brigadier A.P. Campbell, OBE. His brother, Michael, was a Major in the Royal Artillery during the War, after which he and his wife lived for some time in Kenya. Their sister, my cousin Helen Friend, was recently widowed. She and her two married sons live in Australia.

The Purdons came to Ireland in 1540 and were granted land in Co. Louth and in Co. Westmeath. An ancestor Sir Nicholas Purdon, of Baltimore, was knighted on the field of Knockranos when Lord Inchiquin defeated Lord Taaffe's army in 1647. My cousin, Captain Denis Purdon, late Rifle Brigade, lives in the family seat, Lisnabin, Killucan, Co. Westmeath. My branch of the family moved to the north of Ireland in about 1820 when my ancestor Henry Purdon was made Staff Surgeon for Ulster and bought a property in Belfast. There he married the beautiful Anne de Lacherois, from where our association with Donaghadee began.

The family soldiered in the Rifle Brigade, the Guards, the Gunners; some were Army surgeons, while others served in Irish regiments - the Royal Inniskilling Fusiliers, Royal Irish Regiment, Connaught Rangers, Leinster Regiment, and Royal Ulster Rifles. My younger son, Tim, currently commanding 1st Battalion Welsh Guards, is continuing the Service tradition. Colonel Sir Edward Purdon made a name for himself in one of the earlier Ashanti wars, where his timely use of a troop of Congreve rockets won the decisive battle of that particular campaign at Dodowa near Accra.

The Purdons are reputed to have their own Banshee, that keens when one of the family is about to die, and I remember how, when the Banshee was reputed to have been heard, telegrams were sent to all members of the family to see if they were all right.

My mother was a saint and a very beautiful woman. Her father, who was a Coates from Herefordshire, had moved to Ireland where he met and

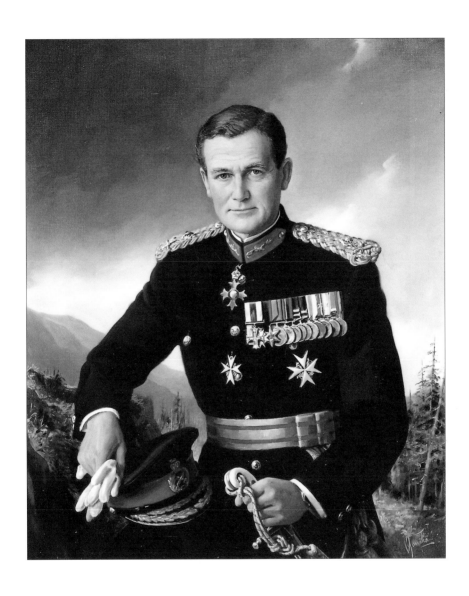

The author: Major General Corran Purdon

My mother, Myrtle, 1904

My father, Brooke Purdon, pictured at Buckingham Palace
having been invested with the DSO and MC

A regular little workman; the author, August 1926 (India)

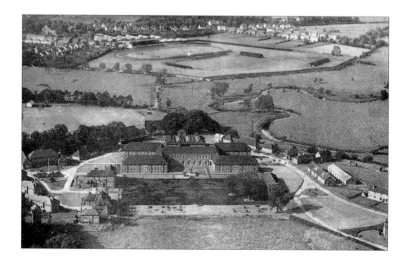

St Patrick's Barracks, Ballymena, the regimental depot
of The Royal Ulster Rifles

married my maternal grandmother, a Miss Ward, whose ancestors lived at Kilmanahan Castle, Co. Waterford. She was descended on her mother's side from the O'Cahan's, ancient Princes of Limavady and the Roe. Ireland is full of ghost stores and legends and my mother's family had a spectral coach and horses with a headless coachman, which foretold the death of anyone who, looking out when it was heard, saw the headless coachman turn towards them. My mother heard the wheels on the gravel outside the castle but did not look out lest she was noted by the coachman!

My grandfather, William Coates, had a large house in Belfast. His wife, my grandmother who used frequently to be taken for Queen Alexandra, died early and their elder daughter, Aunt Molly, virtually acted as a mother to the rest of the children. My mother had a terrific sense of humour and was full of tales of her childhood.

The children had two pet monkeys and one day they gave them a bath and put them in an oven to dry. Before they could warn her, the cook opened it. Out flew the monkeys and bit the woman, who gave immediate notice and left, followed next day by the monkeys, who were given by my grandfather to the Belfast Zoo!

There seem to have been some real characters in Belfast at that time. There were two brothers who shared a house but were not on speaking terms. They went for walks at the same time, but one behind the other - as the local people said 'in tandem'! Then there was the family that hated callers so always wore their hats in the house. If anyone called, they would answer the door, but always looking as if about to go out!

Another family who also hated callers used to hide if anyone came to the house, and my mother remembered being made to lie up against the wall under the windows when the door knocker sounded!

My mother's sister, Aunt Molly, married the Reverend Clifford Wall and lived most of her married life in Kelmarsh Rectory in Northamptonshire. Her two sons, my cousins Richard and Denis, served in the last war. Richard ended up as a Lieutenant Colonel in the Royal Engineers with an OBE and the Order of Orange Nassau, having taken part in the Allied Landings in North Africa, Sicily, Italy and Normandy. Denis was a Flight Lieutenant in the Royal Air Force and served in France and Italy.

My mother's two brothers, Charters and Hojel, served in the Great War. Uncle Charters served in the Royal Field Artillery and won the Military Cross, while Uncle Hojel served on the Western Front with the Canadians. Uncle Charters served again in the Second World War, this time as a Squadron Leader in the Royal Air Force.

My father's greatest friend was my godfather, Uncle Billy Tyrell. Like my father he became very well known in his native Ulster. Uncle Billy and my father got up to the most amusing escapades and were always pulling each other's legs. Uncle Billy was not only an Irish rugby international but he represented Ireland at four other sports. He was amazingly tough and fit, and became Air Vice Marshal Sir W. Tyrell, KBE, DSO, MC.

My father told me of how, in thick snow, on the day he was about to take an all-important oral medicine examination at Queen's University Belfast, he saw walking about ten yards in front of him the imposing, top-hatted figure of the professor who was to test him. Suddenly Uncle Billy appeared, bent and made a snowball with which he knocked off the professor's tall hat. He then dashed up with the hat to the great man, brushing off the snow and saying, 'For shame, Brooke Purdon, for shame!' It says a lot for the professor that my father passed his exam!

Another time my father somehow managed to buy off all the taxis at Buckingham Palace in the 1930s on the occasion of a Levée given by HM King George V. This meant that my godfather, by then an Air Vice Marshal, had to walk the whole way from the Palace, in full dress, via Green Park, down Piccadilly to his club. He was more upset when he received an anonymous letter (written by my father!) which he showed indignantly to my father. The letter accused him of becoming so vain at his exalted rank that he 'had been seen peacocking down Piccadilly in full fig'!

After my father returned from India he commanded the Military Hospital at Holywood, Co. Down and we lived in nearby Craigavad. Then in 1930, when he was posted to the War Office, we lived in Wimbledon and I went to preparatory school at Rokeby as a day boy. I loved Rokeby: it was a very happy school run by Mr Olive and Mr Battersby and I learnt a lot there, and was encouraged and taught to play rugby, soccer and cricket and to take part in athletics.

When my parents went to Egypt I went to a preparatory school, Cabin Hill, near Belfast, because my father wished me to be brought up as an Irishman. I spent a year there and then went to Campbell College, the well-known Irish public school.

While my parents were abroad I spent my holidays, apart from our summer holiday in Egypt, with my father's sister, Aunt Gwen and Uncle Joe, at Ardee, Co. Louth. It was an idyllic time as I had a pony and used to hunt with three neighbouring packs, the Louth, the Royal Meath (both foxhounds) and the Dundalk Harriers. I also learnt to shoot and fish and generally to love country life. In those days you were allowed to collect birds eggs, but never to take more than one egg from a nest. I had a large collection of eggs and in the course of finding their nests I learnt an enormous amount about birds.

In the summer holidays in southern Ireland there was always something doing. All the big houses had tennis courts and there seemed to be tennis parties every afternoon at such places at Darver Castle, owned by Colonel Brabazon Booth who had served with my father, at Stameen, home of Colonel Cairns, whose daughter Anne is married to my cousin Denis Purdon, and at Milestown, home of another Anglo-Irish Army family, the Barrows. We used to have bathing parties at the nearby seaside at Annagassan, where Vera Henry had railway carriages and a caravan, and at Baltray where there was a splendid golf course.

At these gatherings there would be sons of the various families on leave from Sandhurst and Woolwich ('the Shop'), and from time to time a subaltern home from the North West Frontier of India or from Palestine. I used to listen avidly to their tales of life at the Royal Military College and the Royal Military Academy, and of active service abroad, and long for the day when I, too, could be a soldier. I was determined to be a soldier, and used to read all the books of that era extolling the manly virtues and the British Empire. Far from exploiting it, as modern day little Englanders would have our youth believe, men and women were proud to devote their lives to serving its peoples abroad.

Every 24 May was Empire Day, and at Campbell College the OTC led by the Pipe Band would march into the quadrangle in front of the old, red brick school buildings, outside which the rest of the school would be assembled. The Union Flag would be hoisted to the top of the flagstaff and three cheers would be given for the King Emperor after the National Anthem.

By the end of my school days I was in the Army Class, a member of various school teams, a sergeant in the Pipe Band and a platoon commander. My Irish education made such a difference to me when I joined my Regiment (and my ability to play the bagpipes was another asset!). To satisfy my ambition I worked hard at school to prepare myself for the Army Exam. In those days there were no Regular Commission Boards. Candidates sat written examinations in various subjects, after which they attended an Interview Board. If I remember rightly, this was at Burlington House and consisted of a civil servant, a headmaster and senior officers of the Services.

When my turn came I was questioned as to my scholastic record, what school teams I was on, my interests and any Service connections. I found it a bit awe-inspiring, but they all seemed fair-minded and kind.

I had a friend with me, Melville Leggett, Captain of Boxing at my school, who stayed with me at Commandant's House, Millbank and I remember my father inspecting us both before we started off for our interviews and how he ensured that we wore dark suits and bowler hats. We both passed, Melville into 'the Shop' to become a Gunner, and I into Sandhurst to be trained for my heart's desire, which was to be an infantryman.

I had taken the Army Examination in 1939 and that summer, whilst we were fishing for trout on Lough Currane, Co. Kerry, we heard that I had passed into Sandhurst. I remember my father saying to my mother, 'There's only one Regiment for the boy, the Royal Ulster Rifles. I'll speak to Jimmy Cooke-Collis and see if they have a vacancy.' (General Sir James Cooke-Collis was one of the Regiment's most distinguished officers at that time.)

Before going to Sandhurst I packed away my collection of lead soldiers which had been such a joy to me as a boy. When my brother Pat died I had inherited about a thousand or more lead soldiers and sailors from him. I trebled this amount, having saved my weekly pocket money so that I could buy boxes of Britain's Soldiers; eight gleaming, painted figures in a long, flat box. They cost 2 shillings and 6 pence. Nowadays you would be fortunate to buy such a box for £40! I used to walk to and from school at Rokeby to save the bus fares to buy still more soldiers, and eventually I had several thousand of them to arrange in their many regiments, in fighting and ceremonial order. I had been allowed to use the floors of two box-rooms in Aunt Gwen's house in Ardee as parade grounds for them, but now I carefully put them away into several old fashioned, hoop-backed, iron-ringed trunks. Alas, they all want up in the London Blitz.

Now I was going to learn how to lead real soldiers as a Gentleman Cadet at the Royal Military College, Sandhurst.

CHAPTER TWO

FROM SANDHURST TO THE RIFLES I.T.C.

In July 1939, escorted by my father, I reported to the Royal Military College, Sandhurst, where I was greeted by a seemingly most helpful, friendly and attentive Cadet Corporal, dressed in 'blues'. My father, who was carrying out an inspection in Aldershot and was therefore in general's uniform, dropped me and my kit in front of the Old Building, where I was joining No. 5 Company ('Lovely Five' as it was known).

I had thought what a charming chap the Cadet Corporal was. However, my father had hardly departed when a marked change took place and I was made to feel like a new boy going to school for the first time!

'Do up ALL your buttons. Put the flaps OUTSIDE your jacket pockets. You may ONLY use THAT door!' etc.

In fact I loved my all too short time at Sandhurst. The NCO Instructors were outstanding. Naturally the Guards took us for drill, which I enjoyed. Line Regiment NCOs taught us weapon training and other infantry skills, and NCOs from various arms and services taught us riding (discontinued after war was declared), vehicle maintenance, field engineering, etc. They were the cream of their regiments and corps.

In those days the Army Physical Training Corps instructors seemed rather 'harder' on people than they are now. I have always enjoyed P.T., but they used to give us the most terrific 'benders' at the 'P.T. Palace', as the large gymnasium was called. I have memories of endless press-ups, and double marking time ('Knees UP, UP, UP!!') in dreadful long, blue serge P.T. 'shorts' that used to chafe the backs of our knees.

Everything was split-second timing and we learnt to change from one sort of uniform and dress to a totally different outfit in an incredibly short

11

time. We rode everywhere on 'Bog-wheels', and did bicycle drill. We paraded on the Square to ride to the Gymnasium wearing brown, highly polished shoes, blue woollen stockings, white flannel trousers under which we wore our long, blue serge P.T. 'shorts'. We had red and white striped Sandhurst 'Square' scarves round our necks, red and white striped blazers with polished brass buttons bearing the Sandhurst crest, and red and white striped pillbox hats worn over the left eye, held in place by a black elastic strap.

'Parade, parade 'Shun! By half sections left, LEFT! Prepare to mount, MOUNT!' and we swung off the near side pedals onto the saddles of our bicycles to ride away in file to the 'P.T. Palace', where we changed into P.T. kit. In those days P.T. in the Army was not so enlightened and enjoyable as it has become now, although it was certainly effective, even then, for enhancing our strength and agility. Officers taught us such subjects as Tactics, Military Law and Administration.

Our Commandant was Major General (afterwards Lieut. Gen. Sir) Ralph Eastwood, KCB, DSO, MC late Rifle Brigade, and the Adjutant was Captain (later Major General) E.H. Goulburn, DSO, a Grenadier. We saw quite a lot of the Adjutant. His manner was gruff and disapproving, his appearance immaculate. His field boots were like brown glass so highly polished were they, and his bushy moustache grew fiercely out horizontally, parallel to the ground.

I grew to enjoy College parades as our expertise increased. We drilled to the RMC Band which we were told was the smallest regular unit in the British Army. It was an excellent band and it was a pleasure to drill to its music. It is sad that it was disbanded, owing to the seemingly endless Defence cuts, in the 1970s.

The old Duke of Connaught was a fairly frequent visitor to Sandhurst at that time and I remember the rhythmic clack of rifles as we presented arms to him. One day he came seated as usual in the back of a large black car and was driven down to what were then called the Car Maintenance Workshops, outside where my term in 5 Company was being taught to ride motor-cycles for the very first time.

When the Duke arrived we were riding slowly and rather unsteadily in a circle, some of us still finding it a little hard to remember which hand controlled the throttle and which the brake.

Just after the great man had been driven off, one cadet applied throttle instead of brake and in an effort to remain on his heavy motorbike left the circle, shot onto the road adjoining our practice area and disappeared in the direction of the Ranges. Unable to stop he eventually found himself hurtling along a track beside the rifle range when, to his horror, he saw H.R.H. Field Marshal The Duke of Connaught's car approaching him on that same narrow track! The Cadet was still determined not to fall off, and, unable to stop, and in desperation to remain on the tiny space between car and boundary ditch, managed somehow to kneel on the seat with one leg stretched out behind him. In this position he flashed past the Royal car, before wobbling at last into a five-foot ditch, there to lie upside down beneath the weight of his motorbike, whence he was eventually extricated. The Duke who had not seen the crash, is reported to have commented unfavourably on 'Gentlemen Cadets who show off by trick riding!'

During the afternoons a wide variety of sporting activities was open to us, according to the time of year - cricket, tennis, squash, hockey, rugger and soccer. There was a pack of beagles, which I used to whip in and help exercise, as well as fencing and playing rugger and squash.

In the evenings we would change into 'blues', blue tunic with button-up high collar, Mess Wellingtons and blue mess overalls, and after a couple more hours of classroom work would dine in our Mess. On occasions there would be Guest Nights when the officers would be invited to join the Gentlemen Cadets, and it was then that we would see the great variety of mess kits worn in the pre-war British and Indian Armies.

Our Company Commander, Major Jerrard, was in the Guides, my father-in-law's Regiment. The Guides wore khaki mess kit, which contrasted with the scarlet of the Guards and Line Regiments, the dark green of the Rifle Regiments and the blue of the other Arms and Administrative Corps, each with their distinctive coloured facings.

These occasions made joining our own Regiments seem nearer. My platoon Commander was the future Major General Henry Alexander of the Cameronians. But it was really our Guards Drill NCOs who impressed us most as they seemed to be with us most of our working hours. Large, erect, immaculate, with stentorian voices and an inimitable sense of humour, we Gentlemen Cadets owe them a lot.

After war had been declared on 3rd September 1939, 161 (Inns of Court) OCTU formed at the Old College, and our Senior and Intermediate terms were commissioned early. Those of us pre-War Gentlemen Cadets who remained were re-formed into two Companies and moved to Victory College, into the 'new buildings'. These companies were commanded respectively by Bernard Fergusson, later Brigadier Lord Ballantrae, Black Watch, of Chindit fame, and the delightful Jock Goodwin, Welsh Regiment, later killed in action as a lieutenant colonel commanding a battalion of the Parachute Regiment at Salerno. We were lucky in having these two grand men as company commanders and we all liked and respected them very much.

We retained a number of our Regular NCOs, especially the Guardsmen, but the platoon commanders were now former schoolmasters, who had been commissioned in public school OTCs. Now that it was wartime we painted windows with blackout paint, and it was during this chore that I had a chat with the Regimental Sergeant Major, Brand, nicknamed 'the Bosom'. Although he was a fairly terrifying figure on parade, I found him a kindly and affable person to talk to.

We dug slit trenches, sited weapons, carried out practical tactical exercises, did map reading, fieldcraft, night work, weapon training and generally were trained to be platoon commanders.

I enjoyed it all enormously, having always wanted to be a soldier, and I did all I could to learn as much as possible about my chosen profession. I was sorry, and still am, that our time there was cut short. I was very happy at Sandhurst.

The GCs of my Term behaved pretty well, but on one occasion one amorous cadet, destined for a well-known county regiment, asked assistance from some of us to pull up to our floor a laundry basket containing a comely young lady who was an usherette in one of the local cinemas!

Our only other misdemeanour, apart from dodging the 'bluebottles', as the local RMC police were called, when we came in late, was one Saturday afternoon when the ticket inspector at Camberley Station was so unpleasant that the eight of us, who were travelling up to see a performance at the Windmill Theatre, Shanghai-ed him, stuffed him under one of the seats and kept him there until we reached London. How we got away with this I can't think, unless the official was too frightened to report us.

My Term produced a field marshal and four major generals – Field Marshal Sir Roland Gibbs, Major Generals V.J.S. Carpenter, R.S.N. Mans, Sir Jack Younger, Bt. and myself.

After a short leave in London with my parents, where my father was still Commandant of the Royal Army Medical College, Millbank, I joined the Depot of my Regiment, then at Armagh, Northern Ireland.

Having joined Sandhurst pre-war I was kitted out for peacetime as well as wartime soldiering and had no less than fourteen items of kit, including uniform trunk, canvas bedding roll, *chilumchi*(a metal basin with a leather cover containing my washing and shaving kit), saddle and bridle, shot gun, sporting rifle, fishing rods, various suitcases, helmet box and Bill, my white English Bulldog. The phoney war was still on otherwise, I feel sure, I would have made a radical reduction in my kit! However, in those first few months in Ireland we did in some ways live a pre-war life in so far as sport went.

I had no opportunity to ride, but instructed by my then Company Colour Sergeant, Ben Matthews who was later to become Major A.E. Matthews, Second in Command of our 70th Young Soldiers Battalion, I shot snipe and duck in the local bogs and later fished the rivers for trout. Ben was a marvellous teacher of field sports, especially rod and gun. Later, when the Royal Ulster Rifles Infantry Training Centre was established in Ballymena, Ben used to take me ferreting in the grounds of Ballymena Castle in the summer evenings and I acquired my own ferrets, one a greyhound ferret, the other a polecat ferret, which I used to carry, one in each jacket pocket, keeping my hands in the pockets so they could get used to me. At first they bit me a lot, but in the end they knew me and rarely nipped me. There were also point-to-points and a lot of parties and dances.

The Infantry Training Centre was teeming with men, and we trained very hard. Like all new subalterns I owe a tremendous debt to my platoon sergeant, in my case Sergeant Duggan, and the two senior NCOs, Cpl Harknett – a Londoner and former Army Boxing Champion – and L/Cpl Willie Kines, like Sergeant Duggan, a Northern Irishman. They were grand soldiers, I admired them and they all wore the ribbon of the General Service Medal for Palestine, so had that extra aura of having been on active service.

Our C.O. was Lieutenant Colonel Victor Cowley, DSO, MC, a friend of my father's, and he and Doss his sweet wife were kindness itself to me. My company commander was 'Crook', Rollo Crookshank. He and his wife, Babs, befriended all us new subalterns.

A number of Great War vintage officers had come back, many of whom had served with my father, and they gave me a lot of useful advice, although some were a bit crusty, especially at breakfast. We always quickly got out of the easy chairs in Mess when they came in, and sat on hard ones!

I had travelled over with my two Sandhurst contemporaries, Teddy d'Arcy, whom we thought no end of a swell for smoking black, gold-tipped Balkan Sobranie cigarettes, and Bill Hanna, a fine athlete against whom I had played matches for Campbell College when he was at the Royal Academy, Armagh. Bill had represented Ulster at rugger, cricket and hockey. I remember being tackled by him - it was like being hit by a charging bull! Tragically both of them are now dead. Bill was killed in action serving with the Royal Irish Fusiliers, and Teddy died after the war – he had joined our 2nd Battalion shortly after we got to Armagh and had displayed great sangfroid with them at Dunkirk.

I looked very young for my age (18½), and was especially conscious of this when I was with my platoon. They mostly came from the north and south of Ireland, but some were English – usually with Irish names.

We subalterns drilled, did P.T., dug, marched, shot and carried out fieldcraft and battle drill with them and grew to know our men well.

The day I joined I was informed I was Orderly Officer. Normally one was under instruction first but I missed out somehow. I had only a sketchy idea what my duties were from reading the Orders concerned. The Adjutant was not available to elaborate so I asked a Regular subaltern who had left Sandhurst two months before me. This I realised later was a mistake.

'Don't accept complaints at meals,' said he carelessly, 'and when you inspect the Medical Centre, if the windows are shut in the ward tell them to open them. If they are open have them shut!'

Fortunately the Orderly Sergeant was a thoroughly helpful, grizzled veteran wearing Indian North West Frontier and Long Service and Good Conduct Medals, and he was probably infinitely more value to me than an officer would have been.

I was appalled at the food, especially at lunch when each man had a small portion of gristly, grey meat set in a sweaty looking border of yellow fat, soapy potatoes with 'black eyes', and watery cabbage – an incredible contrast to the current very high culinary and presentation standards and multi-choices provided by our excellent Army Catering Corps. I learnt a lot that day and saw things from the point of view of the Riflemen as opposed to that of the officer. This was of considerable help to me in becoming a more useful Orderly Officer in the future.

I was quartered in a former granary in the Mall at Armagh where a number of us subalterns shared stone-floored, freezing-cold, bare rooms, sleeping in our bedding-rolls on wooden-framed, canvas camp beds. Our washing and lavatory facilities were spartan but we were lucky enough to have batmen to clean our kit, tidy our accommodation and – what I certainly appreciated – to bring us a large mug of hot, sweet tea at reveille.

I still remember some of the names of my first platoon – Cooley, a quiet, dark southern Irishman, MacAlorum, a Northerner whose name seemed forever to be exclaimed in exasperation by Sgt. Duggan in something like the squawk made by a hen after laying an egg. I met my former head prefect and another school prefect and cricket captain, riflemen in another platoon, who soon went off to OCTU and commissions.

The Depot at Armagh (now called Gough Barracks) had warm barrack rooms and a fairly large dining hall and gymnasium. There was a big, rather stark canteen, a smallish Sergeants' Mess and a small Officers' Mess, which was then still run very much on pre–war lines.

Perhaps the most useful instruction we received was from the second-in-command, Major Fergus Knox. He and his wife, Ivy, were old friends of my parents. Fergus Knox was a teacher who simplified military instruction marvellously and took us for evening lessons. We subalterns were filled with awe and admiration when Paddy Dunseath visited Ballymena, because he had won the Military Cross with our 2nd Battalion in Palestine.

We did quite a lot of tactical training by night, too, but on other evenings those of us who were wildfowlers were able to go out after the evening flight of duck on the nearby bogs, bringing back what we had shot to be cooked in the Officers' Mess kitchen. Micky Archdale and I used to go out together. A delightful person, he was tragically killed in action with the 1st Battalion in Normandy leading his men.

There were a lot of Territorials of all ranks from the London Irish Rifles, part of our Regiment, whose two battalions were to distinguish themselves greatly in North Africa, Sicily and Italy.

The distinguished Judge, Lord Lawton, was then a captain. There was a tall, thin, wiry subaltern called Tony Dyball, shortly to become a Regular and win an MC in Normandy commanding D Company 1 RUR where he was wounded leading a company attack. Later, having commanded 1 LIR (TA), he was to retire as a Major General after being Chief of Staff Northern Ireland. The legendary Blair (Paddy) Mayne was also there. Paddy went on to win four DSOs, join the Army Commandos and then to command a Regiment of the Special Air Service. I played scrum half for the unit rugby team behind a pack which included him (he was a well-known Irish International Rugby forward), and a number of top class players, among whom were the brothers Eoin and Ambrose McGonigal.

Paddy Mayne and Eoin McGonigal joined No. 11 Commando and went off with it to the Middle East. Eoin was tragically killed on an operation with the SAS, which by then he and Paddy had joined. Paddy was a giant of a man. Eoin was a very good looking chap, as was his brother Ambrose – Ambrose died recently as Northern Ireland's senior Roman Catholic judge. The McGonigal sisters were Irish beauties and one of them, Letty, was married to Jack Carson (later to command 1 RUR in action in France, Germany and Korea), a charming, quiet man and a distant relation of mine.

Letty's two brothers – like most of us subalterns – were wild young men, and it amused them, when full of good cheer, in the small hours of the morning, to ring up Jack Carson. This brought a raging sister to the telephone and Letty would give her brothers a piece of her mind. Little did she know that the receiver was held out for the rest of us, convulsed in mirth, to hear what Letty thought of her brothers!

I remember one guest night in Ballymena Castle where our ITC Officers' Mess was established. The ante room after dinner was filled with uproarious characters and Mess rugger 'broke out'. Our C.O., the burly, gallant Victor Cowley, was bullocking around in the midst of his younger officers. Among them were the huge and enormously powerful Blair Mayne, the McGonigal brothers, the Nixon brothers, the May brothers, Runce Rooney, Desmond Woods, all of whom were to distinguish themselves in the War (Desmond had already won his first MC in Palestine).

In the midst of the mêlée the tall, lean, dark figure of Ambrose McGonigal appeared behind the C.O., a large, heavy oblong silver tray held in both hands. This he brought down with force on the Colonel's head and the burly figure of our leader sank to his knees, but tough guy that he was, he got up again almost immediately. By then Ambrose had disappeared and the slight, wiry figure of my batman Rifleman Henry, former boxing champion of the China Station, was at my elbow. 'Come outside, Sir, and help me with Mr. Ambrose, please.' I went out to where an unconscious shape lay, and with Henry taking his arms and me holding his legs, we carried him down the drive and across the Square to the Depot Officers' Mess where, having undressed him and put him into his pyjamas, we placed him in his bed. 'Did he pass out?' I asked my batman, who had been chauffeur to Mr. Justice McGonigal, Ambrose's father. 'No, Sir, I doped him, Sir, to keep him from any further trouble!' said the champion boxer. Fortunately, Colonel Cowley never knew who or what hit him!

I was most disappointed when I was not allowed to join our 2nd Battalion in France, by now commanded by Fergus Knox, who was to win his first DSO at Dunkirk, because I was only 18 years old, nor could I go to our 1st Battalion in India. I was sent off to England to attend a Mechanical Transport Officers' course, the first part of which was with the London Passenger Transport Board and during which we were based at Putney.

That hot summer Dunkirk took place and we watched troop and hospital trains rattling by at the foot of the garden of the house where we were living, bringing our men back. I learnt to drive heavy vehicles with confidence, including having a session in a double-decker bus on the LPTB's famous skid pan. We then went up to the RAOC Depot at Chilwell to learn the more theoretical aspects of our future jobs as MTOs, and were based at hostelries in Nottingham. On my return to Ballymena I found that I had been appointed Weapon Training Officer!

One morning, as I was crossing the Square, Norman Wheeler, our Adjutant, called me into his office and showed me a notice calling for volunteers for Special Service which he said would be up my street, and I put my name down. My Colonel removed it. I applied again. Again he removed it! I was determined to join, so hearing that one of the Special Service Units, No. 12 Commando, was forming in Northern Ireland and that the C.O. was nearby, I found out where he was, and borrowing a pick-up truck went to see him. He accepted me and 'fixed it' with the War Office.

Victor Cowley was NOT pleased with me. However, he soon forgave me. Looking forward with great excitement to the prospect of active service I left the Depot of my Regiment. I would return to it in 1958 when a Major as Officer Commanding.

CHAPTER THREE

NUMBER 12 COMMANDO

I found No. 12 Commando forming in Londonderry. Officers and men, all volunteers, were still arriving, drawn from the Irish regiments and from the 53rd and 61st Divisions, who were stationed in Northern Ireland.

A Commando consisted of a headquarters and five troops. Each troop was about 65 strong, divided into troop headquarters and two sections of 30 men, each section being divided into two sub-sections, each 15 strong. A captain commanded a troop and a subaltern commanded a section. Lieutenant Colonel 'Peachy' Harrison, who had won the MC and Bar in the Great War with the Irish Guards, commanded No. 12 Commando, and Caryll Cooper-Key, Royal Inniskilling Fusiliers, was Second-in-Command.

I was in C Troop. My troop commander was Tim Forge of the Northamptonshire Regiment, who had had a trial for the English rugby team as a wing threequarter, and the other subaltern was Dicky Garrett, a Sherwood Forester. My men were all Welshmen – Welsh Guards, South Wales Borderers and Monmouthshire Regiment, Royal Welch Fusiliers and Welsh Regiment. Dick's men were mainly from English county regiments. C Troop were a grand lot: Tim Forge was a good trainer and a kind and amusing man; Dick Garrett was great fun, full of high spirits. Our Troop Sergeant Major, T.S.M. Crowther, later to be very deservedly commissioned into the Commandos, was an excellent, sensible and friendly man, liked and respected by us all.

We moved from Derry to Crumlin, a small, rural village in Co. Antrim, where we were billeted on local families. To pay for our keep, other ranks received an allowance of 6/8 a day, and officers 13/4 a day as Army Commandos did not live in barracks. We all liked this arrangement and seemed to get on well with our hosts, all of whom took us in voluntarily.

For my first few months I was billeted in the Mill House, owned by the Scott family, as also were Joe Ryan in my Regiment and Norman Hughes our RAMC doctor who came from Bangor, Co. Down. The Scotts were very kind and tolerant and we were comfortable and well fed. C Troop was based in buildings in the village. We concentrated on weapon training, shooting, direction finding, fitness training, obstacle crossing, tactics including patrolling and ambushing, unarmed combat and a great deal of night work.

We developed a great troop and Commando spirit. My men were terrific and we all got to know each other well. I was taught Welsh songs and played rugger with them – I just made the troop team! For some reason I was nicknamed Dicky, and I remember my Colonel's face when one night accompanying him down Crumlin main street the curtains of a pub were pulled back and 30 Welsh voices called out, 'Come and join us, Dicky.'

We were required to send officers to attend the Commando course at Loch Ailort on the west coast of Scotland, between Glenfinnan and Arisaig. I was one of those selected and arrived at this beautiful, wild spot one winter's day. Although we ate in the big house, we student officers slept in tents in the grounds. This particular six week course was in November-December and I remember feeling incredibly fit and healthy.

The Commandant at that time was Lt. Col. Hugh Stockwell commander of ground forces at Suez in 1956. He was a natural leader whom we all admired and liked. He had recently commanded an Independent Company, (forerunner of the Commandos) during the Norwegian Campaign and had been awarded the DSO.

We had among our instructors officers who had made names for themselves as explorers, rifle shots, etc, before the war, such as J.M. Scott, Jim Gavin, Mackworth-Praed, and there were two marvellous Shanghai policemen, Fairbairn and Sykes, designers of the Commando fighting knife, who taught us close combat fighting. The RSM was called Royle. We were told he had been an officer in the Highland Light Infantry with David Niven, and I believe that after recommissioning he got a DSO and was killed as second-in-command of the Glider Pilot Regiment. He was a fine man with great presence.

We did a tremendous amount of fitness training, and the long exercises over the rugged, mountainous countryside which surrounded us were designed to increase our powers of endurance, to accustom us to direction finding, self-reliance and to teach us battle tactics by day and by night. We fired every type of infantry weapon including the Boyes anti-tank rifle standing, and the 2 inch mortar from the hip. We had been told terrible tales about what happened to those who fired these last two weapons – shattered shoulders, broken hips, etc! – but I reckoned if we were invited to shoot them it must be safe. I made a point of always trying to be first to volunteer on the principle of 'if you've got to fire them anyway why not get it over with?!' This paid off in getting me a good report which pleased my Colonel, who, I suspect, had until then felt that I had been living life too much to the full at night and that I needed a bit of stick!

Led by Colonel Stockwell, we splashed through hip high, freezing sea loch estuaries, forded icy torrents holding boulders to combat the force of the rushing spate, climbed seemingly interminably high mountains and ran down steep scree slopes. We were carefully instructed in the science of demolitions by Jim Gavin and his fellow sapper, Captain Gabriel.

Fairbairn and Sykes, looking like two benevolent, square-shaped padres, took us close combat shooting in their sandbagged, basement range where moving targets suddenly materialised from the gloom. They gave us all great encouragement and confidence. We were taught how to live off the land by Lovat Scouts and on one exercise we had to kill, skin, cook and eat some unfortunate sheep. Captain Shimi Lovat, later to become a legendary Commando figure and a fine Brigade Commander, was an instructor and taught us observation training, including the use of the Scout telescope.

During the course we had one 'free' day when we were given as alternatives climbing Ben Nevis, going out with a shot gun, or stalking yeld hind. I chose the latter as I had done quite a lot of shooting and hill climbing. I went out with a stalker called Chisholm, a tall, rangy man, kind and clearly an expert. Because of his guidance I shot three hinds. Two shots – the first and the last – gave me satisfaction, as I killed the beasts outright, but my second hind I shot through the fore legs, a dreadful thing to have done and although I had had a memorable day, including having to gralloch all the hinds under instruction, I have never felt like stalking again, because of this second shot.

We ended our course with a splendid exercise during part of which I remember following a track, white in the moonlight, round the side of Loch Morar and wondering if we would see its monster in the glittering water! First light found us seated on the platform of a railway halt, the seats of our battledress trousers seemingly stuck to the ground by frost. And how marvellous that hot, sweet porridge tasted, which was brought out on the trucks which came to take us back to camp! No. 12 Commando moved from Northern Ireland to the south coast of England and was based in the Hamble area.

Commando HQ was in either the Golf Club or the Yacht Club and I was greatly impressed to see, present at a cocktail party we gave, the beautiful Vivien Leigh with Laurence Olivier and Ralph Richardson. If my memory is right the two men were RNVR Fleet Air Arm lieutenants at that time.

We continued our training on the same lines as before, but because we had access to landing craft in large numbers on the Hamble River we also carried out a lot of amphibious training.

I was then selected to go up to the Gareloch for training in landing from submarines. I did two such attachments, during the first of which we were based in the old submarine depot ship, HMS *Titania*. We used metal punts which were carried on the submarine's casing fixed to the hull by butterfly nuts and securing stays, one punt carried aft of the conning tower hatch, the other aft of the gun hatch. These punts had screw valves in various places which we opened before the submarine dived, the compartments then filling with water and thereby withstanding the pressure of the sea when submerged. When the submarine surfaced we would emerge from the conning tower and gun hatches respectively, wait briefly while the water ran out, then screw up the valves and seat ourselves with our paddles in the punts. The submarine would trim down while we undid the metal securing stays and floated free, taking care not to get caught under the mine-cutting wire overhead as the submarine submerged.

We practised paddling to the shore, landing, carrying out tasks ashore, re-embarking, and paddling back to the submarine until we were accomplished at this operation both by day and by night. We thoroughly enjoyed – as always – being with the Royal Navy and were greatly impressed with submariners of all ranks. They were highly professional and had a terrific morale.

The second time, in early 1941, I went to train in submarines in the Gareloch, we were based in the depot ship HMS *Forth* and trained mainly in HMS *Thunderbolt*. We discovered that, originally named HMS *Thetis*, she had sunk with heavy loss of life through drowning during her pre-war trials. This time we were using Folbot collapsible canoes which had replaced the steel punts. We were submerged on one occasion, and a sailor was telling us all about the *Thetis* disaster and indicating where the corpses had been found, when suddenly we noticed water gushing in from overhead! We studiously ignored it and hoped we looked unconcerned, our imaginations working overtime! Then there was the sound of whistling and a cheerful matelot came along, screwed something up and the flow of water ceased!

Another time we were returning submerged from a night exercise, and, having been lying on the bed of the Gareloch, were about to surface, when we heard the sound of engines overhead getting louder and louder. We remained where we were and listened to the sound of propellers pass over us and away before we continued with our ascent. When we reached the surface we were told that this was the Free French Submarine 'Surcouf', which had broken its moorings. Later we looked at it with interest: it was huge, with several decks and even a seaplane hangar.

We were alerted to carry out several raids on the occupied French coast whilst based at Warsash. One after another was cancelled at the last moment. On one occasion we had all embarked in our landing craft at Dover harbour and were literally about to sail for a raid on Berck-sur-Mer when we were ordered out of our landing craft and back to base. This was very frustrating, and we became very cynical. However, Philip Pinckney and his Section of E Troop carried out one successful cross-channel operation and we all envied him enormously.

Orders were then received to move to Scotland and we trained around Inverary, in glorious countryside, in April 1941. By now I had joined D Troop, commanded by Captain (later Lt. Col.) Ted Fynn, MC. The other subaltern was Christopher Birney, whose book "Dungeon Democracy" described his years as a prisoner in Buchenwald. Two of my Section, Ken Darlington and Cpl Bowden, were to win the Military Medal.

On one occasion when we were training with several other Army Commandos and the Royal Marines, someone in the opposition appeared to have fired live rounds at us. Certainly the twigs in the bush behind which several of us were standing fell, broken. I was filled with rage and seizing and loading my Very pistol I pointed it at the group of 'enemy' in the fir trees in front of me, whom I suspected of firing, and squeezed the trigger. To my horror, I watched the red, glowing Very light curve accurately towards a soldier I could see across the valley and I thought, 'I've done it this time,' but fortunately he stepped behind a fir tree and the light hit it!

We believed we were training for an operation to seize Madagascar, but were bitterly disappointed when, instead, we were told that we were to be based in Scotland and not go abroad. In fact we all loved being in Scotland. A number of raids on Norway were mounted from there and my own Commando was among those which participated. We were stationed in the country town of Ayr with our Commando Headquarters in Wellington Square. The local people were kind and friendly and I have particular reason for finding it a very special place, because it was there that I met my wife, who lived there with her uncle and aunt. I had seen this terribly pretty girl in the town, but she seemed unaware of my admiring stares. Then one night I was invited to a dance at which she, Patricia Petrie, was my partner. I fell madly in love with her, and have remained so ever since. We were engaged within three weeks, and, had it not been for the Saint Nazaire Raid were to have been married on her birthday, 17 August that year. As it turned out, we had to wait until I returned from Germany in 1945. She has been my sweetheart, my inspiration and my support since the day we met, and has unhesitatingly shared discomfort and danger in far-flung places, and made happy homes for us and for our three children. Any success I have enjoyed is largely due to her.

We continued to train hard over the surrounding Ayrshire hills, in the rivers and in the sea. We were joined in Ayr by No. 2 Commando. Little did I realise that I would go to war with them under the command of their C.O., the cheerful, fatherly Lt. Col. Charles Newman. It was a lovely summer and all the commandos stationed along the West Scottish coast, Numbers 1, 2, 3, 4, 5, 6, 9 and 12, trained to a high standard.

Various raids at troop level were carried out and then in December we, in No. 12 Commando, embarked for 'Operation Anklet', as the second Lofoten Islands raid was called, in the Commando carrier ships *Prins Albert* and *Prinses Josephine Charlotte*. We drew tropical kit and thought we were off to either Madagascar, the Azores or Pantelleria. We were also issued with Arctic clothing. It was not until we were off the Shetland Islands that we were told we were bound for the Lofoten Islands of Norway. It was extremely rough, most of us were seasick, but for me it proved an inoculation and I have never been seasick since.

We had been prepared to remain in the Norwegian area for several months if things went well. On Boxing Day, 26 December 1941 at 0600 hrs, No. 12 Commando, wearing white, hooded overalls, landed unopposed, whilst the German garrison was sleeping off their Christmas feasting. The two harbours on Moskenesöy, the western island, were occupied, but our force, consisting of twenty-three ships, was withdrawn owing to enemy bombing. The newsreel films of the raid were destroyed by some of our subalterns who said they did not want the British public thinking we had achieved a brilliant success. Not everyone agreed with this effort of theirs as we had not seen the film!

Our efforts were certainly completely overshadowed by No. 3 Commando's splendid raid on Vaagso with two troops of No. 2 Commando under command, which took place at the same time.

CHAPTER FOUR

OPERATION CHARIOT – THE RAID ON ST. NAZAIRE

In February 1942 three officers and thirteen NCOs of my Commando were sent on a demolitions course, Gerard Brett, Paul Bassett-Wilson and myself, with Sergeant Deery and Corporals Blount, Jones, Chetwynd, Johnson, Chung, Hoyle, Callaway, Molloy, Wright, Lemon, Reeves and Ferguson.

The officer running the course, Captain Bill Pritchard MC, won the affection, respect and admiration of everyone from the outset. Bill, a Welshman, was a born leader. We would, all of us, have done anything he told us to do without question because he had such a wonderfully happy, cheerful and kind nature and because he was so obviously a master of his subject – demolitions. He had proved this in action at Dunkirk and won a Military Cross in doing so. Furthermore, he made every aspect of our training alive, vibrant and vitally important to each one of us. The success of the Commando destruction of the St. Nazaire dock machinery was due to Bill Pritchard's inspired teaching, coupled with the determination of the Commandos themselves. I am sure that all of us who had the privilege of knowing Bill Pritchard and what is owed to him, wish that his efforts on the St. Nazaire Raid could have been recognised by the posthumous award of a Victoria Cross. Because no one lived to witness his death it was not possible under existing regulations for him to be awarded anything other than a Mention in Despatches.

To help him, Bill Pritchard had his great friend Captain R.K. Montgomery, a tall, powerfully-made sapper captain, also expert in demolitions. Bob Montgomery would demonstrate his ability and resourcefulness and win a Military Cross during the raid.

Our demolitions training started in the bleak Rosyth docks at Burntisland where we learned about caisson and double lock gates, winding houses, opening and closing machinery, steel bridges, cranes, guns, pumping stations and power stations. We were instructed in the use of plastic explosives and made-up charges and where to place them in the most effective way and position. All of us became adept at the various means of ignition and the need for duplication. Bill Pritchard and Bob Montgomery made it all fascinating and our skill, speed and confidence increased rapidly.

There were great personalities amongst us of all ranks. Gerard Brett, who was in my own No. 12 Commando and also in my Regiment, had been a curator at the Victoria and Albert Museum and had written a book on the Byzantine Age. We had joined the Commando together. Bill Etches of No. 3 Commando was another good friend. We had been at the Royal Military College, Sandhurst, together. Bill was at Vaagso with No. 3 Commando while Gerard and I had sailed on the second Lofoten Islands raid.

Ronnie Swayne of No. 1 Commando, huge, black-haired, amusing and a music lover, had just missed his Blue for rugger at Oxford, due to injury. Ronnie had raided the French coast already. Stuart Chant was another fine rugger player, dark, good looking and great fun. Tall, thin Paul Bassett-Wilson was in my Commando and went on to win an MC and Bar. Harry Pennington, the Oxford rugger Blue, was another officer whom I liked very much, immensely fit and tough.

Mark Woodcock of 3 Commando, a delightful, ever-cheerful chap, who had broken both legs mountaineering, really should not have been with us but for his terrific guts and enthusiasm. Chris Smalley, a quiet, reliable man with a heavy moustache and ruddy face, inspired confidence; he and the huge, slightly stooping, powerful extrovert, Bertie Burtinshaw, were both from No. 5 Commando. Bill Bradley of 3 Commando and I had been babies together in India where our parents were friends. Bill always maintained that we had shared the same pram at one stage!

Our men were the pick of the British Army and, like the officers, came from every Regiment and Corps but again, as with the officers, they were welded together by pride and confidence in their particular Commando – and all the eight currently UK-based Army Commandos participated in the St Nazaire Raid – Numbers 1, 2, 3, 4, 5, 6, 9 and 12 Commandos.

As an original member of No. 12 Commando, I knew every man who had been selected for the operation. Sergeant Deery, a fair-haired, cheery Royal Inniskilling Fusilier and Corporal Johnson of the Gordons, a trifle dour and rock-steady, were both to win Military Medals on the Raid.

Corporal Jumbo Reeves, a former RAF pilot, complete with appropriate handlebar moustache and his guitar, extrovert and amusing; Corporal Joe

Molloy, a staunch and dependable southern Irishman; little Corporal Blount of the South Wales Borderers, a tiger in action; Corporal Jones 'the Post', strong, large and, like so many of his fellow countrymen in Wales, possessed of a fine voice; Corporal Chetwynd of the Sherwood Foresters, a tough reliable soldier; Corporal Bob Wright, RE, intelligent, brave, cheerful and strong; Corporal Ferguson and Corporal Lemon, two grand Ulster soldiers from the North Irish Horse; and then the remaining three corporals of the four comprising my own splendid team.

I have mentioned one of them, Corporal Johnson, MM, already. Corporal Ron Chung, RE, was powerful, brave, half-Chinese, with a strong and amusing personality. Corporals 'Cab' Callaway, gallant, reliable and ever-cheerful, and Bob Hoyle, who had a great sense of humour under a slightly serious appearance, very courageous, steady, intelligent and resilient.

These fine NCOs and those from the other Commandos shared in all aspects of our training, and became swift and adept at the work by day and by night in pitch dark.

While we were in Cardiff the news was released that the Bruneval Raid under Major John Frost, later of Arnhem fame, and the renowned Wing commander Pickard, had been a great success, well planned and executed with professional precision and dash. I was shown pictures of it in either the *Daily Mirror* or the *Daily Sketch*, and wondered when our turn would come. We had not long to wait.

We were by now confident as to our speed and expertise in preparing all types of dock machinery for demolitions. It was decided that we should do a two day trip (which took place in vile weather) in Motor Launches (MLs) to the Sicily Isles, followed by an exercise to finish off our training which was a seaborne raid on Devonport docks, codename 'Vivid'. For me, certainly, the 'Vivid' revelation was our vulnerability when we were dazzlingly illuminated by 'enemy' searchlights. We were to experience this for real in the near future.

Our course finished, we went by train to Falmouth, where we joined No. 2 Commando in the *Prinses Josephine Charlotte*, usually called the *PJC*. From here we went ashore for training – P.T., speed marches and shooting.

One idyllic spring afternoon a number of us went ashore and despite it being March, swam in the clear waters of the Fal, and lay on the grass afterwards, in warm spring sunshine, chatting. It was here that that very tough rugger Blue, Harry Pennington, said to me that England was worth dying for, and I wondered afterwards if he had had a premonition of his death.

There was a gripping feeling of excitement when the C.O. of No. 2 Commando, Lieutenant Colonel Charles Newman, who would command the land forces, assembled all officers and briefed us off an excellent scale model on our forthcoming raid, the destination of which was still secret. We were to study and discuss the model and the accompanying maps and diagrams until we could visualize localities and routes almost as if we had already visited the place.

The story of the Raid has been told in 'The Raid on St Nazaire' by Captain Robert Ryder, V.C., our naval commander, in 'The Greatest Raid of All' by the late Brigadier C.E. Lucas Phillips, CBE, MC and by Lieutenant Colonel Stuart Chant-Sempill, OBE, MC, in 'St Nazaire Commando'.

Colonel Charles used a blackboard with a map of a port on it, as well as the model of the docks area. He told us the operation, to be called 'Chariot', was designed to destroy the dry dock and to blow up dock installations. So that this could be executed undisturbed, the land force was to be divided into demolition troops and fighting troops. The fighting troops had two tasks: first to assault and destroy enemy gun positions and hold a perimeter of bridges until the dock demolitions were all completed, the commandos withdrawn and the perimeter bridges blown. The second task was to provide close protection for the demolition teams to ensure they were able to lay and blow their charges.

The strength of the assault parties would be about twelve, including two or three officers, and that of each demolition and protection party would be an officer and four NCOs.

The Force was divided into three groups, two of which would sail in MLs fitted with extra fuel tanks for the voyage; the third group would sail in an old USN destroyer, the former USS *Buchanan*, now called HMS *Campbeltown*. *Campbeltown*, carrying $4\frac{1}{2}$ tons of high explosive in its bows would ram the seaward caisson gate of the great dry dock, the only dock where the German battleship *Tirpitz* could refit, and, having disembarked her Commandos over her bows, would blow up by time-fuse after the raiding force had departed.

To distract the attention of the Germans the RAF were to carry out a three phase bombing attack. In the first, ten Whitley bombers would attack the dry dock area from 11.30pm to 12.30am; in the second twenty-five Whitleys would attack the same target from 12.30am to 1.20am, and in the third phase twenty-five Wellingtons would attack the northern end of the Penhouet Basin and the adjoining shipbuilding slips, (1800 yards north of the Old Entrance), from 1.20am to 4am.

By now we knew that our objective was the great Normandie dry dock at St Nazaire, and its installations. Built between 1928 and 1932 it was 1148 feet long, 164 feet wide and could take a ship in excess of 85,000 tons. Water was admitted or expelled from the dock by sliding in and out a caisson gate at either end. These were huge steel gates 167 feet long, 54 feet high and 35 feet wide, each containing compartments that could be filled with water, sufficient to withstand various pressures.

The caissons were wound laterally on rollers in or out of deep sockets called cambers on the west side of the dock, which lay roughly north and south. Each caisson was wound in and out of its camber by means of two large twin wheels which, with their motors, were situated in a winding house at the extremity of each camber. There was also a large pumping house to pump water in and out of the dock. The pumping house motors were at ground level but its mighty pumps were forty feet below ground.

The objectives for demolition were the two winding houses, one at each end of the dock, together with their great caisson gates and the pumping house; all three buildings being on the west side of the dock. These were allocated as follows: the Pumping Station to Stuart Chant of 5 Commando and his four No. 1 Commando sergeants; the southern winding house to Christopher Smalley and his team; and the caisson itself, should the *Campbeltown* fail to ram properly, to Bertie Burtinshaw and his men – the latter were all from No. 5 commando. At the northern end of the docks, Gerard Brett and his team had the destruction of the caisson gate as their task and I and my four corporals would destroy the windinghouse and its machinery.

Bill Etches would coordinate our efforts. The overall supervision of all demolition tasks was to be under Bob Montgomery.

We boarded HMS *Campbeltown* from the *Prinses Josephine Charlotte* at about midday on 26 February 1942 in tremendous form, everyone very excited at the prospect of the raid. Before we left the *PJC* the Wardroom Petty Officer Steward, Petty Officer Ronald Chilver, gave me a silver horse-shoe that had been on his wedding cake. He and I had first sailed together on the second Lofotens raid and he used to give me cups of tea in the pantry. He took part in every major landing – North Africa, Sicily, Italy and Normandy, as well as the actions at Oran and Dieppe. The horse-shoe, having done its stuff at St Nazaire, was taken off me by Germans after I was wounded so, sadly, I have been unable to return it to him.

The rest of our force embarked in the MLs and the motor gun boat (MGB) at the same time. I remember being immensely impressed with the captain of HMS *Campbeltown*, Lieutenant Commander Sam Beattie, and his officers and crew. Sam Beattie had great dignity and was a tall, good-looking man with an Elizabethan beard and a friendly and calm manner.

We sailed in sunny weather from Falmouth at about 2pm on 26 March 1942. Before we sailed, our Royal Navy Force Commander steamed round our little fleet in his Headquarters boat MGB 314. We looked at him with interest and confidence. Commander Bob Ryder had a reputation as being a really gutsy, tough-egg leader, who already wore the rare Polar Medal's white ribbon, and we were glad and proud to be serving under his command. He and Lieutenant Colonel Charles Newman, together with their immediate staffs then transferred to HMS *Atherstone* which, with HMS *Tynedale*, constituted our Hunt Class destroyer escort.

Atherstone led, towing MGB 314, commanded by Lieutenant Commander Dunstan Curtis, DSO. Then followed *Tynedale*, after which came *Campbeltown* towing Micky Wynn's Motor Torpedo Boat, MTB 74. On either side of the destroyers, in line astern, were the MLs, sixteen of them. A single Hurricane, flying very low, circled our little fleet. Later we changed into the arrow-head formation that was used in anti-submarine sweep operations.

At about 7pm we altered our course from SW to south. Our Hurricane left us before dark, our last link with home, and we changed from anti-submarine order to cruising order, with the destroyers steaming in the centre column and the motor launches, also in column, on either side, and increased our speed to 14 knots. We had our last sleep in *Campbeltown* and next morning, 27 March, we were up on deck early to find a cloudless day and to see *Tynedale*, *Atherstone* and *Campbeltown* each break out the German ensign. We returned to anti-submarine sweep formation. At about 7am *Tynedale*, flying the White Ensign again, attacked a German U-boat which was on the surface, first by gun fire and then by depth charges. She and *Atherstone* hunted the enemy submarine for a couple of hours but it looked as if (as it transpired later), it had escaped. We hoped it had not reported our presence and wondered if we would next see the Luftwaffe. Fortunately the U-boat, although it had seen us, sent a report that led the Germans to think that the British Force was either withdrawing after a minelaying operation or else was heading for Gibraltar.

Our next excitement was the sight of a fleet of French fishing trawlers on the port bow. Commander Ryder, knowing that the Germans often put observers and radios aboard such vessels, ordered *Tynedale* and *Atherstone* each to sink one of a pair of boats well separated from the remainder of the fishing fleet. Both skippers and crew accepted this decision with good will and we heard they were delighted to be taken to Britain, where most of them joined the Free French. They informed Commander Ryder that none of the fishing vessels were carrying Germans nor radios, so he decided to let the rest be.

The sky was now overcast, lessening the prospect of enemy air activity, but we hoped we would not meet up with the five enemy destroyers which had unexpectedly turned up at St Nazaire shortly before we sailed. That day I went through our plan several times with my team. I had the utmost confidence in my four splendid corporals, each of whom could well have had a commission before the war ended had they returned safely from St

Nazaire. They all exuded cheerfulness and confidence and were physically as hard as nails. I knew that with them we could not fail unless we were all knocked out before we got there. I think we could all have found our way blindfolded to our winding house and have laid our demolition charges likewise.

Although we realised that we were taking part in a most audacious operation, most, if not all of us, had made dates for the next weekend with our fiancées, wives or girlfriends, none of whom, of course, knew anything about the forthcoming operation. We were only allowed on deck if we wore naval duffle coats as it was imperative that the enemy should not know that commandos were aboard our ships.

The ships' officers I remember best, apart from Sam Beattie are Lieutenant Nigel Tibbitts, DSC, who was the Naval demolitions expert, Lieutenant Gough, the First ' ' 'tenant and Surgeon Lieutenant Winthorpe, Royal Canadian Na'   :ally, all three splendid officers were to be killed in action on the Raid.

We drank endless cups of 'Kai', sweet, thick naval cocoa, and munched huge bully beef sandwiches, delighting in the scrumptious hot, soft, ship-baked bread, a real treat. Some bought Mars bars, cigarettes, etc. from the ship's canteen, until it was realised that the entire stock would go up with the ship and no payment was necessary! Others made dreadful sandwiches containing such things as Brylcreem, shaving soap and toothpaste and offered them to unsuspecting friends. Many of us were photographed in various poses with the German ensign fluttering above us, but so far as I know, no such photos have survived.

No German ships or aircraft were seen and at about 8pm the Force turned north east straight for the mouth of the Loire. We stopped while Commander Ryder, Colonel Newman and their staffs transferred from HMS *Atherstone* to MGB 314, and Micky Wynn's MTB74 was cast off from *Campbeltown*. We then moved on and at 10pm made contact with the submarine HMS *Sturgeon*, which acted as a navigational beacon.

It was an unforgettable moment when we saw the half-submerged submarine lying with the conning tower showing, the figure of her captain, Commander Wingfield, waving to us and shouting "Good Luck!" We all admired the superb navigation by Lieutenant Green in the MGB which had brought us with amazing accuracy to this tiny rendezvous in the ocean. Our two escort destroyers left us to patrol off the mouth of the Loire while we carried out our operation. We were really on our own now.

We only had forty miles to go. It was cloudy and thickening with a bit of drizzle. We had eaten our last meal preceded by a glass of *Campbeltown's* excellent sherry in which we toasted the success of our enterprise. At 11pm Lieutenant Nigel Tibbitts and AB Demmelweit activated *Campbeltown's*

explosive charge and at about 11.30pm we could hear our bombers droning overhead on their way to their tasks at St Nazaire. Many of us were
standing on deck watching the German searchlights pencilling the sky as
they searched for our aircraft and we could see the coloured tracer of the
German flak climbing, apparently slowly, upwards towards them.

At about a quarter to one on 28 March, we could just make out the loom
of the shore. Speed was reduced to ten knots to lessen *Campbeltown's* draft
in the hazardous shoal waters through which we were now steaming.
Twice *Campbeltown* grounded. We felt her dragging herself, propellers
thrashing, through the mud and were greatly relieved when she was
floating freely once more. I understand our speed was reduced to five knots
during our passage through the mud.

Just before midnight Major Bill Copland had summoned all Commando
officers to a final brief conference, after which he ordered us to our action
stations. Gerard Brett and I with our respective demolition parties moved
to the wardroom, where we sat on the deck with our backs against the
bulkheads to try to lessen the impact of ramming.

At 1am our convoy was caught in the white, pitiless glare of brilliant
enemy searchlights and challenged by two German signal stations. Simultaneously some German guns opened fire. Commander Ryder's reply,
made by Leading Seaman Pike succeeded in stopping the firing and
several searchlights were switched off. Some, however, were still on and
the signal station on the German ship *Sperrbrecher* continued to challenge
us. We were again fired on but Pike and our signaller on the *Campbeltown*
replied, 'Ship being fired on by friendly forces.' This again caused the
firing to stop and in fact we in *Campbeltown* had only six minutes to go
before we rammed the dry dock.

Apparently, had we been a genuine German force we should have stopped
when fired on, so at 1:28am, with only five minutes to go, our bluff finally
failed and every German gun that could see us opened fire. Beattie ordered
speed to be increased to eighteen and a half knots, the German colours were
run down and the White Ensign battle flags were hoisted throughout our force.
Simultaneously all our own guns opened fire and the noise was tremendous as
Campbeltown's eight Oerlikons, 12 pounder and 3 inch mortar split the night
air, combined with the sound of eighty-four Oerlikons from the MLs, the
pompom in MGB 314, the Hotchkiss guns of the MTB, and the Commando's
LMGs. Added to this was the sound of the German guns from 6 inch
howitzers, 170mm, 150mm, 88mm, 75mm, to lighter calibre weapons, while
our little force proceeded, illuminated throughout by the dazzling white glare
of the German searchlights.

We, seated below on the deck of the wardroom, had felt the drag of the
ship's bottom as she threshed over the mud shoal and now we felt and

heard the hammering and explosions of German shells and bullets striking against *Campbeltown's* hull. A shell, glowing red, passed through the wardroom as we sat there, but continued out without exploding.

The intensity of noise increased as *Campbeltown* neared the dry dock. Then came a bump as we hit and passed through the boom, followed by a long shuddering impact as we struck the gate. We had arrived!

Gerard Brett's demolition team and mine made our way up the companion to the exposed deck above, with our heavy rucksacks on our backs. The noise was indescribable and tracer was everywhere, crossing the ship and coming towards us in seemingly slow coloured arcs of whites, yellows, blues, reds and greens, which suddenly whipped past on nearing us. Erect on the deck, rifle slung over his shoulder, stood the confidence-inspiring, lean, soldierly figure of Major Bill Copland. "Off you go!" he shouted, just as if it had been a training exercise, his calm and certain bearing inducive to coolness in a hectic environment.

Forward we went hardly feeling the weight of our explosive-filled rucksacks. The fo'c'sle was exposed to a blinding array of searchlights and to intense enemy fire. An incendiary had burnt a large hole in the deck which was burning, and smoke added to the picture of war. The 12 pounder had been knocked out and nearby Johnnie Proctor lay in his kilt, his leg shattered, cheering us on. The scaling ladders were pushed down over the port side of the bows where we were to land, held in place by the very gallant Nigel Tibbits and Gough, both totally disregarding the intense enemy fire, much of it close range, and directed straight at us. I remember them both cheerfully encouraging us and swearing as they tried to hold the ladders steady. Of my party Corporal Bob Hoyle fell through the burning hole in the deck but was saved from disappearing below by his rucksack which caught on the sides. We pulled him up, burnt, and he landed unperturbed and cheerful.

The ladders were unsteady, and some of us, myself included, jumped most of the way down, stumbling under the weight of our heavy rucksacks as we landed. Our little party consisting of myself, Corporals Johnny Johnson, Ron Chung, Bob Hoyle and Cab Callaway rallied together and made our way at a trot along the side of the dry dock towards our objective, the far winding house. Our rubber-soled boots were almost noiseless. We wore, for recognition purposes, webbing belts and anklets scrubbed white. En route Corporal Johnson was hit and wounded. We came to our winding house and found it had a heavy metal door. I tried unsuccessfully to shoot the lock in, then Ron Chung burst it open with a sledge hammer.

Once inside, following the drill we knew so well, we laid our made-up charges and connected them up. Corporal Johnny Johnson, in great pain, showed a wonderful example of fortitude, determination and efficiency. The other three, Corporals Ron Chung, Bob Hoyle and Cab Callaway, were cool as ice and as cheerful as if on a holiday. When we were ready to blow I sent Ron Chung across to Gerard Brett's party to tell him we were ready when he was, and that once he and his team had completed their task and had passed safely through our area, we would blow up our winding house. Ron Chung ran across under intense fire, fully illuminated by the glare of searchlights. He returned after successfully completing his mission having found the area swept by a hail of bullets and he himself being hit.

The noise of firing was terrific and the place continued to be lit up by searchlights and the fire of explosions. Gerard Brett's party came through us having suffered heavily. Gerard, badly wounded, was carried by Corporals Bob Wright and Ferguson. Once they were through and clear, from what we all hoped was a safe distance, I pulled the pins of our ignitors. It was a memorable sight. The entire building seemed to rise several feet vertically before it exploded and disintegrated like a collapsed house of cards.

In the light of the flames we could see that our task was successfully completed and we moved swiftly back to the RV point, through Donald Roy's bridgehead, running singly over a fire-swept bridge.

I found Colonel Newman, cheerful and kindly as ever, standing near some railway wagons with the imperturbable Major Bill Copland at his side. I reported that our demolition task had been successfully completed, and that my party was present and correct. 'Well done, old boy,' said Colonel Charles. 'Just like some of our exercises, we've been let down by transport again!' We looked over the River Loire, bathed as it was in the white light of German searchlights and criss-crossed by coloured tracer. Heavy pillars of smoke and orange bursts of explosions denoted that there were indeed no ships to take us home to England. I don't think many of us were too surprised. Had the original proposal of sending a second destroyer instead of the very vulnerable MLs been accepted, it might have been a different story, for not only would a destroyer have been less vulnerable, it would have given us all a fighting chance of returning. Because of its robustness in comparison to the little, wooden craft, it might well have enabled a successful landing to take place on the Old Mole, and have resulted in the successful knocking out of the strong points there. The failure to include the second destroyer cost not only the return of the main body of survivors, but the lives of those of our fine commandos and sailors who had to try to achieve their tasks on the Old Mole from flimsy and unsuitable wooden craft carrying vulnerable and highly inflammable extra fuel tanks.

However, there was little time for such thoughts as Colonel Charles told us that we would fight our way into the town of St Nazaire. Having done this, he told us, we would split up into small parties and make our way through France into Spain and Gibraltar and thence home to England. We formed up, and led by our assault and protection parties, moved forward at the double, by bounds. Our progress consisted of crossing open, bullet-swept ground, running flat out, pausing in dark patches of cover to reform for the next bound. Our assault and protection parties did magnificent work, outstanding among them were Donald Roy, nicknamed 'the Laird', moustached, kilted, upright, disdaining cover and holding to the centre of the street; Johnny Roderick and Tiger Watson – who earned his nickname that night, both wounded; and those fearless, tough examples of the finest British fighting man, TSM Haines and Sergeant Challington.

We were being fired on from all sides, some of it coming from very close range, but we charged on rather like a pack of rugger forwards. There was a certain amount of laughter, cursing and calls of encouragement and every now and then someone was hit. Our Commando boots made little sound, the searchlights were no longer able to glare on us and we must have made a difficult target. However a lot of us had some near squeaks and I vividly recall that when I tripped on a strand of wire and had fallen flat on my face, a German bullet struck the cobbles within inches of my head, throwing up sparks and chips of stone, one of which hit my face.

We made our way by a circuitous route that headed towards the little bridge which we had crossed on the way back from our demolition task. Then we turned in the opposite direction and moved back along the quayside of the basin which lay opposite the submarine pens. Here we were fired on from across the water on our right and from close range on our left.

At the end of the quay we came to Old Town Place, an open, broad area beyond which lay what we called bridge D, a girder bridge, about seventy yards off. The bridge and the square were under heavy enemy fire, including that from an 88mm gun. We all went for it like long dogs. I recall Donald Roy, sweeping along the middle of the road, erect in his kilt, the cheerful Colonel Charles Newman and the confidence-inspiring Major Bill Copland who was a rock to us all. Other outstanding fire-eaters included Lieutenant Johnny Stutchbury, TSM George Haines and Sergeant Challington.

A hail of enemy fire erupted as we crossed the bridge, projectiles slamming into its girders, bullets whining and ricocheting off them and from the cobbles. There was a roar of gunfire of varying calibres and the percussion of 'potato masher' grenades as we neared the far end. One of the latter burst at my feet and the explosion, combined with my own forward velocity, lifted me clean off the ground, wounding me in the left leg and shoulder. I remember landing on the back of the sturdy Stanley Day, No. 2 Commando's Adjutant. I could feel my left battledress trouser leg wet with blood, but beyond a sense of numbness, my leg still worked and I quickly forgot about it.

A German motorcycle combination came flying round the corner, I pumped several rounds into the occupants who crashed, dead, into a wall. My feeling of satisfaction at what I thought was my personal success dissolved later on when I discovered that just about every one present claimed to have fired simultaneously on the luckless enemy! Then we saw what seemed to be an armoured car, firing and moving into position at a crossroads about a hundred and fifty yards ahead of us. Seeing that the way directly ahead was barred we turned left. We split into smaller parties and I was among a group with Colonel Newman and Major Copland. We came on a lorry parked by the roadside and Bill Copland tried to get it started. All he succeeded in doing was to switch on the headlights, illuminating, among others, the Charles Atlas figure of Bung Dennison, our protection party commander, to cries of 'Put those bloody lights out!' I was at Charles Newman's side as an armoured car passed us, and then we started what has since been called 'the St Nazaire Obstacle Race', clambering over backyard walls and into and out of houses. In one room breakfast was set, and if my memory is correct Bung had a mouthful or two en route!

Colonel Charles, because dawn was approaching, decided that our party should find somewhere to lie up for the hours of daylight, and then break out under cover of darkness. A lot of us had been wounded by then and Bill Etches had been very badly hit during the initial stages. How he had kept up only his stout heart knows. We went through a door into a cellar fitted out as an air raid shelter with paliasses on the floor. Here the very badly wounded received what little medical attention could be given them, and we hoped to escape discovery.

All too soon we heard raucous, hysterical Nazi shouts. The door burst open and tense-looking, armed Germans appeared. The Colonel, in view of the fact that of his party of sixteen only four were unwounded, decided to call it a day.

We were bundled out and thrust across the road to the house opposite, which turned out to our wry amusement to be the German Headquarters! Others of our number were brought in to join us and then, at about 10:35am, there was a huge roar and concussion as HMS *Campbeltown* blew up and we all gave an enormous cheer. We learnt later that about 150 Germans, including, sadly, some women, had perished in this shattering explosion. The Germans then got very jumpy again and it was obvious that a number of them – probably not their front-line troops – were trigger happy. Firing broke out once more when the two delayed-action torpedoes fired into the outer lock gates of the Old Entrance by Lieutenant Micky Wynn went up. We heard that in addition to Germans killed by Germans, in their mistaken belief that there was a French uprising, tragically a number of innocent French men, women and children were shot in the panicky firing that ensued.

CHAPTER FIVE

WOUNDED, AND A PRISONER OF WAR

Whilst our unwounded went to a Stalag at Rennes, those of us who had been wounded were taken to the Hermitage Hotel at La Baule where we were forced to put on hospital nightshirts and lie on mattresses, closely packed on the ground while German sailors, tommy guns at the alert, moved around, covering us as we lay there. I had Micky Wynn on one side of me. Although he had just lost an eye he was typically brave and cheerful. On my other side was Sergeant Dick Bradley, MM, shot through the body, but also cheerful and gallant. It was the most depressing time of my life: the realisation that we were prisoners of war, that we would not be quickly rejoining our loved ones and friends, coupled with the squalor of our condition and the unpleasantness of our captors, came in massive contrast to the excitement and elation of the operation.

We did what we could to help our severely injured and to keep up our spirits. The behaviour of some of the Nazi medical orderlies and staff, women as well as men, was callous and unpleasant and certainly induced a feeling of hatred that many of us had not entertained up to then. I still recall the moronic naval youth who, when I was injected, presumably with anti-tetanus, threw the hypodermic syringe at my buttock like a dart, and I still remember feeling the point of its needle against the bone.

I was fairly fluent in French and had used it to communicate with French medical staff on behalf of some of our wounded. I suppose because of this, I – with, I think, one other – was taken away to identify a number of our dead comrades. They were already in open coffins, between twenty and thirty of them, and it was a terribly sad and unpleasant task. I remember the body of the superb fighting NCO, Sergeant Tom

39

Durrant, VC, and all the wounds he had suffered in his brave and self-sacrificial final battle.

Those of us who could walk were given back our clothes in order to attend the funeral of our fallen comrades. The Germans were correct and punctilious and obviously wanted to honour our brave men. It was a dreadfully depressing occasion. I was one of four who lowered coffins into the grave and I remember gripping the rope like one possessed as I felt it, slimy with wet mud, slipping in my hand, and the feeling of relief when the act of lowering was successfully completed. We passed in single file by a Union Flag draped coffin, paying our last respects with an Eyes Right.

Whilst we were in hospital we learnt how other members of the Commandos had fared during the fighting. Stuart Chant who, with his four sergeants had the major demolition task of destroying the pumping station, had been badly wounded in the knee, arms and fingers aboard *Campbeltown* during the run in (so badly that he was later repatriated). Despite this Stuart led his team of Sergeants Dockerill, Chamberlain (who had also been seriously wounded during the *Campbeltown's* approach) King and Butler and together they carried out their difficult and arduous task successfully. It was a brilliant operation supervised by Bob Montgomery who had been overseeing demolition tasks and carrying out individual ones of his own, all under heavy fire.

Chris Smalley was killed in the ML in which he was withdrawing after he and his team had successfully destroyed their winding house. Micky Burn had nearly drowned after his blazing ML sank by the East Jetty. Heavily laden with ammunition and, having sunk, he was towed ashore by Lance Corporal Young. He then got separated from the survivors of his party and made his solitary way across the entire enemy-occupied dockyard and successfully reached his objective three-quarters of a mile away. Later he had been one of those who spearheaded the breakout from the docks.

When our wounds improved, we were moved on to an old barracks at Rennes where we were cared for by French colonial troops; these orderlies were blue-black Senegalese and brown Indo-Chinese. They looked after us like brothers and were ever cheerful and kind. The Senegalese were drill addicts and used to delight in demonstrating their arms drill to us, using broom sticks as rifles. The French doctors and nurses were charming and to my surprise one of the doctors, a Commandant Ricquaert, came to me to tell me that he had served on my father's staff in 1940 when my father brought the remnants of the Army Medical Services out of France through – of all places – St Nazaire!

I decided to enlist his help in order to escape and tried to persuade him to allow me to conceal myself in a large wicker laundry basket, under the soiled sheets, to be carried out of the barracks. With my ignorance of existing harsh German reprisals on all who assisted escapees, and with the intolerance of my youth, I was upset at his reluctance to help me. I had hoped so much to be put in touch with the French underground escape organisation and to be on my way home, but it was not to be. What the good doctor did do, bless him, quite unknown to me, was to ask his wife to notify my parents and my fiancée that I was alive and well, having been wounded. His wife addressed a letter to Major General W.B. Purdon, DSO, OBE, MC, posted it in German-occupied Paris, and, unbelievably, it was delivered to my father in London!

Our wounds healed, we were moved from Rennes to Germany and told we were bound for Oflags or Stalags there, depending on whether we were officers or NCOs. We were closely guarded and none of us found any opportunity to escape. We were given German rye bread and French Camembert cheese to eat which did great things both for morale and for flatulence! It was desperately frustrating as we moved inexorably away from France, further and further from its comparative nearness to Britain. A number of us thought we spoke French well enough to make a go of it had we been able to escape into France what with French sympathisers and our ability to pass as French or Belgians.

After a long and tiring journey we entered Marlag und Milag Nord, near Bremen, a wooden-hutted camp ringed with high barbed-wire fences built on the sandy soil of the Luneberg Heath – a desolate, unfriendly spot. This camp catered for officers and ratings of the Royal Navy and of the other navies of the British Empire, its Allies and of the Merchant Navy. I found that we, all ranks of both the Royal Navy and Commandos, who had taken part in Operation Chariot, were to be temporarily housed together and my feelings of depression at the camp were offset by the happy reunion with our comrades who were already there.

I found my other three corporals there – Ron Chung, Bob Hoyle and Cab Callaway (Cpl Johnnie Johnson, who had been severely wounded, accompanied me from Rennes). It was from the example of these four grand men that I really learnt what an honour it is to serve with the British soldier and I have tried to be worthy of them all ever since. Johnnie Johnson, very rightly, received the Military Medal for his part in the destruction of our winding house. I would have wished that my other three comrades-in-arms had each received the MM, for they all deserved it. I wear my Military Cross for all of them, as we were one, and the success of our task was due to the team.

Whilst we were at this camp, at Westertimke near Bremen, I took part in an attempt to tunnel out of the place. It was organised by Bill Copland and supervised by Bob Montgomery, our sapper. We used bedboards to prop up the roof and to shore the sides, and progress was fairly swift because of the sandy soil. It did not succeed. I cannot remember now if it was discovered or if we were moved on before we neared the wire but it gave us valuable experience for working in tunnels in other camps. It passed the time and it gave us some moments of hope and excitement.

One day we were called together by our German commandant, a little, grey, naval Captain with a torpedo beard, who announced the splendid news that Sam Beattie – we who were in *Campbeltown* with him idolised him – had been awarded the Victoria Cross. Whatever one may feel and say about them, those of us who fought against the Germans found that, like all nations, the preponderance of them were good, and a comparative minority were evil, or weak. Certainly they showed their chivalry on numerous occasions, and I for one am glad to have them again as our allies, as indeed they fought alongside us in the time of Wellington. But I did not feel that way then, despite this courteous gesture.

We Commandos hoped our own VCs would be announced, but it was not until after the war was over that Charles Newman's VC and Sergeant Tom Durrant's posthumous VC were gazetted. Those of us in *Campbeltown*, and who were with him, as I was, in the street fighting after the demolition tasks were accomplished, were, I feel sure, disappointed that a VC was not also conferred upon Major Bill Copland. On a night when so many brave deeds took place, his personal example and outstanding leadership ensured the successful, confident landing from *Campbeltown*, and he provided the backbone of the battle through the docks.

I remember my twenty-first birthday, walking in the barbed wire enclosure with another of our superb leaders, Donald Roy. We all looked up to him for his fearlessness and panache, and for his complete lack of side, he was the beau ideal of a fighting leader. Two others in particular we spoke of with awe and respect – TSM Haines and Sergeant Challington, the Germans found to their cost what fearsome fighting machines these two men were. Both were awarded richly deserved Distinguished Conduct Medals.

My other memory is of being marched off to another camp for showers. Here for the first time, we met Russian prisoners of war in abundance. We were horrified at the way in which the Germans treated them, and the Russians seemed overjoyed to see us. Looking back on it, I confess to being surprised that men like these, who seemed in the main to be small and of unimpressive physique inflicted such a crushing defeat on the Germans. When, after the war, I asked a German holder of the Knight's Cross of the Iron Cross how the Germans were defeated by these sort of soldiers, his reply was that the Wehrmacht ran out of ammunition before the Russians ran out of soldiers! However we must never underestimate either the bravery or the toughness of the Russian fighting man, nor must we forget the terrible suffering inflicted on their country by the Nazis and of the vast crushing victories the Russians won by their skill and gallantry.

One morning all our Commando NCOs were sent off to a Stalag: our Naval elements were moved into main Marlag und Milag camp from our segregated compound and we Commando officers went off by train to Oflag IXAH at Spangenberg on the River Fulda near Kassel. Oflag IXAH was a fine old Schloss set on the top of a steep, wooded hill above the little town of Spangenberg. It was surrounded by a deep, dry moat in which the prisoners took exercise, and was entered over a wooden drawbridge covered by a guardroom set on the opposite side of the moat to the Schloss. Armed guards were stationed on the bridge itself, and, also, within sight of each other, around the perimeter, able to cover every side of it by fire including the moat. By night searchlights illuminated the walls of the Schloss and the moat.

This was a comfortable camp and most of the officers had been there since Dunkirk. Many were elderly and a number of the younger ones were working for careers which they intended to pursue after the end of the war. Major-General (later Sir Victor) Fortune, GOC 51st Highland Division and his staff were there, Brigadier Nicholson the defender of Calais, and Brigadier Nigel Somerset, all three charming and dignified men. The Senior British officer, Lieutenant Colonel Ewan Miller won our immediate liking and respect. He was the best sort of British officer; and the Germans obviously held him in high respect also.

We, from St Nazaire, were keen to escape and quickly contacted the camp Escape Committee, composed of Lieutenant Colonels Henry Swinburn, MC of the Sikhs, 'Chatty' Swinburne, a Durham Light Infantry Territorial and W B Broomhall, OBE, a Sapper.

Disappointingly, they did not have many ideas to offer and the only scheme to get our teeth into was a tunnel which was entered under the floor of the music room. This was obviously a very long-term project but one we all volunteered for while looking for other ways out. By then I had teamed up with Dick Morgan of No. 2 Commando. Dick was a very tough chap, full of commonsense and guts. He became my greatest friend, transferred to my Regiment on becoming a Regular, and was Best Man at my wedding, completing his parachute course of eight jumps (including a night jump) in three days to 'get me to the Church on time'!

We found some keen and experienced escapers there, including Tom Acton of the Rifle Brigade and the Hon. Terence Prittie, of the 60th Rifles, both of whom became good friends and advisers; Dicky Lorraine, a Sapper, Robin Snook, a hardbitten Desert Horse Gunner with two DSOs, and Tom Stallard, DSO, MBE, a fair-haired regular Durham Light Infantry captain, later a lieutenant colonel.

Tom was a brilliant organiser and escapist and had planned and commanded the massed break over the wire surrounding the Oflag at Eichstatt.
It was characteristic of Tom that he insisted on going over the scaling
ladders last, in the place of danger. By the time the Germans had discovered the breakout and had opened fire on those last over. Tom was
wounded in the heel by a machine gun bullet, but all the same he reached
the Danish border before he had the bad luck of being recaptured. The other
person I remember particularly as an escape enthusiast was Stewart Walker
who had a number of escapes to his credit. His tales of foreign women
workers whom he met when 'outside' were worth a book on their own!

Spangenberg sold two sorts of German beer in its canteen, and was well
supplied with Red Cross parcels. We who were prisoners of war can never
be sufficiently grateful for them to the International Red Cross and Order
of St John, and for their constant interest and protection. There was a fine
library, as well as games facilities in the moat, particularly for basket ball
and a form of cricket. Dick Morgan and I took advantage of the food and
exercise facilities to really build up our strength and fitness by walking and
running for miles round the moat discussing how to escape.

There appeared in the camp one day a Gefreiter (corporal) a scrawny,
bespectacled, earnest-looking German soldier. He made it his business to
snoop on all our activities in the hope of discovering some escape attempt,
camp radio, hidden maps or other escape aids. He was a dreadful creature
whom the Escape Committee summed up as a man who would crack under
strain. Those of us who were keen escapers were organised into pairs and
told to follow him immediately he came into the courtyard. We were
ordered not to speak to him even if he spoke to us and never to leave his
heels. Dick and I took our turn at this, and he was clearly getting rattled,
especially as he could not shake us off nor get a word out of us. We
christened him 'the Nark', and it became commonplace to see him followed by two British officers, preceded by the cry of 'Nark up' or 'Goons
up'. Eventually he broke and ran shattered out of the courtyard and we
never saw him again.

One day Bill Copland told Dick and me that there was to be a camp play
and that costumes were to be provided from outside sources. These were to
be kept in the guardroom and carried in and out of the camp over the bridge
before and after each performance. There were to be three performances, a
dress rehearsal followed by two shows. Bill suggested that Dick and I
might like to volunteer to be the two officers who carried the large wicker
hamper containing costumes in and out of the camp on each occasion, and
to seize any opportunity to make an escape that might occur.

Dick and I knew that the road away from the guardroom turned sharp
right, the ground fell steeply away to our left, and then there was a narrow,

open stretch of about thirty yards to an archway through which the road passed, continuing straight on for forty or fifty yards more, before it commenced to wind its way right-handed down and round the steep hill on which the Schloss stood. From the Schloss we could see the surrounding countryside spread below us, open and green, rising gently on all sides, like a saucer, on the rim of which were expanses of thick woods. We reckoned the woods were about three miles from the Schloss.

Shortly after the road emerged from the archway which was round the corner from the guardroom, it appeared that there might be a narrow path to the left, that led steeply down the hill. In view of the fact that we would be in the open for at least thirty yards after leaving the guardroom, and that our route would be canalised by having to pass through the arch, the quicker we could remove ourselves as a target for a rifle or submachine gun the better. The Germans had a number of fierce Alsatian guard and tracker dogs – we had seen them – and it seemed to us that the most likely immediate action of the Germans in the event of an escape was to use their lorries to move soldiers and quickly throw a cordon around the limit which they reckoned the fastest movers could reach, i.e. the woods, and then search inwards to the camp leaving standing patrols on likely defiles.

So Dick and I, who were very fit by then, determined to run like Olympic three milers from the base of the hill in order to get into the woods and beyond the likely limit of the cordon before the Germans could get into position. We knew it would be a terrific 'puff', but we believed we could just do it.

After discussing routes with the Escape Committee we decided to make for Belgium and we memorised three addresses where we were told we would be put in touch with the underground escape network. There were no civilian clothes to be had, but this did not particularly worry us as we could neither of us speak German so we did not plan to use the railway or local transport. In fact we preferred to travel by night and to lie up by day, and by wearing uniform we ran less of a risk of being treated as spies if picked up than had we been caught in plain clothes.

We thought it would take at least two weeks to reach Belgium and, as it was then March we were unlikely to be able to live off the land. A harness was made for each of us out of hessian, with numerous pockets into which fitted long, flat cocoa tins. These were filled with cheese, raisins, biscuits and a dry, pounded up mixture of cocoa, sugar, biscuits and currants. We each had our watches, and were given a small escape compass and a map. We both carried a spare pair of thick army socks, a razor and soap, a comb and a toothbrush.

On the night of the dress rehearsal, each wearing his food harness and carrying his escape kit under his battledress, with Commando flashes on his shoulders, and shod in excellent, nearly silent, rubber-soled

Commando boots, Dick and I reported to the Germans. We were escorted by a guard armed with a tommy gun over the drawbridge to the guardroom beyond. We walked up the steps into the guardroom itself, still covered by the tommy gunner, while another armed sentry remained on the drawbridge to open and close the gate into the courtyard.

Wanting to lull the obvious suspicions of the guards we were very cheerful and chatty and quickly established a rapport, particularly when I said I was Irish. Despite this, we were closely guarded on the way back into camp and again after the performance when we carried the hamper back to the guardroom. In camp, Dick and I agreed that on the night's showing there had been no opportunity to escape and that we would have to engineer one if we were to get away.

The next night we went through the same performance, still closely watched, but still pulling the guards' legs and generally being friendly and cheerful. We both felt rather shamefaced having returned to the Schloss at the end of the night's performance and hoped that people would not think we had got 'cold feet'.

On the next night, 26 March 1943, a year to the day when we had sailed for St Nazaire, Dick and I agreed that we must make a go of it, somehow. The guard commander of the first night was on duty again, and greeting me as 'allo Irischer', gave me a jovial clap on the back as we went out to collect the clothes. By good luck he missed contact with my armour plating of cocoa tins, but my harness gave such a rattle that I was sure he would rumble us – but he didn't! After the performance, carrying the hamper, Dick and I joked with the guards on the way back to the guardroom. I noticed that the gate sentry was fully preoccupied with locking the gate behind us, and, as prearranged, Dick and I lengthened our pace without quickening it, leaving him still engrossed with securing the gate. The guard commander said, 'Komm, Irischer' with a laugh and walked up the guardroom steps. As we reached them Dick and I looked at each other in the light of the guardroom lamp – 'Now!' and we quietly put down the hamper while the guard commander had his back turned. Then we ran silently and swiftly round the corner. There came a hysterical shout of 'Halt!' from behind us, and we fairly raced towards that archway, very conscious of the vulnerability of our backs to a burst of tommy gun fire.

In a flash we were through the arch, and judging in the darkness where the path lay, we turned left and literally dived into space as the first shots came. Amid whistle blasts, more shots and raucous cries, we were falling down the steep hill side, turning over and over in mid air, crashing through one bush after another until the 'berg' flattened out a bit. We picked ourselves up and ran through some gardens, climbing over fences, and keeping together.

We took a quick look upward and behind us and saw that the Schloss was illuminated. The searchlights were on, lights were flashing by the top of the hill, more shots rang out – presumably at some unfortunate nocturnal animal – and, in addition to the shooting came the sound of truck engines starting up. Dick and I ran for the forest line as we had never probably run before, uphill all the way but we simply had to be in those woods before the cordon was in position. By the time the edge of the forest loomed up, my legs were beginning to feel like rubber and I was breathing like a puffing billy. We could hear the sound of the heavy lorry engines growing louder and louder and then, thank God, we were among the trees.

Resisting the impulse to flop down on the ground, we forced ourselves to keep going, and we were encouraged in our resolve by the sound of dogs baying behind us. After what seemed like half an hour, but was only probably ten minutes, we stopped and took stock. Our rough descent had resulted in a number of our tins of food becoming dislodged and lost. Worse still, our compass had gone. We remembered that there were two railways, one running from east to west, the other from north to south. We knew the former was on our left and that traffic was fairly frequent so we pushed on, keeping direction by the sound of the trains.

It was exhilarating to have escaped, but we realised that the really difficult part lay ahead of us, the journey across Germany to Belgium and that even then, once in Belgium, we faced the problem of contacting the escape organisation and from getting from Belgium to Britain. However, despite the loss of our compass and the tins of food during our head over heels descent from the Schloss, we felt full of energy and determination and set off at a fast pace leaving the sound of the dogs increasingly far behind us.

We kept going until about an hour before dawn. For quite a time we had been followed by some animal which gave a sinister, eerie howl – we never discovered what it was. At first light we looked around for good cover where we would be safe from woodcutters, foresters and possible searchers. We found a suitable place, ate some rations and had a mouthful or two of water. The only water containers we had managed to get were a small Dettol bottle each, and both of these, despite repeated rinsings, still tasted disagreeably of antiseptic. We had a trouble-free day and managed to sleep for several hours. As darkness fell we moved off again, once more hearing the eerie sound of the mysterious animal behind us. We emerged into a rolling, open agricultural landscape with farmhouses and workers' cottages dotted about and the going was good across country.

We filled our bottles at a stream, had a good drink, and refilled them. We made excellent time and knew we were keeping good direction, not only from the stars, but also we could see the glow from the trains as they passed along the railway on our left. We had difficulty in finding somewhere to lie up before first light on our second morning of freedom as we were still in open country. In the end we had to settle for a small, rather isolated thicket about four hundred yards from a country road. We had some worrying moments, once when children approached us and passed by, and once when a dog ran towards us, but was called away by its owner.

We continued like this for a week. We shaved every day, and, despite having to sleep rough and walk through muddy ditches, tried to keep our appearance tidy as we did not want to look like ruffians when we contacted the Belgian underground. The weather got cold and a biting wind blew. We were feeling tired from our walking, from continually being alert, and from lack of food and sleep – we were rationing ourselves pretty severely. We had not been able to find any water that day. At midnight we came on a wooden barn near a farmhouse and decided we must get a decent, warm sleep.

The barn was padlocked, but Dick put his shoulders to the door and forced open a gap through which I just managed to squeeze. I undid the heavy bolts on the inside of the double door, which made enough space for Dick in his turn to get in. We then bolted the door and found that the barn was piled high with hay, with a ladder propped against it. We climbed to the top of the hay and then discovered that the sides of the barn did not overlap, but were slatted, through which the icy wind whistled. We could not sleep because of the bitterly cold blast which blew piercingly through the open sides of the barn and through the very hay itself.

We were both feeling very thirsty, so we each made a separate night-time journey outside to try to find water. Both of us eventually found some water in a ditch, drank our fill and brought full bottles back. Daylight came, and we heard men's voices outside and the sound of a key in the door lock. We quickly burrowed under the hay, as deep as we could get. I arranged a pile of hay well over Dick and then wound my way down to a depth of about four feet. Both of us went down by the inside of the slatted wall. Soon we heard footsteps on the ladder, and then there were two men walking on top of me, after which they moved to the other end of the barn and started to fork down hay, chatting to each other the while.

Just as they opened the doors on entering, Dick had been seized with a violent stomach cramp and I am afraid I savagely held my hand over his mouth, forcing him to be still despite what must have been an agony of discomfort for him, until he relaxed and the spasm had gone. Thankfully we heard the men depart but we had to lie and freeze for the rest of the day until dark. During this time we got out our water bottles to find both were alive with water bugs. It came on to rain heavily, the wind dropped and the weather became warmer.

When night came we pressed on towards Belgium following farm tracks, crossing a lateral railway track, crouching behind a bush as a train loomed up, drawn by what looked like an enormous engine, the light of the coal fire in its furnace illuminating the edge of the track as it thundered and panted past, after which we came to a cobbled road. We were wet through and, having dodged behind cover each time the sound of vehicles announced their approach, we found ourselves in what seemed to be a mining or industrial town.

Up to now we had skirted towns and villages but as our rations were very low, we had to take chances in order to make speed. We passed individuals presumably going on or coming off shift, and we exchanged 'Gute nachts'. Eventually one man fell in beside us and chatted away and we made various grunts as neither of us understood what he was saying. It was too dark for him to see we were in British uniform but we had to get rid of him in case he had a torch or lit a match. He repeated the same phrase several times, so in desperation, in a rude tone, I said loudly, 'Ach Scheise'. This brought what sounded like a stream of abuse from him, but he forged ahead of us and disappeared down a side street to our relief.

Fortunately we met no military or police during our journey through this town and continued along the main road beyond it. By now, perhaps due to the tainted water we had drunk, we both felt feverish and light-headed and were convinced, although at the time neither of us mentioned it, that we had a third person walking with us. The rain stopped, and although it was night time the sky brightened considerably. We could now see that the road was about to swing left and pass through another large town, but that we could keep to our general line of direction if we left the highway and kept straight on along a farm track. This we did, and found ourselves among fruit trees. Later on the track entered a deciduous wood. The track was covered with wet leaves, water from the recent rain still dripped from the trees and there was a smell of decay and rotting vegetation. Suddenly we were walking through what seemed to be a cemetery, but instead of gravestones there were stone urns and statues. The place had a strange, brooding atmosphere and seemed to us what we would expect the Nazis might have had instead of a consecrated graveyard. We never discovered what it was, nor where exactly it was located.

We passed through yet another town, relieved to find that a bridge which we approached was unguarded, and towards first light came on a fairly thick wood, where we decided to lie up for the coming day. We appreciated that if we were ever going to make it to Belgium we would be unlikely to do so on our feet because our scant rations were almost finished. So we decided we would steal bicycles and cycle the rest of the way by night.

We were not far from a town and as soon as it was dark we set off towards it. When we got there we found eight bicycles on a stand but all

were securely chained to it and locked. We could find nothing with which
to undo them and we had to hide whenever we heard anyone coming. The
night passed and we had still failed to get our bicycles. We knew that the
railway passed through the town and we followed the road until we came
to a large station.

We decided to hop a goods train going to the west. At that moment the
German air raid sirens sounded and the station was plunged into darkness,
apart from a light still shining faintly from inside the ticket office. We had
to pass this office to get on the platform, so I sneaked up to it and I could
just make out a blackout panel that would cover the booking office ticket
aperture. The panel was secured by a hook, so I undid it and swung it shut,
whereupon Dick and I slipped quickly and silently on to the platform. Here
we could make out a number of people standing in the dark whilst a
succession of trains rattled through going the way we wanted. To our
despair they all consisted of high-sided iron-ore hoppers and not one flat or
truck came by. We could hear our bombers droning overhead but no
bombs seemed to be falling in earshot. Eventually the sound of the bombers' engines died away, and we heard another train.

We waited for it and once again it consisted of more ore hoppers. Then
came the 'All Clear' and the faint lights on the platform came on again. We
stood among a crowd of Germans, bareheaded but in British battledress
and no one seemed to notice! Obviously we must leave and try again the
next night, so we moved off towards the exit. 'Halt!' said an unwelcome
and guttural voice, and we turned to face a pistol pointing at us from a
couple of feet away, held by a railway policeman. The crowd quickly
closed around us and our escape attempt was over. Closely escorted, we
were marched to the local jail and handed over to the local bobby, a man
with a Franz Josef moustache. He locked us into a cell with two wooden
benches in it, each with raised, polished wooden neck rests, which served
as pillows. He was quite a nice old country policeman and did not shout at
or threaten us and the cell was very warm. We lay down and quickly fell
into a deep sleep from which we were awoken by shouts of 'Raus! Raus!'
and found ourselves looking into the faces of two soldiers. We were
questioned but we could not understand and were then left alone again.
Our bobby brought in a jug of hot acorn tea, two tin mugs and some dark
brown bread which we received gratefully.

Next day an escort arrived and we were handed over to a Gefreiter and
two private soldiers, all armed – the Gefreiter with a pistol, the two
privates with rifles. These turned out to be decent men who said they
admired us for having escaped and they took us into a troops' canteen on
the station where they bought us each a huge bowl of thick, delicious meat
soup and also offered us cigarettes, but neither of us smoked. Although

they were obviously good chaps we decided we would give them the slip if we got the opportunity. I thought I had a chance when we were on the train and I asked to go to the lavatory. I opened the lavatory window at the top, hoping to squeeze through but the Gefreiter seemed to suspect me and was into the W.C. in a flash, and shouted hysterically at me, brandishing a large ring of keys in my face. After that they never left us.

We returned to Spangenberg and crestfallenly crossed the drawbridge. To our amazement, as we entered the courtyard, every window, and the yard itself, seemed to be filled with officers who cheered us as we were taken through and escorted up the stairs inside one of the turrets to the cells at the top. Here we were placed in adjacent cells and ordered not to communicate with each other. The commandant arrived, Hauptman Roth, a man we respected because he was a real soldier, quiet, courteous and dignified, a veteran of the Great War with the Iron Cross. He congratulated each of us on our escape, said he felt for us that we had been recaptured, and sentenced us each to fourteen days solitary confinement.

We next had a visit from the British padre who gave us a change of clothing, towels and washing kit, smuggled us each a ball of string and told us to let a sock down out of our window into the courtyard below when we heard a whistle. This we did and when I pulled mine up it contained a Red Cross meatloaf, some chocolate and a small tin of cheese.

Whilst we were doing our solitary, another escape attempt took place, made by two officers who had been in a party sent to Spangenberg from Oflag IVC, Colditz. They were caught in the moat, I think, and found their way to the two remaining solitary confinement cells. They were two delightful chaps, one was Jimmy Yule, now retired as a Colonel Royal Signals, the other was Alan Campbell, who had a brilliant and distinguished legal career and is now Lord Campbell of Alloway. They used their Colditz skills to remove a door from its hinges, let me and Dick out, and the Germans found the four of us playing cards in one of their cells, using the door as a table.

We looked around for another means of escape as soon as we had completed our fortnight's solitary and decided that from our own practical experiences we really must travel by train next time, and that we would need to team up with German speakers. Meanwhile we did a lot of fitness training and worked on the camp tunnel. The Germans found the tunnel shortly after, and both Dick Morgan and I were among those caught at work on it. This tunnel owed a lot to the expertise of a delightful South African mining engineer, Captain Jim Rogers, known as 'Horse', who was one of the members of the Colditz party and with whom I was to serve there for the next two years.

Later I was summoned by Hauptman Roth and told that I was a known keen escaper and that he was sure that I was going to continue my efforts to get out. Also, I was 'Deutschfeindlich' and my part in 'breaking' the 'Nark' was known. So, I was 'to go to the Straflager at Colditz for bad boys, Oberleutnant Purdon'. A few days later Dick Morgan, Micky Burn and I were on our way to Oflag IVC, Colditz, together with the recently-arrived former Colditz incomers.

We travelled by train and were closely guarded and saw no opportunity for escape. On the way we discussed escaping with our Colditz friends who were particularly well versed in that subject. As Colditz was so far to the east, we were advised that in the event of getting out of that notorious camp we should aim for Switzerland or Sweden and that the best way to travel was by train, wearing civilian clothes, with a German speaker.

I have recently returned to Spangenberg. Whilst there I remembered the occasion when I was in a small party that broke into a dungeon where there was said to be a well leading down to a tunnel, out of the Schloss. We were trying to see down the well shaft by match light when someone dislodged a huge lamp which was suspended over it. It disappeared with a mighty booming sound into the depths and we just got back into the courtyard before armed Germans came running in. We carried a 30 foot rope made of sheets, down which we proposed to slide. When my daughter-in-law, Angela, and I looked down by electric light into the yawning, vertical tunnel, I was relieved that we had not had time to try out our rope. The thought of dangling at its end with a hundred foot drop tends to whiten the hair!

CHAPTER SIX

COLDITZ

We were marched from Colditz railway station to the Schloss. My first view of this ancient castle was from the bridge over the river and there it loomed above us. It was to house us for nearly two years. To my surprise I could hear the sound of cheering and pieces of material were being waved from the windows – which as we drew nearer, I could see were barred. The noise grew louder and by the time we entered the cobbled courtyard it had grown to pandemonium, sounding like a first class riot.

The Germans had two tables in the yard, each placed below windows, and German officers sat there to take our particulars, photograph us and so on. To my amazement water bombs rained onto the tables, and then a blazing paliasse was thrown down out of an upper window. Grinning faces looked down, roaring insults at our captors. Eventually a riot squad doubled in, wearing coal-scuttle helmets and carrying weapons. The Germans pointed their rifles up at the prisoners above and the proceedings were then completed in comparative quiet. Up until then we had only seen the well-behaved officer prisoners at Westertimke and Spangenberg. Clearly, morale at Colditz was terrific and the prisoners were men to be reckoned with, and respected accordingly by their captors.

Eventually the German guards left and the inmates of Oflag IVC poured down into the courtyard. 'I'm Jack Keats,' said a smiling officer with glasses, 'come and join our mess in the Belgian Quarters.' Dick and I were taken up a spiral staircase with open doors off it through which we could see ablutions and lavatories, to a top floor and along it to an end room. This contained a number of double-tier bunks, plus some wooden tables and benches, and chairs made from Red Cross crates.

Here we were introduced to the remaining members of the Mess. We discovered (not from him) that Jack Keats had been awarded the Distinguished Service Cross and Bar. There were other naval officers, all very friendly, Ernie Champion, Bob Barnes and Dusty Miller. Peter Tunstall, a German 'baiter', was RAF. Don Donaldson was a wise-cracking Canadian pilot and there were two Royal Marines, David Hunter, dark and amusing, and Hugh Bruce, wiry, with a sandy moustache.

After a brew-up we were taken to meet the Escape Committee, the two main members being Dick How, a Royal Tank Regiment captain with an MBE and MC, and a large, cheerful, dark Yorkshireman called 'Lulu' Lawton, in the Duke of Wellingtons.

Colditz Castle has been described numerous times and was built by Augustus the Strong. So far as the prisoners were concerned it consisted of the courtyard, three sides of which housed prisoners of war, a chapel and cells. The fourth side was the cookhouse and ration store, with the German quarters beyond. Also situated on the fourth side was a portion which housed some senior British officers. Down below and outside the castle was the Tiergarten, a wired-off area for exercise, but the cobbled courtyard was the scene of most of our regular outdoor games. Here basketball, volleyball and stoolball were played, and roll-call parades were held. Here also we walked round and round for daily exercise and chats.

At the time of our arrival there were Polish office POWs in one block, very smart on parade in their distinctive square-crowned, peaked caps and polished field boots. The Dutch and the Belgians had just gone, they sounded a fine crowd; and the French, who were a great lot, departed soon after. I remember being shown a bullet hole in the ceiling of a room in the French quarters. It was ringed in pencil, round which was written 'Vous avez tirez le premier', or some such sentence. Apparently the French had been catcalling at the Germans from their windows during a visit by the Swiss Red Cross and one of the German sentries decided he had been fired at by the French! He fired up at the window, one bullet entering the ceiling. Later the Germans said to the French 'You fired first!' The French didn't let them forget it!

We were surrounded by men who had a great deal of escaping experience. Some officers had escaped many, many times, and several had been living for months on end in Poland with the undergrounds. There was still talk of the comparatively recent 'home runs' by the late Airey Neave, Billy Stephens, Pat Reid, Wally Hammond and Hank Wardle. Of course there were a number of escape attempts in the offing but Colditz did seem a very hard nut to crack. Shortly after our arrival the legendary Douglas Bader stumped over for a chat. He was a tonic, ever cheerful and friendly and I admired him immensely. All sorts of interesting personalities came to

Colditz during my time there. Shortly after the Dieppe raid a number of Canadian officers appeared including the commanding officer of the South Saskatchewan Regiment, the very gallant Lieutenant Colonel Cecil Merritt, VC, a pleasant, unassuming person. From Crete and the Western Desert came that superb fighting man Charles Upham, winner of the Victoria Cross and Bar. The founder of the SAS, Lieutenant Colonel Sir David Stirling, DSO, joined us, very tall, dark, sallow and gangling, also Brigadier 'Trotsky' Davies of the Royal Ulster Rifles, who had been grievously wounded leading our mission in Albania where he earned a Bar to his DSO (he already had two MCs) to mention but a few of our distinguished company. Later, after the crushing of the Warsaw Uprising, came General Bor-Komorowski, and his staff – he was a little, seemingly insignificant-looking man until you actually met him, and then you realised he had a personality like a lion. General Bor-Komorowski gave us all a fascinating and enlightening talk about his battle against the Germans in Warsaw. The Russians had cynically halted nearby to allow the Germans to destroy what the Russians considered the disciplined, well-organised anti-communist Polish underground army, which would have proved a major spanner in their own imperialistic red annexation plans for Poland.

The camp abounded with 'characters' too numerous to mention, but if one had to be in a prisoner of war camp, one could not have asked for a finer, braver or more cheerful lot of comrades. When we got there, Lt. Col. 'Daddy' Stainer was Senior British Officer, a charming, kindly man. He was succeeded by Lt. Col. Tubby Broomhall, who had been at Spangenberg. Finally, Lt. Col. Willie Tod of the Royal Scots Fusiliers was SBO at the closing stages of the war, a grand soldier and a fine man to whom we, who were there at the end, probably all owe our lives.

Mike Sinclair stood head and shoulders over everyone in his previous experience of escaping, in his flair for planning and disguise, in his personal bravery and élan, and in his sheer dedication. He was such a nice chap too, redhaired, a regular 60th Rifles subaltern; I am sure he would have gone right to the top had he not been taken at Calais. He was the sort of man who wins the VC and his courage as a prisoner of war escaper was of the highest – calculated bravery, not hot-blooded stuff on the spur of the moment.

Among the inmates there was a Canadian pilot called Don Thom, who had been either an Olympic gymnast or diver. Don dived over a terrace where he had been exercising under the guard of an armed sentry, grabbed the cross bars of the grille over a cell window and then dropped twenty, thirty or more feet to the ground using the tremendous strength of his arms and grip to grab the steel bars on the next successive windows below to break his fall. He then attempted to get through the wire having been fired on by two sentries, but was recaptured.

A small and extremely modest RAF officer, Dominic Bruce, MC, DFM, had escaped curled up in a Red Cross tea chest, which was carried out of camp in a cart to a German storeroom, from where Dominic escaped. Sadly, he was caught in Danzig harbour basin before he could smuggle himself onto a boat and reach Sweden.

Two of our St Nazaire friends were at Colditz, Micky Burn and Micky Wynn. Micky Burn helped run the secret radio which gave us all the BBC news. Micky, who is amazingly diligent and clever, passed a number of examinations from Colditz earning himself university degrees.

Micky Wynn who had lost his eye during the action at St Nazaire was taken out to a German military hospital for treatment. He managed to escape and was to return to Germany towards the end of the War to liberate his own coxswain from a prisoner of war camp.

While the four of us, Micky Burn, Micky Wynn, Dick Morgan and I – were in Colditz together, we had a St Nazaire Dinner on the Anniversary of the Raid, eating what we could provide from Red Cross parcels. John Watton, the artist, very kindly illustrated four individual menus for us. There is a St Nazaire Reunion in London each Anniversary, Billy Stephens and Micky Burn are our Presidents. There is also a Colditz Society, thanks to the enthusiasm of the late Lieutenant Commander Mike Moran, its Honorary Secretary, Kenneth Lockwood, and a very active Committee. General 'Tubby' Broomhall is now its President.

Grismond Davies-Scourfield was another high calibre Regular officer in the 60th Rifles taken at Calais. He, with the clever and experienced Kit Silverwood-Cope, had operated for months with the Polish underground. Wherever you looked there were men with amazing records behind them. Whenever a new arrival came into the gates he was assailed for news and details of his own escaping activities which had resulted in his being sent to Colditz. One French officer was very reluctant to talk about his exploits but persistent questioning eventually elicited the fact that he had not escaped. He had killed and eaten the German commandant's pet dog, or cat, (I can't remember which) and made himself a sort of Davy Crockett hat out of it! Apparently he was unwise enough to wear his headgear on 'appel', when it was recognised by its previous owner, who thereupon consigned him to Colditz!

Germans could not enter a building without the cry of 'Goons Up' and there were various elaborate systems of signalling any movement from outside, so there was almost always timely warning enabling tell-tale evidence to be removed. Everyone assisted with whatever escape activity was going on, and really we all kept our spirits up because each of us was determined to get away from Colditz and to help others to do the same.

Early in my time there a French officer, clad only in running kit, who had been trotting round and round the wired-in exercise area, suddenly ran to the wire, was given a 'chuck-up', got clear over and ran off before any guard could fire. I think I am right in saying he successfully got to France. On another occasion Dick Morgan supervised, and I was one of the assistants, in a successful breakout by Mike Sinclair and Jack Best. In this attempt the bars of an upper window were sawed through, the cut was camouflaged, and, at night the bars were removed to let a polished table be put out twice, once with Mike and then with Jack Best lying on it. One of them lowered a rope which reached the terrace below. After narrow squeaks with guards they cut through the wire, roped down to ground level and eventually got clear out of Colditz. They both managed to reach the German border before, sadly, being caught.

On another occasion Mike Sinclair, Colonel Tubby Broomhall, Lance Pope and John Hyde-Thompson, dressed in German uniforms made by their brother officers, marched out disguised as the guard NCO and relief sentries. This attempt very nearly succeeded but for a vigilant German sentry. Mike Sinclair tragically lost his life in a later, simple and very gallant attempt through the wire, made from the exercise compound. He was through the wire when spotted, but instead of cutting him off and capturing him, as they so easily could and should have done, the German sentries gunned him down. The news of his death was a dreadful shock to us all. We all liked and respected Mike so much and it was almost unbelievable that, under such tragic circumstances, the 'Red Fox', as the Germans called him, who was the beau ideal of escapers and an inspiration to each one of us, had been killed.

Jerry Wood, a burly, tall redheaded, broken-nosed, bespectacled, Canadian engineer subaltern who had been taken at Dieppe, and 'Horse' Rogers had a tunnel going called 'Crown Deep', far down in the castle foundations, and a number of us, myself included, worked on it. I remember hearing that the skeleton of a human hand had been discovered. If true, it was not surprising in view of the history of the Castle. The tunnel never came to anything, but it kept us going and we hoped it might connect up with a passage, drain or conduit leading out of the camp. Certainly it was worth a try, and it was an outlet for our energy.

The Escape Committee had decided, in order to enable various escape activities to take place non-stop, by night as well as by day, that when Mike Sinclair and Jack Best escaped an additional two officers would disappear, and become 'ghosts'. The Germans would (and did) think that they had gone out with Mike and Jack but in fact they would be in the castle, ensuring that unbroken work could be carried out on escape projects throughout twenty-four hours. The 'ghosts' were chosen so as not to be particularly well known or striking in their appearance – officers with red or fair hair, bald heads, scars on their faces, etc., were not selected nor were notorious trouble makers or 'goonbaiters'.

Mike Harvey and Bob Barnes were, I think, the ghosts and there were other officers, superficially like them and not especially well known to the Germans, whose places the 'ghosts' took on shifts.

Although it was extremely difficult to get out of Colditz all sorts of schemes were dreamed up, some long term, some opportunity attempts. I took part in one of the latter with Bush Parker and Checko Chaloupka, a large cheerful, dark, extrovert Czech pilot, who had been decorated for bravery by his own country, by France, and by Britain. Bush let us into a room over the kitchen area from where we planned to get through the ceiling into the German part of the castle, and then out of the place from there. We had a brace and bit among other items, and while making a hole to look through to see if the coast was clear, Bush saw a blue eye looking upwards straight at him, after which we heard the alarm! Apparently we had cut through the German sensor wires in the ceiling. We never found out for certain but we had a mad scramble to get back into the camp itself before the German riot squad dashed into the camp to try to catch us.

Jack Best and Bill Goldfinch, another RAF pilot, were leading lights in a plan to build a glider. I believe the idea behind this was in case the SS took over the Oflag as the war neared its end and it became imperative to get people out to contact leading Allied elements. Or it may have been for a one-off escape attempt. I cannot remember. I volunteered to help in the project. The Escape Committee had rightly assessed that the Germans would not check the actual dimensions of the great, long, wide attics in Colditz Castle, and therefore by building a false wall it would be possible to enclose enough space within it for a hangar in which to construct the two-seater glider. This was most professionally done and we who worked on the glider were let in and out of this 'hangar' by a team of camouflage experts who skilfully concealed our entry and exit. A team of lookouts or 'stooges', as they were called, was posted so as to be able to watch entry into the courtyard and to see into each entrance to the building.

A comprehensive yet simple system of visual signalling was set up which, together with yells of 'Goons up' worked well and we were never discovered, nor was the glider. I believe Bill and Jack designed the machine. Those of us who helped merely did what we were told, including covering the frame with an outer surface made from blue and white checked bed sheets, which we painted with a sort of flour paste, again as specified by Bill Goldfinch and Jack Best. We completed the glider fairly quickly.

The method of launching it, if I remember correctly, was that a bath would be filled with earth, and some stone steps would be removed from the spiral staircase which led to the top floor of the Belgian quarters. The bath would be fixed to a rope and attached (with a quick-release catch) to the nose of the glider. On the earth-filled bath being dropped, the glider and its crew of two would be catapulted from the roof, out towards and over the perimeter wire. I confess I was glad I was not to be one of its two occupants! I heard later, after the war, by which time Colditz was in the Russian-occupied zone, that some officers who knew about it took out the glider and towed it until it became airborne behind a car, but I cannot vouch for this. Certainly I feel fairly confident that the glider would have flown.

A number of officers whom the Germans considered might be useful as bargaining counters and who were called 'Prominentes' were confined with us in Colditz. They were housed in part of the castle on the ground floor, and were specially guarded. They included the Earl of Harewood and the late Master of Elphinstone, who were cousins of the King and Queen; the Earl of Hopetoun (later Marquis of Linlithgow) whose father had been Viceroy of India; Giles Romilly and Felix de Hamel, both of whom were relations of Sir Winston Churchill; Michael Alexander, whom I believe was a relative of Field Marshal Earl Alexander, and others including Earl Haig and Lieutenant John Winant, son of the then American Ambassador in London. Also in this group was General Bor-Komorowski, the leader of the heroic Warsaw uprising whom I have mentioned already, together with certain of his staff.

In addition to, and in preparation for escape attempts, many people did their best to keep very fit. A favourite game was stoolball. As played in Colditz this consisted of two teams, one man in each team sitting on and guarding a stool, one of which was positioned at either end of the cobbled, uneven courtyard. The game was then played like rugger, without the conversions and dropkicks, and the ball could be passed or thrown in any direction, the aim being to touch the other team's stool (the goal) with the ball. It was amazing that playing flat out, including tackling low and falling on the ball, completely ignoring the fact that the pitch was not grass but cobbled stone, no one was ever seriously injured. It was a most exciting, tough sport and it helped expend our energy. Douglas Bader, who was game for anything, used to play guard on a stool, and jolly tough he was.

When the news of D Day came we were all very excited, and at one time felt we might be liberated within a few months. However, that was not to be and we continued our efforts to escape so as to try to 'get in on the act' before the war ended. Among the most impressive and heartening sights were the daylight raids carried out by the Fortresses and Liberators of the United States Army Air Force and we used to gather in the courtyard and cheer as we gazed up at their majestic air-armadas droning overhead in massed formations, easy to see by their white condensation trails and, at times, by the sunlight reflecting on their polished surfaces. From time to time we would see their fighter escort, and the puffs of dirty smoke as German flak exploded among them. It made us feel very imprisoned to think that probably an hour after passing over us on their return trip, those who had safely completed their missions would be sitting down to tea in their bases in England and taking girls out in the evening.

We became resigned to the fact that the war would go on into 1945, and that food supplies would lessen. Also the fuel situation was such that some officers went out on parole in order to gather wood. Red Cross parcels had ceased to arrive and German rations consisted of bread, potatoes and either turnip soup or cabbage soup. We supplemented these rations with what remained of our camp store of Red Cross parcels. The RAF were bombing Leipzig, Chemnitz and Dresden with great effect and we were heartened by the sound of our bombers at night.

Four French generals and a horde of French army officers, most of whom had been captured in France in 1940, arrived in Colditz. Many wore khaki-hooded cloaks and some pushed little wooden carts bearing their belongings. They were crowded into the chapel and a cellar under the building.

On 11 April 1945 the Prominente were removed from Colditz. They were taken away by night, despite the strongest protests from the SBO, Colonel Willie Tod, and from Brigadier 'Trotsky' Davies. Hauptmann Eggers, the English-speaking camp Security Officer, a decent man, accompanied them to their destination, Königstein, from where General Giraud had successfully escaped some three years earlier. Hauptmann Eggers returned to Colditz with a signed certificate of the Prominentes' safe arrival. This had been stipulated earlier by Colonel Tod and Brigadier Davies.

By now artillery and tank fire could be heard from the west and each day it moved nearer to us. On Saturday 11 April 1945 the German commandant was told that all prisoners of Oflag IVC were to move out of the camp eastwards. Colonel Tod refused point blank, the German commandant passed this back to his superiors and eventually it was agreed that Colditz Castle should be surrendered to the Americans when they arrived, but that the SBO must accept responsibility for any casualties suffered by us in the process of our liberation.

That night as we lay in our bunks we heard the firing of artillery from both sides, very near. At first light we were at the windows and shortly after 9am we saw five US Army tanks emerge from the woods to our west. American shells came close, one hitting the window of Group Captain

Campbeltown embedded in the dry-dock gate at St Nazaire. This photo was taken by the Germans between daylight on 28 March 1942, and the time she blew up that morning at about 10.35am. The photograph was taken from a German soldier in North Africa by a British Serviceman who, on learning a few years ago that HRH Prince Andrew was serving in the present HMS Campbeltown, sent the photo to the Prince.

Prince Andrew, Duke of York is now Colonel-in-Chief of The Royal Irish Regiment, of which my previous Regiment, The Royal Ulster Rifles, is a component part.

The remains of the winding hut blown up at St Nazaire. Photo taken in 1947

The funeral of a British serviceman killed in the St Nazaire raid (April, 1942)

Forged Ausweis or pass, made in the PoW camp

Veterans of the St Nazaire raid parade through the town, with Colonel Charles Newman VC and Captain Bob Ryder VC at front.

THE PRISONERS' QUARTERS

The prisoners' quarters in Colditz Castle

A post-war exercise in Northern Ireland. The author makes a point to Brigadier Nelson Russell, DSO, MC, commanding 107 (Ulster) Brigade of the Territorial Army. Brigadier Russell had been one of the commanders of The Irish Brigade during the war

Wedding Day

1st Royal Ulster Rifles about to search Varosha, Cyprus during the EOKA campaign, 1958

1st Royal Ulster Rifles, Vickers medium machine-gun training, Hong Kong, January 1964. The Vickers had been in service with the British Army since before the First World War

Exercise "Iron Hand", 1960. Saracen armoured personnel carriers of 1st Royal Ulster Rifles cross a pontoon bridge over the river Weser in Germany

The Staff College Rugby XV, 1955. Author sitting at front right

Battalion Headquarters, 1st Royal Ulster Rifles, about to fly to Sarawak from Hong Kong for the Indonesian emergency

On foot in the jungle. A patrol of 1st Royal Ulster Rifles crosses a stream in Sarawak

A Wessex helicopter of 845 Naval Air Squadron adds its support to my battalion in the Borneo jungle

9 Platoon, C Company, 1st Royal Ulster Rifles on jungle patrol in the Third division of Sarawak. As roads were almost non-existent in this 25,000 square miles area, river patrols formed a large part of day-to-day operations

Searching for terrorists in a kampong or village

On the alert in a swamp

Terrorists could be anywhere. Corporal King leads a patrol through a jungle swamp in Sarawak.

Corporal Matata checks his position in a jungle swamp. He is one of a number of Fijian soldiers in the Ulster Rifles. Note the shamrock badges in the soldiers' hats

Ready for the jungle. Commanding Officer, 1st Royal Ulster Rifles, Sarawak

An ambush team in a covered bunker at Tepoi. Cpl Deignan and his ambush team killed a raiding party of three Indonesians in a night action from positions including this one

Second Lieutenant Niall Ryan, leading a patrol, interviews a local resident while a kampong is checked for terrorists

On the alert for terrorist infiltrators. Four riflemen cover a track

Iban tribeswomen play the drums and dance for soldiers of The Royal Ulster Rifles

The letter from home. That important contact takes the full attention of a young rifleman

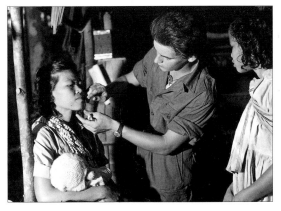

Hearts and Minds. A medical orderly of the Rifles treats a Dayak woman in the Serian area

I escort General Sir Walter Walker, Director of Operations in Borneo, to my Battalion HQ at Sibu in Sarawak. Behind us, Commander 'Tank' Sherman

Rfn Moore, a medical orderly, treats a small cut on Rfn Barr's hand. Even a minor cut needed immediate attention in the damp heat of Sarawak to prevent sepsis, or worse

The Sultan of Oman

Commander, Sultan's Armed Forces

A quarter guard of Desert Regiment at Nizwa, 1967. Ivor MacEwan is on the right

In the Empty Quarter

Mike Peele, MC, with a company of Muscat Regiment
at Sur, 1967

'The Hard Men'. Conference at Bid Bid, 1967.
L to R: John Clarke, Sandy Gordon, Jim Sheridan,
Mike Harvey, John Cooper and Peter Raven

"After Operation Lance. L to R: Guy Sheridan, Richard Kinsella-Beran,
Peter Thwaites and Simon Sloane

A 5.5-inch howitzer of the Sultan's artillery in action, 1969

Recapture of Sudh, St Patrick's Day, 1970. Included L to R: Lt Col Fergus MacKain-Bremner (CO, Muscat Regt), Signaller Suleiman, Maj Peter Bennett (OC, B Coy, Muscat Regt), Cpl Brown (Queen's Own Highlanders), the author

Investiture after Wadi Jizzi battle

General Officer Commanding, Near East Land Forces

Douglas Bader's room. Early next morning, 16 April, as we crowded into the courtyard some American GIs entered through the courtyard gate to an ecstatic welcome. They rounded up the German guards and I remember one GI who said 'Any guy who has been bad to you, just say, and we'll kick his ass!' In the confusion of the moment, my recollection of the exact chronological order of events is hazy. I know I was bitten on the hand by a Frenchman who was trying to see the first GIs entering the castle court-yard!

Dick Morgan and I went into town, joined up with a sub-unit of the American battalion that had liberated us and went out on an operation to clear the next objective. The Americans armed us and we found ourselves members of a section commanded by a rugged NCO who told us he was a Mexican. There was some fighting and we were both impressed with the aggressiveness and élan of our American allies. During this operation I recall one unfortunate tall German officer in a greatcoat who refused to surrender and who used his little pistol. He was shot down.

We entered a camp for Hungarian Jews and were horrified to see the four remaining inmates. We were told that the rest had been shot by their SS guards. I particularly remember their huge eyes seemingly burning in their emaciated faces. Eventually we were given transport back to Colditz Schloss in time to get ready to join the rest of our comrades for our return to England. American trucks driven by huge, friendly, cigar-smoking American negroes drove us at great speed to an airfield and I recall passing three regiments of 75mm guns firing massed in an open field at their German objective. At the airfield we embarked in US Air Force aircraft which lumbered along the grass and were quickly airborne, en route to England. It all seemed like a dream.

It was a great moment seeing the English coast below, and it seemed only moments later that we landed, I think, near Aylesbury. We were greeted by soldiers who disinfested us, puffing powder from projectors up our battledress sleeves and legs. We were given a cup of tea by kind, welcoming members of the WVS and then driven off in lorries to our reception camp. Here I was delighted to meet again Rifleman McGuiness of my Regiment and he quickly kitted Dick and me out with new battledress, Commando shoulder titles and green Commando berets.

We were issued with travel warrants but were then told we were to remain in this camp overnight. This was too much for some of us and we simply walked out, and made our way home. In my case this was to Queen Mary's Hospital, Roehampton, where my father was Superintendent and where he and my mother lived in a little house designed by Lutyens. Here I found out my fiancée's telephone number and rang her up.

Patricia was on the train from Scotland that night! It was wonderful to hear her voice, and to be with my parents again. Next morning I was at Euston Station where I met Patricia and it was as if we had never been apart. We then had the joy of leave together, while I awaited my posting, and we made our plans to be married.

I knew Patricia's Aunt Mary and her Uncle Kenneth, with whom she lived in Ayr, best of any of her family. I had also met her mother and grandmother before they had gone to the USA for the rest of the war, and her brother Hamish, who was a pilot in the Fleet Air Arm. I did not meet her father until considerably later. The Petries come from Aberdeenshire and although a number of Patricia's forebears were in the Church, her father was in the Indian Army, in the Guides. For a time he was seconded to the Tochi Scouts and Patricia spent her early childhood in Peshawar. Her mother was a Dundas descended from 'Old Pivot' who, as a Field Marshal, was a former Commander-in-Chief of the British Army. Another forebear was an Admiral at the time of the Crimean War. Her grandfather was in Indian Railways for thirty years and he and her grandmother, who was also a Scot, were stationed in such places as Lucknow and Gorrakpore. We were to carry on the tradition of overseas service after we were married, spending nearly half of our service married life abroad.

CHAPTER SEVEN

1ST BATTALION THE ROYAL ULSTER RIFLES

I had hoped to return to the Commandos and lost little time in reporting to Combined Operations Headquarters at Richmond Terrace. Here I was told that the Army Commandos were virtually on the way out and that the Commandos of the future would be provided by the Royal Marines. My great friend Tom Stallard then asked me if I would join the Special Air Service Regiment, saying that David Stirling would be taking an SAS unit out to the Far East and that there was a place for me. I liked and admired David, with whom I had been in Colditz, and jumped at the idea of serving with him. I told my father my plan.

Shortly afterwards my father said he would like me to have a chat with the then Major General 'Jas' Steele who was in my Regiment. He was Director of Staff Duties, and had known me since I was a baby in India. I presented myself at the DSD's office and was duly ushered in. The General who was about my size had the shrewdest eyes and had not lost his northern Irish voice. He sat me down and said, 'Sonny, you have been away from the Regiment long enough.' When I started out to tell him my ideas about the SAS he just said that the 1st Battalion of my Regiment was in the famous 6th Airborne Division, that I would be joining it shortly and that that was an end to it!

Patricia and I had a wonderful leave and early one morning my mother told me that I was wanted on the telephone. The caller was the commanding officer of the 1st Battalion, Lieutenant Colonel Gerald Rickcord, DSO, whom I had last seen in 1940 when he was a subaltern. He told me he wanted me to be his adjutant and asked me to join the Battalion at Kiwi Barracks in Bulford in a few days time.

I arrived and was given the kindest of welcomes. The battalion was clearly a 'crack' unit, morale was at top level, and the officers and men were tough, fit and experienced. I was issued with my red beret and set about learning how to be an Adjutant. Gerald Rickcord had always been one of my great friends. I was to learn a tremendous amount from him, not least what it takes to be a successful battalion commander. I have never ceased to admire his efficiency, depth of knowledge, coolness and unflappability.

We had a number of interesting members of the battalion at that time. The Second-in-Command was Major Stuart de Longueuil MC, brother of the only – I think – Canadian peer in the Commonwealth. The company commanders were an experienced team and included Major Huw Wheldon, MC, later to find fame in the BBC as Sir Huw. In the Signal Platoon was Rifleman Bill Eckersley the English soccer international. Sons of Stanley Holloway and Victor Sylvester were among our subalterns.

We were very happy under Gerald Rickcord's command. We trained hard, as although the war in Europe was over, we were destined for Burma. Then the atomic bombs were dropped on Nagasaki and Hiroshima and the Far Eastern War came swiftly to an end.

On 28 July 1945 Patricia and I were married at St Paul's, Knightsbridge. It was a Regimental wedding and Dick Morgan, who had transferred from his Regiment to a Regular Commission in mine, was my Best Man.

Our Brigade Commander was Hugh Bellamy, CB, DSO, a vivid personality, seemingly always in great form – the Riflemen adored him. He was for ever up 'at the sharp end' in Germany and they couldn't get over how he would ask some surprised and bemused section commander 'Where's Gerry?' when seeking our Colonel. Major General Eric Bols, CB, DSO, was our Divisional Commander, small, wiry and with lots of panache. There was a great *esprit de corps* in the Division and everyone seemed to know everyone. It was a highly decorated collection of officers and men with a fine fighting reputation. My cousin, Lieutenant Colonel Terence Otway had won his DSO commanding 9 Para in their epic capture of the Merville Battery on D Day.

In the evenings there were a lot of parties, and in our own Mess we seemed to have a great old hooley each night – mainly on beer – and a tremendous singing of Irish songs. I had a marvellous batman, Rifleman Nixon, who also served behind the bar in the Officers' Mess. He used to keep an old tunic of mine under the counter, and once we reached the singing phase, when we were prone to gesticulate with flowing tankards of beer, Nixon would say firmly to me, 'Captain Purdon, Sir, give me your good jacket and slip this on,' whereupon he would neatly fold my good tunic, put it safely away and help me into the older one. However, despite all our jollity in the evenings, we would be out running up Beacon Hill at 5am next morning, returning to eat an enormous breakfast before another day's hard work.

Every Friday afternoon we had a battalion run for everyone save the sick and one telephone orderly in battalion Headquarters and each company. I used to chase round the officers' rooms to hurry them up changing beforehand. I remember one day when I found that charming Welshman Huw Wheldon absentmindedly about to get into his pyjamas instead of his PT kit!

Patricia and I lived in Amesbury and several other officers had their wives with them in the Bulford area. The battalion was then ordered for service in Palestine with the rest of 6th Airborne Division. Patricia went to Ayr to live with her uncle and aunt who were second parents to her, and I sailed with my battalion for Haifa in HMT *Duchess of Bedford*. After an excellent journey we landed at Haifa and I remember the night of our arrival – the stillness, the balmy heat and the clear water by the ship's side, where we could clearly see hundreds of fish swimming close to the surface, attracted and illuminated by the bright gangway lights.

Next day we moved in lorries and jeeps to Gaza where we were in tents, in a very spartan camp, just some huts and a few water standpipes set in a waste of sand, and little else but lizards, and the ubiquitous sparrows seemingly endlessly cheeping in the corrugated iron roofs of the Battalion and Company Headquarters huts and dining halls. There was quite a good club for the men in Gaza and a pleasant but small Officers' Club.

Although we had all come from Germany feeling profoundly sympathetic with and concerned about the sufferings of the Jewish people, it was not long before we saw how tough and aggressive they were in Palestine, fanatical in their will to establish their National Home there, and we became sorry for the Palestinian Arabs who were outclassed by the ruthlessness of the Jews. The Jews with their international background, their superior education, their years of surviving cruel and inhuman oppression, and with many of them having had combat experience in the British, U.S. or Russian armies, quickly gained the upper hand over the Arabs in what was – for the majority of us – our first Internal Security operation. I can say, though, that the British Forces were, and continued to be despite the action of the Stern Gang, the Irgun Zvai Levmi and the Haganah – all Jewish armed organisations – thoroughly impartial.

We were not in Gaza long as we were ordered to Lydda to guard the airport there from terrorist action. From Lydda we moved to Camp 22 at Nathanya, where we had the sea and lovely beaches on one side and orange groves on the other, a delightful spot. We had the 52nd Oxfordshire and Buckinghamshire Light Infantry with us, a fine battalion with whom we were good friends.

Jewish immigrants were sailing into Palestine above the permitted numbers allowed to enter that country under the Mandate, and, while the Royal Navy strove to intercept them at sea it was the task of the land forces to prevent any of those who got past the Navy from landing from their beached ships, and to round up any who had already succeeded in getting ashore. The Jews were very tough and they rigorously and forcefully opposed our efforts. The battalion, like the rest of 6th Airborne's units, was busily employed in foot and mobile patrols, road blocks and ambushes, and in patrolling the railway which was blown up on a number of occasions by Jewish saboteurs.

On 13th November 1945 Ernest Bevin, the Foreign Secretary, made a statement on British policy on Palestine which bitterly disappointed the Jews as it failed to increase the Jewish immigration quota over the existing monthly rate of 1,500. As a result the National Council proclaimed a twelve hour protest strike for the next day, 14th November, and hooligan elements started rioting in Jerusalem and Tel Aviv. Jerusalem was quickly brought under control but in Tel Aviv the situation deteriorated rapidly and as a result the town was occupied by a reinforced 3rd Parachute Brigade for five days. British troops were heavily stoned in Colony Square by large crowds but behaved with the highest standard of restraint. A number of police and soldiers were injured. After repeated warnings to the crowd fire was opened, a small number of rounds, specifically directed by an officer, being fired. At this the crowd withdrew but then attacked the Post Office, the Income Tax Offices and other government buildings, which they set on fire.

On the 16th November our battalion moved into Tel Aviv under the command of 3rd Parachute Brigade and we were allotted a sector of the town. A curfew had been imposed and we enforced this in our sector. We all welcomed having something exciting and worthwhile to do and we were very busy indeed. Our Battalion Headquarters was established in the Ark Dance Hall and I remember I had my camp bed behind the counter. The Parachute Regiment battalions were first-class and the commanding officer of one of them, a real tough character, was credited with having personally shot three ringleaders – the only shots fired by his battalion, thus bringing the situation in his battalion area under control.

My own battalion, being in 6th Airlanding Brigade, was very much among friends in 3rd Para Brigade and our soldiers were most workmanlike and effective. Although I was Adjutant and extremely busy, I managed to get a stand-in for a few hours and went out myself with my batman on foot and on mobile patrols with our rifle companies, which was useful experience. We got stoned by Jewish crowds and I was hit by a rock thrown by a woman who had her skirt tucked into her knickers, revealing a pair of thighs worthy of an Olympic shotputter! Fortunately my Denison smock absorbed much of the impact.

Despite the behaviour of these elements, a number of us who had seen liberated Jewish concentration camps in Germany, were full of compassion for what that dreadfully persecuted race had gone through at Nazi hands. At the same time we felt great sympathy for the Arabs who had lived in Palestine for centuries and who clearly had so much to lose. On 20th November we returned to our tented camp in Nathanya, the curfew having been lifted and law and order restored in Tel Aviv.

We found time to train between operations and to keep extremely fit. We used to run before breakfast, and the scent from the orange trees in the early mornings was delightful. We also swam from the lovely beach by the camp, and played games, in particular rugger, hockey and soccer.

On the night of the 24th/25th November the coastguard stations at Givat Olga and Sidna Ali were attacked by armed bodies of Jews in well planned, well executed attacks which were covered by heavy fire from automatic weapons. The wire defences of each station were penetrated and the buildings were blown up. The Jews, who wounded fourteen police in these attacks, withdrew taking their casualties with them. They also mined the roads around Givat Olga in order to delay any pursuit.

The Palestine Police traced the Jews who had attacked Givat Olga to the two Jewish settlements of Givat Haiyim and Givat Hogla, which were close together to the southeast of Hadera. The Jews who had attacked Sidna Ali had been traced to two other settlements about fifteen miles away, at Rishpon and Shefayim which were within about two miles of the coastguard station.

On 25th November the Palestine Police supported by troops, entered these settlements. The Police told the inhabitants that they had come to find those who had attacked the coastguard stations and that they would therefore screen all males. The Jewish settlers opposed the police attempts and used stones and clubs against them. The police, who made a number of baton charges, could make no progress in their search and were forced to withdraw. The Jews in the nearby settlements poured across to help their comrades and a number got into the four suspect settlements before British troops had established cordons round them.

We had just got a new Brigade Commander, as our popular Brigadier Hugh Bellamy had left us to take command of 2nd Parachute Brigade. Brigadier Roger Bower had taken over and won our respect and affection by his obvious professionalism and kind nature. Our battalion formed part of a force of extra troops brought in to strengthen the security forces around Givat Haiyim and Givat Hogla. This force consisted of the 1st Battalions of the Loyal Regiment, the North Staffordshire Regiment,

Argyll and Sutherland Highlanders, 2/7th Battalion of the Middlesex Regiment, 1st Reconnaissance Regiment, 6th Battalion The Gordon Highlanders and a company of 1st Battalion The Hertfordshire Regiment.

As a result of our previous experience with the inrush of Jews from neighbouring settlements, an outer cordon of British troops had been established. Within the outer cordon was an inner cordon to prevent egress from the settlements. The rest of the force was to provide support for the police searchers. In addition, a squadron of 3rd King's Own Hussars and our own Brigade Field Ambulance was deployed. A similar operation took place simultaneously in the two settlements of Rishpon and Shefayim under 3rd Parachute Brigade.

The second day of the operation the Palestine Police tried again to search the northern settlements on their own but once more they clashed with Jews armed with clubs and bricks. We were then called in and entered the settlements. Resistance became passive. Jews from neighbouring settlements then tried to break through the outer cordon. Despite our warnings that fire would be opened if the would-be reinforcers did not desist, troops were forced to open fire and the Jews sustained a number of casualties. In one case a crowd of about three thousand Jews approached a platoon in the outer cordon led by a man on horseback. The situation was restored when this gentleman was shot.

By the evening of that day the operation was successfully concluded and police and troops were withdrawn from all four settlements. The Jews were highly organised; for instance, their reinforcements moved in response to signals from watchtowers, gongs and sirens, and they had a highly efficient medical organisation.

One weekend my CO and I took a break and went shooting on Lake Hule. This area has now been drained by the Israelis but at the time it was a marvellous place for duck and snipe. The scenery was delightful, overlooked by Mount Hermon. Gerald Rickcord brought his batman and his driver, and we camped on the edge of the marshes. Gerald and I got up before first light each morning and while it was still dark were each seated in Arab boats being paddled through the reeds to catch the first flight of duck, a young Arab boy in each boat acting as a retriever and leaping into the water to pick up the bag. After the dawn flight we walked the marshes for snipe, and at dusk we were out again after the evening flight. I cannot recall how many duck and snipe we shot but we each got an enormous bag. Hule was a wonderfully relaxing break. Other times of relaxation were over the Christmas period when some of us, myself included, visited Jerusalem and Bethlehem, and saw the Holy Places. However, we were upset to find how much they had been commercialised.

Another occasion was when I was selected as scrum half for Ireland in the Middle East Rugby Internationals. Dick Morgan had been chosen to play as a wing threequarter so we drove across the Sinai Desert to Cairo and then on to Alexandria, where we were very kindly put up by 1st Royal Irish Fusiliers at Mustapha Barracks. The 'Faughs' were then commanded by my first company commander, Lt. Col. R.F.A. Crookshank. 'Crook' had invited all the Irish team to stay and we had a great time. We had several good training sessions, but I don't think the very kind entertainment we enjoyed in 'Alex' – in marked contrast to our Spartan life in Palestine – did much for us as we were beaten by Scotland at Bewsher Park Stadium on a hot afternoon! The Scots had a number of 'pukka' Internationals in their team and they outclassed us. I remember successfully tackling that fine Scottish wing threequarter Graham Jackson as he thundered down the touchline, his legs seemingly like two telegraph poles.

After we returned to Palestine we played another international, this time against Wales at Mount Scopus in Jerusalem, on a ground with sharp rocks protruding through the grass, and we certainly felt it when we fell. This was one of the best matches in which I have ever played. The Welsh team contained a number of true Internationals and it was a very tough but clean game. Wales won but we all thoroughly enjoyed the match and had a terrific party afterwards in an Arab restaurant with plenty of Welsh and Irish songs to follow.

Afterwards I gave a lift in my jeep to my stand-off half who was called Cosgrove, from the Palestine Police, and dropped him at Beit Lid Police Station not far from Nathanya. As I drove into our camp firing broke out and we could see tracers arcing overhead. I stopped the jeep outside the verandah of the Battalion Headquarters hut, went straight to my office and got on to the radio to find out what was going on. It was, in fact, a false alarm of intruders in the lines of a neighbouring unit, but it gave our immediate action drills a useful and realistic practice.

Spring came and the lovely flowers in Palestine transformed the scene. Gerald Rickcord told me that he was leaving the battalion and that a previous commanding officer was returning in his place. I was to be posted, on promotion, to command our Regimental Company at the Irish Group Infantry Training Centre at Omagh, Co. Tyrone. Gerald was a splendid CO, loved and respected in the battalion. He was imperturbable under fire and earned our great respect for his thorough knowledge of his profession. Under his wise and kindly leadership morale was skyhigh and discipline was of the highest standard. I learned a tremendous amount from him.

In April 1946 I heard that I was to go to the School of Infantry, Warminster, to give a series of lectures on International Security operations in Palestine. I always felt that this honour was thanks to the typical kindness and thoughtfulness of my Brigade Commander, Brigadier Roger

Bower, who knew I had only got married a very short time before we sailed for Palestine after three years' separation from Patricia.

The news also came that the battalion was to leave 6th Airborne Division after a distinguished and happy career in this élite formation, which included the D Day and Rhine Crossing airborne landings, the fighting in the Ardennes and the advance to the Baltic. It was sad news indeed. I was sorry to leave the battalion, but it was shortly to move to Austria under its new commanding officer to a very different life to that of the active service of Palestine. I had learnt a lot about Internal Security operations and this was to be of great use to me in the future. It had been a wonderful experience to visit the Holy Land and I had seen at first hand what an almost insoluble issue was posed by the Palestine problem. Finally I had come away tremendously impressed with the impartiality and the good humour of the British Serviceman.

Once again I drove across the Sinai Desert to Cairo along the black tarmac road that shimmered in the mid-day heat, with portions occasionally half covered in desert sand blown across it by the hot wind. For the last time we stopped at the wayside NAAFI marquees to drink tea from thick brown glasses made from cut-down Stella beer bottles and to eat welcome 'egg banjos' to sustain us for the next stretch of desert. After a night in Cairo and my first swim at the Gezira Sporting Club since I was a boy of thirteen, I flew home in a Dakota, seated behind a friend who had the silk for his fiancée's wedding dress wound round himself, under his clothes!

After a second honeymoon with my wife, I reported to the Commandant of the School of Infantry at Warminster in Wiltshire. He was Brigadier (later General Sir) Michael West, a relaxed, friendly officer with a distinguished war record, who quickly put me at my ease. I had to lecture to very large audiences of both officers and NCOs which was useful experience if a little unnerving at first. We lived at the Bath Arms and had a very happy six weeks. I could not foresee at the time that not only would I attend a Company Commanders' and a pre-Staff College course at Warminster but that I would return there one day as Chief Instructor, and later still as Commandant.

CHAPTER EIGHT

NORTHERN IRELAND

My father had recently been appointed Agent in London for the Government of Northern Ireland, and Patricia and I spent our last few days in England with him and my mother in their large and comfortable flat in Oakwood Court, Addison Road. They saw us on to the Irish boat train at Euston, and then we, with Patricia's Pekinese and my bull terrier, were on our way. We had to sit up all night as we had not been able to get a cabin and my poor wife was very tired by the time we reached Omagh by train.

On arriving at our hotel where we had booked rooms and having already said we had dogs, we were horrified to be told that dogs were not allowed. However, we were informed that Mrs Porter who kept a small hotel near the barracks would be sure to take us all. Bless Mrs Porter, she did. We loved her, and her hotel was like something out of 'Some Experiences of an Irish R.M.' She immediately sensed that Patricia was having a baby and sat her down in front of the kitchen stove with a glass of hot milk. We were given a comfortable bedroom and were told we could house a pack of hounds in it if we so wished! We were very happy there.

I found that I was to take over the Royal Ulster Rifles Company from Gerald Going in my Regiment. I took over a very happy company but a number of the officers and NCOs soon changed over so I had a fairly new team. Eventually WO II 'Stoker' Lynch, MM, came as my CSM. He was a tremendous asset, an iron man, incredibly tough and strong, but wonderfully good with the Riflemen who thought the world of him. 'Stoker' had won his MM in Burma with the 82nd West African Division.

My Second-in-Command was Captain Dick Gage, a grand, dependable man whose family owned Rathlin Island. Among my subalterns were Jack

71

Wheeler, a former RSM in the Army Physical Training Corps, Gerry Murphy (the Irish International rugby fullback later Chaplain to HM the Queen at Sandringham, officiating after that in the Falkland Islands and now at the Tower of London, one of the finest men I have ever met), Hugh Brett and Pat Newport. All, like me, were mad keen on physical fitness as were my NCOs. We decided we would be the best trained, fittest company in the unit, and also win at everything! Whatever we were doing – Battle Efficiency Tests, Battle Shooting, Pokey Drill, we all took part. We won everything, and the Commanding Officers of the 1st and 2nd Battalions of my Regiment both expressed themselves pleased with the Riflemen we sent them.

Patricia and I by now were sharing a lovely old Irish country home called Mullaghmore House with Joe and Joan McCausland. Joe commanded the Royal Inniskilling Fusiliers company and was an experienced soldier having served in North Africa and Italy in the Irish Brigade.

A number of social functions were held at the ITC and one night the Sergeants' Mess invited us to a dance at which we were introduced to a Major dressed in the uniform of a certain Guards regiment, who wore the VC and the MM at the beginning of his full double row of ribbons. He told me which battalions he had been in, but he seemed unfamiliar with the location in Palestine where I had last seen his unit. He also wore a different formation sign to the Division they were in and later, when we left the dance together, I remarked to him that his peaked cap was not Guards' pattern. He told me that his had been stolen in Belfast. I had found him unlike the VC holders I knew, because he talked a lot about how he had won his supreme decoration for valour to the enthralled sergeants. He had, he claimed, knocked out several German panzers with a PIAT in Italy and I remembered reading about such an incident. He said he had won his MM when a sergeant, for shooting down a Stuka dive bomber over the Dunkirk beaches with a Boyes anti-tank rifle. Somehow I couldn't believe he was genuine and I mentioned my feelings about the VC to my superiors but was pooh-poohed. A few days later, after we had been staying overnight at the Grand Central Hotel in Belfast, a complimentary copy of the daily paper was delivered with our breakfast. Its headlines were 'Phony VC Arrested'. Our friend at the Sergeants' Mess Dance turned out to be a lance corporal in an English county regiment who had pinched an officer's cheque book, gone absent and had been having a whale of a time for a fortnight! Sad to say, his father WAS a VC.

Early on in my time at Omagh the Victory Parade took place in London. The Irish Group ITC sent a contingent and I commanded the Royal Ulster Rifles component. The Victory Parade was an unforgettable occasion. Not only were there contingents there from every country in the British Empire and Commonwealth but from all our Allies. The atmosphere was terrific and small towns of tents were set up for all of us taking part, in the nearby Royal Parks. On the day of the Victory Parade we were up very early and took some time in forming up as the procession covered such a long way. From the moment we debouched onto the streets the sound of cheering never ceased. It was a long march but we none of us would have missed it. I managed to catch a glimpse of Patricia and my sister Biddy in the crowd, and also of Their Majesties The King and Queen, and Queen Mary, and of Sir Winston Churchill. The colours of the regiments were massed and carried wreaths of laurel. I remember being very amused at seeing an officer in the Welsh Regiment, who wore the ribbon of the Victoria Cross, place his wreath on his head; with his Roman profile he looked like Caesar. I believe that that Major may now be the famous judge Sir Tasker Watkins, VC! We all found on returning to our tents at the conclusion of the great Parade, lying on each of our camp beds, a length of the new War Medal Ribbon, issued for the first time that day – a nice gesture.

Life was busy and exhilarating at the ITC and Omagh was a pleasant town. We used to have Company Passing Out Parades and I remember how proud I was when my father took one of them. Field Marshal Sir Claude Auchinleck was Colonel of the Royal Inniskilling Fusiliers at that time and we were most impressed when the great man walked through the camp.

Our most senior officer in The Royal Ulster Rifles was General Sir James Steele, at that time British Commander-in-Chief in Austria. He was a wonderful character as well as being a fine and astute soldier. He had most amusing and memorable sayings. I remember when, before the war ended (he was a very old and dear family friend) and I was awarded my MC, he saw the ribbons of it and my (what was then the) 1939-43 Star on my battledress. 'Well, Sonny,' he said, 'now you have two, you'll find they breed!' What a great man he was, a wonderful Colonel of the Regiment, and his many acts of kindness will never be forgotten. Few people know that he paid for the schooling of the children of some of our widows, swearing them to secrecy. Jas Steele will never be forgotten so long as there is a Royal Ulster Rifleman alive.

The time was approaching when I would hand over my Company and become the first Adjutant of the 6th Battalion The Royal Ulster Rifles (T.A.), the first Territorial Battalion of the Regiment to be raised in Northern Ireland.

Patricia gave birth to our eldest child, a boy, Patrick, on 25 January 1947, in Belfast (our two sons and our daughter were all born in my native city), and I attended a Company Commanders' Course at the School of Infantry. My Uncle Joe Shannon was at that time manager of the Ulster

Bank, Carlisle Circus, Belfast, and he and Aunt Gwen, my father's sister, found us a flat in the Antrim Road. As the 6th Battalion Headquarters was in Victoria Barracks it did not take me long to get to and from work.

Lieutenant Colonel Jack Carson who had commanded our 1st Bn. in 6th Airborne Division until being seriously wounded when his glider was shot down at the Rhine Crossing was appointed Commanding Officer. Recruiting for the new battalion went well and a number of wartime officers, NCOs and Riflemen joined early on. Our Second-in-Command was capable, experienced John McCann, who had served in North Africa with the London Irish Rifles and Inniskillings Fred Laird commanded A Company; Charlie Gray, B Company, both in Belfast. Robin Morton raised and commanded C Company at Ballymena; Finlay McCance, D Company at Ballyclare and Wyn McCabe Support Company at Lisburn. Frank Hollis, the Quartermaster, and I were the original nucleus of the battalion, with RSM Billy McGregor, a great little man who had been with me in the 1st Battalion when he was CSM to Huw Wheldon. I had two old Regimental friends as PSIs in CSMs 'Stoker' Lynch, MM, and Sam Henry, MM. Sam used to box professionally (and highly successfully) under the pseudonym of Al Somers.

Bob Madocks, another experienced officer, succeeded John McCann as Second-in-Command and Jimmy Brown (later the distinguished judge) and Mike Brown, from our 1st and 2nd Battalions respectively, both served in the early days of our 6th Battalion.

We got a Bugle Section and Pipes and Drums going early. Lance Corporal McCartney was a character. He used to blurt out his sentences, punctuated by a sniff, and when General Sir Ouvry Roberts was GOC Northern Ireland the band put on a Retreat Parade for him at Ballyedmond Camp. The General walked round the ranks and when he came to McCartney he said, 'I was dining in your Officers' Mess last night,' 'I know, Sir,' blurted out McCartney. 'I heard yez was drunk, Sir.' Afterwards I said to him, 'What on earth made you say that, particularly when you know that was not true?' 'I don't know, Sir,' came the reply, 'I must have lost the bap!'

The Officers' Mess was run by 'Kitchener' King, a 'Faugh' who had fought at Omdurman. He wore the Sudan Medal and the Khedive's Star amongst an impressive and colourful 'fruit salad'.

Life in the 6th Battalion was very busy and worthwhile. Jack Carson was a delightful man to work for and was loved in the battalion. We used to visit every company's training night each week, which meant four nights a week – Belfast, Ballymena, Ballyclare, Lisburn, and later Larne. We also trained most weekends, so family life was pretty restricted but Patricia, as befits a true soldier's daughter, was – as always – wonderfully understanding.

Our battalion was one of the units in 107 Independent Infantry Brigade Group. We were lucky to have as our Brigade Commander Brigadier Nelson Russell, CB, DSO. He had been the first commander of the famous Irish Brigade in North Africa and had earned a reputation for quite imperturbable bravery and coolheadedness. He guided the new Territorial formation until it became a workmanlike Brigade Group of high morale. In addition to our other two infantry battalions – 5th Inniskillings and 5th 'Faughs' – we had an armoured car regiment, the North Irish Horse; a Field and an A.A. Regiment of Gunners; a Sapper Regiment; a Signals Regiment; RASC, REME, Field Ambulance RAMC and a Provost Company.

I spent two years as Adjutant, and before I left, Jack Carson had handed over to Lieutenant Colonel Maurice ('Conger') Cummins, an experienced soldier, a charming man, a keen field sportsman and a particularly fine fisherman. We had moved from Belfast to a quarter in Ballykinlar which at that time was a delightful place to live in, only seconds away from the sea. However, it entailed such a long time spent travelling to and from Belfast, and from Belfast to all the far-flung Company drill halls that I was never home before midnight, yet I had to be in my office by 08:30 the next morning. So we moved to a quarter in Lisburn, which was more convenient. During our time in Lisburn our second son Timothy was born, also in Belfast.

In 1949, whilst we were at Brigade T.A. Camp at Ballyedmond I heard from the Military Secretary's Branch that I had been posted to an appointment as a Staff Captain in General Headquarters Middle East Land Forces at Fayid on the Suez Canal.

Before the Camp the Brigade had taken part in the Review of the Territorial Army by his Majesty King George VI in Hyde Park. The King drove round the parade in a Landrover accompanied by Field Marshal Viscount Montgomery of Alamein, that great Ulster soldier. 107 (Ulster) Brigade contingent was led by our Pipe Band. At that time our drummers, as well as our pipers, were wearing the saffron kilt. This was remarked on by either the King or the Queen when we passed the Saluting Base and afterwards we were informed that only the drummers of Highland Regiments were permitted to wear the kilt, so ours wore trousers thenceforth.

The 6th Battalion must have been one of the finest units in the Territorial Army, their morale was sky-high and their military efficiency and sporting prowess were of a very superior standard. I handed over as Adjutant to Dick Morgan and have never forgotten my happy time with those grand Ulster men.

I said goodbye to the RSM's wife. Mrs McGregor was a great friend of mine and ruled her husband with the proverbial rod of iron. I remember him saying to me how highly she polished the floors of their quarter, and insisted that he took off his boots before entering the house – 'like a mosque, Sir!' She had a habit of coming to see me unannounced whenever anything troubled her, and would sit by me, holding my hand, interspersing her peroration with 'Sacred Heart, Captain darling. Holy Mother of God. Sure I'm not putting up with it, now why should I?' She was determined to get herself and her furniture on the all-male, purely military, 1st Battalion troop train to Colchester and succeeded by sitting on the floor of the CO's office until he gave in! But she was a darling, and great fun.

Whilst I was in Belfast my war gratuity came through. It was about £120, so Patricia and I invested this in a navy blue, secondhand, two seater Austin 7. It was a 1932 model and had very narrow wheels. With Patricia and me in the front, we had Patrick, aged about one year old, in his carry cot in the back, plus our Kerry Blue terrier and a Pekinese. We used to get the wheels stuck in the tramlines with sometimes frightening effect as we frantically tried to jerk the wheels out of the rails in face of a careering, advancing tram. I remember at Carlisle Circus, getting embedded in the tramlines and being forced to go round in a complete circle before finally breaking free!

On another occasion the fabric hood came undone and we drove down Belfast's Royal Avenue with the hood standing up vertically behind our heads. My father was very worried about the car, particularly since his first grandson travelled in the rumble-seat with two dogs. I left the car outside the Manor House, Donaghadee, where my parents were visiting my cousin Gina. When my parents came out all four wheels of the car were leaning drunkenly inwards which did nothing to increase my father's confidence in our car!

We went for a drive through the Mourne Mountains one day, and as we were bowling along enjoying the lovely scenery, we were singing 'Where the Mountains of Mourne Sweep Down to the Sea'. Suddenly the complete bonnet took off and flapped into a nearby bog. I put it back on again and we commenced a downhill descent. A jerk to the left took us into a bank and we watched our nearside front wheel bowl rapidly down the road and into the front garden of a cottage surprising a man digging there. The running board had moved up on my side so that I couldn't open the door and Patricia's door had jammed so we climbed out of the top amid hysterical barking from the Kerry Blue. Helpless with laughter we asked for our wheel back at the cottage and had just trundled it to the Austin Seven when a good Samaritan drove up and insisted on putting it back on for us. We both agreed to keep these episodes from my parents who had returned to London, but Murphy's Law had it that our good Samaritan was a cashier in Uncle Joe's bank! He had recognised us but had not said who he was and next day Aunt Gwen was asking archly if we had enjoyed our drive in the

Mournes! After my sister-in-law had almost given herself curvature of the spine from travelling in the rumble-seat during her stay with us, and after some mechanical failures, I reluctantly sold the car for the princely sum of £32 and relied on public transport!

CHAPTER NINE

TWO YEARS IN EGYPT AND A YEAR IN HONG KONG

I went out to Egypt in Autumn 1949 by what was called the MEDLOC route travelling by military train across Europe to Trieste where I embarked on a boat for Port Said. On arrival Mike Mulligan in my Regiment kindly collected me and my kit in his big, blue Lincoln saloon and drove me along the Canal Road to Fayid, where he and Pauline his wife had a bungalow in a small compound of a dozen similar dwellings by the Fayid Officers' Club, on the shore of the Great Bitter Lake. I was to live, temporarily, in the Royal Army Pay Corps Officers' Mess in the Headquarters area, where I found a kindred spirit in David Swiney, an amusing Gunner with whom I played rugger as halfback for the GHQ 1st XV.

I had been appointed staff captain AG3, dealing with the posting of infantry officers and I had a charming boss in Major Herbert Munden of the Gloucestershire Regiment. Tragically, Herbert died of poliomyelitis shortly afterwards, a great shock and loss to us all. In his place we got Major Mike du Boulay, MC, a Gordon Highlander who had fought with 51st Highland Division from the Battle of El Alamein to the Baltic.

General Headquarters was a very large organisation, responsible for an area including Ceylon, British Somaliland, Eritrea, Malta, Cyprus, Libya, Egypt, the Sudan, Aden, the Gulf States and East Africa Command. There were British Military Missions in Ethiopia and in Saudi Arabia; in Jordan the Arab Legion was commanded by Glubb Pasha and included a number of British officers.

Britain still had powerful armed forces in those days and all three services were represented at Fayid. H.M. ships were to be seen regularly passing up or down the Suez Canal, the RAF had a number of airfields nearby, and the Army was present in strength in Egypt, Libya and in East Africa. The staff worked very much on pre-war Eastern hours and we were in our offices by 7am and worked until 2 or 2:30pm. In the afternoon a variety of games was played and sporting facilities catered for every taste, with several rugger grounds and hockey and cricket pitches in abundance. There were many simply made but effective concrete squash courts, open but roofed with chicken wire to keep the squash balls in and large complexes of tennis courts and at both the Old Victorian Lido and at the Olympic Stadium waterpolo was played.

When I first got there General Sir John Crocker was Commander-in-Chief; he was succeeded by General Sir Brian Robertson, son of the Field Marshal. Under Sir Brian polo flourished and the C-in-C was to be seen playing most afternoons, surrounded by 'centaurs' from the Cavalry, Horse Gunners and other equine enthusiasts.

Servicemen of all ranks and their families could, for next to nothing, sail on the Great Bitter Lake and, of course, swimming was very popular. In the cold weather one of the big sporting events at Fayid was the Big Flea Race. (The Big Flea and the Little Flea were hills of soft sand near Fayid.) I suppose the Big Flea was about 100 feet in height and I can't remember how long the Race was, I think it was about six miles there and back from GHQ. I ran in it and captained our AG (and later MS) teams each year I was there. I and one other officer and six clerks made up our entry. We got very fit training for it and a tremendous crowd always turned out to watch. It was run at a very fast pace and climbing up the soft sand of the Big Flea was leg sapping. We all enjoyed it and it certainly helped us to get to know our clerks who were a grand lot.

One day a Royal Signals sergeant who was an excellent swimmer swam the Great Bitter Lake at its widest part where it was $7^{1}/_{4}$ miles wide. I decided it was time for the officers to show that they, too, could cross it and did some swims along the Lake to practise. Then, having asked my DAAG for time off to do the swim, I arranged with a friend in the RASC for one of their motor launches to accompany me across. I decided that I would probably get thirsty so Patricia made up a mixture of fresh orange juice and glucose.

Lance Corporal Spratt of the RASC, a national serviceman, came to see me and said he would like to join me in my attempt, and so did Corporal Margerison, also RASC. So very early one morning, about 4am, while it was still dark, we entered the water on the Sinai side of the Great Bitter Lake. Fortunately the water was warm and we glided past the white shape of the RASC launch and settled down to our swim. It was a pretty amateur effort looking back at it, as we all swam breaststroke, but our sole aim was to cross the Lake. My intention was that we should not get caught in the shipping lanes when the daily traffic consisting of liners, tramps, tankers and warships began to pass through. So we pressed on hard and as it grew light we were obviously going to make it, which was a great relief.

Although the water had appeared warm when we entered, it seemed colder as we got into the deeper water towards the middle of the Lake. I was by now quite a long way ahead of the boat which was standing by Cpl Margerison. He was having eye trouble with the very salty sea water of the Great Bitter Lake. Sadly, he was temporarily blinded by it and had to be taken out of the water into the launch. Suddenly I was seized by cramp in my legs. Automatically I pressed one foot down on the other and this eventually relaxed my taut leg muscles. Then I got a terrific stomach cramp and I knew the launch was at least half a mile away. On impulse I turned on my back and extended my arms and legs rather like a starfish. This did the trick as my tummy muscles relaxed and I was able to continue swimming.

By now I could see the far shore and was just able to make out the Big Flea. Behind me I could hear and feel in the water the throb of the powerful engines of the big ships passing along the deep water of the shipping lanes. Then, seemingly for hours, the far horizon hardly grew nearer. Lance Corporal Spratt and I swam on and on. It became incredibly boring and later we began to feel tired. The sun beat down on our heads and necks, and the salt content of the water was so blinding that I swam with one eye shut to keep my vision.

We chatted away to each other to keep our minds off our task. From time to time we trod water by the launch and were handed down a glass of ready-mixed orange juice and glucose. We made certain not to touch the launch so it could not be said we had used it to support us. The swell was such that every glass contained a great salty slop of sea water which did little to refresh us! We closed our minds to boredom, effort, heat and thirst and at long last we saw the buildings of the Old Victorian Lido a few hundred yards ahead of us. All the same it seemed an age before we both waded out of the water and sat on the wooden jetty, where we drank copious draughts of delicious, fresh lemon juice brought by Patricia.

The Canal Zone was a good place to serve in and we were all pretty fit and healthy. In addition to excellent sporting facilities, the social side for all ranks was well catered for with well run and inexpensive NAAFI Clubs. We lived by the Fayid Officers' Club in one of the tiny little bungalows made from whitewashed mud bricks; each had a verandah which was a great boon. Inside was a sitting room where we ate in cold weather and for the rest of the year we had our meals on the verandah.

Water was carried to the bungalows and stored in oil drums on the flat roof. The contractor who had built the bungalows had bought an old generator from an RAF surplus auction, so we had electric light from dusk until midnight when the power was switched off. The electric wiring was also mixed up with the plumbing and I found out for myself that anyone pulling our metal lavatory chain when the lights were on got an electric shock! I substituted a piece of string for the chain and all was well. However, I also found that if I pulled the cord and held it, all the lights in the compound went out until I released it! I never managed to cure that.

Peter and Margaret Dowse, both childhood friends of mine, whose fathers, like mine, were RAMC generals, lived on the other side of the compound. When Moussa, their cook-suffragi, turned on their kitchen sink tap during lighting-up time, he always got an electric shock. He never mentioned this thinking it 'par for the course', and it was only found out when Margaret turned on the tap on his day off and got a shock herself.

We had fly netting on all our doors and windows and one night Patricia and I went to a dinner party on the Dowes' verandah. They had asked an elderly bachelor colonel among their guests, a charming but rather prim man. We were all seated facing the bungalows opposite and, of course, could see through the fly netting into the lit rooms in front of us. To our amazement, the couple who lived directly opposite, who were both – like the bachelor colonel – rather prim, appeared in their hall, floodlit and stark naked! Apparently they did not know that their fly netting was transparent! The colonel had clearly rarely seen a naked woman before and sat trans-fixed, his fork motionless, half-way to his mouth. Because they had not fitted in to our little compound 'family', no one could bring themselves to tell them about it, and the result was that dinner parties on that side of the compound had their own built-in 'strip show'!

There was no air-conditioning but we got used to the heat, although we never got used to the bed bugs which lived in the mud walls. They gave a beastly bite and our two poor little boys used to be a prime target for them. We stood our steel beds with their legs in tins of kerosene which helped a bit but whenever we thought we had got rid of the bed bugs back would come a new team from our dhobi, concealed within the fresh laundry! This was called the 'Fayid Electric Steam Laundry', and although our laundry invariably came back spotlessly clean we always had to search each garment for unwelcome visitors.

Halfway through my tour of duty I was made Staff Captain in the Military Secretary's Branch where I dealt with the posting of all officers to and from the Staff. Suddenly I found that every senior officer knew me by my Christian name!

However, my task was a lowly one, mainly providing information to help my boss the Deputy Assistant Military Secretary, Major Rodney Lyall, Royal Signals, in the selection process, and in issuing the necessary posting orders. It was an enjoyable job and it was interesting to be 'in' on confidential matters relating to officers and to Honours and Awards.

One of my tasks was to ring up and congratulate all officers who had passed into the Staff College – not much fun that year as I was one of those who failed! The experience, however, hardened my resolve to pass, as I did – at my next attempt.

Before we left Fayid, Nahas Pasha had abrogated the Treaty with Britain and there had been considerable unrest in the Canal Zone during our last few months. There were a number of unpleasant incidents caused by anti-British Egyptian elements to British personnel travelling or shopping by themselves. One friend of mine, a captain in the RASC, was grabbed by a mob who put a rope round his neck and dragged him to the Sweet Water Canal. On arrival at its banks it was clear they were going to drown him. Happily a small patrol of Egyptian police turned up, under a stout-hearted sergeant, who released him and escorted him back to safety in Ismailia. Yet it was that same Egyptian police force who refused to be disarmed in the Caracal in Ismailia and it took elements of a British infantry battalion which, I think, was the XX Lancashire Fusiliers supported by tanks of the 4th Royal Tank Regiment to overcome them. Sadly, a number of people on both sides were killed, including a British subaltern, before the police laid down their arms.

In 1951 I was posted to the 1st Battalion of my Regiment, and my family and I were told we were to go to 156 Transit Camp at Port Said to wait until the troopship arrived for Hong Kong. Instead we spent a few days in Ismailia with our friends Alma and Badger Terrey in their nice flat. For our journey, about twenty of us, travelling by an army 3 tonner from Fayid to Ismailia, were given an armed escort. We were shouted at by Egyptians en route and rocks and stones were thrown at us. We were dropped off at the Terreys' flat and had a most enjoyable night.

Next morning a train load of hooligans arrived from Cairo intent on making trouble. Gangs roamed the streets, chanting slogans and beating up any isolated Europeans they met. We looked over our verandah and saw a crowd of yelling galibiyah-clad Egyptian yobbos battering at the door of the NAAFI shop where a number of British wives were inside shopping. We saw others push cars over and set fire to several of them, but shortly afterwards the Royal Military Police arrived and escorted the Service wives to safety. A spotter plane circled round but, despite the obviously worsening situation, no troops were brought in.

I went down onto the street to see if I could help anyone. Two Gunner jeeps drove up and halted near me. A sergeant in one of them said, 'The mob are into the Other Ranks' Married Quarters at Arashiya, breaking them up'. So I jumped into his jeep and off we went, forcing our way through the crowd. I was sitting by the Gunner sergeant who had just spoken to me and noticed that his ribbons were headed by the George Medal.

We got to the quarters to find a milling crowd of young Egyptians smashing all they could lay their hands on. Using our fists and our boots we made our way into the first house. Inside we found a terrified British woman, wrapped in one of her curtains, ear lobes bleeding. She told us her husband was a REME sergeant and that those hooligans had stripped the very clothes from her and torn off her ear-rings. The mindless creatures had even taken sledgehammers to the bannisters. I can tell you that we really got a move on these uninvited guests! Some straight lefts and right hooks had the cowardly creatures streaking for safety, helped on their way by forcibly applied ammunition boots.

Jeep loads of British soldiers were taking similar steps to restore the situation in the other quarters. Armed British servicemen then arrived to guard the quarters, and eventually we were able to leave knowing that those poor girls would be safe. Someone at Headquarters British Troops Egypt had 'sparked' and we had troops on the streets from that night onwards and a curfew was imposed.

Next morning with the curfew lifted, trouble started again with more looting. In came that fine unit, 1st Lancashire Fusiliers with their dynamic CO, Lt. Col. Geoffrey Bamford, DSO, in command. I was able to lead one platoon to where a lot of trouble was going on and we had the satisfaction of seeing it sorted out most efficiently. By now the 'Powers That Be' had taken a grip of Ismailia, troops were camped throughout the area and a typical Internal Security situation was in hand. However British officers and other ranks were to be killed and wounded in the subduing of the disaffected Egyptian police at the Caracal before order was finally restored. Still, all was fairly quiet on our journey to the docks at Port Said to embark in HMT *Empire Fowey* for Hong Kong. Patricia told me afterwards that while I was leaning over to talk through the window at the back of the cab to the driver, a rock the size of a pudding basin had narrowly missed my head.

The Master of the *Empire Fowey* proved to be a delightful and unusual man. The only passengers disembarking at Port Said were a major general and his wife who had occupied the best cabin on the ship with its own little private deck. They had also sat at the Captain's table. Apparently there was considerable lobbying by other senior passengers to get this cabin. The Captain said that whoever came on board, irrespective of rank would have the general's cabin and would sit at his table. In this manner the Purdon family had No. 1 Cabin on A Deck and Patricia and I were fortunate enough to sit at this marvellous man's table.

As we sailed down the Canal past Fayid, I had happy memories of GHQ MELF where we had made so many friends and where I had learnt about the functions of the different branches of Staff. We had had a lot of fun as our senior officers were a kind and friendly lot. I remembered a leg pull of mine and the forbearance of my Brigadier when it went wrong. A friend of mine, an Irishman in the East Lancashire Regiment who was a fellow Staff Captain, had the habit of saying when he was exasperated that he wished he was out of the Infantry and in the Army Catering Corps. I managed to get some War Office official paper from England, copied exactly the type of formal letter for an inter-Arm transfer and had it sent through the GHQ Registry to Paddy.

That morning Paddy had come in as usual and wished aloud that he was in the ACC. He went through his IN basket and I watched him from my desk across the office. He stiffened and stared at a piece of paper. 'They *have* transferred me to the Army Catering Corps!' Paddy spluttered. 'It must be a joke, Paddy,' I said. 'Someone's pulling your leg because of your well-known saying.' But Paddy would have none of it, and with trembling hands took the War Office letter in to our respected DAAG, Mike du Boulay. Mike had a terrific sense of humour but this letter made him blazing angry and before I could get over to his office I saw his kilted figure haring across the sand to the office of our AAG, Lt. Col. Kim Woods, OBE, an ex-CRASC of 6th Airborne Division. This was getting out of hand! I then had to take an incoming telephone call which meant I couldn't leave my desk and by the time I had finished the Colonel 'A' had taken the letter to our DAG, Brigadier Bill Cox. I could see the C-in-C coming into this so taking my courage in both hands I went to the DAG's office and was ushered in to see him. I told him what I had done and thought I was in for big trouble. However, the Brigadier was amused and incredibly kind and I heard no more about it.

One of the most respected Senior Officers at GHQ MELF was the Chief of Staff, General Sir Ewan Miller. General Miller had commanded the 60th Rifles at Calais in 1940 and received the DSO for his gallant leadership during that heroic stand. He and Lady Miller were kindness itself to us; he had been the Senior British Officer at Oflag IXAH when Dick Morgan and I escaped from Spangenberg. When we first arrived at Fayid my cousin, Brigadier Jack Napier was DQMG, and he and Muriel, his wife, were very good to us both. My sister Biddy was also working in GHQ, another bonus.

In 1950, after about a year, we had gone to Cyprus for leave and spent a week at Famagusta in Golden Sands Leave Camp, and then a week at Pine Tree Leave Camp, in the Troodos Mountains, where we saw the colour come back into our boys' cheeks in the clear, cool, pine-scented mountain air. People used to travel to Cyprus in one of two small ships, *Empire*

Comfort and *Empire Peacemaker,* known respectively and predictably as the *Empire Discomfort* and *Empire Sickmaker.* We really enjoyed our leave and it set us all up for the rest of the year. Before we went to Cyprus we had seen HMS *Amethyst* on her way home through the Canal under the gallant Commander Kerans DSO, after her escape from the Yangtze River.

While we were in Egypt I had a bitter blow when my father died. He never spared himself and despite being told by his doctor to rest after suffering from more than one massive heart attack, he had refused to let up. One day he had come home from the Ulster Office in Lower Regent Street and as he stepped out of the lift outside his flat, he died in my mother's arms. How I loved and admired him. My sister Biddy was by then stationed in Cairo and she and I flew home for his funeral and remained for his memorial service. I flew back to Egypt to rejoin my family, but my sister remained in London to be with our mother. About six months later, Biddy married Colán MacArthur, son of my father's friend, the former Director General of the Royal Army Medical Corps, Lieutenant General Sir William MacArthur who, like my father, was an Ulsterman.

A visit by the then Defence Minister reminded me of his visit to the 6th Battalion when I was Adjutant. I had never met Mr Emmanuel (later Lord) Shinwell before. He had come to Victoria Barracks Belfast, which was an antique red-brick, out-dated and unlovely place. The architecture of the main Officers' Mess was supposed to have been muddled with that of Victoria Barracks Hong Kong as it had verandahs and lofty ceilings.

I was taken by Mr Shinwell's strong, engaging personality. This man was a leader and a student of human nature and I could see why people said he was one of the best-ever Secretaries of State for War. He was keenly interested in us all, asked searching questions, did not talk down, and had a sense of humour.

I was taking him around and we passed the little building that was our Officers' Mess. In the doorway, wearing a spotless white coat, blazing with a long row of shining medals with colourful ribbons, smart blue trousers and highly polished shoes, stood dear old 'Kitchener' King, the Mess Steward. Mr Shinwell did not see him and passed by still talking. As soon as he finished his sentence I said, 'Do you know, Sir, you have completely ruined what should have been a great day for a grand old soldier?' As soon as I told him about 'Kitchener' he said, 'Well, we can't have that, can we?' He swung round, walked straight up to 'Kitchener' and said, 'I believe I nearly made a great mistake.' 'You nearly did, Sir,' replied dear old 'Kitchener', beaming all over his face. Mr Shinwell admired his medals, '...and this one, is the Queen's SOWDAN Medal, Sorr, and this one the Khedive's Star,' 'Kitchener' explained. Mr King was delighted and Mr Shinwell once again had shown why those of us soldiers who met him thought so highly of him.

After an enjoyable voyage we arrived in Hong Kong, the troopship *Empire Fowey* slipping past lovely green islands in the early morning to a berth in Kowloon where my good friend Robin Charley was waiting with a smart Rifleman driver and a truck to take our kit. We had been allotted a sub-standard married quarter in Whitfield Barracks off Nathan Road on Kowloon side so we did not have far to go. After Egypt, with its surly, hostile locals and its arid scenery, it was heavenly to be among smiling friendly Chinese in surroundings of lush green with flowers and lovely trees, and to hear the singing of all sorts of birds, bulbuls and golden orioles among them. The shops in Hong Kong are fascinating and we had endless enjoyment browsing in them.

The 1st Battalion The Royal Ulster Rifles was stationed near the Border as part of 27 Infantry Brigade commanded by Brigadier Billy Burke, DSO, a Kingsman. The other battalions in the area were 1st Royal Northumberland Fusiliers, 1st Middlesex Regiment (The Die Hards), 1st Argyll and Sutherland Highlanders, and 1st Wiltshire Regiment.

Our Battalion Headquarters was located by the Fanling Golf Course, with companies at Fan Gardens and at Dodwells Ridge, while D Company, of which I had just taken command, was at Ho Tung House, a very pleasant spot. Lieutenant Colonel Jack Carson had been evacuated ill from Korea and Regimental history had repeated itself, as the Second-in-Command who had succeeded him when his glider was shot down on the Rhine Crossing had once more taken command. This was Gerald Rickcord who, to his DSO, had now added the United States Silver Star for his gallantry in action in Korea. I was so pleased to serve under Gerald again. He taught me so much about commanding a rifle company, particularly tactics. Not only did Gerald know his stuff but he knew how to put it over. It was indeed a happy battalion; we trained hard and one night each week we took it in turn to be inlying company, ready to turn out for whatever emergency occurred.

The threat from China was such that a tremendous wiring programme right across the New Territories was set in train, and we spent several days a week, in all weathers, out on the mountains putting up a deep belt of wire. We also carried out some interesting long tactical exercises in the mountains between Kowloon and the Frontier, shot on the ranges and generally improved our infantry skills. On St Patrick's Day the Battalion celebrated with a parade beside the Fanling Golf Course. The shamrock had arrived from Ireland in a rotting condition and could not be worn, so Au Wai Lam, our local contractor, quickly made seven hundred green cardboard bunches of our national emblem! The GOC of our Division was mystified – as were

we all – by the regimental water truck, which was found after the celebra-
tions, two hundred yards from the road upside down in a paddy field, *with
no tracks whatsoever leading to or from it.*

Gerald Rickcord left us for the Malayan Campaign, to command 1st
Battalion 2nd Gurkha Rifles. In his place came Lieutenant Colonel John
Drummond, DSO, formerly CO of our 2nd Battalion. John Drummond
was a highly efficient CO who set, and expected, the highest standards. He
also taught me a great deal, particularly about attention to detail! During
John Drummond's time in command, Hong Kong had a visit from the
Defence Minister, the renowned Ulster soldier, Field Marshal Earl Alexan-
der of Tunis. I commanded his Guard of Honour, complete with our Band,
Bugles, Pipes and Drums, and we were all very proud to be selected. After
the parade I was driving up in the dusk towards Fanling along the West
Coast Road. We were approaching Jubilee Reservoir – my driver, myself,
Brian Wadsworth, who was the subaltern of the Guard, and our RSM, Alex
Patterson. To our astonishment, a tigress crossed the road in front of us,
from right to left, with two half-grown cubs and vanished as quickly as
they had appeared.

Every year the Cross Harbour Race took place, from Kowloon on the
mainland to Victoria on Hong Kong Island. I decided to enter, called for
volunteers from my company and two subalterns and twelve NCOs and
men joined me. One Sunday morning the fifteen of us stood among
hundreds of other entrants, mainly Chinese, on the wooden jetty near
Kowloon railway station. We were marshalled, given the command 'Go!'
and dived into the flotsam and filth-covered waters of the harbour. My
head bumped against something as I surfaced and I saw that it was a dead
dog.

There was great confusion, thrashing arms and legs and a phalanx of
jostling bodies. Then the mob sorted itself out as the faster swimmers
surged ahead leaving the slower competitors astern. I suppose it was about
a mile across in those days before reclamation narrowed the gap between
the Chinese mainland and Hong Kong Island. It was spring tide and on top
of that it was a freak one with very high water so that we had an unusually
strong lateral current to contend with to avoid being swept away from the
winning post – which, I think, was Victoria Steps.

I made quite good progress and then about half way across I was
grabbed from behind and pushed under. I fought my way back to the
surface and found that a Chinese swimmer was the cause. He was ex-
hausted and rather panicky, so had clung on to me. Fortunately a motor
sampan came up, so he grabbed its stern, was held there by one of its
Chinese occupants and towed away towards our finishing point. I heard
later that when within a couple of hundred yards of the finish our hero let

go and was among the first swimmers to land! It was not a well organised race that year! There was supposed to be a string of rescue boats all the way across, every hundred yards but I never saw one, only commercial and passenger sampans such as had removed my clutching friend.

I was swimming past a floating dry dock which rose like a rusty red and black wall above me, when I was sucked down by an eddy nearby. I had just time to turn on my back and, as in my crossing of the Great Bitter Lake, extended my arms and legs like a starfish. As the waters closed over my face I looked up into a blue sky with one or two very small white clouds, thought 'I picked a great way to spend my Sunday!' and then I was spinning down, held in the grip of this powerful whirling current. Shortly afterwards I felt myself rising to the surface again. As quickly as I had been sucked under I was free and able to continue my swim.

In those happy days when we had a large and powerful Royal Navy, a number of our warships were stationed in Hong Kong. I remember the strong current bearing me past HMS *Black Swan* and the chi-yiking I got from the cheerful sailors leaning over the side. I arrived at the steps and climbed out. I suppose I was about half way up the finishing order and I felt it was all worthwhile. All but two of my team completed the course, including the two subalterns John Cave, the English international sprinter and hurdler, and Michael Mulholland, another fine young man of spirit, tragically killed when his jeep crashed on a precipitous mountain track.

Another essay in endurance my Company took on was to march right round the New Territories. Continuing throughout the night we completed the 60 odd miles in twenty-three hours. This, although tiring, was good for morale and we ran the last couple of miles home.

We were given the interesting little task, for a time, of intercepting and arresting smugglers on the Border which practised and improved our night ambush techniques. Another task was manning Observation Posts overlooking the Chinese Border. This was a fascinating experience as we were able to study our opposite numbers in the Chinese Army through binoculars and telescopes and watch them manning their own OPs, drilling, playing basketball and, of course, watching us!

There were civil disturbances in Hong Kong and once again we became involved in Internal Security duties. This was the first time I had worked with the (now Royal) Hong Kong Police and a very smart and efficient Force they were – and are.

In those days Hong Kong was unspoiled, the New Territories were green and cultivated, with traditional Chinese villages and were a delight to be in. The only high buildings I can recall were the Hong Kong and Shanghai Bank and the Bank of China on Hong Kong Island itself. As is the form today, the Clubs were very kind to officers, and we were members of the Hong Kong Club, a real privilege. In 1951, unlike now, lady members were pretty well confined to the 'Snake Pit', and were not welcome elsewhere in the Club.

Norman Fraser who was a senior officer in the Police, very kindly gave me an Alsatian dog pup. We called him Watchman and he was our family friend for thirteen happy years. He died while I was away commanding my battalion on operations in Borneo. I loved that dog; he was like a shadow to me, and apart from my unaccompanied tours in Cyprus and Borneo, he was my constant companion.

I learnt a lot about commanding a rifle company during my time in Hong Kong. I had a great team of officers and men. Robin Charley, my Second-in-Command, and Denis Lucy, my enthusiastic senior platoon commander, were to be two of my company commanders ten years later when I became CO. Both are related to me.

After two years in Hong Kong I was selected to be Training Major of 1st London Irish Rifles (TA) at Duke of York's Headquarters, Chelsea. We sailed home in the *Empire Trooper*, a journey that took six long weeks and we arrived in England during a horribly cold February in 1952.

There were some Argyll and Sutherland Highlanders on board. Our two regiments had become great friends after a tremendous fight at Fanling Crossroads when, so it was said, the respective RSMs (both Irishmen) had hurled in reinforcements by the lorry load! Next day Brigadier Billy Burke had both battalions on parade; gave us both a tremendous rocket; had the two Seconds-in-Command, who were then both acting COs, shake hands publicly, and then dismissed us all. After the parade the Brigadier was taking off his puttees and, turning to his orderly, Lance Corporal Downey in my Regiment, said 'I hope the Stickies and Jocks will now be friends, Downey.' 'Indeed they will, Sorr, I've heard tell that they're getting together this weekend to do up the Middlesex!'

CHAPTER TEN

1ST BATTALION THE LONDON IRISH RIFLES

I had an uproarious introduction to this renowned battalion which I joined in early 1952 and which was full of 'characters'. I returned home after my initial visit to Battalion Headquarters at Duke of York's Headquarters, Chelsea, where my bowler hat suffered an attempt to boil an egg in it! Cecil Nixon was Adjutant having succeeded his brother Sir Christopher. Both Nixons had won MCs with the Gurkhas in Burma and were very popular with the London Irish. They, with Colonel Lord (Monty) Stopford, OBE (later the Earl of Courtown) a previous CO, and Lieutenant Colonel John Cantopher, OBE, GM, the Commanding Officer, were a formidable quartet and each one dearly loved a party.

Basil Irwin, who got his MC for gallantry with the partisans in Italy was Second-in-Command and the company commanders had also all had distinguished service in one or other battalion of the London Irish in North Africa and Italy, as had a number of the warrant officers and NCOs, such as Archie Evans, Bruce Cortis and Pipe Major Johnnie Franklin, BEM.

During my time as Training Major it was the rule that former national servicemen had to complete a specified number of compulsory attendances in Territorial battalions, including the fortnight's annual camp. This was a great mistake as most of them had had enough of the Army and resented having to give up their spare time to the T.A., an essentially volunteer organisation. However, during their annual camp, they accepted the compulsory fortnight with good grace, and – because we did our utmost to make camp interesting – did well and were 'proper soldiers' again.

We were brigaded with 7th Middlesex Regiment and the London Scottish, and our Brigade Commander was Brigadier Victor Paley, a wise and

experienced soldier, with Bill Brooks in my Regiment as his Brigade
Major. Bill had had a very gallant record in the war, when he had been
gravely wounded, and been decorated with the Military Cross and Bar. He
and the Brigadier were an excellent team. Johnnie Johnson, an old friend
of mine came as Adjutant. Johnnie was an experienced and balanced
soldier, and I was lucky to have him with me. He was to be my Second-in-
Command in Borneo where he was decorated for his distinguished service.

Continuity was the most difficult thing to achieve in a T.A. battalion, but
we prepared a basic programme that produced as sound a standard of
individual training as we could, and then did our best to raise the standard
of tactics at section level and above. Johnnie and I used to run evening
sand-table exercises for officers and for NCOs, followed by TEWTs
(Tactical Exercises Without Troops) at weekends, which were succeeded
by actual exercises to practise what had been learnt. Company and battalion training took place at Annual Camp.

Sport was another activity we encouraged. We used to play basketball
and badminton in the drill hall, and Colour Sergeant Vic Farrant ran our
football teams which played matches on grounds he booked at Croydon for
the weekends. We went in for boxing, too, and I fought my last battalion
fight at the age of 32 against a charming corporal who could easily have
knocked me out, but I think he felt he couldn't bring himself to treat an
officer like that! Instead he kept hitting me under the heart which was far
worse! However I lasted the three rounds and managed to score some
points too. We had a cross country team and I took them up to Formby in
Lancashire to compete in the T.A. Championships. We had only just
enough members for a team and one failed to turn up. I filled his place and
will never forget what it felt like running up the soft, steep sandhills on the
course.

Johnnie and I played for our basketball team in the finals in the T.A.
Cup. I'm afraid I can't forget my rugger background when on the basketball court and tend to play too physical a game. I was sent off having
incurred the maximum number of personal fouls.

During my second year I determined to pass into the Staff College and
worked from 5am to 7am every morning, for two hours every night and for
six hours each weekend. Patrick, my eldest son, bless him, then aged only
five, used to get up and make me tea, boiled eggs and bread and butter for
my breakfast every morning. I had taken the entrance examination twice
before, once in Northern Ireland, when I hardly did a tap of work, and
again in Egypt when my down-to-earth Scots wife said I didn't work hard
enough. In those days you were allowed three attempts and as I had only
just failed one paper in Egypt I made up my mind I would do everything in
my power to get through on my third and last try. I attended an excellent

pre-Staff College Course at Eastern Command when my Director of Studies was Major Eric Penn. Thanks to his help I learnt a lot. However, when I sat the examination I was convinced I had failed. I went over my estimated marks again and again and I just could not even on my kindest self-assessment believe I could possibly have passed. I began to make plans as to what to do. Should I perhaps transfer to a Corps where my future advancement would not at that time have depended on the magic letters PSC, or should I seek a career outside the Army? Both courses, especially the second, were unthinkable. I loved my Regiment; I could never cease to be an infantryman. The Army was my life. I just could not leave it. I was very depressed indeed.

One morning Bill Brooks walked into my office with a copy of *The Times* in his hand. 'Have you read this morning's *Times*, Corran?' he asked me. I said that I had not yet done so. 'Well, you had better read it then,' said Bill, handed me the paper and walked out. Published inside was a list of those fortunate officers who had successfully passed into Staff College and to my utter surprise and delight, my name was among them. I was also glad to see that Johnnie Johnson had passed, as had Donald MacIntyre and James Majury all in my Regiment.

One of the last events I took part in was a divisional exercise which had been badly run insofar as our battalion was concerned, and everyone felt we had been messed about inexcusably. John Cantopher, at the end of his tether, said to our formidable and fierce-looking GOC, later General Sir Otway Herbert, 'Any more of this, General, and I will take my battalion straight home!' To our surprise and relief, the GOC reacted mildly and reasonably!

I was told a story about a social climber who was keen to be known as a friend of Monty Stopford and Chris Nixon when they were respectively Commanding Officer and Adjutant. His cup ran over when he was invited to lunch with them, and he let it be known that he was about to be entertained by Lord Stopford (he had not at that time succeeded to his Earldom of Courtown) and Sir Christopher Nixon ('the Baronet, you know'). Our friend turned up for pre-lunch drinks and these went on for quite a time. Eventually they left the Mess and walked along the King's Road until they came to a food stall, a sort of barrow on wheels. Its Cockney owner greeted them with 'Ullo, Monty, wotcher Chris,' and the guest was then invited to choose between pie and chips, sausage and chips or hot dogs and coffee!

The time came for me to hand over my job as Training Major and go to the Staff College. The London Irish have a terrific ésprit du corps and an enviable war record, and I had greatly enjoyed my two years with them.

My great-great uncle, Colonel James Ward, CB, VRD, had been their Honorary Colonel at the end of the last century. I held the same proud honour from 1986 to 1993, having taken over from that legendary Irish fighting soldier, Major General 'Bala' Bredin, CB, DSO MC.

CHAPTER ELEVEN

THE STAFF COLLEGE, CAMBERLEY

In December 1954, my family and I moved into a married quarter in King's Ride, Camberley near the sandy, pine-covered Barrosa area. I used to run there most days to keep fit accompanied by Watchman. We had a very good vintage year. Major General 'Splosh' Jones was our respected and popular Commandant and his Deputy was Sir John (now Lord) Hunt, the victor of Everest. We had a sparkling Directing Staff, which included a number of authors. Among these were Lieutenant Colonels Arthur Campbell, Rex Whitworth, Dair Wilson and Tony Deane-Drummond. I think eight instructors had written books. Perhaps the most successful writer of them all was our star student, Tony Farrar-Hockley. Among all the distinguished personalities (including Field Marshal Viscount Montgomery of Alamein) who lectured us, many of us believed that Tony Farrar-Hockley who talked without notes on 'Communism' was the most arresting and outstanding speaker.

The year's course was divided into six terms and we had a different DS (Director of Studies) for each term. There were three Divisions of the Staff College. 'A' and 'B' Divisions were at Camberley itself and 'C' Division under Colonel 'Tubby' Butler was at Minley. Ours was the last course where students could be 'sacked' during its progress. Three unfortunate officers left at the end of the first term. When we reassembled after the break to begin our second term, our kindly Commandant addressed us in the Rawlinson Hall and told us that 'provided none of you throw bricks through the Headmaster's window!' we were successfully through the course. He told us not to worry but to work hard and to take the opportunity to learn and to better ourselves as professional officers. I enjoyed the course; it was hard work but we had a happy atmosphere at Camberley and pleasant staff and students.

We used to play games on Wednesday and Saturday afternoons and I played for the Staff College rugger XV, first as a scrum half and later as wing three quarter, with my good Regimental friend James Majury, who was a first class back, on the other wing.

We went on an interesting battlefield tour in Normandy in the summer when a number of 'guest artistes' were present to give us their own first-hand experiences of the sub-unit actions in which they took part. They included a Sherman tank troop commander, and a rifle company commander in a Highland regiment. The latter could point out on the ground the very position of the slit trenches his company had occupied in one particular battle. We were billeted in a girls' school (it was holiday time!) and there was a certain amount of jollification in the evenings.

Among our distinguished lecturers was Field Marshal Viscount Montgomery of Alamein. We all knew about his views on coughing and we on the rugger team were discussing this in the dressing room after a match. I bought a tin of Zubes to be sure I did not transgress. On the morning of the lecture I sat fairly near the back with a number of my rugger-playing friends, where we hoped to be well away from the reputedly terrifying speaker. The great man entered, I put a Zube in my mouth. I took another in my hand and passed the tin to our enormous rugger captain, a Rhodesian called Theo Passaportis. The Zube tin flew along the line, I never saw it again, but none of us coughed!

We had a splendid Staff College Ball that summer, colourful with the dresses of the girls and the Mess Kit of the men.

Then came the day when we were all told where our postings were to be. To my joy I was going to a Grade Two Staff appointment in the Far East – with the Malayan Campaign in full swing I was to be DAAG at GHQ Far East Land Forces based in Singapore. I was determined to get out on operations in the jungle, not only to be able to understand and 'speak the same language' as the operational battalions but to fit myself for jungle warfare as a professional soldier.

Our nice bank manager was away on leave and his stand-in decided to foreclose on all overdrafts. We had a modest one in order to pay the education insurance for our two boys. We had to sell everything not utterly vital to us in order to repay our £500 overdraft. This included our car. I wonder how many people realise how few luxuries were possible to us captains and junior majors in those days? Our financial life was changed when Patricia's Aunt Ethel died and left her some money. Also my mother made over to me a small legacy from my father. These would assure our children's education and also enable us to buy a small, new car in Singapore.

I discovered that no less than twenty-five of us were to be posted to the Far East and also that our two Malaysian students would be on the staff of the Federal Army in Malaya. This was one of the marvellous things about the Staff College; your fellow students were contacts for the rest of your professional career. I was soon to find this in the Far East, where I had Staff College friends in all branches of the staff from the various Brigade Headquarters to the Headquarters in Malaya, Singapore and Hong Kong. This certainly not only oiled the works efficiently but made the lives of all of us considerably easier. Because of education we had to leave our eldest son, Patrick in England as a boarder at a very good preparatory school in Reigate, the Hawthorns. He was then aged nine. Timothy, our younger son, aged seven, came out to Singapore with us.

Before sailing in HMT *Dunera* in May 1956, I and my A Division co-students attended a three month course at the Royal Military College of Science, Shrivenham.

The *Dunera* was a small but comfortable troopship and I volunteered to run PT, sport and weapon training. The King's Dragoon Guards were the major unit being brought out; they would be equipped with armoured cars in Malaya.

This was one of the last times we went through the Suez Canal and we were allowed to go ashore at Port Said, a place I remembered well from my youth and from recent service in Fayid. We visited Simon Arzt's emporium and saw the resident mongoose playing with eggs and later the 'gully-gully' man came abroad and pulled chicks out of passengers' hair and clothing, as usual. Next morning when we got up early to see our progress down the Canal, camels were swaying along the road beside it and the Great War Memorial at Ismailia to the Anzacs was silhouetted against the dawn sky.

As we passed through Lake Timsah we saw bougainvillea-wreathed Canal Company houses and with field glasses looked at our old bungalow and at the GHQ buildings at Fayid. We did not stop at Suez but Aden was our next port of call. Patricia, Timothy and I had time to swim off a shark-netted beach. I was horrified when swimming underwater close to the shark net I found a hole big enough to allow a small submarine to enter. I reported this but I don't think the news galvanised anyone into quick action. Certainly when I visited Aden ten years later and was in the same shark-netted area, a shark got in and passed my legs so closely and with such speed that it felt like a near miss by a torpedo!

After a pleasant journey with sightings of porpoises and flying fish we came to Ceylon and went ashore at Colombo. My wife and I had first been there as children. As a result of our friendship at the Staff College we were met by Jerry Van Reyk and his wife Elizabeth. Jerry was in the Ceylon

Light Infantry and had been the star foreign and Commonwealth student on our course. There was quite a lot of anti-British feeling in Ceylon just then yet the Van Reyks made it quite clear to their country folk that we were their good British friends and they gave us a very happy day. Our last sight of them was standing at the very end of the breakwater waving up at us as we sailed out of Colombo harbour on the last leg of our journey to Singapore.

The night before we arrived at Singapore we had a fancy dress party and at about midnight a number of us were standing on deck in the Malacca Straits, a bright moonlit and balmy night. One officer, who was the life and soul of the party and who was going out to the 23rd Battalion King's African Rifles, was dressed in a nappy and clutching a baby's bottle of milk, heavily diluted with gin. He was having an absorbing conversation with someone quite oblivious of an enormous moth that had settled on his forehead, almost between his eyes! It had been a great evening!

CHAPTER TWELVE

COUNTER INSURGENCY OPERATIONS AGAIN – MALAYAN AND CYPRUS EMERGENCIES

Major Tim Robinson MC from whom I was taking over, met us at the boat and took us to 4 Tanglin Hill, formerly the Austro-Hungarian Embassy close by GHQ at Tanglin. It was a large, rambling, attractive building. We had a huge bedroom and a sitting room. The house stood in its own grounds with a small bandstand in the gardens. The staff were very pleasant, the food was good and we liked the other residents. I used to walk to the office in a few minutes. Thanks to Patricia's Aunt Ethel, we could afford to buy a rifle-green Morris Minor Traveller shooting brake, a great joy to us.

I took over as DAAG PA3, the section which dealt with terms and conditions of service and with the manpower of infantry battalions. I had two staff captains, Mary Morley, WRAC, and a Gunner captain who had been at the Staff College with me, Arthur Sisson. They both proved to be first class, dedicated and dependable. The Colonel AG was a Grenadier, Colonel (later Brigadier) Peter Miller CBE. The other DAAGs were a pleasant lot – Douglas Donnelly, Cheshire Regiment, had been at Sandhurst with me; he and Derek Baynham (who had also moved into 4 Tanglin Hill with his family) had been my fellow students at the Staff College.

Colonel Peter Miller seemed a stern taskmaster and for my first few weeks I wondered if I would ever succeed in pleasing him. Then one day at one of his DAAGs Conferences he praised something I had done. I felt as if I had been decorated! After that, he never criticised my work and trusted me utterly. I realised that he had been training me up to his very high standard. He was the most wonderful boss, we all loved him. He would never allow anyone, no matter how senior, to criticise us, backed us to the hilt and we would have done anything for him. If he felt anyone did deserve criticism he could deliver a blistering rocket, but no one else was permitted to discipline his staff. As part of my duties I took the minutes at the DAG's weekly conferences; I had never taken minutes before and I learnt the hard way. I sat enthralled during my first meeting and quite forgot to note the conversation! I spent the next 24 hours dashing from one kindly major general and brigadier to another, asking him what he had said! I made sure that I was on the ball at the next meeting!

The DAG, Brigadier Ian Buchanan-Dunlop DSO, OBE, MC, was a charming man and a real Infantry soldier.

I was anxious not to be a 'gaberdine swine' out of touch with the officers and men it was my task to serve, most of whom were operating in the jungle, so I decided I must arrange not only visits but attachments to infantry battalions in the jungle on operations. I was lucky enough to have a great Regimental friend, Brigadier Tommy Harris commanding 1st Malay – later 1st Federal – Infantry Brigade. Thanks to him I spent a month with 1st South Wales Borderers (24th Foot) commanded by that magnificent leader of men, Lieutenant Colonel, later Brigadier, Richard Miers. The 24th were an outstanding battalion and very highly regarded. I have a particular feeling for the Regiment because when they were raised in Ireland in 1689, three of their first-ever officers were Purdon ancestors of mine. I always felt completely at home with them, so much so that Patricia always referred to them as 'Your Second Regiment'.

Alun Gwynne Jones commanded B Company and had won his MC in a gallant jungle exploit. Rollo Price, Second-in-Command, was later awarded the DSO as a Brigadier in the Congo. The Adjutant was Tony Sharpe, whom I was to have the pleasure of serving alongside in Sennelager when we were commanding our respective 1st Battalions. Tony, like Rollo, was promoted to Brigadier, and then retired and became headmaster of a public school which under him became most successful. Tony Sharpe's successor as Adjutant was Lennox Napier who became a Major General. Blethyn Elliott, an old family friend of mine, was another company commander, loved by his men. Their padre Ned Kedward who had been in the Merchant Navy, was just the sort of down-to-earth, understanding chaplain that soldiers think the world of.

The 'feel' in the battalion was tremendous. They were a grand lot and they knew it. Under Richard Miers, their 'basics' were a hundred per cent. They were a very thoroughly trained battalion; they practised their Immediate Action drills for the jungle; they practised their shooting; and they were determined to eliminate all the enemy in their battalion area.

I knew nothing about the jungle and wanted to learn everything I possibly could about it and about Malayan counter-insurgency operations and techniques. Richard Miers started me off with Headquarter Company who were carrying out a food control operation at a village by a rubber estate. Each day we were in position before first light in order to check everyone leaving the village. Villages were wired in and entry and exit were through guarded gates. The South Wales Borderers were always smartly turned out and the soul of politeness.

Each rubber tapper leaving the gate was carefully searched for any food that he or she might be carrying out to the Communist Terrorists (or CTs). Rice, the staple diet was taken out in a variety of disguises, hidden within the women's brassieres, inside bamboo poles, in the hollow frames of bicycles and even in bicycle pumps. Food denial played a major part in the successful conduct of operations against the Chinese communists. In its uncooked, raw state rice will keep indefinitely and storage is easy. Colonel Richard Miers explained that rice is eaten by the Chinese in some form at every meal. It has little taste so that the human body which would object to any other food as an unchanged diet, can accept rice day after day. He went on to point out that rice as a diet must be balanced with some form of vegetable if beriberi is to be avoided.

The soldiers were also looking for other articles of value to the CTs such as medical items, electric torches, plastic cloth to use as roofing material for jungle shelters, and material for clothing. Although the CTs had food stored away in dumps, these stocks could not last forever and with a firm grip by the security forces on their potential chief source of food supply they would be forced to come into the open to try to get more, giving the security forces chances to inflict casualties on them and eventually eliminate them. Furthermore, some of the weaker, more timid CT sympathisers tended to fall away saying it was too difficult to get food past the soldiers.

Having had a very instructive time with the food denial operation, I spent some time being briefed on the intelligence picture, both from the military and from the Special Branch point of view, after which I was given instruction, together with newly-joined officers and soldiers, in the rudiments of jungle soldiering. This included immediate action drills, patrolling, ambushing, direction finding and shooting by day and by night. After this I was considered ready to be attached to the rifle companies in the jungle on operations against the CTs.

That night I was kitted up and went off to spend some time in the jungle with D Company, commanded by Major Dixie Deane. This was a very happy company, Dixie was a quiet, smiling, heavily-built man, very much at home on jungle operations. I arrived at D Company's camp in a Landrover accompanied by an escort in a 1 ton truck at about 7.30pm. The Welsh driver said to me, 'If we are ambushed, Sir, I drive straight through the ambush, then we stop, you and Pte Jones (one of the escorts) out the left hand side, me and Pte Davies out the other, and then we come back after the CTs with the lads from the one tonner.' We hared down the road, headlights blazing, but arrived without incident. Although the road along which we travelled was 'black', the battalion had only been ambushed on it once. I was sure that this was because the Welshmen always looked so alert and ready to use their weapons that CTs preferred to await less vigilant, less aggressive looking convoys.

At every village we came to, uniformed Malay policemen opened the gates to us at each end, closing them after we had passed through. After being greeted by Dixie on arrival, I was shown my tent where I slept like a top. The tent was on the edge of a rubber plantation and after early breakfast I heard the sound of our artillery engaging targets in the jungle. I was attached to a platoon commanded by a pleasant young national service subaltern, Nick Thompson, who had served his other rank service in my regiment, and we embussed in a $8^1/_2$ ton armoured truck en route for the jungle area. Inside the vehicle the seats faced inwards and there were armour-plated doors at one end and in the middle of the vehicle. There were oblong loopholes for firing out of, which could also be opened to let in the air; the men, all Welsh, were very cheery and friendly. Officers do not wear badges of rank in the jungle and only Dixie's batman knew who I was, so as a newcomer I had my leg pulled and we all had a great laugh as they questioned me on what I had learnt as a recruit at the Depot in Brecon.

We passed through a rubber estate, along a red laterite track and over a wooden bridge which surprisingly stood up to the weight of the heavy armoured troop carrier with its fifteen fully-equipped occupants. We debussed, the men formed up and looked to their front, rear and sides. Then at an order from Dixie we moved off up a track, four to five yards between men, everyone with weapons at the ready. After about half an hour we came to a bridge over a stream on the other side of which waited a group of soldiers.

This was one of D Company's ambush parties which had been lying up for several weeks covering a hidden store of food which had been concealed by tappers for the CTs, the whereabouts of the dump having been revealed by a police informer. This informer had got the wind up because the CTs had not come to collect the food and he thought they may have suspected him. To save his bacon and his further usefulness, the police had helped him to write a letter warning the CTs of the presence of the ambush and the men were now being removed.

We moved off over this bridge and along the track for about four hundred yards and then cut up through lallang (elephant grass) to the top of a feature from where we had a fine view of Mount Ophir to our north west.

Our route then went downhill through more lallang to a small river which we crossed by a fallen tree trunk after which a short distance forward brought us to the edge of the jungle. We were each carrying a full water bottle, two days rations, a change of clothes, rubber-soled canvas hockey boots, a poncho wrapped round a sweater, boots, socks, shirt and slacks, a dry bag containing, in my case, matches, a couple of paperback books, dry tea, sugar, milk and sweets, while a field dressing, tommy cooker, mess-tin, knife, fork, spoon, washing kit, insect repellent, paludrine tablets and water sterilising tablets were all in a pack carried on my back.

I will never forget my first entry into the jungle. One moment we were in bright sunlight, the next we were in a hot, humid, green gloom. The air was filled to bursting with noises. Predominant among these was a very high, trilling note like an alarm bell which got louder and louder until it seemed to fill the whole jungle. High in the trees birds called from time to time but it was the insects that made most of the noise. One sounded like an electric razor, finishing with the musical click made by a typewriter when it reaches the end of a line; it then started afresh and continued seemingly endlessly. Navigation in the jungle was by following the contours and the water courses and I was impressed by how well we kept direction.

At about 4pm we arrived at a flat piece of ground some thirty yards long and fifteen yards across, situated by a clear running stream. On the far side the ground rose steeply for about fifty feet and on our side of the stream it rose to three or four times that height. Everywhere was a tangle of trees and undergrowth. Dixie said, 'We'll make our base here, basha up!' In no time the ground had been cleared with matchets, branches were cut and laid across other branches and these, covered by and floored with ponchos, made good shelters. Soon tommy-cookers were going and tea was brewed, followed by hot stew, cooked individually on our hexamine cookers. Two Iban trackers who were accompanying us quickly put a long vine round the camp perimeter. This would not only stop anyone entering the camp unheralded but would enable each of us to move around the camp after dark.

The positions of the platoon commander's and platoon sergeant's bashas were indicated by phosphorescent buttons tied to the tree beside each. As daylight faded we stood to, and then when it was dark stood down, leaving double sentries on guard. (Two security patrols had been sent out by Dixie directly we arrived at the position to clear the area for enemy around our camp site.) The remainder of the party went to their bashas to sleep until it was their turn for guard duty.

We had changed out of our jungle kit which was sopping wet with sweat and swamp water. I had a stripped-off bath in the stream, dried myself on a jungle-green towel and put on my dry change of kit. I for one was not sorry to stretch out with my head on my pack and look up at the stars through the trees. The night is long in the jungle, from about 7.30pm to 6am. Once we were alerted by the sound of what seemed like automatic fire but it was a tree falling, away in the distance. From midnight, and on the hour thereafter, a battery of 25 pounders from 48 Field Regiment fired a number of rounds into the jungle to the north of us.

At about 6am we stood to, and by the time it was light enough to see, hot tea was on everywhere in the camp. Drinking mouthfuls of the welcome, hot, sweet brew we changed back into our previous day's clothing which, although we had hung it out to air the previous night, was disagreeably cold, damp and slimy to put on. After we had eaten our individually-cooked breakfasts, I moved off with a patrol commanded by Nick Thompson, the national service subaltern who in civilian life had been studying at RADA. We wore light patrol order with jungle green belt, bandolier of ammunition, water bottle, and one pouch on the belt containing some biscuits, salt tablets, sterilising tablets and a field dressing.

We moved off, first the leading scout, then Nick, then the Bren gunner, then me, then three private soldiers. We climbed up the steep hill behind the camp on a bearing of 40°. The jungle was full of noise, insects predominating. Our aim was to patrol the stream and its tributaries to our north and east to see if we could find any CT camps near the water. In places the jungle was quite easy to move through, but for most of the way there were deceptive, shiny palm like leaves on the backs of which were serrated thorns. These pulled at jungle hats, clothes and equipment. It was hopeless to fight against these gripping leaves; the only thing to do was to patiently move back far enough to disengage the thorns and then, when free, to proceed again. Loops of vines caught at our legs and necks. When you are fresh these are easy enough to slip through or round, but when you are tired they are swine.

In the watercourses inside the jungle it was green and gloomy and the heat was like a hot, wet blanket of cotton wool. It was heartening to look upwards and see bright blue sky and white scraps of cloud through gaps in the jungle canopy. A troop of monkeys crashed through the trees overhead; from their howls they sounded like gibbons. A toucan or hornbill, or some such large bird, croaked, the noise sounding like a human voice. To get to the stream which we were to search, we went by a compass bearing which took us now uphill, now downhill, but nearly always through these gripping, thorn-covered belukar leaves. The Bren gunner told me they were called 'Wait a while', which was sufficiently descriptive but not nearly abusive enough!

We found the stream and followed it, walking sometimes in it, sometimes above it, on one side or the other, constantly crossing and recrossing.

We followed it, with ten minute halts every hour, for about two hours, when we turned for base. I was feeling fine. Getting back to base was over very different country and by 4pm we were still a long way from camp in terms of time.

Then, by chance, we hit the tracks made by a previous outgoing patrol and Omar, the Iban tracker who was attached to our patrol, took over to lead us back to camp. Nick would have got us back all right but this saved time. By now we were all feeling a bit tired as we had been going solidly for eight hours over rough country. Omar led at a cracking pace and after an hour I found that my time on the staff had not helped my jungle fitness! Half an hour more and I was flogged and for me the journey became purgatory. Had we only kept to the original patrol pace I could have gone on indefinitely but this colossal speed set by Omar, crossing over logs, through looped vines, belukar and thorns, then over fallen trees, through swampy stream edges, had me wondering when we would ever get to camp. At our next halt I ate two salt tables, finished what was left of my water and felt greatly revived.

We resumed our patrol, and dragged on. I could not believe my eyes when we arrived in a clearing and saw the neat bashas of our camp. I had certainly relearned the need for constant physical fitness. After a hot, sweet brew of tea I felt grand, had an invigorating cool bath in the stream, changed into my dry clothes and cooked myself a meal of stew, raisins and biscuit, my comrades individually cooked their evening meals at the same time.

After stand-to and stand-down I slept gloriously until stand-to at 6am next morning. A dear black labrador tracker dog was part of our group, with a SWB handler but dogs have not always proved a great success in the art of jungle tracking, as opposed to the Ibans who are amazingly good.

Next morning our group carried out a shorter patrol during which we found plenty of signs of Security Forces but none of CTs. We heard over the radio that B Company under Alun Gwynne Jones had killed another CT.

The Iban trackers were very much part of the Regimental family, any English they spoke was with Welsh accents. They seemed to know all the Army swear words, too. Next morning it was chilly and Omar, who with Cpl Hodges was on guard before stand-to, said to me in what must have been a true Brecon accent, 'Morning, Sir, f– cold day!' After breakfast we demolished the camp and moved off up the hill. The jungle, though thick, seemed less antagonistic than on Friday's patrol.

We arrived at the head of the stream on which our camp had been based. By now I felt really fit and was revelling in being in the jungle. Around us huge trees soared skywards and with a vast croaking and cracking of vegetation, a large hornbill settled into the top of one jungle giant. We continued, alert, weapons at the ready, glad that the route after we had reached the head of the stream was downhill. For another hour we pushed on through the jungle. Once, when negotiating a fallen log, I felt an excruciating nip in my backside as it touched the bark and I discovered that a bulldog ant had bitten me.

Then we were in a clearing at the jungle's edge and ahead of us was Mount Ophir rising out of the distance. We crossed a wire fence and walked down a slope covered with black, charred tree stumps until we reached a track, on both sides of which Chinese men and women were clearing the ground preparatory to planting young rubber, helped in their task by a bulldozer and its Tamil driver. We advanced across the broken ground in extended order, coming into line when we came to a track over a bridge, and eventually arrived at a rubber estate. Here transport was waiting which took us back to D Company's Camp at Batu Anam.

I then joined B Company, commanded by Alun Gwynne Jones at Pekan Jabi and went out on a patrol with him. The aim was to move out to where he and his ambush party had killed a CT the day before. Pausing at C Company's range at Bulok Kasap to fire our weapons, we drove to a point on a rubber estate where we debussed and the jeep, the scout car and 1 ton truck returned to Pekan Jabi camp. (Alun is now Lord Chalfont, OBE, MC, PC.)

We moved off as follows: leading scout, Bren gunner, Alun, myself, two riflemen, Mr Tan the JCLO (Junior Chinese Liaison Officer) and the CSM. The battalion were determined to get the leader of the local Selampur gang, Lee Ming, and his men, and as this was his area we hoped to meet him. It was a lovely sunlit morning and our route followed a track into a swamp with clumps of bamboo and trees to our left, while to our right, from a distance of about 200 yards, rose the jungle on higher ground.

We investigated a track through the undergrowth but it petered out in a clump of bushes. Twenty minutes later we came to the rubber and opened out in extended order, moving quietly. We stopped various tappers whom we found moving silently through the trees, inspected their identity cards and passes and, through Tan, asked if they had seen any CTs – invariably they said they had not! As we were moving down the hill, we heard male voices from the other side of the swamp and we could see several figures in a tapper's hut.

Under cover of high, thick bushes we proceeded until we found a series of round logs, end to end, overlapping in places, connecting with the other side which was a rubber estate. We stole across and when the patrol was assembled, quickly advanced to the hut – but we only found a woman and two youths and, of course, they had no knowledge of the owners of the male voices we had heard! Their passes were in order and I had a look at their work. They poured the white rubber latex into trays 4 to 5 inches deep, added a coagulating acid and left it for 20 minutes. The substance was then put through a mangle whence it emerged as a white sheet, a quarter of an inch thick and about the dimensions of a handtowel. This was then hung up to dry.

On we went, stopping to listen every now and then, till we reached the top of some high ground from where we looked down across the jungle edge onto a field of coffee which joined the jungle. We came quickly down into the field and up another slope moving through the coffee bushes. Whereas from the high ground we could see clearly into the coffee, once we were inside the plantation, visibility was limited to the bushes in front. There was a shelter half way up the hill where coffee was being roasted. We encircled it and entered, looking at the identity cards of its occupants. Alun recognised one pale, pockmarked Chinese as a man who had been caught in an opium den the previous week. Having left them we investigated a fire and then crossed some green, creeping undergrowth which had recent elephant tracks across it and moved into the next coffee field.

We were now approaching the tapper's hut where Alun and John Mitchely had shot Yap Kow the CT the day before. Arriving at the bottom of the hill where the swamp began, we saw the silver, corrugated-iron roof of the hut before us. Here Alun put out sentries and then had a quick brew-up. He showed me the positions of the ambush party. Yap Kow's blood was still on the dark red earth and where he fell near the hut the soil was black with it. He had been carrying a Japanese hand grenade when he died – he'd been trying to get it out to throw it but John Mitchley's shot from his FN rifle had cut the CTs belt and Yap Kow's pants had fallen down. When Alun Gwynne Jones 'filled him in' with his FN, Yap Kow was only a few yards off and was too slow to use the gun he was carrying.

We went to where Alun had buried the grenade and the CSM got ready to blow it up. It went off with a good loud bang, startling a troop of monkeys who were swinging through the trees uttering guttural cries. There was no sign of CTs so we patrolled the rubber. Near the jungle's edge we came to a filthy-smelling collection of tappers' huts. These we searched but only one shifty looking, middle-aged Chinese woman was there. There was a strip of cultivation; chillies and mangosteens, and this was forbidden. The crone denied all knowledge as to who worked it but it was obviously CTs as it was only 50 yards from the swamp at the edge of the jungle.

I covered Alun with my rifle while he searched a dirty hut then I heaved myself up a broken-runged ladder and burst open a door so as to search the upper floor. As I stared into the gloom three pairs of beady eyes met mine

– bats! Alun reported this suspicious area on our return so that it would be watched and ambushed. We continued our patrol. It was very hot, the sunlight splashing through the trees and not a breath of wind. We crossed several swamps over hundreds of yards of planks set on piles.

After another eight miles of patrolling we came to a track through a rubber estate near the Muar River. Right on time our transport met us and another day's patrolling was over. No kills had been achieved; alas, not even a contact, but we had at least discovered a CT cultivated strip and had demonstrated that Security Forces could appear unexpectedly, anywhere, any time.

My education in jungle operations progressed and by the end of my attachment to this fine battalion I felt at home in the jungle and confident in my operational skills. I returned to GHQ and next Sunday morning, beside the pool of the Tanglin Club, the pallor of my skin was in marked contrast to the deep bronze tan of those staff officers who had not had my good fortune. From then on I was the South Wales Borderers' link man at GHQ FARELF and whether their problems were operational or administrative Major Tony Sharpe the Adjutant and Colonel Richard Miers the Commanding Officer knew that they only had to pass them to me and I would contact the appropriate staff officer and ensure that their problem was speedily dealt with.

I used to get myself into the jungle about once a month, adding to my infantry knowledge, meeting the fighting regimental officers, NCOs and men in their own environment, taking back with me any matters they wished resolved by the Staff. I began to take some clerks with me, the keenest among them being WOI 'Topper' Brown, later Major Brown, and WOI Paddy, later a Lieutenant Colonel. One of my good friends, Malcolm Campbell, was commanding a squadron of Gurkha Engineers and I learnt about jungle sappering from him. I patrolled in the armoured cars of the King's Dragoon Guards, watched the Singapore Regiment Royal Artillery shelling a CT camp, visited various RASC and RAOC installations, an RAMC field hospital in Malaya and patrolled with various Gurkha battalions, with 2nd Royal Welch Fusiliers, and with the Singapore Guard Regiment.

I also flew in an Auster light aircraft when it put down markers for a strike by Lincoln bombers on a CT camp in the depths of the jungle. The pilot, Captain Peter Myers, was a delightful man, and expert at his job. He pinpointed the CT camp after we had taken off from Sembawang and put down his markers, calling up the Lincolns on his radio as he did so. We then remained flying close to the target area. I had my cine camera with me and got some good shots of trees hurtling into the air from the heavy bomb explosions – which also threw us all over the place as is apparent from my cine film! Peter then flew back over the CT camp to photograph and report back on the damage, and we stared down at great gaps in the trees, huge craters and debris.

We later had an Internal Security situation in Singapore and 18 Infantry Brigade took command. I was in charge of a road block near Tanglin; my men were GHQ clerks, well known to me, and we all enjoyed the change in routine. Once again, it was good down-to-earth experience and reminded us all that we were soldiers first and members of the staff second.

Singapore was a great place for sport and we used to play a lot of tennis and squash and swim at the Tanglin Club. I won the GHQ plunge title each year I was there and the breaststroke races. I also took part in the Singapore to Johore Bahru Road Walk.

I loved Malaya and Singapore and the jungle fascinated me. One of our treats was to get away from Singapore up country to Mersing on the east coast and to bathe in the gloriously pleasant sea. On one visit Tony Tighe had us all picked up in a police launch and taken out to a tiny white sand-encircled island called Pulau Baba Kechil, covered with tall, graceful palm trees. We spent a happy day there swimming in crystal-clear water and returned to the rest house at Mersing almost too sleepy from sun and sea to eat a dinner of the inevitable mulligatawny soup, curried chicken, and créme caramel, before falling into our beds, wonderfully and healthily tired.

On another occasion Brigadier Tommy Harris who had won his DSO commanding 2 RUR in Normandy invited us to Fraser's Hill to stay with him in the Sultan of Pahang's bungalow. Up there in the cool air it was bliss after the hot humidity of Singapore and reminded me, with the brightly coloured flowers and Tamil labourers, of my early Indian childhood in the Nilghiri Hills. We had to have an escort on the way up, as part of the roads were 'black' but once at Fraser's Hill, we were able to wander into the jungle, or through the hillsides, at will. Patrick, our eldest son, had gone down with pneumonia the previous Christmas holidays so it was good to see him now so fit and well, with his younger brother Timothy, both with red cheeks because of the high altitude and the clear air.

One of the duties that came round to us staff officers in Singapore was that of OC the night mail to and from Kuala Lumpur. The Duty Officer was in charge of the train and took command if it was ambushed. There was a signaller with a radio who was in contact with the main stations and a warrant officer was detailed as the Duty Officer's right-hand man. Through him, soldiers travelling were organised into sub-units so that immediate action could be taken in an emergency. The engine mounted a searchlight to illuminate the track ahead and an armoured Wickham trolley, also with a searchlight and radio, preceded the train to protect it. I carried out this duty several times. We would leave the train next morning, in daylight, at Kuala Lumpur and then catch the night train back to Singapore that same evening. In the meantime, I would visit either Headquarters of Malaya Command or of the Federation Army during the day. In Federation Army Headquarters I would call on my two Camberley friends Shaharim and Ibrahim bin Ismail, both experienced operational soldiers – Shaharim had been Mentioned in Despatches for his gallantry against the CTs, and 'Ib' wore an MBE for his work in Force 136 in Burma when he had held a commission in the Indian Army. I would also see my friend Digger Tighe-Wood who was in my Regiment. Digger had been a splendid, down-to-earth wartime company commander in our 2nd Battalion in France, Holland and Germany under Tommy Harris, and had commanded 3rd Parachute Regiment and then, as a brigadier, 16 Parachute Brigade (TA). After Malaya, Digger was offered yet another brigadier's staff post and is reported to have said to the Military Secretary's Branch that he joined the Army to serve with soldiers not to shuffle paper. He was a delightful person, a fine shot, an exceptional fisherman; he loved the outdoors, yet was an expert in restoring watercolours. When he retired he ran the Watercolours Department in the Victoria and Albert Museum. Sadly, he died several years ago.

One evening as OC Night Mail, I was on my rounds of the compartments while the train clattered and swayed through the hot, humid Malayan darkness. I had noticed a Royal Navy petty officer with a detachment of ratings bringing back under escort a small number of sailors from the Military Detention Centre. I then saw him drinking in the first class refreshment compartment with a planter. I went over to him and asked him why he had left his charges, if he had a first class ticket to be where he was, and why he was drinking on duty. He could not answer any of these queries and was extremely surly. I took his name, rank, number and unit and ordered him back to his compartment. Later on I found him back in the bar plus his escorts, having left his prisoners unattended, so I escorted them all back again, the petty officer surlier than ever. I was chatting to another officer in my compartment when I heard a commotion outside, and into the car burst this same petty officer, brandishing a rifle and calling for 'that bastard Purdon'! He was very drunk and said 'I'll swing for you, you bastard!' However, I had no difficulty in wresting his rifle, which by now he was pointing at me, from his grasp. I asked my friend to witness what had happened and to accompany me with this disgraceful creature to his compartment. I released his charges to open arrest (they were extremely well behaved) disarmed his escort as well as him and put them in the custody of their former charges. I alerted the Royal Military Police at our next stop by radio and personally handed over the petty officer and entourage to them in the small hours of the morning on the platform of Seremban Station. I was later called on to give evidence at the petty officer's trial at which he denied everything and said he had had a blackout from the time he had first entered the train and remembered nothing. The Captain asked me my opinion and I said that the man was undoubtedly drunk, whereupon he was found guilty, reduced to the ranks and sent to the cells. The Captain told me that this particular ex-petty officer had always been under suspicion but that had trodden a disciplinary tightrope so that they could never catch him out. He thanked me warmly for helping them to get rid of such a rogue.

On another occasion I was handed over a large party of Australian private soldiers who had completed their time on jungle operations and were due to catch a ship back to Australia next day. In a loud, hectoring voice for all the Aussies to hear, a blustering, portly and elderly British Major advised me to lock them into their carriages without any drink and not to stand any nonsense. I agreed with the last injunction but could see no reason for the rest of his rude and unasked for advice and told him so. I got the Australians into their large, open compartment and said to them that I knew they were all excited at the prospect of returning home and also that I knew some of their battalion. I said that I was not going to place them under any restrictions whatsoever, they could drink as much beer as they wanted, but if there was any drunken behaviour by ANY of them I would put them all out on the first station we came to, as I would do to anyone else travelling with us. I told them I had no reason whatsoever to think they would misbehave, congratulated them upon the success of their battalion on operations and wished them a pleasant journey and a good voyage back to Australia. Not only did those men behave perfectly but next morning in Singapore Station they sought me out to say goodbye. I have always had the highest regard and great affection for this nation of fine fighting men and I was disgusted with the overweight major's attitude to them.

Another interesting assignment I had was to organise under the direction of Brigadier Walter Walker, the equivalent of the Westbury Regular Commissions Board for Gurkhas and Malays. This was the first time that I met the dynamic fighting soldier who was to be my General eight years later during confrontation with Indonesia in Borneo. Among the successful candidates was a young Rifleman Lalbahadur Pun who, after completing his course at Sandhurst, went on to receive a Regular Commission into the 2nd (King Edward VII's Own) Goorkas (The Sirmoor Rifles). He was to be decorated with the OBE, the Military Cross, be ADC to General Walker in Borneo and become Commanding Officer of the Brigade of Gurkhas Depot as a lieutenant colonel.

GHQ Far East Land Forces was a happy place. The respective Commanders-in-Chief during my time there were both impressive men. General Sir Charles Loewen and after him General (later Field Marshal) Sir Francis Festing known as 'Front-line Frankie' from his leadership of 36th Division in the Burma campaign. We worked hard, played a lot of sport and had excellent clubs where we enjoyed ourselves with our families. At weekends we would usually alternate between the Tanglin Club and the Changi Club, or perhaps go for an early morning swim off Changi beach, followed by fishing in Pongol Ponds.

Most Saturdays we would take Tim, our younger son, to Robinson's in Raffles' Square where out of his weekly pocket money he bought boxes of Britain's soldiers to add to his growing collection – this is still one of his hobbies.

My kind and forbearing Brigadier continued to allow me to go off into the jungle on operations at frequent intervals so I was never bored and obtained quite an insight into what went on in the many different Gurkha and British battalions and in the Singapore Guard Regiment on their operations up-country. A good friend in my Regiment, George de Stacpoole was commanding D Company in the latter unit, whose CO was an Ulsterman, Lt. Col. Freddie Cunningham OBE of the Royal Inniskilling Fusiliers. I had some interesting patrols with George's Malays, including one by boat down the Johore River. George, now the Duke de Stacpoole, lives in the West of Ireland.

We were now living in Claymore Drive, five minutes walk from the Tanglin Club, and ten minutes from GHQ. Patricia was teaching at Miss Griffith-Jones' Kindergarten School in Orange Grove Road and Tim was at the Army School in Pasir Panjang. In the evenings we often walked in the nearby lovely Botanic Gardens where we were amused by their monkey population and enjoyed feeding the great carp in the lake.

Tom Laister in my Regiment was Director of Public Relations and an excellent and experienced one he was. We used to meet to update each other on the latest Regimental news and he and Queenie, his wife, and Patricia and I saw a lot of each other socially.

Eventually the day came when my time on the GHQ staff was over and I was appointed to command my Regimental Depot (in those days a Major's command) at St. Patrick's Barracks, Ballymena, Co. Antrim, in my native Northern Ireland. For our last few days Patricia, Tim and I moved into the Rex Hostel (well known by another name to Somerset Maugham).

I remember how, after returning from a farewell party, Patricia found an enormous black, hairy spider on her bed and told me to get rid of it. I, by that stage of the evening, only wanted to go to bed and, the spider by then having gone under the pillow, I said I would change beds and sleep with my head on the spider and as many others as cared to join it. Patricia would have none of this, saying it might well transfer to her side later on and that I must pick it up and put it right out of the room. I did not relish touching its thick, hairy body and legs and in cowardly fashion wondered if it could be a tarantula or some other deadly insect. Putting on a pair of her cleaning gloves, I gingerly picked the insect up. I was sure I could feel the hairs on its evil body through the cotton gloves which were far too short for my fingers anyway. I advanced towards a sort of large, steel door on rollers that led out from our quarters, rolled it back and threw the great black spider as far away as I could. I hastily rolled the door back shut. I could swear that from my last glimpse of the spider it was about to hurl itself against the steel door!

We embarked in the excellent troopship *Oxfordshire* for our voyage home. Again I ran the sport and PT, so kept fit myself. We had an enjoyable trip home, stopping at Ceylon where we visited the zoo at Mount Lavinia, had a swim in the sea and a wonderfully hot curry at the Galle Face, Colombo with Dixie Deane (late of D Company 1 SWB) and his wife Margaret. We also went ashore at Aden, Port Said, Limassol and Gibraltar. Troopships gave one an easy build up to service abroad and a pleasant run down on one's way home.

We docked at Liverpool. It was February, and once again it was snowing.

Before leaving Singapore in 1956, I said goodbye to our Chief of Staff, Major General William Pike. I told him that I was determined to join the first battalion of my Regiment, then on operations against the EOKA terrorists in Cyprus. I wrote to the CO, Lieutenant Colonel Norman Wheeler, told him that I had four months to spare before taking command of the Regimental Depot and asked if he had a slot for me. Norman replied saying that he needed a company commander for Support Company which was to be employed as a Rifle Company because of the battalion's internal security role.

General Willie Pike had given me a letter to the Royal Air Force to help me get out to Cyprus but, I should only use it *in extremis*, so I felt I must do as he said, particularly as I was sure we would meet again, and whereas I was a major, he was a general! So, having got leave of absence from my long-suffering wife, I went along to see the RAF and true to my instructions from General Willie, my letter was never opened – BUT, I admit, I did produce it in its envelope, say who it was from and announce that I had his approval, which I knew to be true, to join my Regiment in its theatre of operations! I was given a form to sign, which Patricia insists said that in the event of my untimely demise she would not receive a pension – she still has not forgiven me for that! – and was told to report to RAF Brize Norton.

I had an uneventful flight to Nicosia. As we came in low to land we flew over a cemetery where a military funeral was in progress. I heard later that it was of a soldier who had been killed as a result of an accidental discharge. Wherever I had been, since the Second World War, on active service, I had come across instances of accidental discharges of weapons and I took, and still take, a harsh view of anyone responsible for causing death under such tragic and irresponsible circumstances.

I was met by my good friend, Paddy Liddle and taken off to join the battalions at Dhavlos on the 'Panhandle' of Cyprus and was made very welcome by that fine regimental soldier Norman Wheeler. It was wonderful to be back 'in the family' again and surrounded by friends of all ranks.

Next morning was glorious, with a blue sky, blue sea and cool air despite a hot sun, and Norman, Paddy, Dennis Lilleyman (OC C Company), Johnnie Watts (OC A Company) and I went for an early morning swim in the 'submarine pens', as we called a collection of lagoons in the rocks where the clear sea was enclosed in long, narrow pools. Then, after breakfast, I took over S Company. John Weir a very strong and reliable officer, was my second-in-command and my three subalterns were Jeremy Knox, Robert Carson (both of whom I had known since they were tiny) and Denis Gallwey, the last two of whom are distantly related to me. I could not have had better officers and with 'Dolly' Gray as my CSM and Micky Byrne as my Colour Sergeant, I was truly lucky with my team.

We moved south to Famagusta shortly after my arrival, to Karaolas Camp. Nearby Varosha was a hotbed of EOKA activity as were the surrounding villages of Akhiritou, Asha, Vattili and Athna. We had an RUC officer called Paddy Freeborn attached to us: he was serving with the Cyprus Police on secondment. Paddy was a real character and being himself an Ulsterman became very much identified with the Battalion. Colonel Wheeler quickly took the initiative in our new operational district and companies carried out detailed reconnaissances of their company areas. We worked hard to dominate our allotted areas, patrolling by night and by day. Every night we carried out what we called 'soft-shoe' patrolling in our various villages, with blackened faces and wearing gym shoes. We would slip quietly through the narrow streets and suddenly appear in some café where the locals were drinking, and look at their means of identity. At that time it was the Turkish Cypriots who were friendly to the British and the Greek Cypriots, many of whom were EOKA sympathisers, who were surly and unfriendly.

EOKA had a habit of murdering non-EOKA, leaving the dead bodies in churchyards and ringing the church bells. As our patrols turned up anywhere, at this time, this evil habit ceased in our area. Slogans were painted on roads and walls, the Greek Cypriot equivalent of 'Brits Out'. We suspected the older students in the gymnasia of our local villages, but we were not lucky in catching them. One particular village gave a lot of trouble with slogans, which said 'Cyprus is Greek', but one morning, after one of our NCO-led patrols had failed yet again to ambush anyone, the local gymnasium headmaster complained of a white-washed message on the school wall, announcing that 'Cyprus is Irish'! Strangely, that did the trick and there were no more painted slogans.

By day we patrolled partly on foot and partly in vehicles in order to cover our considerable area, but we dropped off ambush parties covertly to lie up and observe suspect locations. I used to take a 'soft-shoe' patrol out every night, as did all my officers, and I got to know our villages well. We carried out a number of stop-and-search operations on vehicles and, working in close co-operation with the police, put on snap road blocks to catch terrorists and their weapons.

We were all very fit, sunburnt and healthy with our energetic outdoor life. Although we had little time to spare for sport, we used from time to time to take armed bathing parties down to swim at Golden Sands Leave Camp as a change from operations. The Director of Operations when I first arrived in Cyprus was Major General Douglas (Joe) Kendrew, the former English rugger captain, and holder of four DSOs.

General Kendrew handed over as Director of Operations to Major General Ken Darling, who had known the Battalion well in 6th Airborne Division. We had a great regard for him also and were to continue our happy association with him later when he commanded 1 (BR) Corps and, later still, Southern Command; on both occasions when I was CO.

The atmosphere in Cyprus grew increasingly more tense, particularly in Varosha. One day Norman Wheeler sent for me and told me had received information from Special Branch that there was to be a meeting that night of the leaders of Red Soil Group North in the village of Asha in my Company area. There was one snag. The informer would not give the location of the building concerned, and refused to reveal its whereabouts until we got there when he said he would shine a torch on it! This was most unsatisfactory, as we could neither hold a rehearsal on a mock-up house, nor make a proper plan. We had some outstanding men serving in Special Branch at that time, especially John Prendergast, so we knew that when we got information it was going to be good, that every effort would have been made to get the detailed location of the meeting place, and that the informer was probably acting as he was through fear of discovery by the EOKA.

I selected two officers and twelve men to accompany me, the officers being Jeremy Knox and John de Courcy Ling. Our plan was to travel in a Landrover and a one-ton truck and as soon as the informer shone his torch on the building to jump out of the vehicles, surround it if it was a detached house, and then burst in and search for our quarry. The informer would not even tell us if the house was detached or not, nor on which side of the road it lay, so we would need all the luck in the world to catch our men. Obviously we also made a plan should the house be semi-detached.

We assembled in Karaolos Camp, blackened our faces, checked our arms and equipment for rattling, tested weapons by firing them at a target and, then when it was time – I think about 10pm – drove quietly out of camp. Just before we left, Paddy Freeborn, who was coming with us in his big black American limousine accompanied by his huge Turkish Cypriot bodyguard, said to me with a grin, 'Corran boy, I think maybe there'll be a bit of gunplay tonight.'

It was a moonless night but the stars gave enough light for us to make out buildings and trees. I chose a route away from Asha then followed a cross-country track that joined the road through the village. We sat ready to jump out as, with our car lights extinguished, we rolled quietly down the main street led by Paddy's saloon. It was infuriating not knowing to which side to look. Suddenly Jeremy hissed to me, 'There's the torch light, right!' We leapt out and dashed noiselessly to the building indicated. Alas, it was NOT a detached house so we couldn't surround it. We burst open the door and sprinted inside. One small group of our men made their way round to the back of the buildings, but I doubted if it could be in position quickly enough.

With our pre-assigned parties of riflemen, we went quickly into the downstairs rooms and a party under Sergeant Cairns moved off upstairs. I found myself on my own in a room with one Greek Cypriot man in it. I covered him with my Sterling and ordered him to hold his hands up. The room had all the classic signs of sudden flight – the window was open, the table in front of it was laid with an unfinished meal, the plates still held warm food, and a chair had been kicked over by its fleeing occupant. Had our informer been persuaded to say that the house was one of a row and where, I could have positioned a cut-off party behind it in advance and caught the lot. As it was I had caught one of the four wanted leaders.

I found later that my captive was a schoolmaster, a wiry tough man who kept yelling 'EOKA'. I made him face one of the side walls and warned him that if he tried to escape I would shoot him. I was infuriated that because of the confusion of our unrehearsed entry I was on my own and I did not want to be tied to guarding this one man when I could be co-ordinating a search. Suddenly there came a great crash of breaking glass and woodwork and through a hitherto-closed window swung the welcome figure, glass, frame and all, of ginger-haired, tough Rifleman Taffy Roberts, one of my best men. Taffy covered the prisoner while I searched him.

The man pretended not to understand English. I was pretty sure he could speak it, so we took him outside and handed him over to Paddy Freeborn and his Turkish Cypriot bodyguard. Paddy drove him away for questioning. The captured man later said that he and the other three leaders were having a meal when they heard the muffled sound of vehicle engines and decided to jump for it. The schoolmaster was slowest so I caught him, and I just missed seeing his companions. If the wretched informer had not been so windy, we should have got the lot!

Special Branch had warned us that a Greek Cypriot Cyprus Police sergeant at Vattili was an EOKA man but that he was too clever to give proof. We fixed his duff by always ostentatiously being friendly with him in public, singling him out for handshakes and chummy claps on the back! We heard later that the EOKA began to suspect him of being pro-British, as he asked for police protection.

After four happy months back with my Regiment the time came for me to leave the 1st Battalion and return to the United Kingdom to take command of our Regimental Depot. I was sad to leave the Battalion but at least I had shared in their successful operational tour and knew from first-hand experience what sort of special training our recruits at the Regimental Depot required.

On a sunny morning I took my leave and set off in a Landrover for Nicosia to catch my Royal Air Force aircraft, accompanied by my batman Rifleman Dandy, my signaller Rifleman O'Toole and, of course, my driver Lance Corporal Carbery. As we drove along in the hot sunlight we passed a vehicle with a couple of Greek Cypriot priests as passengers. One looked rather like Archbishop Makarios and I directed Carbery to drive alongside while I subjected the two increasingly uneasy looking bearded priests to an intense scrutiny and compared their faces with the photographs in my 'Wanted' album. Sadly, neither of them was Makarios. It would have been a most satisfying coup to have captured Makarios on my way home.

CHAPTER THIRTEEN

COMMAND OF THE REGIMENTAL DEPOT, ST. PATRICK'S BARRACKS, BALLYMENA, CO. ANTRIM, 1958-1960

Patricia and I stayed at the Adair Arms in Ballymena while I was taking over from Bill Brooks, who was being promoted to command our 6th (Territorial Army) Battalion which had its Headquarters in Victoria Barracks, Belfast.

I was fortunate in my staff, Major Tom Smith, MBE, my Quartermaster, had a very strong personality, a great sense of humour, and was an outstanding Quartermaster. He was full of ideas as to how to make life better for the Riflemen, yet he was no 'softie', and no one could take advantage of him. It was he who introduced the Sportsman's Dinner in the Depot, when every member of all our teams sat down together to a tremendous feast, which engendered a great feeling of camaraderie and ésprit de corps. Tom had been a Regimental footballer and was a skilled trainer of our teams.

Major A.E. (Ben) Matthews was my PRI. Ben had been a friend of mine since my earliest days as a subaltern in Ballymena, when he was Colour Sergeant of my Company. Under Ben's expert instruction I had learnt to fly-fish, shoot and ferret. He not only ran all the depot and regimental accounts meticulously, and the Regimental Museum – for which he deserves the greatest credit, but he also ran the Depot shoots and fishing. Ben is a charming man, a great raconteur, and he and Debbie, his wife, had been kind to me since I was eighteen.

My Adjutant Captain Michael Henry, quiet, efficient, and well liked by the Riflemen, was succeeded by large, tough, cheerful Ken Boyd who had recently been awarded the MC after being wounded in a gallant exploit

119

in Cyprus. Major Robin Bruford-Davies who commanded Training Company was a reliable, conscientious and capable officer who had fought in Korea with our 1st Battalion and had eventually been taken prisoner. Despite what must have been an unpleasant couple of years he returned as cheerful and determined as ever. Robin's father was a colourful Regimental character, Brigadier Trotsky Davies, whom I have already mentioned.

We had rather a changing population of subalterns and, as we trained them up, they took their place in the 1st Battalion. Among them were Michael Mates, later Minister of State, Northern Ireland, and Philip Mooney, a fine officer from Kilrea who, like Michael, had had recent Cyprus operational experience against the EOKA. Another was Tony Kelly who had had a rugby trial for Ireland, a charming, robust man. Tony, who married my cousin Caroline Johnston, told me of an experience he had had with the recruiting sergeant of the Irish Guards in Belfast, Sergeant (later CSM) Kenny, BEM. It was early morning and Tony was disembarking at Donegall Quay from the Liverpool boat when Kenny, who met every boat in his quest for recruits, saw the powerful figure of Tony Kelly running down the gangway. 'Good morning, my grand fellow,' says Sergeant Kenny. 'And would a big strapping lad like you be thinking of joining the British Army?' 'I might,' replied Tony. 'Well then, me lad, there's only one Regiment for you, the Irish Guards!' 'Oh,' said Tony, 'I have always liked the Rifles.' 'That heap!' replied the recruiting sergeant. 'Never think of them!' 'Ah, well,' said Tony, 'I'll be seeing Major Purdon when I return to Ballymena, where I'm the Training Subaltern. I know he'll be interested in your opinion!'

Patricia and I moved into the OC Depot's house, with the river at the end of our garden. Across the other side of the river lay a bog where the Depot had shooting rights and where you could usually put up a couple of brace of snipe and quite a few duck. Over the fields adjoining it there was a good chance of bagging a hare or two. Looking to the east stood Slemish, the table-topped mountain where Saint Patrick had tended his sheep. I love that mountain and many is the time that I have climbed it.

I remembered as I stood looking at its familiar and distinctive bulk dominating the flat plain around it, an occasion when I had been Adjutant of our 6th Battalion and had led a party of soldiers up it one Saturday. Lieutenant Colonel Conger Cummins, my CO at that time, had expressed doubts about the cloudy weather but I had pooh-poohed them and pressed on. Of course, Conger was proved right, down came the cloud and I lost all sense of direction. I was concerned lest I lose my party (and my name!) and I quite frankly prayed to God to guide me. As I climbed upward I had a glimpse at my feet of what looked like, in the swirling mist, a silver sixpence. I bent down and picked it up and saw that it was a small silver St

Christopher medallion. As I held it, miraculously, the rolling clouds vanished and I and my group stood in blazing sunshine with the way to the summit clear ahead of us. Saying a quiet prayer of thanks to the Almighty I completed the climb with a happy team of Riflemen. I have that St Christopher medallion to this day.

Shortly before we left the Adair Arms for our house in the Depot, we were fast asleep one night when one of the hotel maids tapped at our door to tell me that Footie MacMaster, Master of the Mid Antrim Harriers, wanted me on the telephone. Blessing Footie for waking me from a deep and sound sleep, I stumbled along the corridor to the telephone booth, struggling into a dressing gown. Footie said, 'Corran, Vera and I wondered if you and Patricia would come over for a drink?' 'What day?' 'Why now, to be sure,' replied Footie. 'But for goodness sake we're in bed, Footie!' 'Just throw on some clothes then, and we'll expect you in twenty minutes!' We went, of course, and had a great crack. We were certainly back home in Ireland!

I used to exercise hounds before breakfast with Footie, who always lent me a horse. This would be one or other of a pair, with Footie riding the one I didn't choose. One had an awkward trot and its saddle, no matter how tightly you girthed it, always slipped to the left. The other horse was simply terrified of traffic and would try to bolt each time a vehicle passed us on the road. My worst moment mounted on this steed was when I was riding over a bridge across the railway. Just when we were in the middle of it a train thundered below us. As the terrified horse bucked and reared under me and the pair of us were enveloped in clouds of steam, the engine driver blew an earsplitting and piercing blast on his whistle. Never have I been nearer falling off, and at one time I wondered if the frantic animal was going to jump over the parapet onto the railway below, on top of the still passing train, so great was the horse's panic.

An officer back from Cyprus came to join us from the 1st Battalion, which increased the operational expertise on which we based our continuation training for our recruits. This officer, unbeknown to me at the time had, to his embarrassment, discovered a primed 36 grenade in his kit, which had been packed by his batman in Cyprus. He wore it, à la General Mathew B Ridgeway, on his equipment for an EOKA-type exercise with recruits in the Antrim Hills. To his horror it became detached and he could not find it, despite searching for hours. Being a transparently honest person, he telephoned Headquarters Northern Ireland District and reported himself and his loss. He then returned to the Depot and reported himself to me. I told him that he would search the area every day until he found the grenade and meanwhile we warned the local Royal Ulster Constabulary and the schools. The poor chap was terribly worried and every day he was out from first to last light. It had snowed on his first day, and thickly. The GOC-in-C, Lieut. General Sir Douglas Packard, KBE, CB, DSO, to whom I spoke on the telephone wanted to court martial him. However, I persuaded the GOC-in-C who was a very nice, kind person and a distinguished soldier, that the officer was already being punished by his conscience. It was therefore agreed because he was very shortly leaving the Army and emigrating to New Zealand that, provided he found the grenade and brought it back to me, the Commander-in-Chief would confine himself to giving him the biggest bollocking of his life.

One day the thaw set in and at about lunchtime I was immensely relieved to receive a telephone call from the officer to say that he had found the live grenade. What had happened was that, with the heavy snow, the grenade which had originally rolled into a runnel under a hedge, was literally flushed out by a fierce freshet of water onto the tarmac road – not far from a school, and the officer recovered it just before the children came out at lunchtime. So I rang the GOC who was very good about it all and told me that he wanted to see the officer the next afternoon.

I had the officer into my office and said to him 'Whatever you do, do not argue or explain, just tell the C-in-C what a clot you have been, and how very sorry you are'. Next afternoon the officer reported to the GOC-in-C's office at Lisburn. The GOC-in-C had his two Norfolk terriers under his desk and told me to call the officer in. In he came, smart, very contrite, making no excuses, no explanations, just expressing his sincere apologies. Every few minutes, interrupting one of the best rockets I have ever admired from the sidelines, the Norfolk terriers burst into frenzied barking, interrupting the GOC-in-C's tirade, whereupon the GOC-in-C would say to the officer, 'I am so sorry, my dear chap – Shut up!! (to the dogs) – Now as I was saying…' and the blistering tongue lashing went on.

Again and again the Norfolk terriers burst into their paroxysms of barking, again and again the GOC-in-C politely apologised to the officer, before returning to the slaughter. Eventually it was all over, the contrite officer saluted and departed amid a final storm of barking from the irate terriers. The GOC-in-C turned to me as I stood beside his desk. 'I don't think,' he said, 'that he will forget today.' 'You're quite right, Sir,' said I, with feeling, 'and neither will I.'

We had our Annual Inspection and a change of GOC-in-C as, sadly, General Packard left and I carried out my own preliminary inspection of the Depot. As I visited the butcher's shop my old friend Corporal Davis showed me round his immaculate premises. As I knew well, there was a box, cushioned with a blanket, which housed a black and white cat, and this I did not think would go down too well with our new GOC-in-C. However, I knew also that Corporal Davis was aware that I possessed three dogs, two pheasants, four fantail pigeons and twenty-six bantams, so all I could in fairness say was, 'Square up that blanket, Corporal Davis,' and hope that the general would be kind. I had also given my permission to the handlers of our guard dogs to keep a litter of Alsatian puppies in a small brick building which they had furnished with straw-covered sleeping benches and this was something else he might not like. However, the GOC-in-C went into neither building during his visit, so all was well.

We paraded for our new GOC-in-C and he inspected us. He seemed annoyed that the harps in some of our issue cap badges were surmounted by the old King's Crown and that not all had the Queen's crown. He was right but Tom Smith, our peerless Quartermaster, had been trying for ages to persuade Ordnance to issue the modern badge. The GOC-in-C brushed aside my attempted explanation. A commander worthy of his salt, he intimated, would have bought new badges out of his own pocket. He appeared not to hear me when I murmured we had paid for all our black Rifles buttons. Nothing we could do seemed to please him and this was clear to my officers and men. We knew that our barracks were spotless, our turnout impeccable and that we were the fittest, best trained, best shooting, most successful Minor Unit in Northern Ireland, and that we held the trophies to prove it.

With the Depot drawn up on parade I escorted the General to the saluting base, burly Tony Kelly acting as his ADC. RSM 'Scrape' Kennedy had placed some steps from the dais leading to the parade ground, made from ammunition boxes and covered with a strip of red carpet. After the GOC-in-C had inspected us and found fault he returned to the dais. We marched past him in quick time, in slow time and after that we doubled past. We then formed up and advanced in Review Order. The GOC-in-C stepped forward to leave the saluting base. Horror of horrors, the ammunition boxes gave way under the red carpet and before our stricken eyes, we saw that the Inspecting Officer was lying on his back.

'Quick, Tony, we'll pick him up,' I murmured, hastily striding forward. Although the General was wearing service dress, the rest of us wore battle dress and somehow I clumsily trod on his outstretched brown leather gloved hand with my highly polished, heavily studded ammunition boot. Tony and I (both of whom were keen on weightlifting) had not realised how light the General was and we lifted him right up into the air with abandon. After lunch in the Mess the GOC-in-C said to me, 'Well, at least I enjoyed my meal.' So my cup of bitterness overflowed. He departed and I got into my Landrover to visit Robin Bruford-Davies' company which was on a training exercise near the coast. My driver, Rifleman Magee, said 'How did the inspection go, Sir?' 'Not well, I am afraid, Magee.' 'No Sir, that's what we all thought. But the way you trod on his hand as he lay there on his back, indeed the boys all said you did it out of spite, Sir!' But next time the General came, for some reason it was a different matter and from then on, apparently, we could never do wrong and always received compliments.

Two French officer cadets spent a few days with us. We took them out on a Saturday to the Depot shoot near Cushendun. They seemed to enjoy it as we tramped over our heather-covered mountain and we shot a few grouse. Our guests had shot nothing that morning and we sat eating our sandwich lunch in bright sunshine looking down on the sparkling blue sea off the lovely Antrim coast, hoping they would 'break their duck' after lunch. We resumed our walk-up, and suddenly a hare got up almost under our feet. Both our French guests fired simultaneously and wounded the poor animal which screamed like a baby. They were horrified and stood aghast. 'Put the poor thing out of its misery,' called Ben Matthews. One of the cadets, small, slight, bespectacled and earnest, sprang forward, seized the hare by its ears and began raining rabbit punches on its neck. The screaming increased. Suddenly flinging one hand dramatically across his eyes and averting his head, the cadet stretched out his arm, hare clenched by the ears in his hand, 'Tirez!' he screamed at his friend who stood, irresolute, not a yard away. Someone quietly moved his shotgun barrel away and cleanly killed the poor hare. The thought of the fate of the caller of 'Tirez!' if his friend had fired appalled us all!

At that time the IRA were raiding various establishments and made an attempt at the Royal Irish Fusiliers' Depot in Armagh. As a result of their bravery in removing a ticking bomb from the Depot, Harry Baxter, the CO, was decorated with the George Medal and Hal Chavasse, his Adjutant who gallantly drove a one-ton truck out of the barracks to a safe area in the countryside with Harry sitting beside him with the bomb on his knees, was awarded the MBE.

Everyone had to keep very much on their toes; sentries were armed with live ammunition, machine guns covered entry points, camps were wired-in and armed riflemen and guard dogs patrolled the barrack perimeters. In our Depot we had a scout car mounting a searchlight that patrolled sporadically throughout the night, and always on an alarm being sounded.

We in the North Irish Brigade had a co-ordinating Headquarters at Lisburn, where our Brigade Colonel at the time was Colonel 'Smudger' Maxwell of the Royal Inniskilling Fusiliers. One day, we three Depot Commanders, Percy Blake, Harry Baxter and myself were at a meeting there. Harry Baxter had found another suspicious suitcase near the wall of his Depot and was telling us about the incident. Dramatically Harry said, 'I ordered the grip to be opened,' he paused, 'and what do you think was in it?' 'George Medals?' asked Percy sourly!

Whilst I was at the Depot, the Colonel of the Regiment was Brigadier Ian ('Rupert') Good, DSO, who introduced the black hackles worn in our rifle green caubeens. Until then our headgear had, to me, looked too heavy, but the hackle set off the caubeen and gave it more proportion. This brought us into line with the London Irish Rifles element of the Regiment who wore a St. Patrick's Blue hackle, and the Inniskilling and 'Faughs' who had worn hackles, of grey and of green respectively, for some time.

It was whilst Patricia and I were at the Depot that our daughter Angela was born in Belfast in February 1959. Angela was baptised and christened in the Church of Ireland church in Ballymena by Canon Craig.

I have always found the Press in Northern Ireland most helpful and interested in the Army. We welcomed them to the Depot and we had particularly close relations with both the *Belfast Telegraph* and with the *Belfast Newsletter*. We used to exchange visits and got to know some fine people in whom I had complete confidence.

On the social side we had an annual 'At Home' in St. Patrick's Barracks for the people of Ballymena when we would stage excerpts demonstrative of our skills in soldiering and in sport. We also had Guest Nights to which we invited VIPs and other friends of the Regiment. Colour Sergeant 'Shufti' Dawson ran the Officers' Mess and we had a wonderful civilian cook whose only weakness was that he would occasionally embark on a drinking bout or, as 'Shufti' would say, 'Go on the batter.' Then we didn't see him for days until, ashen-faced and repentant, he would return. We never sacked him for we liked him too much. Also he was a peerless chef and had a sad home life.

Whenever a Guest Night was due we would anxiously question 'Shufti' as to whether our genius was likely to be sober. 'Shufti' knew all the signs and on one occasion when a very, very important person was to honour us with his presence, I discovered that 'Shufti' had kept our cook locked in the Squash Court, complete with meals, comfortable bed, radio, heating and literature, for several days until the time came to prepare and cook dinner! The cook accepted this equably and I only discovered it because I wanted to play squash and so had to be let into the secret!

The 1st Battalion returned from Cyprus and moved to Iserlohn in West Germany as a component of 5 Infantry Brigade in 4th Infantry Division. My time at the Depot was coming to an end and I was to be posted to the Battalion in June 1960 as Second-in-Command.

I had loved my time at St. Patrick's Barracks, Ballymena. I had known it since it was being built in January 1940. Indeed at one time the present ante-room of the Officers' Mess had been my bedroom. The Depot was a grand independent command for a Major and as a result of my two years there not only had we made many friends locally but I knew a tremendous number of Riflemen for whose training I had been responsible and who were now serving in the First Battalion.

The local people had all been so good to us: Lord and Lady Rathcavan at Cleggan Lodge, the Chichesters of Galgorm Castle, the McLarens, the Martins of Craigdun Castle – Tubby (Commander R.P. Martin, DSC) was married to my cousin Doreen – Robin Morton, his sister Ruth and husband Maurice Taylor (also 6 RUR), the Reades and the Casements, among others.

I took a party to climb Errigal in Co. Donegal one day, it was only about three hours drive away and we had a wonderful view from the summit. My sister Biddy and her husband Colán MacArthur live not far from there at Marble Hill, and my cousin Jacqueline Day lived at Fort Stewart, Rathmelton, another lovely house in that most beautiful county.

Before I left Northern Ireland, I was talking to the Irish Guards recruiting sergeant, my old friend, CSM Kenny, BEM. He told me that when Mr Profumo visited Northern Ireland as Minister for War the Minister said to him, 'Would you take me into the Micks, Company Sergeant Major?' To which – to the consternation of the accompanying officers, Kenny said, 'No, Sir'! When the War Minister asked why, CSM Kenny said, 'Well, you see, Sir, in Irish Regiments we like the O at the beginning of our names!'

The Wives' Club used to run a Bingo Session each week which we always attended and enjoyed a lot. We had a Wives' .22 rifle shooting club, and I suspect that a number of them could have beaten their husbands had their spouses been pinned down to a competition.

In our last week at the Depot, we had an All Ranks Ball, during which I was dancing with one particular Senior NCO's wife, whom I had known for years – she was a great girl. She told me that her husband had annoyed her before the dance so she had hit him over the head with her handbag. As we continued to dance, she told me that she had 'flu, holding me the closer the while. 'But, Major, darling,' she breathed into my ear, 'I mean to sweat it out!'

CHAPTER FOURTEEN

1st BATTALION THE ROYAL ULSTER RIFLES, BAOR

My Commanding Officer, Sam Sturgeon, and Milly, his wife, very kindly met us at Dortmund railway station where we arrived after travelling on the ferry from Harwich to Hook and on by train from there. They took us to our married quarter in Rembrandt Strasse, Iserlohn, and told us that they expected us to dinner that night. Such kindness was typical of them. We found fresh flowers in vases, beds all made up, refrigerator stocked with food and drink and a cold lunch already prepared.

Regimental officers will know the very happy sense of homecoming on returning to the Regimental family when you are back with old friends, where you want to be. The battalion was the first post war unit – I think – to be equipped in a trials role with armoured personnel carriers (APCs) of which it had ninety-six Saracens, together with a number of supporting vehicles. The battalion was housed in Aldershot Barracks, a former Luftwaffe Flakartillerie Kaserne, which had excellent, well built, airy, warm barrack blocks, NAAFI and messes. There were still the original stained glass windows in the Officers' Mess, with Nazi swastikas inset. It is typical of the British Army that these had never been defaced nor damaged.

To support our mechanical role we had under command a large Light Aid Detachment of the Royal Electrical and Mechanical Engineers (REME) commanded by Captain Tim Inman, and a Royal Corps of Signals detachment to help look after our large number of radios, commanded by a Royal Signals subaltern Mike Spence. Headquarters 5 Infantry Brigade was also lodged in our barracks and this obviously had its advantages and its disadvantages. Communication was easy but Brigade HQ could see us always, warts and all!

Sam Sturgeon had appointed a Trials Officer, Major Ken Neely, MBE, to oversee, monitor and write up each stage of the trials and to prepare the final report. A most efficient soldier. Ken was a natural choice to carry out this important task. We trained hard. Company training was carried out at Haltern and battalion training took place at Soltau, at that time a much bigger training area than now. Encroachments by German farmers on to the dwindling area took place before our eyes. This, because it was unchecked, has reduced the area available for training and such areas, alas, are now limited.

Our quarter was about a ten minute run from the Seiler See, a charming lake with round-topped wooded hills beyond it. Beside the Seiler See was an outdoor swimming pool, surrounded by grass lawns and beds of lovely roses. Some of us used to run down there in the summer before breakfast, do some exercises, swim a number of lengths and run home. It was a good way to start the day.

For evenings out, there were two restaurants we particularly liked. One, in Iserlohn, was the Haferkiste which had white-scrubbed tables and excellent food and service. The other, outside the town, was Zum Bären, in a rural setting and this was very good too. Iserlohn was a pleasant town with some lovely old timbered buildings and a friendly population. When we weren't training we played games and I found time to play rugger, hockey, basketball and swim for the battalion.

General Sir Charles ('Splosh') Jones was our Corps Commander and that year he staged a large practical exercise called 'Spearpoint' which apart from the absence of live ammunition, really simulated war. It was a most valuable exercise, realistic, exciting and tiring. We covered a lot of ground and crossed two major rivers, the Aller and the Weser. This was where we got to know the other battalion stationed in Iserlohn, the 1st Battalion of that fine Regiment, The Green Howards. Their Second-in-Command, John Scott and I became great friends. He was a sound, experienced soldier who stood 6 ft 7 inches tall and towered over me. Jeanne, his wife, was very tall too. His very efficient Adjutant is now General Sir Peter Inge, Chief of the General Staff.

Sam Sturgeon detailed me to go up to Neumünster near the Kiel Canal to attend the formation ceremony of a German Panzer Grenadier division. Like all German parades this was most efficiently carried out. It was a night-time, torchlit parade and very impressive. I had with me Johnnie Watts and Mervyn McCord and we had been told to wear No. 1 Dress. In our case this consisted of a dark rifle green patent-leather black peaked cap, dark rifle-green tunic which had woven epaulettes bearing black metal badges of rank, black tight-fitting overalls, black patent-leather crossbelt, mess Wellingtons with spurs, and we wore decorations and medals. We were escorted by a German Bundeswehr officer who was attached at that time to our battalion, Major Dieter von Drabich and by Marianne, his pretty wife. At the end of the ceremony, as we made our way to the Officers' Club escorted by the von Drabichs, we noticed that the German crowd fell back – we couldn't think why. Later Marianne told us that they had never seen Rifles officers before and believed we were Russians!

At the party we met two distinguished Bundeswehr officers; one was a Major Muller, the other a Major Müller! Both were Ritterkreuzträgers, winners of the Knight's Cross of the Iron Cross and were two very interesting men. We sat up talking throughout the night about their experiences fighting against the Russians, the British and the Americans, which were fascinating.

Next morning – we were staying in the Wappenklause Hotel – we were all, Germans and British, having breakfast together when we were joined by two amusing US Army officers. Eichmann, the Nazi war criminal, had recently been abducted by the Israelis and was on trial. All went well until one of our American friends said, 'Did you hear the news this morning? It seems they have sent Eichmann his gas bill for 1944!'

Back at Iserlohn we had a mystery. Every morning, before the Commanding Officer arrived, there was an occurrence which perturbed the staff at Battalion Headquarters. A tombstone invariably was to be found placed against the door of the Colonel's office. The RSM, (later my MTO, Major Tim Moloney) came to see me and we laid ambushes but failed to catch whoever was responsible. So every morning, until it ceased, I made certain that I always arrived at least ten minutes before the Colonel and then a small party, consisting of the Battalion Second-in-Command, Regimental Sergeant Major, Orderly Room Quartermaster Sergeant and the Provost Sergeant could be seen carrying a large tombstone into the orderly room. From here, after the arrival of the Commanding Officer, the tombstone was smuggled out, beyond the camp gates where it was returned to the grateful, if long-suffering owner of the nearby monumental mason's establishment! I don't think Sam ever knew about this and it went on for several months, before whoever was responsible tired of it.

We used to get out on to the training areas as often as we could and I recall one occasion when I was visiting Mervyn McCord and his C Company. I was greeted by a livid Mervyn who announced that a battery of Royal Horse Artillery (mechanised) was in the middle of the allotted space. I went to see the battery commander who turned out to be a young Brevet Lieutenant Colonel called John Douglas-Withers. He was a very relaxed officer and seemed vaguely amused that anyone should object to finding that another sub-unit of equivalent size had, unbooked, unheralded, unasked, calmly moved into someone else's training area! He was a delightful, charming man and I have to admit he and his battery were nearly allowed to remain. However, Mervyn was still spluttering with rage and, despite John's plea 'There's plenty of room on the maidan, old boy!', we managed to persuade him to move off but by then he had had half a day's use of the place. I often wonder what they both thought when, after attending Staff College, Mervyn was appointed Brigade Major to an Infantry Brigade commanded by Brigadier John Douglas-Withers, CBE, MC.

Our battalion owed a big debt to two non-Infantry officers. The first was Major Alan Parks, who commanded A Squadron 1st Royal Tank Regiment. We learnt from the example of Alan and his officers and men, how to quicken up our hitherto pedestrian thinking to armoured speed, to give quick, concise, clear and confident orders on the radio – and not to be frightened of talking 'on the air'. He taught us the importance of meticulous maintenance of our vehicles – officers, NCOs and riflemen – and he taught us to drink beer at each halt! We used to say jokingly A Squadron even carried cans of beer in their gun barrels. But they never drank to excess and nor did we.

Major George Arnold who commanded Imjin Battery, 45 Regiment Royal Artillery was the other. George helped our ability and speed in selecting and calling for our targets and DF (Defensive Fire) tasks; the importance of ALWAYS 'Being through' on the air, and of accurate map reading.

Serving in Germany made holiday weekends and local leave easy to enjoy as we were so near to places and countries of interest. We visited the memorable Dutch tulip fields at Keukenhof and I will never forget the sight of the small, flat-bottomed barges floating on the narrow canals that ran through the bulb fields, and of the reflection on the dark, still water of their loads of massed tulips in all their glorious colours – flaming reds, bright yellows and deep mauves. Sometimes we took a tent and drove down the Moselle visiting the vineyards on the steep slopes running down to the river and stopping to taste the Moselle wines at charming German riverside inns, set in picturesque timbered villages. At other times we would drive along the Rhine, seeing its romantic Schlosses and the famous Lorelei.

I had been officially told that I was to succeed Sam Sturgeon as Commanding Officer. I felt that the battalion would be bored with Germany after another year and that we would probably have got all we could out of it professionally. In fact, it was high time we went on active service. So I lobbied every VIP who visited us. I remember 'bending the ear' of my sympathetic Divisional Commander, Major General Desmond Gordon and also that of my Brigade Commander, the kindly Brigadier Philip Pope, and of various visiting War Office generals. Whether this had any effect, I don't know but we got what we wanted in 1964, when I had the honour, privilege and pleasure of taking my battalion on operational service against the Indonesians during the Confrontation Campaign in Borneo.

Sam's tour in command came to an end with the production of Ken Neely's comprehensive and valuable trials report which was based on all our experience under the Colonel's direction. Sam Sturgeon earned a well deserved OBE, was promoted Colonel and appointed Brigade Colonel the North Irish Brigade.

THE COLLECT OF THE ROYAL ULSTER RIFLES

Almighty God, whose summons strikes a chord in loyal hearts; so awaken in us, The Royal Ulster Rifles, the ancient echoes of thy call to service; that quick in step and spirit, no onslaught of nature or man may separate us from trust in Thee, and in one another, through Jesus Christ, our Lord. Amen.

In April 1962 I took over command of 1st Royal Ulster Rifles in Iserlohn. As I had been Second-in-Command for two years I decided to go on leave for three weeks as a clean break and also to give the Battalion a chance to get used to the change. My family and I went off to the south of France and Donald MacIntyre, who had arrived only a day or two previously from the West Indies was catapulted into running things in my absence. I think I am correct in saying that Donald had not even been measured for his battledress when he heard I was off!

When I returned from leave there was one thing I wanted to do, and that was to get rid of a number of men who were a disruptive influence in the battalion. These were the sort of men who could turn out immaculately on a Quarter Guard but at night would get drunk and beat up their fellow Riflemen. There were about thirty of them. The best soldier must be tough and hard on operations and training but he must be well disciplined and well behaved both on and off duty. These men fulfilled my first criterion but not the second, so I decided that they must go. As there were so many of them, I went to my recently appointed Brigade Commander, Brigadier John Thomas and asked him to support me when I put their names forward for discharge under the appropriate paragraph of Queen's Regulations. He didn't know me, but he backed me.

When these men had left the battalion, I had young Riflemen and senior NCOs alike coming up and thanking me, and men were saying they could sleep in their beds without the fear that they might be awoken by some drunk threatening to strike a broken bottle into their faces. My Brigade Colonel was not pleased with me because he had to produce the replacements for these discharged soldiers but I would rather have done without a platoon of soldiers than been up to strength with men like them.

I wanted to get the battalion away for some practical down-to-earth training and was lucky enough to be allocated the splendid training area at Sennelager. Here we fired all our weapons from lightest to heaviest calibre on realistic ranges. Every one of us, from myself to the most junior Rifleman, fired every weapon Sterling, SLR, LMG, the short, medium and long range anti-tank weapons, the light and the medium mortars – with each of us taking over all the gun numbers and firing positions in turn. We did a lot of shooting on the ranges by night as well as by day and we came back to Iserlohn feeling really confident in our ability to fire all our weapons with accuracy. By 6.30am each day Donald MacIntyre and I would be out running, after which we were ready for breakfast in the comfortable mess, having looked in beforehand at our Riflemen enjoying their own excellent multi-choice meals.

There were three other battalions using Sennelager at the same time, 1st Cameronians (Scottish Rifles) commanded by my friend Reggie Kettles, 1st South Wales Borderers commanded by another friend, Lieutenant Colonel Tony Sharpe. There was also an English county regiment, 1st York and Lancaster Regiment commanded by yet another friend, Lieutenant Colonel Donald Creighton-Williamson. I got my battalion on parade and told them that I knew we would get on well with the other Regiments. There were ironic cheers, so I said, 'The Cameronians are brother Riflemen and, furthermore, my uncle was killed with them in the Great War. The South Wales Borderers are the battalion I served with in Malaya, and three Purdons were among their initial set of officers when they were formed in 1689. As for the York and Lancaster Regiment, my father was their Regimental Medical Officer in the Great War. So,' I said, 'I know we will all get on.' There was another great cheer and indeed, in a place where there could be, and had been, trouble, our four battalions got on brilliantly. (The South Wales Borderers are now part of the Royal Regiment of Wales. Both The Cameronians and The York and Lancasters refused to amalgamate into 'large' regiments and disbanded in the late 1960s.)

Shortly afterwards we went off in our APCs to Belgium to train at Bourg Leopold Training Area. We camped among trees on grassy ground and again we fired our weapons and practised minor tactics. Brigadier John Thomas spent several days with us. He was a delightful friendly man and a first-class soldier. We all loved him, all ranks got to know him and he got to know the battalion well. Later he was to become General Sir Noel Thomas, GCB, DSO, MC, Master General of the Ordnance.

We had a dreadful tragedy at Bourg Leopold when one of our finest young NCOs and sportsmen, Cpl McHugh, was killed by a hit-and-run car as he was walking along the road in the dark. This cast a black cloud over us all. I will always remember the bravery and the dignity of his family when they came over for his funeral.

Unhappy events seem to feature in the story of Bourg Leopold. The menfolk of one of its villages were massacred during the war by the Nazis in a clearing in what is now the training area. I was out for my early morning run on our first day there and I came to a clearing where the grass looked blood red yet, on closer examination, I could see that it was green. I noticed a large wooden cross there and on enquiries from our Belgian liaison officer at breakfast on my return, I discovered that I had unknowingly visited the very scene of the slaughter. There was a miasma of hopelessness and grief about it that most of us noticed, as well as the uncannily red appearance of the grass.

We had missed our Regimental Day owing to a Divisional exercise and so I decided to celebrate it during our Bourg Leopold camp, to cheer the Battalion up after Corporal McHugh's tragic death. I planned that we would spend our Day at the battlefield of Waterloo and I made each company produce an officer to describe the conduct of the battle from each of the main view points. We hired a fleet of air-conditioned coaches, each with inbuilt taped music, to take us there. We had delicious pies, baked by our excellent Army Catering Corps' cooks in Iserlohn, included in special packed lunches sent down to us and we booked a road-house restaurant near Brussels for a steak and chips, apple pie and ice cream dinner with crates of beer and soft drinks to follow, that evening. We had a terrific day and all enjoyed ourselves enormously.

The Duke of Wellington's maternal grandmother was a direct ancestor of mine, so I had a particular family interest in that great battle. As we drove off to our restaurant for supper we all felt that a casual onlooker who did not know his military history could be forgiven for thinking that it was the French and not the Allies who had emerged as the victors of the Battle of Waterloo. The Belgians are realists when it comes to tourism and many more French than British visit Waterloo!

Our next battalion exercise was in the area of the Kiel Canal and once again we drove to it, in our ninety-six APCs and back-up vehicles well supported as usual by our peerless Light Aid Detachment. We were all very interested to view the Kiel Canal and the surrounding Schleswig Holstein countryside and to visit a part of Germany we would otherwise probably never have seen. By now we had lost our popular GOC, Major General Desmond Gordon but in his place we had welcomed another very distinguished soldier, Major General Jean-Victor Allard, an extremely tough French-Canadian with three DSOs. We soon had a tremendous rapport with him and everyone in the battalion looked forward to his visits. General Jean-Victor was not only a soldier of distinction but a man of great culture. Before he retired he had become a full general and Chief of the Canadian Defence Staff.

We were very keen on sport and the battalion won the 4th Divisional cross country and were runners-up in the Rhine Army boxing. As an Irishman I know full well that Irish soldiers do best when busy and interested. When I took over command I told myself that I would keep the battalion more tired than I was throughout my tour as commanding officer! To lessen people drinking in Iserlohn as well as to keep ourselves fit, we had a battalion cross-country run of five or six miles every Friday evening, with only telephone orderlies and sick exempted. I found that after this run and a bath, Riflemen who wanted to drink tended to be too tired to walk into the town and preferred to use our good NAAFI. To further encourage this we arranged social events there for every Friday night.

Then on Saturday mornings I would always have a battalion drill parade first thing, with the band, bugles and pipes playing to make it more enjoyable. We would have an RSM's Parade one Saturday, Adjutant's the next, Second-in-Command's after that, then Commanding Officers' Drill Parade, followed again by RSM's Parade and so on. After the drill, I would inspect one part of the barracks for twenty minutes. The part to be looked at was never specified in advance, and then from 11am everyone had to take part in some sporting activity. We organised trips to Winterberg on Saturday afternoons and after church on Sundays, to swim in summer and to ski in winter, as well as laying on tennis, squash and angling.

My Roman Catholic Padre, Father Topping, had considerable success in ensuring a big turnout at Mass on Sundays. One of his flock was our battalion middleweight boxer, a tough and gutty Rifleman called McConkey. Father Topping suspected that Rfn. McConkey was not always his keenest parishioner and he used to go into the barrack rooms – with my willing prior permission – to encourage the faithful.

One Sunday morning there was no sign of McConkey when Father Topping entered. However, our Padre who was well used to dealing with Riflemen strode to McConkey's locker and flung it open, to find an almost fully-dressed McConkey inside. 'So there you are, McConkey!' he exclaimed. McConkey stepped out smiling and adjusting his tie, 'Just getting ready for Church, Father,' said our battalion middleweight!

We, as befits a Rifle regiment, and one that had produced in Lieutenant Colonel Dick Parsons and in Major Billy Baudains MM, winners of the coveted Queen's Medal (Dick won it twice), were extremely keen on shooting. During our two years in BAOR we were 3rd and 2nd respectively in the British Army of the Rhine Shooting Championships. Our greatest rivals, who defeated us were the Rifle Brigade, commanded by Grismond Davies-Scourfield, and another very fine shooting regiment, 1st Queen's Own Highlanders. By now we had been fully re-equipped with the FV432 range of tracked armoured personnel carriers. The technical trials of the FV432 had been carried out by Douglas McCord, under Ken Neely as Trials Officer. Both Ken and Douglas had left and we as a battalion were in the process of carrying out the full tactical trials of an infantry battalion equipped with tracked APCs. This was a fascinating task and, as we were the first battalion in the British Army to have the FV432, every one of us felt we had a personal stake in ensuring the success of the trials.

The tactical trials, covering all the phases of war, culminated in the various Brigade and Divisional exercises taking place. Germany was a grand country in which to train and we all learnt a great deal, individually as well as collectively.

Brigadier John Thomas went off on promotion to Major General and in his place came Brigadier Hugh Davies MC, an experienced cavalryman whom I had known when I was a student at the Staff College and he was a Director of Studies. Once again we were lucky and found another good friend to the battalion. Like Jill and John Thomas, Audrey and Hugh Davies were very kind to us all and were greatly liked.

One day a very nice Major, John Mathewson, in my Regiment, stationed as DAD Public Relations at Rhine Army Headquarters died and his widow said that he had especially asked for a regimental funeral. Apparently he had wanted the dress to be green No. 1 Dress and medals. We determined to carry out his wishes and I and a regimental party travelled up to Hanover for the funeral. It was the coldest day I had ever known in Germany, incredibly, bone-chillingly freezing. To carry out our brother officer's last wishes, we did not wear greatcoats but I was worried about our bearer party, bugler and piper in particular, and the whole party in general, in this gnawing, bitter cold. I therefore arranged for a large but discreet rum ration for all ranks just before we appeared at the church and for hot tea laced with more rum to be served afterwards which did the trick.

Our LAD ran some excellent car rallies which not only gave us much enjoyment but invaluable practice in map reading and mobile navigation. As a contrast, during the Easter break we had a battalion competition to see who could travel the farthest from Iserlohn and back, using any form of transport. All who entered had to send a postcard from whatever destination they finally reached. Postcards came in from such places as Paris, Brussels, The Hague and Luxembourg, but the winners sent theirs from a town in the USA! They had travelled to a USAF base in the United States

Sector of Germany and had persuaded the powers-that-be to arrange for them to fly to the USA and back in one of their aircraft in time to be in Iserlohn for first parade on the Tuesday morning after Easter Monday!

We developed close relationships with the local Bundeswehr units, in particular with a panzer battalion commanded by a one-armed Prussian, Oberstleutnant Karl Matz, and a panzergrenadier battalion commanded by a former 1936 Olympic Games athlete, Oberstleutnant Karl Bless. We had West German army officers attached to us for quite long spells and they were very popular with all ranks. I remember one Bundeswehr lieutenant colonel coming in to breakfast in our mess tent, remarking conversationally to me – it was a Sunday morning and pouring with rain – before an audience of goggle-eyed subalterns, how much rather he would still be in bed, stroking his wife! Another officer, Major Dieter von Drabich and his wife Marianne thought nothing of travelling right across Germany in order to be present at our special regimental occasions to which they were always invited.

At one of our guest nights at which a number of German army friends were present, an embarrassed silence hung over the room, when one guest said in a loud voice, 'Do you know what Hitler's biggest mistake was?' to one of our senior German officers. 'No,' said the Oberstleutnant politely and guardedly. 'He didn't have any Irish regiments fighting for him!' replied the guest. A roar of relieved and approving laughter followed. At another guest night, during the Cuban crisis, one panzer commander who had been enjoying Irish hospitality stood up and urged all concerned to get our men into tanks and APCs and drive with him to meet the Russians. We soothed him by bringing in the pipers!

We had a strong team at all levels in the battalion. The Second-in-Command, Donald MacIntyre, had not only a fine military brain and strong personality, but a great sense of humour. The company commanders were keen and energetic and all had operational experience; Pat Winter, Allen Hill, Robin Charley, Johnnie Johnson and Denis Lucy. Jeremy Knox was a most efficient and imperturbable Adjutant and Micky Byrne and Mick Estridge were pillars of reliability as the QM and Technical QM respectively. The capable Mike McGuinness now commanded the LAD having succeeded Tim Inman, and Nigel Vandyke commanded our Royal Signals elements.

Michael Toomey continued as our own first rate Regimental Signals Officer. Having been a company commander in Hong Kong and in Cyprus, having commanded the Regimental Depot and then been battalion second-in-command, I knew every officer and man in the battalion, many of them since the day they had enlisted. The warrant officers, indeed the NCOs in general, were a vintage crop. Tim Moloney (whom the Riflemen called 'Softly Softly') was the RSM. He was to be my MTO and second Quartermaster in Hong Kong and Borneo and then to retire as a major. Micky Byrne, who retired with a well-deserved MBE as a Major, left the battalion after our exercise in Australia and was succeeded by Mike Estridge, who also became a major. We had a fine team of CSMs and CQMSs and we ran a constant series of NCOs' cadres to train and promote our up-and-coming leaders. Sixteen of our officers and over a hundred of our NCOs and men had had fathers in the Regiment. We had seven pairs of brothers. Six of my officers were related to me. We were a close Regimental family, and our wives were very much part of it.

Whenever we had a visit from some really important VIP to our training exercises, the RSM would offer, as 'elevenses', a tall glass of Irish coffee. I remember one distinguished visitor, now a field marshal, saying firmly, 'Corran, I'm tight,' as we stood together in Pat Winter's tracked APC and bucketted across the sandy hillocks of Borkenberge towards our objective, while the future field marshal belaboured the side of the vehicle with his stick to make it go faster!

The Sergeants' Mess was a happy one and full of characters, a number of whom have since been commissioned.

In early 1963 we were warned for a move to join 51 Gurkha Brigade, then stationed in the Tidworth-Bulford area. The 1st Royal Welch Fusiliers was replacing us in a direct swap and their CO came over on a visit. We thought we know about Welsh Regiments and offered him spacious accommodation for their goat mascot. We suggested that he bring it over early on as we felt the local Germans would be fascinated by it and that such a tangible form of tradition would help in making a good initial impression. Our suggestions were politely turned aside. The goat, it appeared, had many public appearances to make in its native Wales, etc. etc. It was only after we had arrived in Bulford that we heard that the painting green by Cpl. Williams in my Regiment of the Welsh Regiment's goat in Hong Kong had become a very well-known cautionary tale in Royal Welch circles – and I must say I don't blame them!

One of our visitors from Bulford, where we were to be stationed, drew a dreadful picture of a military hierarchy under which we would be serving. From what he said, Beelzebub himself commanded overall, our GOC was Mephistopheles while Satan was our Brigade Commander. 'You'll not last,' he warned me earnestly, 'and as for an Irish battalion…!' He rolled his eyes and departed, leaving Donald MacIntyre and me with misgivings. I hasten to say that this description was exactly the opposite of what we found and we formed the warmest regard and respect for all our 'bosses' from the time we arrived in Carter Barracks.

In fact our new Brigadier came to see us and we all took to each other. Brigadier Brunny Short was – and is! – everything a soldier should be: tall,

lean, silver-haired but youthful looking, and erect. He was a very professional soldier, with the highest possible standards and a reputation for not
tolerating slackness or inefficiency. He had been decorated for gallantry
and had a great deal of operational experience. He came to see us in
Iserlohn and fired off numerous questions at me and at my second-in-
command, who finally said, 'Brigadier, I just can't give you an answer to
that.' 'Why?' asked our slightly surprised future Brigade Commander.
'I've run out of cuff, Sir,' replied Donald with a shout of laughter – to
which I was relieved to see the Brigadier respond in kind!

CHAPTER FIFTEEN

51 GURKHA BRIGADE, ENGLAND AND AUSTRALIA

In May 1963 I found myself, with my battalion back in Bulford. We had last been there in October 1945 when I was Adjutant in Kiwi Barracks whence we had left for operational service in Palestine. Now we were stationed on our own between the military cantonment of Bulford and the village of Bulford, in a wooden hutted camp called Carter Barracks. The huts were excellent and our isolated position insulated us from unexpected visitors. Our families were housed in good married quarters in the cantonment. The battalion had now changed from a mechanised to an airportable role and officers, NCOs and men went off on the appropriate courses. The other two battalions in 51 Gurkha Brigade were 1st Royal Scots commanded by Hugh Taylor, and 1st 6th Gurkha Rifles commanded by Bruce Stanbridge, OBE. Our brigade formed part of 3rd Division, which was commanded by Major General Mike Carver.

A lot of my contemporaries seemed terrified of our GOC. I found that provided you ran an efficient happy unit and never tried to bluff him, you could not have asked for a better commander. I think he liked us – we certainly liked and admired him, and we liked and respected our Brigadier, Bunny Short. We were also lucky in our Army Commander, General Bobby Bray, who was a tough and forthright soldier but a grand man to work for. The wives of our three 'bosses' were all delightful and most hospitable and kind, and we have very happy memories of Lady Short, Lady Carver and Lady Bray, and of their friendliness and generous entertaining.

We settled down to get ourselves militarily more efficient and to perfect our airportable techniques. During this time we were selected to represent the British Army in Exercise 'Sky High', to be held in the Blue Mountains of New South Wales that autumn. Donald MacIntyre and I flew out to Sydney and spent two weeks in Australia, meeting the leading personalities with whom we would be working, and calling on the Governor General Lord de L'Isle VC; the British High Commissioner, General Sir William Oliver, and his staff; the Chief of General Staff of the Australian Army, Lt. Gen. Sir John Wilton and the GOC Australian Pentropic Division, Major General Hans Andersen; under whose command we were to operate.

We got to know Colonel Sandy Pearson who commanded 1st Royal Australian Regiment with whom we would be operating on the exercise, and his staff. I called on various civic dignitaries, including the Lord Mayor of Sydney, Mr Kramer, who was later knighted. I also found time to spend a day with my cousin Helen Friend, her husband Paul and their delightful family, and our close family friends John and Jan Cooper. John is now retired, his last diplomatic post having been Australian ambassador to Portugal.

Among the pre-exercise publicity was an article from the London Correspondent of an Australian newspaper, entitled 'Blarney in the Army'. Donald and I both 'fell' for Australia, and for the Australians.

Having found out what we were required to do, we flew home via Singapore where we were royally entertained by Major Dick Connell MBE, formerly of our Regiment, Quartermaster of 1st Bn 2nd Gurkha Rifles at Selerang.

On our return to Bulford at the end of July we got down to training for Australia in a very intensive way. 'Exercise Sky High' was designed to practise the techniques of counter-insurgency operations mounted from a Task Force defensive area and supplied by a Logistic Supply Force operating primarily on air support under conditions as envisaged in South East Asia. We had three months in which to get ready and we concentrated on physical fitness, jungle skills (using the thickest country we could find around Bulford), patrolling, ambushes, jungle bases, searches, use of helicopters, administrative self-sufficiency and air support. I note that I added to my Directive 'at the same time skill at arms and wireless communications must not be neglected, each man will fire his 10 rounds a week, and officers' radio training will take place each Thursday morning as organised by the RSO (Regimental Signals Officer).' Captain Denis Gallwey, an outstanding officer, SAS-trained, ran a Counter Insurgency Operations Day for officers and NCOs, and courses in the same subject for platoon commanders and platoon sergeants. We carried out a month's section and platoon training followed by an air move to Dartmoor where we had a ten-day battalion exercise in ghastly weather. It poured with rain every day!

This was followed by a month's company training after which we went up to Otterburn in Northumberland and had a fortnight's exercise based on 'Sky High' in mostly cold and windy weather. We were visited in Bulford by Mr Joe Godber, Secretary of State for War, a nice, friendly man, later Lord Godber.

We also found time to win the 3rd Division Athletics Championship before we left for Australia. I was in attendance at a conference at which a very 'English' general expressed doubts about sending an Irish regiment to Australia as ambassadors for the British Army. He ended his objections by saying, 'Well, if things go wrong, at least the Australians will realise they are Irish and not English'. I was talking to my battalion the next day and repeated the general's remarks to stress the need, not only for impeccable behaviour, but in order to get my boys on their mettle so that they could pull out all the stops. I gave our Wives' Club an illustrated talk on Australia, after which we said *'Au revoir'* to our wives and sweethearts and set off from Royal Air Force, Lyneham in seven Britannia aircraft. Our 12,000 miles flight was broken by halts at Royal Air Force El Adem in Libya, Royal Air Force Khormaksar in Aden, at Royal Air Force Gan, that delightful tropical atoll in the Maldives, and at Perth, before arriving at the Royal Australian Air Force base at Williamtown in New South Wales. From here we moved by road to Singleton Camp in the Hunter River valley to prepare ourselves for the exercise which was to be held in the Blue Mountains 150 miles north east of Sydney.

I think we all fell in love with Australia, with its fascinating bush, the gum trees, the rugged mountains, the hot sunny climate, and the friendly forthright people. Although we had flown 12,000 miles in two and a half days and then completed quite a long drive from RAAF Williamtown, within minutes of our arrival at Singleton the riflemen had footballs out and had endless kickabouts, punctuated only by supper, until it was dark.

Our visit fell into three distinct parts: first, arrival and acclimatization, next, participation in the Australian Army annual exercise 'Sky High', and finally relaxation and 'Showing the Flag' in and around Sydney.

For the first phase, from 3 to 16 November 1963, we immediately set ourselves a gruelling series of exercises in difficult wooded and mountainous country during a very hot period. This proved to be the toughest test of the whole visit, but the battalion emerged confident in its physical fitness and its ability to endure much hardship. This fitness was to be the key to our success in 'Sky High'.

Exercise 'Sky High', the second phase of our visit, took place in the Colo Putty area of New South Wales in terrain and under conditions even more difficult that those near Singleton. It was designed as a counter-insurgency operation under South East Asia conditions and after a few days of patrolling and defensive activities we carried out an advance of some 40 miles on foot in conjunction with Australian units and captured a complete enemy company. "The highlight of this final action was an attack by the Rifles Battalion Headquarters on the 'enemy' position and the capture by Colonel Purdon of the enemy commander, and by his batman of the enemy RSM, a matter which I imagine the Sergeants' Mess will not allow him to forget for some time!" (Quote from Gen Sir William Oliver's Report.)

On 28 November we moved to quarters with the Australian Army at Holdsworthy, about 25 miles west of Sydney for the third and last phase of the visit in which our role was largely one of public relations. Sir William Oliver said in his Report, 'They proved to be splendid ambassadors who enjoyed themselves into the bargain'. Whilst we were there we beat 1st Royal Australian Regiment at boxing in a succession of hard-hitting fights fought in the cleanest and most sporting spirit and which cemented the bonds of friendship between our two battalions. We also beat them conclusively at cross country. On the other hand, they beat us at Athletics and, as befitted Australians playing against Irishmen, thrashed us at cricket!

We were entertained by the Mayor of Liverpool, by the Returned Servicemen's League and by numerous other organisations. Some of us visited our Allied Regiment, the Adelaide University Regiment. I was keenly disappointed that my official programme kept me from taking part in this, particularly as Lieutenant Colonel John Twopenny, their CO, was a friend of mine and we had served together in 1st London Irish Rifles.

Many of us went on picnics and fishing expeditions with Australian people, and the appeal to Australians to have members of the battalion to stay with them was oversubscribed on its very first day. Some of the riflemen stayed with relatives who in many cases had been previously unknown to them and had been specially traced, while others took the opportunity of short leave to visit Canberra, Adelaide, Brisbane and Melbourne. I had brought out the Band, Bugles and Pipes with me, under Bandmaster Maurice Clarke, Bugle Major Willie John Brannigan, and Pipe Major Andy Wilson BEM. They proved to be worth their weight in diamonds. Willie John's fierce, ginger handlebar moustache received front page treatment in most Australian papers. Maurice Clarke arranged selections brilliantly to include such popular tunes as 'Waltzing Matilda', 'Tie Me Kangaroo Down Sport' and 'The Road to Gunda Gai', while the Pipe Major had not only adapted a number of Australian airs for the pipes but he had trained up a team of very popular Irish dancers. I had also brought out, despite advice to the contrary, the Officers' Mess Silver, including our wonderful Peninsular War Candelabra. I had all of this on display the night we entertained a thousand people to a searchlight Retreat Parade followed by buffet supper at Victoria Barracks, Paddington, and the silver was an outstanding success.

We mounted guard at the Cenotaph in Sydney and the leading Australian weekly commented, 'The men were smaller than ours, but livelier. They marched as if hurrying to destiny. And never has the Cenotaph had a guard mounted on it with such parade ground precision or at such pace.' It went on to say, 'As for the Ulsters, they were not here long enough for Australia to slow them down, but the Antipodean blush on their fiery skins indicated that it may be a few weeks before they forget the Australian sun which makes us take things in a slower, longer stride.'

We also carried out a Retreat Parade in Singleton and ceremonial marches in the towns of Maitland and Cessnock. It was all a terribly busy time and I had a total of three hours off during which I managed to shop in David Jones and buy some gifts for Patricia, my children and my mother, and to have a swim off Bondi beach, accompanied by Johnnie Johnston, Donald MacIntrye, Jeremy Knox and Pat Winter.

We took part in a morning service at the Garrison Church at Miller Point where I read the Lesson and had the pleasure of the presence of my cousin Helen Friend and her two fine sons with me in my pew. The elder of these two young cousins had spent some time with us in our camp at Singleton, in his capacity as a lance corporal in Barker College OTC. The last British regiment to worship at that Church, and, indeed to serve in Australia, was the legendary 18th Foot, The Royal Irish Regiment. Their Old Comrades Association entrusted us with a Regimental Plaque before we left England, to present on their behalf to the Garrison Church, which we did, together with one of our own.

My cousins also attended our Retreat Parade and it was a happy coincidence that they were also related to our chief guests, the Governor of New South Wales and his wife, Lieutenant General Sir Eric and Lady Woodward. A number of other Australian VIPs were kind enough to find the time to accept our invitations, among whom were Lt. Gen. Sir Thomas Daly, the then GOC Eastern Command, his wife and pretty daughter, Lt Gen Sir John Wilton, the CGS and Lady Wilton, and Major General (later Lt Gen Sir) Mervyn Brogan, with whom I had served on the Staff during the Malayan Emergency. As always with my Regiment, they really rose to the occasion and never have I seen the Band, Bugles and Pipes smarter nor more full of swagger, nor have I heard them play better. Similarly, the Officers' Mess Staff, under Colour Sergeant Willie Fay, and the Regimental Police under Sergeant Downey, excelled themselves. For this and other ceremonial occasions we wore No. 3 Dress – white, high-collared tunics, with black woven epaulettes on the officers' shoulders bearing black metal badges of rank; black buttons and black crossbelts, black overalls and black Mess Wellington boots. It looked very smart and distinctive.

The High Commissioner in his Desptach is kind enough to go on to say, 'But the greatest credit obviously goes to all ranks of the Rifles, for no impressario could have wished for better performers. Their bearing on duty, both in field and on parade, and their behaviour off duty, within the bounds of enjoying themselves, were impeccable. Not one man got into trouble with the police and not one stayed behind although some were certainly urged by Australian friends to migrate in the future. Knowing their local Irish population the Sydney police were amazed.'

We had had an unforgettable time. Never could I forget that vibrant, dynamic, sunny country and the friendly, forthright Australians. Sydney reminded me so much of my native Belfast on a white-hot, sunny day and the Sydney-siders of my own, straight-spoken Northern Irish folk. What a country for our children and our children's children to grow up in! They would be about 6 inches – at least – taller and broader, and we Purdons could certainly do with the extra height!

While we were breakfasting at Holdsworthy the day after the end of the Exercise we were shattered at the news that President John F Kennedy had been assassinated. To be snatched away after he had saved us from World War 3 because of his firmness with Kruschev over Cuba was a bitter blow to the free world.

I thought back over our time in Australia, and so many memories flooded in, of seeing a koala bear high up in a blue gum tree near Singleton, and kangaroos, and the national emblem of New South Wales, that glorious flower, the waratah. I thought of the night that we arrived in the 'Sky High' exercise area, cut out of virgin jungle by the Australian sappers, and of the 'O' Group held by Colonel Sandy Pearson in a dug-out. Here I and my senior officers learnt of the dreaded Funnel Web spider, and how it liked sleeping bags! Lights were forbidden in the area at night, but (whisper!) what Royal Ulster Rifles officer who attended that Orders Group that night did not take out his pencil torch before going to bed in his 'hootchie' outside, without, by its thin yellow light, searching his sleeping bag and shelter for one of these potentially lethal insects?!

I remember still the brilliant navigation of my Intelligence Officer, Brian Gallagher (his father had served in my father's Field Ambulance in the Great War); Robin Charley eating parrots and wichity grubs; the colourful flocks of parrots, parrokeets and lovebirds; the hot sun; the attack on one of my 'O' Groups by the enemy, and how we collared the lot of them; of Allen Hill, OC D Company taking a flying rugger tackle at one of them and bringing him crashing down. Of that early morning when, assisted by the Australian SAS and their swash-buckling commander Al

Garland, we threaded our toggle ropes together and roped our way down the sheer walls of a 300 foot canyon, down to its virtually virgin jungle bed, as we moved to capture our enemy.

My next remembrance is of standing, unseen, on a ledge some 15 feet off the ground, my batman Lance Corporal McCormick and a number of men at my side, and with the unwitting enemy passing below – of dropping on to the enemy commander while 'Cormick' squashed the RSM and the rest of my men 'bagged' the remainder. How superbly fit we all felt, most of us had lost at least half a stone! I remember my TV and radio appearances, my twenty public speeches. I remember the kindness of the Australian Press for they all were on our side. And above all I remember my pride in my officers and men, which is with me still, and always will be.

On our return flight, we stopped at Perth at 1am and there Major General Sir Joe Kendrew, Governor of West Australia bore us off to where tables were laid out covered with white cloths on which were arrayed armies of bottles of chilled champagne – what a kind final gesture! We hated leaving so many new found but firm friends. They loaded us with generous gifts, even just before we took off. We gave a lot of remembrances too, such as a large circular, silver shooting shield to the Australian Army, ash trays, silver salvers and shillelaghs. We were so drawn to these wonderful Australian folk.

I recalled the 1 RAR officers' Christmas Party, which we all attended wearing No. 3 Dress. We found that in Australia the men tended to talk among themselves at one end of the room, while the women were segregated at the other end. I had told my officers that they must look after the womenfolk and dance every dance. Was it our imagination, but were our, until then, warm friendly and generous hosts getting a little like dogs, hackles raised over delectable bones? Unsmiling faces stared at us as we waltzed our way round the dance floor with their laughing wives in our arms!! No sooner was that dance over than these husbands suddenly rediscovered the charms of their neglected wives! After that we never got a look in although we were warmly thanked by the wives at supper! We knew then how the Poles and the Yanks must have felt in the last war!

I think we all slept the entire way back to England! Just before we took off on 11 December I received a signal to say that the battalion had been selected for a year's unaccompanied operational tour fighting the Indonesians in Borneo: that we would stage in Hong Kong for three months whilst rotating companies through the Jungle Warfare school at Kota Tinggi in Malaysia; and that our advance party would fly to Hong Kong on 3 January 1964. Happily I nodded off and woke again at Gan. Here the captain of a visiting frigate HMS *Lincoln*, who had been to school at Glenalmond with my wife's brother, and the RAF station commander, entertained us until we took off.

We sent everyone on Christmas leave when we got home, apart from the Adjutant, the Quartermaster, the ORQMS and myself. All four of us managed one day (I was in bed with a streptococcic throat on mine!) before we flew out to our next assignment. My lobbying of senior officers seemed to have worked, as operational service, to our delight, lay ahead. And we were all determined to emigrate to Australia one day! Each one of us felt tremendously honoured to receive a letter from Sir Michael Adeane conveying Her Majesty The Queen's approval of our Australian mission, together with one from the then Secretary of State for War.

CHAPTER SIXTEEN

HONG KONG AND MALAYA –
PREPARING FOR OPERATIONS IN BORNEO

Before I left England for Hong Kong, arrangements had been made for my battalion to be trained, a company at a time, at the Jungle Warfare School at Kota Tinggi in Johore, Malaysia. We were required to go to Hong Kong to temporarily replace 2nd Bn 7th Gurkha Rifles who were in Borneo and who would return in three months thus releasing us for operations in Borneo.

My second-in-command was now Johnnie Johnson who met me at Kai Tak airport and took me to Far East Farm Camp where our battalion was to be stationed. Johnnie was an old friend of mine and I was happy to have him with me. Shortly after my arrival I went off to the Jungle Warfare School in Malaysia to get back into the operational groove and to see my boys learning all the jungle techniques and tactics.

I attended an official cocktail party where I was talking to Lady Walker, wife of Major General Sir Walter Walker. When Lady Walker heard that I and my battalion were training for the war in Borneo she took me along to her husband whom I had not met since the Malayan Emergency. General Walker has always been a hero of mine. He is a tremendous leader. All he wanted from the units he commanded was efficiency, no bluffing and a bit of dash and personality, and regiments that provided that mixture were sure to find his approval. General Walker was Director of Borneo Operations and I asked him where we were to serve. Was it to be Sarawak, Brunei or Sabah? The General told me that he had not yet decided for various reasons but he then and there wrote me a chit authorising me to fly out to the theatre of operations and to visit certain battalions which he specified and which were operating in each of the three main states, Sabah, Brunei and Sarawak.

Taking with me my Intelligence Officer, Brian Gallagher, I flew off to learn all that I could at first hand about the enemy, the task in hand, the terrain and the various techniques and tactics applicable.

Meanwhile those companies of my Battalion which were not at the Jungle Warfare School were training in the most 'jungly' areas of Hong Kong that we could find, with special emphasis on navigation, IA (Immediate Action) drills, patrolling, ambushes, shooting by day and by night, physical fitness and setting up jungle bases including the use of claymore mines, wire, trenches and panjis (sharp pointed bamboo stakes).

Brian Gallagher and I first flew to Singapore for another visit to Kota Tinggi, and then one morning, just before first light, we drove from RAF accommodation in Changi to the airfield. The warm, humid air was already full of the rich calls of golden orioles and bulbuls. Soon we were airborne in a Royal Air Force Hastings and droning off to the island of Labuan. From there we were flown by a Chinese pilot of the Royal Malaysian Air Force to Brunei in a Twin Pioneer aircraft. We were met by an officer from Headquarters 51 Gurkha Brigade, commanded by Brigadier Harry Tuzo who had succeeded Brigadier Short while we were in Australia.

We called on Brigadier Jack Glennie who was General Walker's deputy at that time and he and his wife kindly invited us and Brigadier Tuzo for drinks that night. I also visited the various heads of departments including several old friends in the Director of Borneo Operations Headquarters. Next morning I went round Headquarters 51 Gurkha Brigade and I must say I did hope that we would have the good fortune to serve under Brigadier Harry. He was one of those people who always ran such a happy, contented, helpful show and we wanted very much to be a part of it.

He sent us off to see the 2nd Bn 7th Gurkha Rifles which was commanded by an old friend of mine and fellow Irishman, Lieutenant Colonel Runce Rooney, MC, who had originally been commissioned into my Regiment. He was very helpful and informative. We lived in his Headquarters camp for several days and he arranged for us to visit his companies so as to 'pick the brains' of his leaders at all levels. We flew into one of his jungle bases one evening and were greeted by the British Company Commander and his Second-in-Command, a Gurkha Captain. News that one of the Royal Princes had been born that day, HRH Prince Andrew, now Royal Colonel-in-Chief, the Royal Irish Regiment, had just come in on the radio and we were led straight to the Gurkha officers' bashas and handed half-pint tumblers full of neat rum. Brian and I had not eaten since breakfast as we had been too busy to do so. We were terribly thirsty and hungry and it is still my belief that we each drank at least three tumblers of that (delicious) undiluted rum and I maintain that we were both quite unaffected! We then ate an enormous goat curry with mounds of rice and drank more rum. I went to bed early and was woken at about 2am by a beaming Brian who informed me that he had not yet gone to bed and that he had just written and proposed to a girl in either Denmark or Norway, and wanted me to be the first to know! We played basketball on the company airstrip at 0500 next morning. I bet I felt better than Brian did!

Next, we flew to Sabah to visit 1st King's Own Yorkshire Light Infantry. The battalion was commanded by John Saltonstall OBE who was very kind to us and arranged for us to visit his posts on the Indonesian border. Among the places we saw was where a Scottish subaltern of his had won an MC knocking out an enemy machine-gun post. At each place we visited we were able to learn about enemy techniques and tactics at first hand. The last unit which we visited was 42 Commando Royal Marines in Sarawak's 1st Division, commanded by another friend, Ian Gourlay. His second-in-command was Bob Loudoun, and their companies were located along the Indonesian border. Commando Headquarters was at Semengo Camp, Kuching. At that time the pilots of their affiliated Royal Air Force helicopter squadron lived with the Commando officers. As a result there was a terrific Joint Services spirit, and morale, operational cooperation and mutual confidence were admirable.

We visited all the company bases and saw the difference between the terrain in the 1st Division of Sarawak to that in Sabah and in Brunei. I particularly remember Tim Priest, large and cheerful, and the advice he gave us; and Alex Higson who not only gave us valuable operational advice but took us swimming in a flooded gold mine at Bau. I know it was extremely deep water but apparently it had no 'bugs' in it because of the arsenic it contained from the old mine. Bob Loudoun was commanding at that time and was extremely good to us. At the end of our visit which took about three weeks, I had a much better idea as to what lay ahead in Borneo and was confident that we would make a real success of our tour of operations there. Also, I was certain that our training was on the correct lines.

Brian Gallagher and I returned to Hong Kong direct from Kuching by Cathay Pacific. I remember we had a brilliant menu and I chose a delicious Chinese meal. Seated beside me, my neighbour Brian Gallagher showed his independence by tucking into steak and chips! Back in Hong Kong and full of plans for Borneo I was surprised to hear that the battalion had been ordered to take part in the Queen's Birthday Parade in Kowloon. As we were due to fight a war within a few weeks I couldn't believe that anyone thought we had time for ceremonial when every minute spent on operational training was vital. I formed up to my Brigade Commander who sympathised with me and referred me to the Chief of Staff, a nice man but who was adamant we must participate. So I asked to see the Commander British Forces, General Sir Richard Craddock, KCB, KBE, DSO.

General Craddock explained to me that for political reasons he had to have a particular number of troops on this parade and whereas he fully appreciated my feelings it was only because of this factor that he had to have my battalion on parade. I understood this and after my return to Far East Farm Camp, I addressed my battalion. I told them we would carry out drill parades until I was satisfied that we had reached a really high standard of excellence, but that as soon as we reached it (which we did after a very short time), I would dismiss the parade.

When the day of the parade came I was very proud of my battalion. There was a reception later that day at Government House and I was standing chatting to some of my brother commanding officers. General Dick Craddock came up to us and in front of everyone congratulated me, saying that my battalion had been the smartest and best on parade. This was typical of him and no wonder we all thought the world of him. He and Lady Craddock used to call in at Far East Farm Camp at Castle Peak Bay for tea and we used to say Lady Craddock was our Pin-up Girl, so popular was she. The General had been desperately badly wounded in the last war and was in perpetual pain with his leg but few people knew this.

My great friend Tony Tighe was the General's Military Assistant at that time and it was very pleasant to have him and his late wife, Elizabeth, nearby. A pleasant interlude for me was when the Chaplain General Ivan Neill, CB, OBE, QHC visited Hong Kong. He had already been to see us at Iserlohn and he had been our 2nd Battalion's padre at Dunkirk. We all looked forward to seeing him, myself in particular because he is my cousin. General Sir Richard and Lady Craddock very kindly invited me to dinner at Flagstaff House where Ivan and his wife Pat were staying with them.

The Chaplain General spent next day with the battalion where he met a number of the NCOs and Riflemen for coffee, also our Brigade Padre, John Northcott. John had been a subaltern in the Coldstream and had fought in north-west Europe. He was also a parachutist. He was extremely tall, lean and erect and everyone loved him. He used to do card tricks for the Riflemen which went down very well but they were so impressed with his bearing that they seemed unable to help themselves standing to attention whenever he addressed them. He was coming to Borneo to join us as our Battalion Padre when he suddenly became grievously ill and died; such a tragic loss and we all mourned his passing deeply. I still have in my possession the St. Mark's Gospel he gave me prior to our departure for Borneo, inscribed by him inside the flyleaf and I always think of John when I open it.

My battalion athletes asked me if we could put a team in for the 48 Gurkha Brigade Championships and I agreed, provided they trained in their own time as we were busy preparing for jungle warfare. They won the Championships which was good for battalion morale. We trained hard and in the evenings everyone played games. We had an inter-platoon championship which included basketball, football, hockey and volleyball. Battalion headquarters was split into several platoons, the idea being that every member of the battalion took part and not just the 'gladiators'. It was great fun and we played games until it was dark. All that people wanted to do then was have a couple of drinks in their Messes or in the NAAFI and go to their beds. But several nights a week we had night training and we shot at night time regularly, both in the dark and with the aid of various flares and lights.

We trained on Saturday mornings, after which Saturday afternoon and all day Sunday were holidays. Most people went into Kowloon and Hong Kong in battalion coaches, saw the sights, did some shopping and had a meal. Behaviour was excellent and everyone had their sights set on the war in Borneo.

We celebrated St Patrick's Day with a short, traditional parade at which I presented the shamrock. We chartered a large Hong Kong Yaumatei Ferry Company boat and went off in her to Silverstrand Bay on Lantao Island. Here we swam, played volleyball and football on the sand and the battalion cooks prepared an enormous and delicious barbecue on the beach. I was handed a set of bagpipes when we got back onto the ferry and invited to entertain the battalion on the way back. Piping and singing a solo of 'MacNamara's Band', with actions, were my particular 'turns' – most of us had our party pieces and were ready to do our stuff at concerts and parties. Pipe Major Andy Wilson and I often gave a bagpipes 'duet' after guest nights. We had our battalion swimming sports at Sek Kong. The officers beat the sergeants and I swam the final lap winning by more than half a length so the Sergeants' Mess stood the winning team drinks!

Now it was time for us to fly out to Borneo. I had managed to 'acquire' eight Vickers medium machine guns and thanks to a nucleus of trained MMG members in the battalion had turned the Defence Platoon (consisting of the Bugles and Pipes) into an MMG platoon. Furthermore, I suggested to Lieutenant Colonel Leslie Fleming, MC, commanding 1st Durham Light Infantry that he might like to send, in rotation, a platoon at a time to serve with us in Borneo, as at that time it did not look as if his battalion would be going there, although it did later. He jumped at the idea. Learning that we were going to have either Gurkha or Malaysian sappers with us, I turned our assault pioneer platoon into another rifle platoon and with these three platoons formed an extra rifle company. Major John Cave, an experienced jungle soldier who had been Mentioned in Despatches in Malaya when serving in the Royal Malay Regiment became the Company Commander.

By now we had completed our training at the Jungle Warfare School and in Hong Kong, and early one morning we took off from Kai Tak airport in RAF troop-carrying aircraft and flew into Sibu in the 3rd Division of Sarawak to take over from 1st Bn 7th Gurkha Rifles.

Whilst in Hong Kong I had got to know Ronnie Somerville well. Ronnie, a high calibre officer, was commanding 4th Light Regiment, Royal Artillery and he and Jean, his wife, were both very kind to me. One evening I accompanied them to an evening at their NAAFI at Fanling. We were joined at our table by their quartermaster who was a Major and his wife. I kept wondering why the QM looked so familiar and told him that I was sure we had met before. However, he denied having set eyes on me. Suddenly I remembered – he was wearing uniform and I noticed that his first medal ribbon was that of the George Medal – yes, we had met in Ismailia when he was the sergeant with the GM whom I had accompanied to rescue the terrified REME sergeant's wife in her pillaged quarter in Arashiya!

CHAPTER SEVENTEEN

BORNEO – THE THIRD DIVISION OF SARAWAK

Our overseas tour was to be unaccompanied but some officers' wives asked to accompany their husbands to Hong Kong and Borneo. I explained that if one wife was allowed to be with her husband, we had four hundred more in England or Ireland who could claim an equal right to accompany their spouses. There was absolutely no married accommodation for us either in Hong Kong or in Borneo and in any case we had a war to fight. Despite my explanation, one very attractive wife refused to accept my reply of 'No' to her letter enlisting my support, and wrote to my Adjutant to say that she was arriving anyway! Despite my Adjutant's and her own husband's exhortations not to come, this mettlesome, pretty girl arrived in Borneo. She was not allowed to remain in Kuching and was sent on to Brunei from where I got a signal from the Brigadier telling me I owed him a sum of money for helping her to get to Hong Kong or Japan. Her nice, embarrassed husband settled up with the long suffering, busy operational Brigade Commander. I am sure she has never forgiven me.

My first action on arriving in Kuching was to call on my new Brigade Commander at his 99 Gurkha Brigade Headquarters. Brigadier A.G. (Pat) Patterson was a wiry, very fit looking, dark-haired officer with a clipped moustache who appeared to be full of boundless energy. He exuded dynamic enthusiasm and fixed me with an intense gaze. 'I didn't ask for your battalion in my Brigade,' said my new Brigadier. 'I wanted the Argylls.' 'I quite understand, Sir,' I replied. 'We hoped to go to Brigadier Tuzo's Brigade!' Brigadier Pat grinned at me in the most friendly way, and thus began my service under the command of a man for whom I have the highest respect and admiration and who became a great friend. He was a superb leader, tough, courageous and tireless and I learnt a great deal from his example.

The 1st Bn 7th Gurkha Rifles which we were to relieve had had a distinguished operational tour in the 3rd Division of Sarawak. Battalion Headquarters, Headquarter Company and one rifle company were located at Sibu on the Rajang River, a deep, wide, brown, mighty jungle waterway, full of powerful currents and navigable by sizeable coastal steamers up to a hundred miles from the sea. There was a rifle company at the little town of Sarikei towards the coast which had a platoon at the village of Binatang. Another company was at Song near the highest navigable limit of the Rajang River. A rifle company and the reconnaissance platoon were based respectively at Bangkit and Katibas, both bases situated on the Katibas River, a large, powerful tributary of the Rajang. We had one more company, and this was operationally responsible for perhaps the wildest and certainly the remotest portion of our battalion area, with platoons stationed at Nangga Gaat, at Belaga and at Long Jawi.

Once again I was participating in a jungle war but this time in the enviable position of commanding officer of the 1st Battalion of my own Regiment, The Royal Ulster Rifles. The Borneo War, or Confrontation, as it was styled, took place in Eastern Malaysia and Brunei. The theatre of operations comprised the 47,000 square miles of Sarawak, the 29,000 square miles of Sabah, and Brunei which has an area of 2,226 square miles. These territories are situated on the north and north western side of Borneo which is the third largest island in the world. Sarawak, the largest state, was divided into five administrative Divisions, and Sabah was divided into four Residencies. Tooth-shaped Brunei which lies between the 4th and 5th Divisions of Sarawak, is governed by a Sultan and forms no part of Malaysia. The terrain consists of an enormous area of jungle and mountains. It had few roads, the main means of communication being the many rivers, the jungle tracks and, with the advent of war, helicopters.

The main towns and villages lay along the coast which was bordered by low-lying plains with some small hills interspersed. Most of the lowlands are swampy and there are vast, thick areas of mangroves on the river estuaries and muddy foreshore, with flooding at high tide.

Much of Eastern Malaysia between the coast and the mountainous terrain of its border with Indonesia was covered by an almost unbroken canopy of tropical rain forest with trees a hundred feet or more in height. This border from Sabah in the east rises gradually from three thousand to eight thousand feet, continuing at this height into Sarawak and descending to three thousand feet in the west, dropping sharply to the coast. There are tracts of fairly level land between the mountain and hill ranges which are cultivated and settled by the local hill tribes. Most of the inhabitants of

Borneo live near the rivers which are the main artery of transport, or on the coast.

There are a number of different races; Malays, the ubiquitous Chinese, and the various indigenous tribes, perhaps the best known to the British servicemen being the Ibans. Among others are Kayans, Kelabits, Muruts and Punans. The climate, as on the Malaysian mainland, is hot and humid becoming cooler and less humid in the mountains. It is a very beautiful country with a profusion of birds, animals and insects and with attractive, friendly peoples.

Confrontation had stemmed from President Soekarno of Indonesia's dislike for the concept of Malaysia and from his ambition to establish a Malay empire embracing Indonesia, Sabah, Brunei, Sarawak, Singapore, the Malayan mainland and the Philippines, which would bear the composite name of Maphilindo. This empire, presided over, of course, by himself, would (Soekarno hoped) because of its unlimited natural resources and combined population of some 150 million, rival any of the three Superpowers. The rebellion in Brunei had affected the 4th and 5th Divisions of Sarawak and had spread to the remainder of Sarawak. Here there was a real danger from the Chinese Clandestine Communist Organisation (CCO) which had not participated in the rebellion but was sympathetic to it. In Sabah uniforms similar to those worn by the Brunei rebels were discovered near Tawau. All this led to the whole of Sabah, Sarawak and Brunei being occupied by British and Malaysian security forces.

The military formations now stationed there consisted of East Brigade, commanded by a Malaysian Brigadier, (my old Staff College friend, 'Ib' who retired as General Dato Ibrahim bin Ismail, Commander-in-Chief Malaysian Army) in Sabah; the Centre Brigade was Brigadier Harry Tuzo's 51 Gurkha Brigade based in Brunei but also with responsibility for the 4th and 5th Divisions of Sarawak; whilst in the West was Brigadier Pat Patterson's 99 Gurkha Brigade which had its Headquarters in Kuching and covered the 1st, 2nd and 3rd Divisions of Sarawak. The task of my battalion was to take over the 3rd Division with Headquarters at Sibu from the 1st Bn 7th Gurkha Rifles, commanded by Brian Heelis who had been at Sandhurst with me.

As I flew in the aircraft carrying my advance party, I looked down on the terrain over which I and my soldiers would be operating. We had crossed a coastline of mangrove swamps and nipah palms intersected with inlets, creeks and great brown, powerful-looking rivers which, with their narrower offshoots, writhed beneath the green canopy of the jungle. Scarcely a road or logging track was visible and I already knew from my reconnaissance earlier on that until the arrival of our security forces with their helicopters the main means of travel had to be by the waterways or along jungle trails. We flew over longhouses where whole villages lived under one long roof inside a building built on stilts high above the river bank to escape the flooding waters, access being by notched tree trunks leant against the building and leading up to a long, wide, communal verandah. The domestic animals lived below.

Sibu was a sprawling town on the Rajang situated about thirty miles from the coast. The houses within a quarter of a mile of the river were built on stilts to avoid the flooding at high water. Battalion Headquarters was in a group of atap buildings near a school, with the Officers' Mess across the road in a pleasant bungalow. The Resident's house was by the river not far off and every morning the Divisional War Executive Committee met in the school. This Committee was chaired by the Resident and included the Senior Police Officer, the Battalion Commander, the Commander of the Sarawak Police Field Force, the Special Branch Officer (SBO) and certain staff officers, among whom was the Battalion Intelligence Officer. Also present would be the commander or his representative of the helicopter squadron, with the District Officer. Specialists, such as the head of the Public Works Department (PWD) would be invited to join the Committee when their particular expertise was required.

We were met at Sibu airfield and quickly made to feel among friends. The Resident, Murdo Grant, was a pleasant, intelligent and commonsense Scot, and the Police Commander was Roger Edwards who later became Commissioner of Police in the Solomon Islands, and later still was to serve with me as Director of Personnel when I was Deputy Commissioner of the Royal Hong Kong Police Force. Roger and I quickly became friends and worked together happily.

The helicopter squadron's commander, Lieutenant Commander 'Tank' Sherman was one of the legendary characters of the Borneo War. A natural leader, of a piratical disposition, he was a swashbuckling flier with the Nelson touch. I was to serve with 'Tank' again when I was General Officer Commanding Near East Land Forces based in Cyprus and he was in charge of naval intelligence at Joint Headquarters in Episkopi where he did a fine job. The Company Commander of the Sarawak Police Field Force was a tough, experienced character, Bill Crenell whom we got to like a lot and who was the soul of loyalty and cooperation.

The 1st 7th Gurkhas were a fine battalion. Brian Heelis, their CO, was very experienced and helpful. His Second-in-Command, Birdie Smith was greatly loved by his Gurkhas and he and I lived in the local guest house until the handover was complete. He gave me a lot of useful advice. Birdie was to be involved in a horrific helicopter crash in Borneo when his arm had to be amputated with a penknife by the Regimental Medical Officer, Captain Crawford. He had to operate while Birdie hung upside down in his safety harness, with high octane fuel from the Wessex helicopter pouring out and the threat of a fatal explosion ever present. Birdie and the Gurkha soldiers with him were eventually freed – I believe some were killed in the crash, and others badly injured – thanks largely to Captain Crawford, who was awarded the George Medal for his gallant work. Birdie's bravery and disregard for acute pain throughout his ordeal came as no surprise to those of us who knew him. I am happy to say that he went on to command a very happy battalion; to continue to play a good and vigorous game of tennis; to be the author of numerous articles and books and to become Colonel of his Regiment.

Together with my Quartermaster Mick Estridge, my Intelligence Officer, Brian Gallagher, and my Regimental Signals Officer, Bill Clements, I carried out as detailed a reconnaissance as possible of the Third Division which was an area about the size of Wales. Most of the journeys I made were in the Wessex helicopters of Tank Sherman's 845 Naval Air Commando Squadron, Royal Navy, seated in the co-pilot's seat beside the pilot from where I had a good view of the terrain over and through which we would be operating. For some of the shorter journeys we travelled in longboats with powerful outboard engines or in speed boats. These trips could be quite exciting as enormous logs would be met, semi-submerged, rolling and dipping in the powerful river currents. I was told that Tank and his officers would waterski up the Rajang from time to time behind their Wessex helicopters. I never saw them doing so but it would not surprise me if they had!

Tank had a peerless team of officers and men, their enthusiasm and dedication an inspiration to us all. Their efforts were recognised by the award in 1964 of the coveted Boyd Trophy presented for the finest contribution of the year to naval aviation. In order to cover the limits of the Third Division, Tank had a forward helicopter base at Nangga Gaat which was situated on the uppermost reaches of the Rajang River. Nangga Gaat is the seat of the Temenggong Jugah, the Paramount Chief of the Ibans, who at that time was also Minister for Sarawak Affairs in the Malaysian Government. Nangga Gaat, situated on a small, grassy promontory surrounded by primary jungle, is a wild and beautiful place where rivers rush between mountains, and when it rains hard have been known to rise thirty feet in six hours. The Temenggong loved his naval airmen and they, to a man, were devoted to him and greatly enjoyed being there. The Navy had taken the place over in their own inimitable way.

The advance party had had to land and take off on the river bed as there was no room anywhere else, but with the help of local labour, trees had been cut down and ground levelled so that up to six helicopters could land, be serviced and refuelled. Two more landing pads were cleared on nearby hilltops for maximum-weight take-offs. Living accommodation was in huts on stilts. These huts had atap roofs and split bamboo floors and the squadron also established The Anchor Inn in an atap hut, with a bar and a couple of rooms. The Navy's ground crews worked extremely hard, as helicopters returning from the last trip of the day had to be serviced and refuelled and, if necessary, repaired, ready for take-off at first light next day or, in an emergency, at any hour. However, they rightly relaxed and enjoyed themselves when they could before starting work again at first light.

Digby Lickfold was commanding the detachment when I called in. He was another colourful character who also became a good friend of mine – Digby looked rather like that bearded sailor on the Player's cigarette packet! Later when I was Chief Instructor and OC All Arms Battle Group Division at the School of Infantry, Warminster, Digby and some of his pilots would come and give life, colour and realism to the day in each course when we studied operations in Borneo. The main body of the squadron was based at Sibu where there was a large airfield and full facilities for major maintenance and repair work, as well as a recently constructed camp for an infantry company.

In addition to Bill Crennell's Sarawak Police Field Force Company, we had a company's worth of Border Scouts dispersed throughout the border area as the 'Eyes and Ears' of the Security Forces and, of course, we had Roger Edwards' Police. There was one other component, Naval Party Kilo which comprised seven assorted vessels including a Landing Craft and various launches. This Force was very useful for patrolling the creeks, inlets and coastal estuary of the Rajang.

I set out to learn as much as I could from 1st 7th Gurkhas while my three henchmen picked the brains of their opposite numbers. George MacKenzie, the Scottish Intelligence Officer of 1/7 GR, was very helpful to us, with a great sense of humour and a strong personality. I was glad to meet him again fourteen years later in Hong Kong, when George had become a successful businessman and I was a Colonial Policeman.

The two company commanders I saw most of, because the handover was in full swing and some companies had already left, were Richard Holworthy and Denis O'Leary. Richard was a small, wiry, tough officer, a Light Infantryman serving on secondment to the Gurkhas and he was able to give me a lot of valuable tips from recent practical experience. The next year at Warmister he was one of my best students on the All Arms Course. Denis O'Leary who was older than Richard and a veteran of jungle warfare, was the other company commander. In January that year a mixed group of Indonesians and Sarawak Malaysians who had received military training in Indonesia sailed in a kotak (native craft) into the mouth of the

Rajang but split up into three sections when they were informed by the local CCO that Denis and his A Company were alerted to their presence. Two Indonesian sections went upstream and the third lay up on a swampy island on an offshoot of the Rajang. Denis mounted an operation whereby two of his platoons assaulted one side of the island, covered by fire from a launch which carried his company headquarters.

The two Gurkha platoons were landed at 1700 hrs. on the island which was covered with close mangroves and which consequently had very limited visibility. A tough fight took place at close quarters among the twisted mangroves and in the stinking black mud of the swamp. The Gurkhas and the Indonesians inflicted casualties on each other and Denis who had been directing covering fire from the launch, came ashore as soon as he saw his two platoons were held up. The enemy were virtually invisible among the mangroves but Denis led one of his platoons almost up to the concealed enemy, inspiring his men by his personal example. The Indonesians had three dead, two wounded and one captured by Denis. Denis had three Gurkhas wounded but all made good recoveries. The rest of the incursion party, sixteen of them, were captured eight days later in the hold of a fishing boat sailing up the river.

Denis took me to meet the Pengulus (headmen) at Bangkit and Katibas on the Katibas river and they became friends of mine. One evening we were sitting on the slatted bamboo floor of the longhouse at Bangkit being entertained by the Pengulu and his people. The Pengulu eventually said how much he wished that he had a watch as he had none. On impulse I took mine off and handed it to him and Denis nodded approvingly. The tuak (strong Iban equivalent of poteen) was handed round but I didn't sample it (I had sworn off alcohol for the duration of my time in Borneo, this was part of my quid pro quo for restricting my battalion to two cans of beer per day in the jungle) but the welcome was warm and songs (Pantuns) were sung in our honour. The tuak began to take effect. The Pengulu had not noticed that I was not drinking and at the height of the party he arose and went over to a heavy metal safe, opened the door and locked my watch away in it. Before he closed the door I could have sworn that I saw hanging inside a large number of watches!

The Gurkhas left for a well-earned reunion with their families and friends in Hong Kong and we took over the Third Division. I had put Denis Lucy, the fiery, enthusiastic commander of B Company, at Sarikei, with a detached platoon at Binatang village. The imperturbable Robin Bruford-Davies and his C Company were in the airfield camp at Sibu, and Battalion HQ, as well as Pat Winter and his Headquarter Company, were stationed in the main Sibu Camp on the Rajang. A Company under John Cave, with Mike Henry as second-in-command, and Allen Preston, another cousin of mine as a platoon commander, were at Song and Kapit up river, the reconnaissance platoon under Robert Carson was at Katibas; D Company, under the clever and ebullient Bill Benson was stationed at Bangkit also on the Katibas River. Then, considerably further afield, was my attached Company of 1st Royal Green Jackets with one platoon at Nangga Gaat, one at Belaga on the river of that name, 60 miles by river from Kapit and the same by air from Nangga Gaat, and the third platoon at Long Jawi on the Balui River 20 miles from the Indonesian border, a good 60 miles from Belaga and 70 from Nangga Gaat. Their company HQ was at Belaga. We were very fond of the 1st Royal Green Jackets who were commanded by my good friend David House, who became, after a most distinguished career, Black Rod in the House of Lords.

The company commander was a charming man, Martin Cracknell, and two of his subalterns, Hugh Dumas and David Roberts, who was shortly to be awarded the Military Cross, were to serve on my staff at the School of Infantry, and were both high-class professional soldiers. We set to work to dominate our area by constant patrolling, varying our routine, timings, routes and areas so as to keep the initiative and be unpredictable. The enemy were not just the Indonesians, because in the Third Division of Sarawak we had the strongest and most active elements of the Chinese Clandestine Communist Organisation in Borneo. The importance of winning the Hearts and Minds Campaign was well known to us all and we realised that we did not have an easy task in Sibu, with its largely Chinese population.

As we walked or drove about the town we were greeted with stony, indifferent looks, even from the children. I told my battalion that whatever the response we would always, without fail, wave and smile at the locals. By the time we left Sibu the local people were smiling and waving at us, often before we waved at them! The behaviour on and off duty of my men impressed everyone; they not only maintained the high standard of our predecessors but added their own special 'Rifles' spirit and charm which won the interest and hearts of the Chinese in Sibu. We had two threats. One was in the areas of the towns where there was a Chinese population and where the Clandestine Communist Organisation flourished. The other was from the Indonesians who could appear either from across the Kalimantan border or else come in from the sea as did those who had been disposed of by Denis O'Leary and his company.

To take the threat posed by the CCO first. Our main centres of Chinese settlers were in Sibu and around the area of Sarikei and Binatang towards the mouth of the Rajang River. Denis Lucy and his B Company dominated the Sarikei-Binatang area by vigorous patrolling by day and by night. In conjunction with Naval Party Kilo and thanks to the mobility given by

Tank Sherman's helicopters, Denis also had patrols and ambushes near the coast ready for any sea incursions. Robin Bruford-Davies and his C Company similarly dominated Sibu and the surrounding area and both companies achieved considerable success. C Company was also my battalion reserve, ready, grouped with 845 Squadron's helicopters, to fly to reinforce our troops dealing with any cross-border Indonesian incursions.

There had been two incursions into the Third Division from across the Indonesian border. In September 1963 about 150 Indonesians crossed the border and made their way to Long Jawi where they persuaded the locals not to give them away, and to let them conceal themselves in their longhouses. They then attacked the very small security forces' garrison which consisted of six Gurkhas, twenty-one Border Scouts and three policemen, at first light, knocking out both the Gurkha and police radios. They killed some of the Gurkhas, a policeman and a Border Scout. Most of the Scouts withdrew and were captured in the jungle and although the surviving Gurkhas continued to fight, they ran out of ammunition, withdrew to the jungle and eventually reached safety.

Johnny Clements a sound and experienced soldier who was the CO of their battalion the 1st 2nd Gurkha Rifles used helicopters to lift in his ambush parties on what he reckoned was to be the raiders' escape route. He caught them on their way out by boat down the Balui River and killed all twenty-six raiders in the two boats. There were several enemy lines of approach into this company area along the various river routes from the frontier.

The other cross-border incursion into the Third Division occurred in August 1963 when about sixty Indonesian raiders moved on Song on the Rajang and clashed with a patrol of 2nd 6th Gurkhas which had been alerted. This Gurkha patrol killed six of the enemy but their own platoon commander was hit in the knee during the battle. He ordered his party to continue and told his orderly who had stayed with him to return to camp for assistance. The rescue party found the platoon commander dead, having been shot through the shoulder in a gallant fight.

Our jungle-based companies quickly made friends with the local people and with the Border Scouts operating in their areas, and set about patrolling the likely enemy lines of approach which were mostly along the rivers, via 'gaps' in the Border. Helicopter sorties along likely entry routes were also carried out. I hoped that we would receive information about any enemy incursions in time for me to not only ambush their approach route, but, by using the helicopters, to lift in troops behind them to intercept and ambush on their way back to Indonesia any enemy who had escaped our 'welcome committee'. We had news of a possible incursion that might come in using the Sungei Bangkit and follow a trail crossing the high

Gunong Sepali, a mountain thickly covered in primary jungle. D Company would take on the main Indonesian force in ambushes chosen by Bill Benson, while C Company would provide the troops to be helicopter-lifted in behind any enemy incursion to ambush likely withdrawal routes. C Company also provided a 'stop' on the very top of Gunong Sepali and Corporal Keating and his section walked in up jungle trails to establish this position. They had been in position for about a week with supplies air-dropped by helicopter because Wessex helicopters could not land on the little, vertiginous ledge where the trail crossed the mountain summit, near which, concealed in the thick jungle, lurked Corporal Keating and his section. I wanted them to know they were not forgotten and decided to try to land on their narrow ledge in the little Hiller helicopter that Tank Sherman so kindly always put at my disposal.

I had – as was to be expected from 845 Squadron – a skilled pilot, Lieutenant Mike Thompson, RN. He put the helicopter down beautifully with the skids balanced on the stone outcrop of the narrow ledge and with the trail projecting dizzily over the abyss below. We got carefully out and handed the astonished Corporal Keating and his, by then, bearded section their mail, two cans of beer each, cigarettes, sweets and some fresh food from the cookhouse.

Corporal Keating and I had a look at the track from our (and from a possible enemy) point of view. We all had a chat and then Mike very skilfully and carefully took off vertically, hovered for a moment and then sent the little Hiller swooping down the near-perpendicular face of Gunong Sepali. As we rushed over the dark green tops of the huge trees I noticed splashes of scarlet, mauve and yellow which were orchids growing in the trees. Great rhinoceros-billed hornbills flapped heavily from one jungle giant to another. We hovered over another patrol in deep jungle but couldn't land, so I threw out their mail to Lieutenant Derek Bird and his platoon, exchanged waves and continued on our way. I remember Mike bringing the Hiller down one narrow vertical tunnel into the jungle, the tall trees so close that it looked as if the little helicopter's rotor blades must strike the branches. We gradually descended as if in a lift and when we came to the foot of the shaft there, glorious in a great beam of sunlight which struck the ground at an angle, rose a cloud of large green and black Rajah Brooke butterflies. Amid such beauty, at times it was hard to concentrate on the operational side of things!

One evening on our way back from one of my visits to companies and other sub units Mike flew low over Sibu swimming pool. Taking a well-earned half hour's break from his Officers' Mess duties was our Mess Sergeant, Colour Sergeant Willie Fay from Dublin, with the Mess Corporal, Corporal McMahon, another Southerner and several men from Headquarters. On spotting my helicopter, the vigilant Bill Fay came to attention in the middle of the pool and called the other occupants up – all out of their depth – at the same time – I never saw it, but the RSM enjoyed telling me about it later!

The RSM and my orderly Lance Corporal Haveron used to accompany me on patrol provided – if I was flying in to the jungle – there was room in the helicopter. They both used to be quite stiff with me if I ever had to leave either of them behind and I was rarely allowed to fly in the Hiller if a Wessex could be obtained. I remember one patrol through the swamps, rivers and jungle with a platoon of Robin Bruford-Davies' C Company, which ended in a surprise swoop on a small settlement of CCO Chinese. A number of Riflemen sought me out and said how good it was to find the RSM and the CO's orderly joining in any operations that the jungle companies undertook. I was very lucky in both these grand soldiers. I was most upset when the North Irish Brigade would not accept my RSM for a QM's commission. I took him along to see Brigadier Pat Patterson and my Director of Operations, General Walter Walker, both of whom knew Charles Cardwell's true worth from first-hand observation and they welcomed him into the Brigade of Gurkhas to the loss of the North Irish Brigade. Having had Major Dick Connell, MBE, of my Regiment as Quartermaster of the 1st 2nd Gurkha Rifles where Dick had been a tremendous success, Charles Cardwell followed in his footsteps.

Everyone living in company bases fired his personal weapon every day as we all knew that jungle targets can be fleeting, rarely giving one an easy or a second shot. Before leaving base for a patrol or any other operation, every man tested his weapon and practised immediate action drills. No one was allowed to wear aftershave or hair-oil or to use scented soap prior to going into the jungle. One of my officers was a tough young man but he invariably wore a famous West End barber's well-known hair preparation and was quite upset to receive the edict forbidding the wearing of this odorous concoction in the jungle! Those who live and operate in the jungle become like wild animals and smell such artificial odours as tobacco, hair-oil, soap, deodorant and aftershave before the owner appears. The best thing is to totally immerse oneself in swamp water, clothes and all, to kill these aromas.

Some of the previous battalions had had cases of leptospirosis, a serious illness caused by flukes from the urine of rats and other animals and our medical officers advised us not to swim in the river pools. I forbade anyone to bathe therefore but of course we had to wade through rivers or even to swim them on occasions for operational reasons. However, forbidding bathing in streams and rivers would lessen the chances of any of my battalion catching the horrible disease. The sailors had no such inhibitions especially Naval Party Kilo who were not under my disciplinary command. Sometimes my Riflemen used to point this out to me, especially if I had been with them on an operation and, hot, tired and sweaty, we had come to some inviting, cool, clear stream gliding over a sand or gravel bed. I don't know if any of the sailors ever got leptospirosis; probably by Sod's Law they escaped it but not one member of our battalion ever caught it.

The story is told that there was a platoon of a certain Regiment garrisoning the advanced helicopter base at Nangga Gaat. They were young soldiers and had a young and inexperienced platoon commander. On several nights the tired, bearded, warlike flying sailors of 845 Squadron awoke to bursts of LMG fire and automatic rifle shots. The enemy never fired back. About the fourth morning the weary platoon were surprised to see a large bull buffalo on whose flanks the word FRIENDLY had been painted in large, white capital letters by 845 Squadron. This was Temenggong Jugah's prize bull, whose amorous nocturnal visits to his bovine harem had conjured up the 'enemy intruders'!

We had a number of important outside visitors, all helpful, all welcome. General Sir Reginald Hewetson, GOC-in-C Far East Land Forces came to Sibu and I took him by speedboat to see Denis Lucy's B Company at Sarikei and his platoon under 'Tander' Shooter at Binatang. Mr James Ramsden, the Secretary of State for War, who wrote a very kind letter afterwards, came to Sibu accompanied by General Sir Alan Jolly who was General Hewetson's successor and I took them both up to Song to see John Cave and his A Company. Denis Bloodworth from the *Observer*, whom I took up to Sungei Bangkit to see Robert Carson and his reconnaissance platoon's base at Katibas and to Bill Benson and D Company at Bangkit, wrote a thoughtful and interesting article later on. Another popular visitor was JAK who delighted us all with a series of amusing and topical cartoons covering his visit, including two 'featuring' The Royal Ulster Rifles, each with an excellent commentary by Tom Pocock.

It was a wonderfully exhilarating life and I was away from my Headquarters practically every day, either visiting company bases, accompanying a patrol, or carrying out a reconnaissance – usually by helicopter, but sometimes by speed boat, longboat or on foot. I used to stay overnight in the jungle bases and remember so well standing-to an hour before last light and an hour before first light at Bangkit, and at Katibas, listening to the sound of the powerful river as it flowed by close to our stand-to positions.

On some evenings we would be invited to a longhouse for a chat with the headman and his elders. We would be warmly welcomed when we had climbed up the notched tree trunk which led to the split bamboo floored communal longhouse, not only by the men, but by their comely barebreasted women. Tuak, the Iban equivalent of poteen, would be pressed on us. They simply couldn't understand why I always refused alcohol until someone explained that I was a holy man who had forsworn alcohol until the Indonesians were defeated!

On these occasions songs would be sung, Iban musical sagas telling of the prowess of bygone headhunters (whose shrivelled trophies hung above us). These native songs would be interspersed with such Irish airs as 'MacNamara's Band', 'The Wearing of the Green', 'The Star of the Co. Down' and 'The South Down Militia'! A special pantun (song) was composed in my honour which included the lines '...and though the Indonesian bullets fall on him like rain, yet he shall be victorious...'!! Not to be outdone, Pipe Major Andy Wilson composed a march before we left called, 'Colonel Purdon's Farewell to Sarawak'.

A tragedy struck the battalion at Bangkit when a boat came adrift and a fine young Rifleman, Rifleman Huddleston who was trying to recover it, was pulled down by a violent undertow and drowned. We were such a Regimental family that it grieved each one of us. The RSM and I stood sadly by the airfield as the Royal Air Force Argosy aircraft carrying the body of our friend took off from Sibu. A party of his comrades, including a piper, accompanied him on his last journey, to be present at his military funeral at Singapore.

Prior to our arrival in Borneo, because in all the towns of Sarawak there were known to be cells of the Clandestine Communist Organisation, all licences for twelve-bore shotguns had been cancelled – all 8,500 of them – and most of these weapons had been successfully collected by the Security Forces. This process was codenamed Operation Parrot. In the Third Division these shotguns and other recovered weapons were held in corrugated buildings separated from the main road only by a single-strand barbed-wire fence about ten feet in height. Special Branch told us that the CCO were very much alive in our area and I wanted these weapons out of the way before they tried to get hold of them. Our police chief was away and I could get absolutely nowhere in persuading the police to move them.

I decided to take responsibility myself. However, General Walter Walker was paying us one of his welcome visits so, to salve my conscience I told him my problem and what I intended to do. It was typical of him that he immediately and wholeheartedly supported me. So it was with a clear conscience that when the steamer MV *Auby* came to Sibu from Singapore a day or two later I had all the weapons removed from police custody, boxed and carried aboard. They were taken away to storage in Changi, and the constant threat of a CCO sudden raid on the vulnerable store of captured arms was removed.

One morning at about 2am the radio operator called me to say that the platoon at Nangga Gaat had reported enemy movement in the vicinity. It was pelting with rain but within a few minutes I was at Sibu airfield where an alerted immediate readiness platoon of C Company was already waiting and three Wessex helicopters were running up their engines. We took off in pitch darkness and followed the River Rajang which we could see shining below, with the torrential rain lashing the windscreens. After a bit the rain ceased and we could see the stars as we thundered and thrashed on our way, the great river gleaming and rolling below us.

We passed Song and Kapit and eventually came to Nangga Gaat where we landed and quickly disembarked. A tense platoon commander reported to me that he and his men could hear the sound of radios, of talking and of movement. With the Immediate Action platoon following I accompanied him to his stand-to position and listened. A rushing sound very like that made when a Pressel switch is pressed was to be heard, together with a murmur of voices and rustlings. I blessed the previous all-weather jungle experience I had had in Malaya, because what the young officer and his men had heard was the aftermath of the tropical storm, the rushing water was the 'enemy radio', the 'murmuring' came from a runnel still flowing, and the 'enemy noises' were caused by great drops of rain falling on the flat surfaces of large leaves. I told the crest-fallen young officer that he had been quite right to summon our assistance – he was very inexperienced – and I was reassured, not only at the quick reaction within the battalion but also at yet another proof that 845 Squadron could go anywhere, at any time, in any weather.

By now the local people in Third Division were 'sold' on our battalion and our Riflemen had clearly won the Hearts and Minds campaign. Our medical officer together with the Company medical NCOs and the 'medics' in each platoon were treating ailments as they found them – often with only a codeine tablet, paludrine or even 'Smarties' – the latter being very popular! Casualties were quickly flown to hospital and Iban chiefs were taken up for rides in the little Hiller. Pengulu Mangai of Katibas particularly appreciated this honour. He was a stout-hearted man who had already played a major part in defeating an enemy incursion and was decorated for his bravery and quick thinking.

Robert Carson at Katibas taught his locals how to improve their farming and market gardening. In towns we were now met by smiling faces from the Chinese whose children ran to the Riflemen to get sweets and to examine military equipment. We really felt on top of our jobs. Then Brigadier Pat Patterson my Brigade Commander flew in unexpectedly to see me. Once inside my office he said to me, 'Corran, what is the worst thing I could do to you?' 'Sack me, Sir,' I replied. 'No, no, of course I don't mean that!' said my Brigadier. 'What if I should tell you to pick up your battalion from all its dispersed locations and move it to another area?'

he asked. 'No problem, Sir,' I replied, 'we are well used to moving in this battalion.' 'Right,' he said, 'I want you to move down to the 1st Division and relieve a battalion of the Malay Regiment. They will replace you here. The Indonesians are very active in their battalion area, the local people are worried and frightened because the Malay battalion is as yet too inexperienced to take the war to the enemy.'

I knew that the 1st Division was currently a very active area and that this move would mean that we were almost certain to see some fighting which is what we all wanted. 'The battalion will be thrilled, Sir,' I said. 'When do we go?' The Brigadier told me and I flew down to carry out a reconnaissance of our new area of operations accompanied by Brian Gallagher, Bill Clements and Mike Estridge.

The CO of the Malay battalion wore the ribbon of the MC he had won as a platoon commander during the Malayan Emergency. The area for which he and his battalion were responsible had its battalion headquarters at the little town of Serian, with company headquarters respectively at Tebedu, at Balai Ringin and at Gunan Gajak. Unlike operations in the Third Division where battalions operated from company bases, we discovered that in the First Division we would operate from platoon bases. We had a walk round the battalion headquarters camp which was located on both sides of the main road which ran from Semenggang in the Second Division to Kuching on the coast in the First Division.

The CO had arranged for the local helicopter squadron to fly me and my party around the Border area in a Whirlwind which would land at various villages and enable us to have a look at the ground as well as to meet the locals. I was rather surprised and put out when the pilot refused to allow me to sit up front to see the ground. He was quite adamant that I and my officers must sit in the body of the aircraft. No amount of cajoling or pointing out that an oozlum bird type of recce facing backwards or even sideways, was not so helpful as a direct head on view, would shift him. Nor would he depart from his scheduled landing stops to enable me to visit other Kampongs that I thought might be sensitive. It was apparent that his squadron operated in a different way to Tank's 'press on' 845 and that 'flexibility' was not in his vocabulary. We took off and flew near to the border which was much more open and less wild than in the Third Division and craned our necks doing our best to see the ground. We landed at one village and were greeted by a group of chattering locals who seemed very excited. The pilot suddenly took off and flew away. We could see him circling around. We tried to converse with the locals who gestured wildly and tried to pull us into a building. Eventually we discovered they were saying 'An Indonesian patrol has entered the other end of the village!' What a start to our first day in our new area! We had visions of a close quarter fight, our four pistols against Indonesian rifles and LMGs or, worse still, being wounded and taken off over the border. When *was* that bloody pilot going to come back for us? And would we all be jumped once he did? Anyway, we acted the part of being totally unconcerned and said we would like to be taken to a place from where we could attack the Indonesians. The jabbering and arm waving lessened and a calmer atmosphere prevailed. Thank heavens the Indonesians were apparently a small party and thought we had landed to deal with them, so being unable to see how few we were and presumably believing the helicopter pilot was observing them, they withdrew from the village! Then, at last, the helicopter landed and bore us safely away. I told the pilot he would remain on the ground at future stops and that one of my officers would 'guard' him and the chopper!

I had a long chat with the Malay CO and told him frankly that there was a considerable antipathy to Malays in the Third Division and that the locals were worried about their comely women receiving unwelcome attention from his soldiers because, rightly or wrongly, Malays had a reputation for womanising. I said that we had had to fight and win the battle for their Hearts and Minds and that as he and his battalion would be the first Malaysian soldiers the Ibans in the Third Division had ever seen, they would have to be scrupulously well behaved. I told him all this in plain language because I genuinely wanted him and his men to succeed and I knew I was being outspoken. He appeared to take this in the spirit in which it was meant and I then asked him for an operational briefing on his battalion area. I did not get a lot from this. I told him to keep his room door locked in Sibu, as the Oily Man was still at large! This was advice based on personal experience. We had had a long atap-roofed hut built on stilts opposite the Officers' Mess. This was divided into seven rooms. I never locked my door so that my early morning tea always reached me without hindrance. One night something woke me and as I lay with moonlight flooding through the window, I heard a click at my door, which slowly opened. The figure of a man noiselessly entered, naked except for a loincloth. He carried in his hand a dagger or knife, the blade of which gleamed in the moon's rays. I lay motionless affecting sleep, but I had to make up my mind like lightning as to what to do as I was unarmed. Suddenly in one movement I sprang out of bed with a roar and went straight for the intruder who was covered in what looked like oil or grease. Probably fortunately for me, he turned and ran straight out of the door and along the wooden catwalk that led between the huts (all of which were on stilts because of the flooding from the tidal River Rajang).

We pounded along, the near naked intruder leading and me, barefoot and in my sarong, flying after him. I was not gaining on him so I bellowed, 'Turn out the Guard!' There was a sudden splash of orange light as the door of the radio room opened and Corporals Skilling and Magee came out, blinded by the change from electric light to darkness. 'Follow me,' I said but by then it was too late. Other people came out, we combed the camp but the Oily Man had vanished. Although the Camp proper was guarded, the Officers' Quarters were not included. Now that the horse had bolted, I took steps to shut the stable door!

Another lesson learned and perhaps I had been lucky. Roger Edwards commanding the police told me years later that although the Oily Man was known about he was never caught. Anyway the Malay Regiment CO said he would see that everyone locked their doors and that the perimeter was properly guarded, and we parted. What I did not anticipate was how bitterly he resented my outspokenness and perhaps also he was smarting at the battalion changeover. But the outcome was that the Malaysian CO sat down and wrote a letter of complaint to the C-in-C of the Malaysian Army, who was then General Tunku Osman. The C-in-C apparently was most upset about the changeover and with my candour. We heard that the C-in-C Far East, Admiral Sir Varyl Begg whom we all liked and respected enormously, had had to spend two days pouring oil on troubled waters. Pat Patterson received a signal expressing displeasure, which I gather concluded with something like, 'Purdon 1 RUR, extremely tactless officer'!

With light hearts we made plans for our move. Pat Patterson had warned me not to try to take over too soon and stressed that I must not do so until I had two rifle companies and battalion Headquarters deployed in the Serian Area.

I sent off my first company, C Company, commanded by Robin Bruford-Davies. Robin had a fine team of officers, all six-footers. David Emmett, later succeeded by Paddy Blake, was his Second-in-Command and his platoon commanders were George Boucher, Niall Ryan, Paddy Doyle and Tony Vosper, all winners and first-class fighting leaders.

Robin moved his company headquarters and one platoon into Tebedu – the scene of previous battles with the Indonesians – and disposed his other two platoons, one to Tepoi – right on the border – and the other to Pang Amo. The very night that Robin had arrived he rang me up and told me some unusual news. A Malaysian General had arrived in Kuching, where a series of cocktail and dinner parties had been laid on in his honour. Every officer in the battalion had pushed off to Kuching including the CO, except for one young subaltern who had just returned from a Signals Course in Malaya and they were not expected back for at least 24 hours! Hoping I could explain matters satisfactorily to my Brigade Commander I flew down with my Headquarters next morning and took command. Fortunately there were no more accusations such as 'extremely tactless officer' and although our hosts were patently surprised to see us on their return, we took over without further acrimony.

We had left behind some very nice and helpful people in the Third Division – the Resident, the police, the Sarawak Police Force, 845 Naval Air Commando Squadron, Naval Party Kilo, Border Scouts and PWD. The local people there were delightful and we felt great affection for them and interest in their future, but action in the First Division beckoned!

CHAPTER EIGHTEEN

THE FIRST DIVISION OF SARAWAK

The Serian area was much different from the wild, jungle-clad area of the Third Division with its rushing rivers and comparative scarcity of population. Here, although there was plenty of jungle and mountains too, it was much more open, with stretches of cultivated land and longer ranges of visibility.

The Indonesian border was very much nearer and enemy incursions frequent. The Royal Green Jackets, commanded by David House, was responsible for the coast to inclusive Bukit Knuckle with Battalion Headquarters at Semengo camp in Kuching. We took over responsibility for the remainder of the border up to the edge of the Second Division. From here 2nd 2nd Gurkha Rifles, commanded by tough, experienced Nicky Neill, dominated the border with their headquarters in Simanggang. I visited both COs to establish contact in our new area and to exchange notes, and then set about getting to know our area, visiting each of my company headquarters and their platoons and going out on patrols, which meant, of course, taking with me the RSM and Lance Corporal Haveron as often as possible!

Sadly, my Adjutant left us. Jeremy Knox had been a tower of strength in Cyprus, BAOR, Australia, Hong Kong and Borneo. Jeremy's successor, Denis Gallwey I have mentioned before. Like Jeremy Knox and Robert Carson he had been in my company in Cyprus where he had been Mentioned in Despatches for gallantry.

I called him 'The Reluctant Adjutant' because he had just come from the Special Air Service Regiment and his only wish was to get stuck into the Indonesians. I tried to persuade him that it would be helpful to his career to get different experience from his new and very important appointment of

Adjutant. Denis heard me out politely, but I could see I had failed to convince him! Despite his preference for a fighting job he did well as Adjutant and I sympathised with his natural wishes for action. Johnnie Johnson had left too; in his place I got Patrick Winter, a big man in every way and always cheerful.

We sent our 'card' over the border from Tebedu, to tell the opposition that the place was under new management and that visitors would be warmly welcomed. Meanwhile, our platoons settled in to their bases and made them strong enough to be held by a section whilst the other two sections were out on aggressive operations, ambushing and harrying the enemy. Each platoon cleared the area around its base so as to get the best possible all round field of fire and to deny the enemy close approach or observation. Wire was put out, low wire entanglements and Dannert-wire barriers, and pits were dug, filled with sharp pointed panjis – needle-ended bamboo stakes, points uppermost. Slit trenches with reinforced overhead cover, Claymore mines and grenade necklaces to cover possible enemy forming-up places completed the preparations.

At night trip flares were positioned which would either be set off by the unsuspecting enemy or controlled from platoon or section headquarters. Aiming and distance marks were put out and targets set up and engaged for practice every day and night.

Our District Officer was a pleasant Malaysian and our police presence in the First Division was less in strength than in the Third Division. Lieutenant Colonel John Cross visited us to see his Border Scouts and to discuss tactics and enemy intelligence. John was another old friend, bubbling with humour, a brilliant linguist who spoke many different tongues and dialects. As always he was full of amusing and interesting stories and quite put us off our dinner with his account of sharing a communal stew in some remote longhouse when he found what looked like a baby's hand in his portion – in fact it had belonged to a monkey!

We were delighted to learn that our old friends Imjin Battery of 45 Field Regiment Royal Artillery, who had supported us no less than eleven times since 1944, the last time in action being Korea – and who had been with us in peacetime less than two years before in BAOR – were to support us yet again. I hope they were as pleased as we were. George Truell an old friend and an Irishman, was the Battery Commander and he lost no time in coming to visit me. Not only were his guns in our support, but he detached one to Tebedu, where it was sandbagged in, inside the police station compound in Robin Bruford–Davies' camp.

Early on I spent a night at Tebedu and it was interesting in the evening at stand-to to see how easily the fireflies that abounded around the perimeter could be mistaken for hand torches, but we had learnt that lesson much earlier on at the Jungle Warfare School. General Walter Walker came to see us and I took him to see Niall Ryan's platoon, then stationed at Tepoi. Niall had been at Sandhurst with one of the General's sons and rather to my surprise, on being introduced to our awe-inspiring Director of Operations said, 'How is he, Sir? Is he still bluffing his way?' However, the General loved it and was much amused by this fine, big, soft-spoken southern Irish boy – one of my very best platoon commanders. It was indeed tragic that after the battalion's return from Borneo, Niall and his great friend Hamish Shaw (son of the gallant Major John Shaw who was killed in action in Korea), and who was another of my 'ace' young officers, should both be killed in a car crash near Bulford. I still think of them. They would have made first class regular battalion commanders had their grand young lives been spared.

We had brought our battalion charwallahs with us from Hong Kong thanks to our excellent contractor Dr Aslam Khattak. Not only had each company headquarters and each platoon their charwallahs but we had a number of them at Battalion Headquarters as well. I used to enjoy discussing the operational situation with my company commanders over a cup of hot, sweet tea and an 'egg banjo' prepared by our faithful camp followers.

Major Bob McGonigal was now commanding Headquarter Company. Bob was a most reliable, conscientious and amusing officer. He suffered badly from very severe migraines but never let them interfere with his work, even though some attacks nearly prostrated him. He was our 'No. 1 Hearts and Minds' winner.

One complete Indonesian village, fed up and disillusioned with the perpetual pilferings and outrages that they were suffering from their own soldiery, decamped and walked *en masse* across the border into our area. Bob quickly obtained marquees, bedding, cooking equipment and food and set up a tented village for them on the banks of a clear, fresh river. I went to see him there, and we stood, politely averting our eyes as a collection of very shapely young Indonesian women sported in the water, each wearing nothing but a slender, coloured belt round her tummy! The British press christened Bob's village 'Kampong McGonigal'.

The remainder of the battalion was based in the camp at Serian from where we lifted them by helicopter to patrol areas remote from platoon bases and to ambush entry points or gaps on the border. It was my policy that all frontier villages were visited frequently and that patrols should often stay nearby overnight, ambushing approaches to the kampong. The morale of the border peoples soared and we started getting more and more information about the enemy. Bill Benson had a very strongly fortified jungle base at Gunan Gajak, with a platoon under Colin Hughes at Plaman Mapu. Plaman Mapu was overlooked by a large jungle-covered mountain called Gunong Rawang. Although its summit was at times covered in mist, we knew that the Indonesians had an observation post up there. It is always an uncomfortable feeling to be watched by the enemy. In our time the post was never attacked and Colin Hughes and his men made it as impregnable as possible. But later on, after we had departed and it had been occupied by various battalions, the post was eventually attacked most gallantly in great strength by some two hundred Indonesians. However, it was defended even more bravely by a small number of soldiers of 2nd Parachute Regiment splendidly led by their CSM, and they successfully beat off the attack inflicting severe casualties on the enemy.

Bill Clements my Regimental Signals Officer had done a fine job in the Third Division in keeping a 24 hour radio link open to all stations even though this had been adjudged by previous units to be difficult, if not impossible, during the small hours. He now set up radio relay stations on high features in the First Division and, once again, we never had to worry about communications. We were always 'through' loud and clear. With closer proximity to the border, our chances of clashes with Indonesian raiders were increased. The enemy had a greater choice of incursion routes whilst the more open terrain favoured quicker movement on foot than in the Third Division.

One village that had received more than its fair share of visits from the Indonesians was Kujang Sain which was situated on a spur jutting into Indonesia. I established a platoon there covering the approaches to the village, with Vickers medium machine guns and a detachment of 81mm mortars. The platoon position had a good field of fire and there was a large, saucer-like depression between it and the hills of Kalimantan opposite. The whole area was covered in jungle but in the saucer there were bushes and thick undergrowth and only a few trees. The presence of this platoon made all the difference to the villagers who ceased to be so jittery and unhappy.

At that time our air support used to insist on us having soldiers physically on the ground before they would fly in troops. This meant that if an incursion took place, and we wished to airlift a cut-off force behind the enemy invaders, the only way to fulfil this requirement was to walk troops in and then to augment them by air! We just did not have the time to do this. I discussed this with my Brigade Commander, whose reaction was to allocate to me, virtually permanently, a Scout helicopter of the Army Air Corps. I had some excellent pilots flying our 'battalion chopper' and the one who was mostly with us was Staff Sergeant, later WOI, Hall, formerly of the Royal Welch Fusiliers. He was a superb pilot and, as he had been an infantryman, he and I were 'on the same net'.

One day we had news of a suspected incursion and I decided to fly a platoon in to a particular spot right by the border. When I asked for helicopters to fly in my platoon we were told as usual that we had to have troops on the ground first! It was quite impossible to get anyone on foot in time so I took with me Brian Gallagher and one other Battalion Headquarters officer – I think it was Jeremy Knox – and L/Cpl. Haveron, and S/Sgt. Hall flew us into the place where I had decided to place my ambushing force when it arrived. At the same time, my Second-in-Command had confirmed to the air authorities that there would be troops on the ground to protect their arrival with our air-lifted platoons.

I flew in with my scout party, landed and took the opportunity of having a good look around while the remainder of the small party kept a look out. Then came the sound of helicopter engines and the 'choppers' appeared. I had rehearsed my henchmen and we took it in turns to appear from various bushes and pieces of undergrowth, rifles in hand, and successfully gave the impression that we had a platoon on the ground already! Meanwhile Staff Sergeant Hall was circling around, keeping an eye on the border approaches. The first helicopter landed its load of men and lumbered away, and the next did likewise. After I had personally briefed the platoon commander, who then positioned his men, Staff Sergeant Hall returned and flew me and my 'ground holders' away. This was no way to win a war! This difficulty was overcome as the squadron became used to working with us, thanks mainly to their new squadron commander who, I believe, later was awarded a Distinguished Flying Cross. I used to fly with a box of primed 36 grenades at my feet and Staff Sergeant Hall nobly put up with this whim of mine. On our way to and from our daily round of visits we used to fly over likely looking areas and he would part the tree tops with the wash of his rotor blade so we could see if there were any enemy below to be able to bomb them. Looking back on it, perhaps it was just as well there were none.

One afternoon I heard over the radio that our platoon at Kujang Sain was engaging the enemy. Staff Sergeant Hall and I, with Brian Gallagher armed with a GPMG as passenger, were airborne and on our way there in no time and we landed near the platoon. There was a terrific noise of Vickers gunfire and the barks and crumps of the 81mm mortar. The platoon commander was a young Belfast subaltern, Nigel Taggart, who was clearly enjoying himself, as were the beaming Pipe Major Andy Wilson BEM, and the rest of the platoon. Nigel briefed me at the top of his voice on what was happening. The firing stopped but we continued our conversation, Nigel still bawling at me at the full extent of his lungs and vocal chords until I drew his attention to the fact that I was not deaf and I could hear him loud and clear! Nigel had inflicted casualties on the enemy.

However, he told me that there were still some enemy in the saucer-like area between him and the border and he was unable to reach them with either his 81mm or 2 inch mortars. He and Pipe Major Wilson and Lance Corporal Morrison indicated the area in which the Indonesians were concealed, so Brian and I returned to the Scout. Brian already had a belt of ammunition on the GPMG and I took out some grenades. Staff Sergeant Hall and I had discussed my aerial hand grenade bombing before, as we wanted to be sure that the explosion of the grenades did not blow off our tail rotor. We also wanted to be sure we hit our target. As the Scout got airborne I indicated where the raiders were to Staff Sergeant Hall. Brian poked the barrel of the 'Jimpy' out of the window, close behind my head. I pulled out the pin from a grenade and Staff Sergeant Hall brought in the Scout low and fast. I had asked him to shout 'Now' when we were at the correct distance from the enemy's position whilst I had my hand out of the window holding the grenade, pin removed.

'Now', he yelled. I let go of the 36 grenade, whilst Brian was firing the GPMG to keep the raiders' heads down. We were swinging round for our next pass when we heard, and felt, the explosion of my first grenade. We repeated our grenade attacks several times, the spent cases from Brian's GPMG striking me and Staff Sergeant Hall on the head and neck as the machine gun chattered away. I was satisfied that we had hit our target successfully and we landed to see what Nigel and his platoon had to say. 'Spot on Sir!' grinned Lance Corporal Morrison. 'Well done, Sir!' said Nigel. So the next thing to do was to get to the spot to see if we could find any dead or wounded enemy. Nigel gave me a corporal and four riflemen and we squeezed them all into the Scout.

Daylight was fading as we flew to our erstwhile target in the saucer, got to a piece of bare ground nearby and disembarked the men. We hovered by ready to support them by fire. They searched the bushes and then headed towards the border. They returned to the base after daylight had gone. They had found no bodies on the spot but had followed heavy bloodstains which led towards and across the border. We learnt later that we had killed and wounded some of the enemy but that whilst we were emplaning our patrol, the enemy had dragged their dead and wounded the remaining few hundred yards into Indonesia. This was their normal form. They tried never to leave their dead or wounded behind. The enemy never returned to Kujang Sain during our time in Sarawak. Nigel and his platoon had done well.

My battalion were working like Trojans and I wanted to ensure they got some time off in which to enjoy themselves, relax and recharge their batteries. I asked Mike Estridge to find a place where our R and R (Rest and Recuperation) parties could have a short leave. He found a large house in Kuching which had its own swimming pool and garden. I decided to fly out a platoon at a time for ten days R and R, and I gave out my orders for it.

A bar would be set up in the leave camp, also a cinema room with the latest films and a games room including table tennis, while a volleyball court was made in the garden. The platoon was free to go anywhere within bounds in Kuching and they could drink all that they wanted provided they did so in the house bar. However, if even one man got drunk outside our R and R centre, I would fly the whole platoon immediately back into the jungle. This arrangement worked admirably and gave the hard-worked jungle platoons something to look forward to, and it resulted in them returning to operations alert and refreshed. Mike Estridge ensured that each member of the platoon was fed really well and housed in comfort.

We regularly had ambushes right on the Indonesian border, and one morning I heard that one of my men, Rifleman Sherman, had been shot through the body. Obviously that particular ambush had now been 'blown', so we had to get Sherman out and withdraw the ambush. The new squadron leader had the endearing habit of invariably himself piloting any helicopter engaged in anything that could be a 'dicey' mission and I was glad, and not a bit surprised, to see him grinning down at me as I got into the helicopter accompanied by Ken Rooke our MO, with the party to recover Sherman. By the time we reached the ambush position the section there had chopped down sufficient trees to make space for our helicopter to land, and had then taken up positions for all round defence. Fortunately the enemy had not reacted and we got Sherman on to the stretcher and into the helicopter.

Ken Rooke made him comfortable and examined and treated him as we flew back to Serian. Rifleman Sherman and I were old friends; he had been one of my recruits at the Depot and so I had known him from the day he joined the Army. I saw him looking at me rather worriedly so I bent over him and said 'Can I give you my word you're going to make a quick and complete recovery, Sherman?' He grinned up at me whitefaced, 'How can you be so sure, Sir?' he asked. 'Because the good Lord only takes the good lads', I answered, 'They're not ready for you in Heaven yet!' I am happy to say that Sherman did indeed make a quick and complete recovery. I used to drive into Kuching on Sundays to visit him and any of our sick who were in the RAMC hospital there and I was relieved to see that his health and fitness and the clean wound, enabled him to return to his platoon fit and strong, and with his own 'war story'.

But tragedy was waiting for us again and we lost a wonderful young rifleman through an accidental discharge. A member of his platoon was showing off in front of some local girls met near a village, during a break in patrol, pretending to shoot his friend to make the girls laugh. The rifleman was horrified when his rifle proved to be loaded, and his friend, fell, grievously wounded. Our devoted doctor worked through the night helping the hospital doctors and staff to try to save the life of this popular young soldier, who died with a smile on his face. I had not seen doctors cry before.

We had been alerted to carry out cross-border operations. These had to be particularly carefully planned and secretly executed. I accompanied the first one and joined Niall Ryan's C Company platoon on a mission to look at a suspected enemy camp. As we had not far to go we travelled light, just carrying our personal weapons and ammunition, field dressings, filled water bottles and a snack to eat – Mars Bars, raisins and biscuits. The need for stealth and secrecy was stressed. Our men were longing to meet the opposition, confident in their fitness and professional skills as soldiers. We halted by the Border, concealed, for a final check and then crossed into enemy territory. When we reached our objective, Niall sent out parties to encircle the enemy camp and we carefully closed in on it, and entered.

It was empty. On the trees were carved the initials of the enemy regiment and various Indonesian slogans, while on the ground lay empty Indonesian Army ration tins and papers. Leaving a small party to search the camp and others to guard its approaches, three of us went on to see if we could find any other enemy traces. On our return, we entered the camp and prepared to move off. To my horror I saw that carved on top of the Indonesian slogans on the trees were various Irish slogans such as 'up the Irish' and 'RUR'! Time was passing, and we hurriedly tried to scrape out all our misguided riflemen's signs before we had to leave. I could see in my mind's eye the World Press saying that The Royal Ulster Rifles had crossed into Indonesia, and I devoutly hoped that we had left no traces of our visit. That night the guns of Imjin Battery bombarded the enemy camp! Next morning a helicopter sortie proved that the place where the camp had been was now a rubbish heap of torn vegetation, and tossed-about trees. To my relief, the evidence of our first cross-border visit had gone!

We kept getting warnings of an impending incursion by a large group – one hundred to two hundred was quoted – of Indonesian regulars, but we had no idea of their objective. We kept up our patrolling of our villages near the border and practised again and again the helicopter-borne movement of our standby force. We would be as ready as possible when the time came.

The Press continued to visit us. Some reporters promised to send photographs and newspaper cuttings describing their time with our battalion, but few of them did so. However, one man we all took to our hearts was Brian Woosey of the 'Sun'; that was before the 'Sun' became a tabloid paper. He fitted into our battalion way of life and we made sure that he saw anything and everything he wanted. When he left he even wrote to the Director of Army Public Relations to say how well he had been looked after by the

Royal Ulster Rifles and we received a charming letter of thanks from Major General the Viscount Monckton. Brian sent us a lot of cuttings and photographs and we always looked upon him as an ideal war correspondent from the fighting soldier's point of view.

In B Company, Denis Lucy's four subalterns, like himself, had all had fathers in the Regiment – 'Tander' Shooter, Sean Estridge, Donald Mitchell and Roger Wheeler. Roger was already showing the exceptional qualities which have led to his rise to the highest positions in the Army.

At Nibong, in Denis Lucy's area, an explosion occurred in an underground ammunition bunker where white phosphorous and 36 grenades were stored. Without regard for their personal safety, Sergeant (later WOII) Kelly and L/Cpl. (now Major) Gordon Muir MBE entered the bunker and carried out all the boxes of grenades despite the exploding of more phosphorous grenades. As a result of their gallantry, Lance Corporal Muir received the Queen's Commendation for Brave Conduct but Sergeant Kelly, sadly, got nothing although recommended.

Major General Peter Hunt, GOC 17th Gurkha Division, came to visit us and spent the night. This quiet, large man emanated confidence and friendliness and we were all glad to see him. Colour Sergeant Fay looked after him personally and the General told me that Willie Fay even solicitously placed a full bottle of whiskey by the side of his bed. The GOC wondered if he had been expected to consume it all overnight!

I had my own 'bathroom' in Serian camp. This consisted of a small atap-walled and atap-roofed compartment in which, on a ledge, was an aluminium washhand basin and shaving mirror. A large burmail (oil drum) which was kept filled with fresh rain water daily stood on the floor with a plastic dipper beside it and you bathed by standing, stripped, on duckboards by the burmail and sloshing water over yourself with the dipper. You then soaped yourself all over and then sloshed on more fresh rain water to remove the lather. It was a refreshing way to end the day when I came in from the jungle and thankfully got out of my sodden green uniform.

One day I came back, tired, dirty and sweaty, to find that one of our boffin visitors from Whitehall, a colonel on the technical side, had, uninvited, helped himself to my bathroom. To add insult to injury I found him, not washing beside the burmail but actually inside it, up to his neck in the fresh water, which was all soapy with his beastly suds. There was no water left for me. I reminded myself with difficulty of the need to be the perfect host, and of the strange workings of the technical mind!

We acquired numerous pets in Borneo, each platoon having its quota of dogs, monkeys, birds and lizards. We had been presented, whilst in the Third Division, with a bear cub which was christened with the Regimental nickname of Sticky and Mike Estridge took it into his care. I decided we would present it to Belfast Zoo and eventually Sticky ended up there and proved a popular attraction. We were also given another unusual pet by the Ibans, a Rhinoceros Hornbill, which we called Fitch after the first commanding officer of the 83rd Foot and I decided to offer Fitch to Dublin Zoo. Fitch adored raw eggs in their shells. He lived next door to my bathroom in Serian and became a favourite of mine. I used to hand him an egg which he would take, toss into the air, catch, and align to his satisfaction is his great beak. He would then allow it to roll down the two outside edges of his lower bill, rather like a truck down a railway line. Crack! his mighty beak broke it open and the contents, mostly, went down his gullet but invariably left some yellow yolk untidily drooling from his bill. After I had left the Battalion poor old Fitch died for no apparent reason so I never saw him again.

Whilst in the First Division I had a company of Gurkhas permanently under command. One day Major Harkasing Rai, who already had the MC and Bar, and his company of 1st 6th Gurkha Rifles, were in position near Tepoi, where Lieutenant Paddy Doyle and his platoon were also sited, covering the track leading to the village. Two of the village women were our working in an area of hill padi close to the border when a group of Indonesian soldiers contacted them and asked them what security forces were in Tepoi, to which they replied that there were none. The Indonesian commander told them that he and his men would visit their village that night.

Major Harkasing Rai was informed and arranged for a string of tins to be stretched from the longhouse to his position, and Paddy Doyle and his Royal Ulster Rifles 11 Platoon, got ready to welcome the self-invited guests.

The Indonesian party did enter the village that night and following some shouting in the village Harky got his signals on the tins. After a judicious pause he fired a flare and the surprised Indonesians ran down a track beside which, on a steep hill on the other side of the river, Corporal Deignan and his section of 11 Platoon were dug in. At the thud of running feet Corporal Deignan ignited two flares which illuminated four enemy raiders. Corporal Deignan and his section opened fire killing one Indonesian soldier. The other three enemy took cover, and replied with an LMG and rifles. They then bravely tried to recover the body of their fallen comrade, but with the aid of flares and controlled bursts of fire from his GPMG gunner, Corporal Deignan and his section kept the enemy pinned down all night.

When daylight came three enemy lay dead on the track. Our 105mm howitzer from Tebedu was also in action firing shells along the Indonesian main party's likely withdrawal route and we learnt later that as a result of this, more of the raiders had been killed and wounded. I flew into the position shortly after first light to be greeted by a jubilant Paddy Doyle and Platoon, and by Corporal Deignan and his particularly exuberant section. The Riflemen were a bit taken aback when some of the women of the village danced on the dead bodies. As had been the case after our successful action at Kunjang Sain, Tepoi was never attacked again during the time our battalion was in the First Division.

By now my time in command was coming to an end and I felt very, very sad at the thought of leaving my wonderful battalion. We had done a lot together – we had been a mechanised battalion in Germany, an airportable battalion in England and Australia, culminating in our final, and most satisfying task of being an operational jungle battalion in war. I knew every officer, warrant officer, NCO and Rifleman. They were my friends and I dreaded having to leave them.

However, I knew I would be handing them over to an experienced successor in Lieutenant Colonel Hugh Hamill who had been our Adjutant in Korea and a company commander in BAOR. He was known to all ranks, and was liked and respected. Hugh arrived and I took him round all the company and platoon locations. A number of these visits were by helicopter.

At the same time as Hugh said his 'Hellos' I said my farewells to everyone. This I found very hard, more especially when old friends took me by the hand and said, 'We hate to see you go, Sir'. Hugh said, when we got out of the Scout, 'Corran, I turned round and saw your face after you had been saying your goodbyes, I know how you must be feeling.' When the day came for my departure, Lance Corporal Vernor my driver, drove me away from Headquarters Camp in Serian, through lines of cheering, waving riflemen of all ranks. Lance Corporal Haveron was in the back seat of the Landrover.

'Put your foot down, Corporal Vernor', I said as I wanted to get this emotional send-off over quickly while I was still outwardly composed. On our arrival at Kuching Airport, I was 'hijacked' by David House and Edwards Jones, his large, high calibre Adjutant, son of General Sir Charles Jones. Before I went out to board the aircraft from Singapore, I was handed the following message from General Walker:

'From D of Ops. On relinquishing command of your white Gurkhas I would like you to know that you and your distinguished battalion have exceeded my expectations and added great renown to your already high reputation. Thank you for everything. Bon Voyage and best wishes for the future. I rely on you to spread the gospel in the UK.'

As I walked out on to the airfield, the way to the aircraft was lined with members of our Sergeant's Mess, and Pipe Major Andy Wilson played the

Regimental March and 'Lieutenant Colonel Purdon's Farewell to Sarawak'. I found I could not speak. I waved through the window of the Argosy, then the aircraft rolled forward, gathered speed and we whirled up into the air. I looked at a note pressed into my hand whilst I had said my farewells. It was from ORQMS (later Captain) Tommy McCombe.

> 'Sir, Herewith a copy of your 'Special Order of the Day' and your last Part 1 Order. As I write this you will have left only a matter of hours but already there is a very noticeable sadness on everyone's face around Battalion Headquarters. We have a definite feeling, that sort which comes when one has suffered a great loss.

I do pray that you have a safe, although I am sure it will be a most sad and lonely journey, Sir.

T. McC. ORQMS
4th Oct. '64'

CHAPTER NINETEEN

CHIEF INSTRUCTOR (GSO1) & OC ALL ARMS TACTICAL DIVISION SCHOOL OF INFANTRY, WARMINSTER

I spent my first night away from my battalion in Singapore, staying with Colonel Bill Brooks and his wife Elizabeth. The Brooks had been so kind to me and my officers during our tour in the Far East. Bill was Colonel 'Q' at GHQ and we had enjoyed his too brief stay with us in Hong Kong. Another good friend in the Regiment was staying with them, Sam Sturgeon the North Irish Brigade Colonel. In their cheerful company, I found myself unwinding and relaxing, with the sadness at leaving the battalion easing thanks to them.

Next day I flew back to Royal Air Force Brize Norton where Patricia and Angela, our daughter, met me. Patricia had had the vital task of looking after our wives and families during our time abroad and, as I knew she would, had kept them all happy and calm. Before we left for the Far East I had talked to our Wives' Club and explained to them the paramount importance of their husbands being able to concentrate entirely on their operational task. If they had family worries and their minds were in any way taken off the job of killing the enemy, of avoiding walking into an ambush, of looking after their comrades, this would not be helping their husbands to return safely to them. I asked them to go and discuss any serious problems with Patricia and Mrs Cardwell, the RSM's wife, before writing about their worries to their husbands. If they were unable to help, Patricia would contact me and I would do my utmost to solve the problem. But at all costs their menfolk must be left able to concentrate wholeheartedly on their military task.

These grand girls played up brilliantly and although I know Patricia was kept very busy, we only had one compassionate problem during the whole

of our time abroad, and that was unavoidable. I sent the NCO concerned –
he was attached to the battalion – home by air immediately and his son's
serious illness was happily cured not long after his return.

On my return to England I went round all the wives to give them first-
hand news of their husbands. One of them, a Corporal's wife, was an old
friend whom I will call Mrs McIlhagga. She had just burnt down her
second Army quarter! As she bade me goodbye, with a cackle of laughter
she said, 'Sure when Alfie's back, Colonel darling, him and me'll ask ye to
our next housewarming!'

I had been originally informed that I was to be Assistant Military
Secretary MS5 at the Ministry of Defence but this had been changed and I
had now been appointed to succeed Lieutenant Colonel Jack Harman,
Queen's Dragoon Guards, as Chief Instructor (GSO1) and Officer Commanding the All Arms Battle Group Tactical Division (AAD) at the School
of Infantry, Warminster in Wiltshire. Jackie Harman was a brilliant officer
and obviously destined for the highest places in the Army. He was going
off to command a brigade in Germany and he left me a high-powered team
of DS (Directing Staff). These officers were representatives of all the
major fighting Arms – Hugh Browne, a Sapper; John Painter, a Gunner
who had been in the 60th Rifles and SAS; Robin Handley, King's Shropshire Light Infantry; Colin Gardiner, Royal Anglian Regiment; David
Ranft, Royal Signals; and Bentley McLeod, Black Watch of Canada. Later
John Fowles succeeded Hugh Browne; Bill Harrington, Royal Australian
Regiment succeeded Bentley McLeod our Canadian Exchange Officer;
and David Houston, Royal Irish Fusiliers, took over from Robin Handley.

They were a high-spirited, forceful, enthusiastic and energetic team and
worked wonderfully well together. The courses all seemed very popular
and much enjoyed by the students who said they got a great deal out of
them. The courses lasted for six weeks and were designed to train the
students to command a combat team of all Arms. We used to have
infantrymen and other non-armoured officers commanding armoured squadrons, armoured troops and individual tanks; non-infantrymen commanding
infantry companies, platoons and sections; non-gunners commanding artillery batteries and troops; and so on. By the end of the course, students
had practical experience of handling other Arms as well as their own, using
the Demonstration Battalion and armoured squadron of the School and our
affiliated battery and engineer troop from Larkhill and Chatham respectively, during our practical field exercises. Of course there were lectures,
films, presentations, cloth model exercises and TEWTs as well, and we
tried to conduct studies in a relaxed manner.

My predecessor, Jackie Harman, had done away with gradings on
students, which had removed tension, and I continued with this practice.

We merely wrote reports as to how the students got on, for the benefit of their commanding officers. I never ceased to be amazed and delighted by the standard of presentation produced by my DS. So much was put across in the simplest and clearest way, with lots of humour and flair. They took the 'mickey' out of everyone, and this included me. I have always had my leg pulled because of my keenness on physical fitness and my feelings can be imagined when, during my first course with the AAD, a slide was flashed on the overhead projector, showing the figure of a man in bathing trunks doing press-ups over a curvaceous female who was lying on her back, bikini-clad on a beach. The beautiful girl is saying, 'Colonel, would you mind going somewhere else to do your press-ups!' A photograph of my grinning face had been substituted for that of the press-up man!

We ran a number of courses for foreign and Commonwealth students on which we appear to have trained the moving spirits in several coups, Uganda and Sierra Leone in particular!

It was our aim to keep up-to-date in all our teaching. There were two campaigns going on, one in Borneo, the other in Aden and the Radfan. Also British forces formed part of the United Nations Contingent on operations in Cyprus (UNFICYP). So by visits to these operational areas we ensured that we had up-to-date presentations supported by films and slides in order that those of our students who had not served there would know what to expect if they were posted to any of these places.

After six months I sent out two of my DS to Borneo whilst John Painter and I went to visit our troops in Aden and the Radfan. We went out on operations with Tim Creasy's battalion of the Royal Anglian Regiment in Aden, including a night in The Crater, and later we visited the Coldstream Guards at Habilayn. We stayed at Dhala and spent a night with a company of the Parachute Regiment at Al Dibna. There was enemy activity around our base that night and a 105mm howitzer of the Parachute Regiment Royal Horse Artillery was in action from our little fort for several hours. At first light John and I went out with the Paras' clearance patrol but found no enemy. On our return John wrote an excellent presentation. We also saw our old friends from BAOR, the 10th Hussars. Before we left Aden we had a bathe inside the shark net on the beach and a shark got in through a hole. I was standing up to my waist chatting to the AAG GHQ Middle East, Tony Dyball in my Regiment, when I felt something whip past my legs so close that if felt like a blow although it had failed to touch me. I didn't like to comment because Tony went on talking but shortly afterwards there was a cry of 'Shark!' and we were all made to vacate the bathing place.

I took quite a large team with me to update ourselves on what was going on in BAOR and I was lucky in being put up by our sister Regiment, 1st Royal Irish Fusiliers who made us most welcome and took us out on their exercises.

I learnt such a lot as Chief Instructor as when you have to teach you certainly have to learn! I used to work very hard in the evening preparing for the next day, and kept fit by exercises and by running for miles over the wonderful Imber Training Area, thereby getting to know it well.

One day a friend of mine in MS rang me up to tell me that I had been selected for accelerated promotion to brigadier and that I would shortly be leaving for my next job. Two of my friends were also being promoted and later we were summoned to Brigadier Tony Arengo-Jones, OBE, the Commandant, and told our news. Tommy Lamb of the Queen's Own Highlanders was to be a full colonel at HQ Scotland and Peter Litton, a GSO1 at School Headquarters, was off to command 99 Gurkha Brigade. My job was not revealed but one evening Tommy and Peter appeared on my doorstep in Oxendene demanding drinks, dressed as Arabs and accompanied by their wives! They told me that I had been selected to command the Sultan's Armed Forces in Oman. I handed over my job to that experienced Highland soldier and Alamein veteran, Tony Lithgow, of the Black Watch and set off to attend a six weeks Arabic Course in London. This was to be followed by the necessary briefings at the Ministry of Defence.

CHAPTER TWENTY

COMMANDER SULTAN'S ARMED FORCES –
FIRST IMPRESSIONS

I stood behind the pilot as the huge Beverley swooped down, rapidly losing height, towards the tiny airfield. The far end of the airfield was separated by a wire perimeter fence from a dusty road along which I could see a string of camels and, beyond them, a castellated, round-turretted white fort.

On either side, the aircraft's wings seemed almost to brush the harsh grey rocky hills between whose narrow defile we were swooping in to land. A small group of figures outside some low buildings looked up at us, then with a roar we had flashed over. The wheels of the aircraft were on the tarmac and the thunder of reversed engines filled my ears as we stopped in a great swirl of dust short of the airfield perimeter wire. The Beverley turned ponderously round, slowly taxied back towards the control tower building and drew to a halt. We had arrived at Bait-al-Falaj, Headquarters of the Sultan's Armed Forces in the Sultanate of Oman.

My mind went back to the time, a few months before, when Pat Winter, who had been my second-in-command during the latter part of the Borneo campaign and was now in the Military Secretary's Department at the Ministry of Defence, had telephoned to congratulate me on being selected to command the Sultan's Armed Forces in Oman. Pat had told me that not only was I to have accelerated promotion but, what was even more exciting, I was to command a Force which at that time consisted of a brigade of infantry, with its own artillery and supporting services, an air force, and a tiny navy, and with a war on its hands in the province of Dhofar. I had had briefings at the Ministry of Defence, helpful and informative letters from Tony Lewis from whom I was taking over, and from Trevor Alexander who had been a fellow student with me at the Army Staff College in Camberley and who was now commanding the Muscat Regiment in Dhofar. I had studied Arabic for six intensive weeks and had managed to pass my colloquial examination at the end of it, but with a sneaking feeling that the Board had bent over backwards to enable me to do so! I had come out on my own so as to really devote myself to getting fully into my job before Patricia and Angela, joined me to make our new home in Bait-al-Falaj.

The ramp in the tail of the Beverley was lowered and blazing white sunlight filled the rear of the aircraft revealing the dusty airstrip outside. I was invited to alight and found a group of people standing close by. A tall, powerfully-built man with a commanding presence, clipped moustache and thinning hair, shook me firmly by the hand and said, 'Welcome to Muscat. I'm Pat Waterfield. So I met for the first time the man who, misnamed the Military Secretary, was in effect Minister of Defence of the Sultanate. He is a man whom I firmly believe has never received the credit for what he had achieved in Oman during the difficult days before the discovery of oil brought its present wealth and prosperity to that fascinating country which I grew to love so much.

Next to Pat Waterfield was a good-looking, lean, sunburnt man in a blue shirt and khaki drill trousers, with intensely blue eyes, fair hair and a charming smile. He was Tony Lewis the highly decorated wartime Commando leader from whom I was to take over. I knew of Tony's gallant reputation although we had been in different Commandos.

The third member of the group was of medium height, had short, grizzled hair and moustache, was deeply tanned and had the kindest expression. This was Colin Maxwell, ten years older than me, beloved of Arabs, Baluch and British alike, who was to be my Deputy, friend and adviser in the three eventful years ahead. The stocky, smiling man in khaki drill uniform and pale blue service cap whom I met next was Squadron Leader Brian Entwistle, Commander of the Sultan of Oman's Air Force.

We walked through a small flat-roofed building, where customs officers wearing white disha-dashas shook my hand, and out to where some sand-coloured Landrovers were waiting and brown-faced, smiling, black-moustached, lean soldiers wearing red berets and khaki drill uniforms hurried forward to shake my hand and take my kit.

As we drove off in a cloud of dust we came to the gateway to the Headquarters where smart sentries presented arms. We passed the great fort, white in the brilliant, hot, morning sunlight, with the red flag of the Sultanate hanging listlessly from a white-painted pole on one of the round turrets. Some dark green, dusty trees gave shade beside the fort, next to which were buildings which Tony Lewis pointed out to me as the former donkey lines, the hospital and, beyond them, the mosque.

The Landrover swung right where, on high ground above us, were two bungalows, one of which – the nearer – was Brian Entwistle's and the larger one belonged to Pat and Madeleine Waterfield. We turned left and I saw three bungalows on high ground to our front. The one on the left, Tony told me, was where the Force Senior Electrical Officer, Eddie Bailey, lived. the one on the right was the home of the Assistant Military Secretary, Colonel Louis Sanderson, and his wife Joyce, and in the middle, with a deep, shaded verandah, its pillars bright with red bougainvillea and white flowering jasmine, stood our future home. Although it looked rather like two shoe boxes joined together at the ends, I found that it was wonderfully cool and airy inside, the bedrooms had air-conditioners and all the rooms had ceiling punkah fans.

British associations with Oman date back to 1798 when a treaty was signed between Oman and the East India Company and there has been close friendship between the two countries ever since. Britain assisted in the ejection of the Saudi incursion to the Buraimi Oasis in the mid-1950s. This was followed by British support in putting down the rebellion of 1958-1959 which was led against the Sultan by Imam Ghalib, his brother Talib, and Suleiman bin Himyaar, self-styled Lord of the Green Mountain. It was during and after this war, now referred to as the Jebal Akhdar Campaign that the secondment of British Officers and NCOs started, with Colonel David Smiley, a distinguished fighting officer, as the first Commander Sultan's Forces. David Smiley, formerly of the Royal Horse Guards, ex-Commando, ex-SAS, has had a fascinating, colourful life and is the author of interesting books on his experiences in Albania, the Yemen and Thailand.

Oman is situated at the south east corner of the Arabian Peninsula from where part of it dominates the southern entrance to the Arabian Gulf at the Straits of Hormuz, Oman's northernmost tip. This is the mountainous bare Mussandam peninsula which is divided from the rest of Oman by the Union of Arab Emirates. Separated from Mussandam by the states of Ras al Khaimah and Fujairah, Oman begins again at Assouad on the Batinah coast, a green, fertile strip varying from three miles to thirty miles broad, where fruit and vegetables grow in abundance and fishermen thrive, and which stretches to just south of Sib. Behind the Batinah coast curves the great mountain crescent of the Hajar Range, dominated by the Jebal Akhdar which overlooks Oman's ancient capital of Nizwa and its huge, drum-shaped fort. Its highest feature is Jebel as Shams, the Mountain of the Sun, which is over 11,000 feet high.

Polly Lewis, Tony's attractive and vivacious wife, and Emily, their daughter, made me feel welcome immediately and took me in to breakfast.

This was a social meal in Oman, where work started at 5.30am and stopped from 9am to 10am for breakfast. It was an occasion for fresh fruit and cereals, fish, sausages, bacon and eggs, toast and marmalade, tea or coffee.

Later Tony took me over to the Fort to meet the officers. John Crompton of the Worcesters was the Brigade Major; my old friend Tony Adams, Royal Warwickshire Regiment was DAA and QMG; Mike Legg, Queen's Regiment was the GS03 and Tim Herbert, Royal Welch Fusiliers and John Randel, a Sapper, were the Staff Captains 'A' and 'Q' respectively. There was a team of British NCOs. The Confidential Clerk was Bombardier Davis, RA, while Sergeant Spencer of the Grenadiers and Sergeant (later Captain) Beeley, Royal Tanks, worked on the Intelligence side. The GS02 Intelligence, Tony Wallerstein, Royal Tanks, was in the process of handing over to Michael Aris, Royal Anglian Regiment.

The Force Intelligence Officer was Malcolm Denison (relative of the actor), who had been badly wounded in the Jebel Akhdar Campaign. The Garrison Commander was Richard Anderson, rotund, charming, a lover of books, silver and glass, explosive-tempered but generous to a fault, whose imperturbability under fire was a byword. His girth had led to his being nicknamed 'Major Drum' by the men of the Baluch Guard Regiment under his command.

I then met some of the Arab and Baluch officers who were to be my comrades in arms for the next three years. The most senior was 'The Captain Sahib', Captain (later Major) Aziz Ur Rahman, OBI, MBE, Sardar Bahadur, tall, spare and eagle-faced who, after a lifetime in the old Indian Army had continued his military career in the service of Sultan Said bin Taimur. I also met his second-in-command, Lieutenant Shinoon Obeid, another stalwart, and my Chief Clerk, Niaz Ahmed Khan, who proved to be delightful, hardworking and loyal.

The Pakistani clerks seemed friendly and effective and I looked forward to serving with them all. Already Oman had captivated me, whether it was old memories of my early boyhood in India or just the sheer fascination of the place.

As soon as the Lewis's had departed, I got down to visiting my units in order to get to know everyone under my command, and the country for whose security we were responsible. My first visit was to Dhofar, the operational theatre, to have my initial audience with the Sultan, His Highness Said bin Taimur who resided there, and to spend a week on operations with the Muscat Regiment in order to get the feel of the war.

The Headquarters of the Sultan's Armed Forces was located at Bait-al-Falaj about 20 minutes' drive from Muscat the capital. Here also were located the Force Artillery, MT, Signals, Ordnance, EME Workshops, Hospital, and part of the Guard Regiment, the various Messes and Lines,

Guard Room and sportsfields, the Force Mosque, as well as, about a quarter of a mile away, the offices of the Defence Department. The other units comprising the Army component were the Muscat Regiment, currently on operations in Dhofar with its Battalion Headquarters in Umm al Ghawarif Camp near the capital Salalah; the Northern Frontier Regiment with Headquarters at Nizwa in Northern Oman; a Company at Saiq on top of the Jebal Akhdar and a Company further north at Ibri. NFR was commanded by Hugh Sanders, Royal Berkshires, an Australian who had been at Staff College with me, but Mike Harvey of the Gloucesters was about to take over.

The Desert Regiment which had been very recently formed, under Brian Barnes, a tough, dark Irish Guardsman, was stationed at Bid Bid, with a company at Izki situated at the northern end of the Wadi Sumail. This was on the road past the Jebal Akhdar (Green Mountain) that led to Nizwa and beyond, and with another company guarding an approach to the Green Mountain at Rostaq.

The all-Arab Oman Gendarmerie (OG) was the other major unit. this is now called the Oman Coast Regiment and is a normal infantry battalion but at that time the unit, although of battalion strength, had the role of frontier protection. Its headquarters was at Sib on the coast north of Muscat, with a troop at Sohar which was also on the coast; a troop further north at Khatma Milaha on the eastern border; another at Assuad near the eastern border; another in the village of Buraimi; a troop at Sumaini and another at Qabil. The officers, who at that time were all British, came mainly from former Colonial Police Forces. The redoubtable Graham Vivian, MC and Bar, late 2nd Gurkha Rifles was one of the only ex-Army officers in the OG, which was commanded by cheerful Colonel Tony Best, a former Assistant Commissioner of Police in Tanganyika. Tony had commanded an African battalion in Burma in the Second World War.

SOAF, the Sultan of Oman's Air Force, was clearly effective and its piston-engined Provosts and Beavers were flown by a splendid collection of young pilots, some seconded regular Royal Air Force officers and others contract officers who had formerly served in the RAF. Throughout the Force, in the Army, Air Force and Navy, there were Regular and Contract officers in all units. SOAF kept part of its strike and transport force down at Salalah where they were engaged in supporting the ground forces in the Dhofar War. The remainder were stationed at Bait-al-Falaj to carry out training, 'show the flag', transport duties and liaison flights in Northern Oman. I was impressed with the calibre of the pilots who were all to prove themselves gallant in action in the ground attack role in Dhofar and steady and reliable as Beaver pilots, landing on some amazingly short and bumpy strips all over the country.

Finally, the embryo Navy, which was then styled the Coastal Patrol and which consisted of two armed motorised dhows. Between them, these could carry a battalion's worth of infantry. Their Commander was Jeremy Raybould, a large, powerfully-built man who was to earn a reputation both for skill as a seaman and for great physical bravery. One dhow was usually on coastal patrol in the northern waters to counter incursion from Iraq, smuggling and illegal entry and the other, in non-monsoon months, supported operations in Dhofar. The dhows could not operate off Dhofar during the monsoon.

Inland of the Hajar range a gravel desert stretches to the borders of the Union of Arab Emirates and includes Oman's oilfields at Fahud. Muscat lies in the foothills of the Hajar range, beyond it is the province of Sharqiya and further inland is the rolling red sand sea of the Empty Quarter, the Rub'al Khali. To the south is the Province of Dhofar, the land of frankincense, where the waves of the ocean break thunderously on the white beaches in front of its capital, Salalah, fringed by high, dark green palms beyond which stretches the flat Salalah plain. Dominating the Salalah plain is a three thousand foot massif that stretches to the border of South Yemen and here, among steep, precipitous wadis and green rolling uplands, among tangled, thorn-dotted, twisted-lava hillsides, backed inland by a stony, lunar-like landscape, live the Dhofaris. Dhofar, for four months of the year during the south west monsoon, is covered by the Khareef, the rainy season of mists, low clouds and tiny black, savagely-biting flies, when visibility is as little as fifteen yards and the slippery treacherous soil makes the going exhausting and slow.

The Dhofaris are ethnically a different race to the rest of Oman, small, wiry and dark, with chiselled features and matted hair. They tend their flocks of cattle, goats and camels and lived at that time either in conical huts or inside caves. The men had proved their soldier-like qualities in the Dhofari Squadron of the Trucial Oman Scouts. They were fine shots and the fieldcraft of the Jebali enemy was the best I had seen in all my service.

The Dhofar War had started in 1964 with a small uprising and, like a lit match dropped in a dry forest which has not been stamped out immediately, had flared and spread, and from what I had heard, was still spreading.

At that time the only route for bulk supplies and troops to Dhofar from north Oman was by a gravel road. This route ended in the Midway Road stretching from the camp of that name in north Dhofar across the Jebel massif down to and across the plain to the capital Salalah, where lived His Highness Said bin Taimur, the Sultan, and his son, the Sandhurst-educated, charming Prince Qabus. To deal with the rebellion the Muscat Regiment was stationed in Dhofar and enemy ambushes of their soldiers along the Midway Road resulting in fatal casualties were too common-place for my liking. It was to acquaint myself better with their problems, to get to know Muscat Regiment and its area of operations, and its enemy of formidable Dhofaris, who were known as the 'adoo', as well as to have my first audience with my Commander-in-Chief, the Sultan, that I was bound.

On the morning of my departure for Dhofar I was down at the airstrip at first light accompanied by smiling, enthusiastic Mike Legg, my GS03. We took our seats in the back of a Beaver. Our air journey would take between 6 and 7 hours and included a stop to refuel at the RAF base on Masirah Island. The Beaver roared down the runway, took off, climbed upwards and I looked down on my house with the bearers standing waving up from the verandah. We climbed on, circling to starboard over the nearby sea-front town of Muttrah dominated by its fort. Further south was Muscat the capital in its bowl of rocks, the harbour almost circular, the old Portuguese forts of Murani and Jelali standing guard on either side of its entrance, with the British Consulate in the shadow of Fort Jelali, on the beach.

Then we were over the gravel desert, the savage tops of the Hajar Range to our right as we headed south. Far below lay the desert interspersed with green oases, wadis and rocky outcrops, and on our left sparkled the blue sea. Iced loomi – fresh lime juice – was passed round the cabin from a large thermos. Mike Legg, still smiling, was asleep and the pilots chatted to each other over the intercom and kept contact by radio with Bait-al-Falaj and RAF Masirah.

Eventually, when we were getting stiff and bored, the Beaver swung to port and there across the sea, lay the low shape of Masirah Island. As we drew nearer we could make out sinister, bat-like, camouflage-painted Vulcan bombers parked by the runway and a Beverley which had just taken off. An Andover was taxi-ing down the runway having just landed.

We came in, floated down and made a perfect landing, rolling along the black runway which was shimmering in the Arabian heat. The RAF Station Commander met us and took us up to his spacious, cool officers' mess, the anteroom full of aircrew relaxing between trips south to Aden, north to RAF Sharjah or to RAF Muharraq in Bahrain. We had a chat and a welcome cup of tea and then returned to our aircraft which was by now refuelled and ready for the final leg to RAF Salalah. RAF Masirah, like RAF Gan, had a high morale. Both Masirah and Gan were unaccompanied postings and yet station ésprit de corps was remarkably good.

We rolled down the runway, took off and climbed steeply, circling the island. Looking down we could see a circle of sharks swimming round – no wonder bathing in the sea was forbidden! – and then we were crossing the sea heading southeast for the mainland coast again and for Dhofar. The gravel plains gave way to black, twisted mountains, commonly called 'Moon Country', intersected with wide, gently winding wadis, sites presumably of former water courses. At last, there below us was the former oil-prospecting camp of Midway with its airstrip and shack-like buildings. Beyond it ran the Midway Road leading south to Salalah. We followed this route, watching where it climbed the Ramp, a steep incline built on railway sleepers, which was the site of enemy ambushes and attempted demolitions.

Below us lay rolling countryside dotted with trees, hut villages surrounded by stone walls and further out, on either side, were deep steep-sided wadis. It was all covered in grass, burnt a little by the sun but reminiscent of Devon and we could see herds of cattle grazing near some of the villages where smoke from cooking fires climbed vertically into the still air. 'That's Raven's Roost,' said the pilot and, looking down to my right, I saw the shine of vehicle bodies and windscreens denoting an army presence and made a mental note to have all windscreens removed and trucks camouflaged with matt paint instead of gloss!

Suddenly the ground dropped steeply in front of us and below stretched the Salalah plain in a half-crescent. A dark green splash ahead denoted the luxuriant palms and gardens of Salalah, the Sultan's Palace clearly visible, with the blue sea beyond where white rollers curled in to break on the seashore.

We came in low, touched down on the runway and taxied to where a group of officers stood by a cluster of Landrovers. We got out, glad to be free of the small but reliable Beaver. A familiar, khaki-clad, stocky shape came forward, wearing the distinctive scarlet Balmoral bonnet of the Muscat Regiment. Trevor Alexander, the Commanding Officer, shook my hand and welcomed me. I knew him to be a sound officer with considerable fighting experience in France and Germany during the War as a platoon commander in the Duke of Cornwall's Light Infantry.

I was introduced to a tough-looking, shy captain, Trevor's Adjutant Mike Peele, who had been decorated with the Military Cross for bravery on operations with his regiment, the Royal Leicesters, in Borneo, known as 'Captain Shadeed' because of his physical toughness. The final member of the group, whom I was to get to know well, was the grinning Dad Karim, Trevor's batman, later to be taken on by Peter Thwaites when he succeeded Trevor in command of the Muscat Regiment.

The road to Umm al Ghawarif Camp was marked by 'burmails' – 40 gallon oil drums, filled with concrete. I call it a road but the entire surface at that time was corrugated as a result of the constant traffic of military vehicles, and punctuated by boulders and sharp-sided potholes. A cloud of suffocating grey-white dust surrounded us, filling our eyes, noses, ears and mouths as we bounced, bucked and shook our way to the Muscat Regiment's Headquarters, outside which was drawn up an immaculate Quarter

Guard. The Bugler sounded the General Salute, I inspected the Guard, shook hands all round and visited Battalion Headquarters. Then as night was falling, Trevor took me along to his bungalow Kernow Cottage, next door (Trevor is a Cornishman!) where he was putting me up.

My bedroom in Kernow Cottage was to become well known to me as I used to sleep there before going on operations with whichever battalion was in Dhofar and I always found it a welcome place on our return, often dog-tired but almost always after an exciting and successful foray. When I had showered and changed, Trevor took me over to the Mess to meet his officers. Easy chairs were drawn up outside on the verandah and I studied with interest the men who were fighting the Dhofar War.

At this time platoons in SAF were commanded by Arab or Baluch staff sergeants and very good leaders they were. The Commanding Officer, Second-in-Command, Adjutant and Quartermaster, together with the four rifle company commanders and Headquarter Company Commander were all British. Each company had in addition a couple of British captains and one or more Arab or Baluch subalterns. At that time Muscat Regiment's Regimental Medical Officer was a Scot, Iain Hynd, later to render invaluable service as the Forces' Senior Medical Officer. After Iain had left MR we received an Indian Army Medical Corps Captain for each battalion, on deputation or, as we used to call it, on secondment. At the same time we acquired a very good and delightful Indian Army Dental Corps Officer, Major Seifi Vasi. The MTO and the Signals Officers were both Pakistanis and the Army Schoolmaster was an Omani.

B Company was up on the Jebel so I would not meet its officers and men until the next morning, when I would visit them there. The Second-in-Command was Major John Cooper, MBE, DCM, a lean, dark soldier of fortune and a founder member of the Special Air Service Regiment. John had served under David Stirling in North Africa. He had served in many small wars since the Second World War, had participated under Lt. Col. Tony Deane-Drummond in the SAS storming of the Jebel Akhdar in 1958, and had more recently soldiered with Colonel Smiley, the first CSAF, in North Yemen fighting for the Royalists.

Daddy Laurence was the capable Quartermaster who looked after his battalion like a guardian angel. Richard John who commanded A Company was a Royal Scots Grey turned successful infantryman. He was loved by his men and was a brave, active officer. With him as PMC the Mess was always comfortable and the food very good. Wherever the Regiment served there was a Mess garden and when possible a swimming pool of sorts was created nearby. A lean, fit-looking officer came forward, Peter Southwood-Heyton, another fine leader who was, after he had left SAF, to die tragically with his young wife in a car accident. Then there was Simon

Sloane, son of a general and, like his distinguished father, an Argyll. Simon would later be decorated for bravery. Tough young Nick Roberts was another general's son. His father was Major General Pip Roberts, CB, DSO, MC, greatly distinguished in Eighth Army, and north west Europe. Finally, Patrick Brook of the Blues and Royals; whose coolness and military ability would later result in his saving a complete battalion from a dicey situation on a subsequent tour with SAF. I understand that Patrick is the only officer in SAF to have been awarded the Distinguished Service Medal twice, the first under my command, being the DSM for Gallantry. He was later also awarded the MBE.

As we sat out there on the Mess verandah under the stars, I listened to their talk and learned much.

CHAPTER TWENTY-ONE

DHOFAR

Next morning, Trevor took me round the lines where smiling, Baluch and Arab soldiers were enjoying mugs of tea and preparing for the business of the day. Some would be on convoy escort, some on patrol and others would be retraining including firing their personal weapons. In the gun lines I was greeted by Lieutenant (later Major) Mohammad Ashraf, a very experienced former British Indian Army gunner officer. He had fought on the North West Frontier of India and in Burma and later for the Pakistan Army against the Indian Army in Kashmir. Since then he had been the right-hand man to a succession of British gunner officers, first in the Jebal Akhdar Campaign and now in the Dhofar War. He was a fine man in every way.

John Lewis was the seconded Gunner commanding the Sultan's Artillery, which at that time was armed with three different types of weapons; 5.5 inch howitzers, 25 pounders and 75mm light guns of the type I had last seen fired in anger by American artillerymen in Germany in the closing stages of the Second World War. John was an excellent choice for secondment to SAF as he had a natural affinity with the local soldiers, a quiet and effective way of getting things done, and was thoroughly professional.

We called in at Battalion Headquarters to get the latest information from the Operations Room, met the Staff on duty and then went off to the Mess for breakfast, pausing in the Mess garden to look at Bin Sola the silver oryx mascot of the Muscat Regiment. After breakfast we put on green and black checked 'Shemaghs' worn turban fashion, took our rifles and ammunition and got into a Landrover escorted by two sections of the Reconnaissance Platoon commanded by the widely-grinning and enthusiastic Tony Carey, a Light Infantryman on secondment. Then in a whirl of dust we were off, moving north across the wide plain towards where the Midway Road wound steeply up to the top of the scarp.

The old rules of the North West Frontier of India applied in this mountainous terrain and before opening the Midway Road it was neces- sary to seize all main positions of importance dominating the road and to hold them until we were ready to close it again – picquetting the heights. We had not enough troops in Dhofar, let alone in the Sultan's Armed Forces, to dominate the area permanently, so whenever it was decided to open up the road, each vital and commanding piece of ground had to be seized, the first generally by first light, and the picquet that occupied each position built themselves 'sangars' – breastworks of stones and boulders – as protection against enemy fire. The ground was far too rocky to dig trenches. This again, was like the Frontier.

We drove up the winding road, our wheels skidding on loose stones and earth. (Since the conclusion of the Dhofar War in 1975 it is an excellent tarmac all-weather highway but in those days very much open to the vagaries of weather, and of enemy demolitions and mines.) I visited each picquet in turn, walking over to chat with the occupants of the sangar, one of whom would keep an alert watch over his light ma- chine gun while the rest of us talked. Then he would slip away from his gun for a talk with me, after a watchful relief had slid in behind it and gripped the butt of the weapon.

The road along the top of the jebel ran through rolling country inter- spersed with clumps of trees and bushes, with groups of cattle grazing. Now and then, on either side, the ground sheered steeply down into deep, wooded wadis, hundreds, sometimes over a thousand feet deep and often a great distance across. In these instances troops operating on the far side could be beyond the cover of small arms fire from the near side, and the importance of having adequate support weapons to back them up was apparent. We swung off the road into a fortified camp, Raven's Roost, and the man after whom it was named came forward to meet me, Major Peter Raven, late of the Royal Norfolk Regiment.

Peter inspired confidence and was a hard, tough, experienced infantry- man who had had a long time on operations in Dhofar. He took me round to meet his soldiers and I was horrified and angry to see that all of them, including those occupying the picquets, wore brown British Army-type canvas gym shoes which were in almost every case torn and out at the sides and virtually held on by string. The seats of their trousers and backs of their shirts were worn through and Peter and Trevor assured me that such disgraceful conditions were commonplace in SAF where all units were short of uniforms and kit.

Tony Lewis had warned me how difficult it was to get money for the Army and I resolved to speak to the Sultan about this unacceptable state of affairs at my first Audience. (Thanks to Tony Lewis there was no shortage of ammunition.) The 4 tonners and Landrovers in SAF had glass wind-screens and shiny paint and I told Trevor that SAF must camouflage properly, and that all windscreens and driving mirrors were to be removed forthwith and headlights and rear lights covered with hessian.

I looked at the .303 rifles and Bren light machine guns. No cause for concern there as every one I saw was in first-rate working condition and was clearly treated as its owner's best friend. I knew already that the .303s were to be replaced by FN self-loading rifles. We drove the length of the Midway Road, down the Ramp and visited the tatty, ramshackle old camp at Midway. Ordnance Stores, spare fuel for aircraft and spares of all sorts were kept here, administered by Captain Jim Dolphin-Rowland, a fatherly-looking, dependable officer. A resident protection element was supplied by a platoon of the Guard Regiment.

I noted a number of improvements that were needed to make the place properly habitable and then we turned back. As we motored towards Salalah it was plain how easily unwary troops could be ambushed and that picquetting, inquisitiveness and alertness were vital. We passed Ambush Corner, Aqabat al Jasmin, which was the lovely local name for its evil-sounding English nickname and which, to my mind, typified Dhofar. The longer I served there the more I realised how easy it would be to relax one's guard in such beautiful scenery.

As his weaponry improved thanks to the generosity of the Soviets, so the 'adoo's' deadliness increased. The only way to tackle the job was never to relax on the jebal and always remember that the enemy was watching, ready to take advantage of any weakness. Above all we had to have the killer wish, find the enemy, seize the tactical advantage, dominate the theatre of operations, crush his will to continue and so end the war. At the same time we had to win the battle for the hearts and minds of the Dhofar people.

The area swallowed troops. Roads were virtually non-existent and the few tracks were liable to mining and ambush. We knew from experience of numerous counter-insurgency operations in the British Army the folly of being tied to roads; we knew the importance of air power and of close, intimate fire support. I was aware that SOAF lacked adequate short take-off and landing logistic aircraft and that it had no helicopters. I knew also that the only armoured support in SAF were the few Ferret scout cars each infantry battalion had on its establishment and that generally speaking these were mostly mechanically unreliable. Furthermore, we knew from experience in South Arabia the effect that mines had on these lightly-armoured, lightly-armed little vehicles. Before I saw the Sultan I would need to add to my shopping list. But I was impressed with the officers and men I had met so far. Lean, cheerful, keen and wiry, they seemed natural soldiers.

But what was their state of training and what did we really know of the enemy? It did not seem to me that we had the initiative, the information or the will to win but that we merely reacted to ambushes and enemy moves. The longer we allowed the Dhofaris breathing space, the more established they would become, the more they would dominate the jebel and its tribes, suborn the potentially rebellious and terrorise the fencesitters and the loyal. The trees had already caught fire, we would have to act quickly if we were to extinguish the blaze before the forest was consumed.

As we came to the last picquets on top of the jebel on our homeward drive, we looked across the plain three thousand feet below, to where the dark green palms of Salalah flanked the Sultan's Palace, its red flag just discernible through our field glasses. I wondered what the Sultan would be like, and how we would get on at our Audience to which Trevor Alexander would accompany me, in the Palace that very afternoon.

Trevor and I drove from Umm al-Ghawarif Camp at about 3.30pm, dressed in best drill service dress, red berets and wearing swords and medals. We thumped down the corrugated road that ran between the lines of burmails, and leaving the airfield and buildings of RAF Salalah on our right, passed through one of the entrance gates into Salalah town. Salalah was surrounded by a high wire perimeter fence which had several gates, each flanked by mini-forts manned by askars. Wild-looking, shaggy, unkempt, long-haired Dhofari tribesmen passed through these entry points after they and their arrogant-looking camels had been searched by the armed askar guards. The camels usually carried loads of wood destined for the cooking fires of the residents of Salalah. The Dhofaris shopped in the street bazaars and then made their long way back across the plain, up the scarp, to their huts and caves on the jebel. No doubt most of them were active rebels and presumably all bore with them intelligence as to what they had seen and heard of SAF and of the Government.

As we drove into town through avenues of tall palms with, beyond them, verdant green fields where fruit and vegetables grew in profusion in the lush soil, we passed ebony-faced, graceful women clad in brilliantly coloured flowing garments and negroid-featured men in white disha dashas and turbans, curved Omani khanjars (daggers) belted round their waists, for many of these people were of slave stock. Askars threw open the gates of the Palace and we pulled up by a flight of stone steps leading into the building.

A small, slightly-built, smiling figure in grey, gold-edged robes hurried down the steps and we shook hands. This was the Court Chamberlain,

Saiyyid Hamid bin Humaid, a charming person. White-robed Khaddim (slave stock servants), wearing khanjars in their belts escorted us along a corridor to a small room furnished with several fabric-covered easy chairs, a table, a desk and a model of an oilrig in a glass case. After murmuring more greetings, Saiyyid Hamid departed and Trevor and I sat down and waited.

A few minutes later we both rose to our feet as a small, slightly corpulent figure in white robes entered. On his head he wore a large, coloured turban. He had a big, greying beard that covered his neck and upper chest, a rather fleshy nose and large, liquid-brown eyes. He held himself majestically erect, and despite his lack of height, this dignified carriage gave the impression that he was taller than he actually was. He advanced towards me and shook my hand bidding me welcome in flawless English. I noticed that, like Queen Victoria, Sultan Said bin Taimur invariably used the royal 'We'. I don't think I ever heard him say 'I', other than 'I see', in the three years during which I served him!

He motioned us to sit down and took his seat, sitting very erect in one of the armchairs, looking piercingly at me the while. It was obvious that he had a liking for Trevor Alexander and soon we had settled into a pleasant and easy conversation. We discussed the Armed Forces and having been told how difficult it was to secure an Audience with the Sultan I said I would be most grateful if he could spare me the time to see me whenever I came to Dhofar which would be fairly frequent as I wanted to end the war as soon as possible. He said he would always be glad to see me at any time. I then asked him if I might give him my first impressions and he inclined his head, the tassel on the end of his turban nodding, his brown eyes watching me alertly.

'Your Highness,' I said, 'You need more infantry. Your country is large and swallows soldiers. In Dhofar alone I estimate that you require at the very least another battalion as things are at present. This will take time to raise, train and equip, and time is of the essence.'

'I see,' said the Sultan. (I was later to discover that 'I see' meant that he had heard what had been said but did not necessarily agree!) 'Your Highness also requires helicopters in order to give maximum mobility and operational effectiveness to the small amount of infantry available, to quickly evacuate casualties and to enable troops to be logistically self-supporting. At present about five days is the limit for which soldiers can remain away from base and that time is dependent on how much water they can carry. They simply cannot carry more even by using donkeys.' 'I see,' said H.H. 'Also, Sir, I find the kit that your soldiers are wearing is in an unacceptable state.' I proceeded to elaborate and he leaned forward listening intently. I asked him for more kit and better equipment and this time he said, 'Yes, we will speak to the Military Secretary.' I thanked him and told him how much I liked the potential of his soldiers and how I looked forward to the job. At this he smiled, relaxed visibly, pressed a bell in the wall beside him and a khaddim carried in a laden tea tray – tea pot, milk jug, sugar bowl and hot water jug all made of silver, and porcelain cups, saucers and plates. There were three sorts of delicious sandwiches, egg, chicken and cheese, and two cakes, one iced, one fruit.

The Sultan poured tea, questioned me about my family and about how things were in England. Trevor joined in the conversation which was amusing, interesting and informative. The Sultan had great affection and respect for our Royal Family and for Britain and a considerable regard for Mr Heath and the Conservative Party. He had an equally low opinion of the Labour Party of that period and of their policies, which he considered weak, unrealistic and lacking in leadership.

He pressed more sandwiches on us and I found that I was greatly enjoying his company and that I liked him. One could not fail to respect him and though he was autocratic I felt that (whatever his critics may have said about him later) he cared greatly about his people and his country, but found the situation facing him a little bewildering, and that he would like advice. However, he would only accept advice from those he trusted and such advice would require to be very carefully thought out and worded before being proffered to this proud, shy man. I sensed that we had struck up a rapport, and I was grateful to Trevor for his help in this important first meeting.

As we drove out through the gates, waved at cheerfully by armed askars, Trevor said to me, 'He knows you have a lot of operational experience with helicopters and has been expecting you to ask for them. The trouble is, as we all three know, they are so expensive to buy, maintain and operate and he hates spending money! Furthermore the Desert Regiment has only just been formed and here you are saying that we need yet more infantry! Of course, in his heart he knows that this is right but it's going to be a battle to persuade him and his advisers to agree to such expenditure.'

Obviously I would have to earn the trust of the Sultan and his advisers and meanwhile we must equip the Armed Forces properly with decent uniforms and weapons, take the initiative in Dhofar and carry the war to the enemy.

I spent the remainder of the week getting to know Dhofar, flying all over it by Beaver including along the border with the People's Republic of South Yemen, from where the sea lapped the rocky shores below the little village of Hauf, through which place the enemy came and went, and where they based themselves, secure of sanctuary inside the former Aden Protectorate. The premature withdrawal by the British from Aden had been a näive step and the West had paid for it. It seemed to us who were reaping the direct consequences that our political masters were more worried about world opinion and of ridding themselves of foreign commitments than of ensuring the best interests of its inhabitants, before the country to which they were granting independence was really ready to run itself maturely and responsibly, with properly-trained leaders.

The lack of foresight in our post-war 'Scuttle from Empire' has cost millions of lives and has, in most cases, been to the advantage not of those to whom we gave their independence, but to the enemies of the West.

As we droned up the wide, white wadis, with the former Aden Protectorate on our left, towards the Sultanate fort of Habarut, I could see how easy it was for the rebels and their supporters to enter the Sultanate across such an open border. Our aircraft swung back towards Hauf and then over the jebel towards Salalah. Great steep-sided, jagged ravines intersected the terrain in the border area and to the south of the jebel the ground fell steeply three thousand feet towards a shimmering blue sea. The tiny coastal villages of Dalqut and Rakhyut appeared below us, and beyond lay the wide beaches of Mugshail and the wadi leading into it. The top of the jebel was thickly covered with bushes, good cover for the 'adoo'.

Eastwards, away across the Midway Road, lay Darbat where a river flowed after the rains and the water dropped hundreds of feet down a dramatic waterfall. We could see cattle wading in a pool of standing water near the top of the falls and one or two herdsmen and their women looked up from a group of trees beside the water. We flew on eastwards and the country changed to harsher, grassless, rocky terrain. Having passed the two small coastal towns of Taqa and Mirbat we approached the tiny village of Sudh, with its little inlet harbour, dominated by a fort from which flew the Sultan's red flag, caught in a zephyr of hot breeze.

I accompanied foot patrols on the jebel during the next few days and Tony Carey and his Reconnaissance Platoon took me to Mughsail through the hills near where enemy camel convoys were reported to pass. We were able to drive the whole way, leapfrogging our vehicle picquets as we went.

We examined vast caves along the beach, some of which showed signs of recent human occupation. On the way back along the white sand, with big-clawed crabs scuttling sideways to the holes in which they lived and with which they perforated the beach, we halted where the wadi joined the shore in a long pool of fresh, warm water. Here we could see, surprisingly, several sting-rays. The waves thundered down on the beach, sucking sizeable stones and rocks seaward in a rattling, gurgling, powerful undertow.

We drove back to Umm al-Ghawarif, stopping at the camp of Raysut, which then consisted of an embryo harbour, a few ramshackle huts and a small garrison of askars in dirty disha dashas and turbans, waists festooned with cartridge belts.

One evening I lay in ambush with a platoon. The night breeze rustled the grass and foliage and the sound of dogs barking came from a nearby jebali encampment. There was the cry of a nightbird, the smell of herbs crushed where we lay, and of woodsmoke from some village fire. But that night no enemy came. Another night I accompanied the leading picquet to take up a position prior to opening the Midway Road next day. The gymshoes and the rubber-soled chukka boots worn by our party, and the good training of the soldiers, enabled us to move silently along the broken soil and over the twisted rocks. There was a faint light from a myriad of stars and we managed to avoid kicking the stones and boulders, the noise from which could have given away our presence. The ground rose steeply and the drill uniforms clung to our sweating bodies as we made our stealthy progress ever upwards. The lean, fit soldiers moved like silent ghosts. Suddenly the ground flattened as we reached a knoll topped with bushes, and behind and below us stretched the sea, increasingly clear in the growing light.

The shapes of the next platoon behind us loomed up and a line of watchful figures moved silently past, weapons at the ready. As soon as the leading platoon had occupied their picquet, the next platoon appeared and took up its position, and so on until the road was open. Cocks crowed faintly from a nearby jebali encampment; an owl, overtaken by daylight, flapped heavily into a clump of trees, the smell of woodsmoke hung on the air and, then, from the plain below came the faint sound of engines as the north-bound convoy from Umm al-Ghawarif Camp set off on the first and crucial stage of its journey to Oman along the Midway Road.

With a sudden roar a pair of piston-engined Provosts appeared from the direction of Salalah airfield and swept across the jebel heading for Midway. The lazy drone of a Beaver came from where, circling high overhead, John Cooper, the battalion Second-in-Command, binoculars in hand, scoured the countryside with powerful lenses for any sign of enemy movement.

In the gunlines on the plain below, the 5.5 inch medium howitzers and the 25 pounders of the Oman artillery crouched, muzzles pointed menacingly upwards in our support, their gun crews ready to swiftly react to fire orders from John Lewis who was waiting near us on top of the jebel with his signaller in attendance, by the side of the Commander of the road-opening operation, Richard John. The reassuringly competent, distant figure of Mohammad Ashraf standing by the alert guncrews was a guarantee of a fast and accurate response to any call for gunner fire support.

By now the sun was up and, in bumping succession, a well spaced-out convoy of khaki-painted vehicles streamed by, canopies removed, armed soldiers looking out alertly, covering all angles, ready to open fire directly action was joined. On this occasion there was no enemy interference with the progress of the vehicles and once we had heard over the radio that the convoy had safely passed Midway Camp, the picquets were recalled. The one I accompanied having been first in to position, was last to be withdrawn.

At the end of the week I flew back by Beaver to Bait-al-Falaj, calling in to refuel at RAF Masirah and to renew my acquaintanceship with the Station Commander and permanent staff there. In the aircraft I was making notes on the many aspects necessary to be put in train towards the successful prosecution and termination of the Dhofar War in terms of tactics, training and equipment. I would be discussing equipment with Pat Waterfield on my return.

CHAPTER TWENTY-TWO

NORTH OMAN

Sitting in Pat Waterfield's office next morning we discussed my proposed shopping list: another infantry battalion, Iroquois troopcarrying helicopters (excellent work horses in which I had flown with the Australian Army and which had proved themselves in Vietnam), and decent clothing for the men to wear in the way of uniform and footgear. I also asked for proper and sufficient medical, including field surgical facilities in Dhofar with modern-equipped hospitals and staffs throughout SAF, together with a Medical Officer for each major unit. I wanted to have some SAS in Dhofar, not only to give expert instruction in ambush and other techniques but to help us win over the jebalis. 'Hearts and Minds' was not Sultan Said's strong point and we needed the fence-sitters on our side.

As commanders in many campaigns have found so much hinges on finance. Having brought his country to solvency from the bankrupt state in which he had inherited it from his father, and since the money from his oil fields had still not begun to flow in, the Sultan was reluctant to disburse further funds on defence. The Desert Regiment had only very recently been formed and the Sultan just would not contemplate raising another battalion, nor buying helicopters despite the urgency of the operational situation. Pat told me that Caribou transport aircraft were likely to be ordered. These could land and lift considerable numbers of troops on to, and from, short, rough airstrips. However, this would not get casualties out of, or troops and stores into, positions where no such airstrips were possible. Five days was the absolute limit for operations in Dhofar because we could not carry sufficient water for longer periods and I knew that 'choppers' were a 'must', and should have been ordered instead of the Caribous.

207

Pat undertook to get the clothing, small arms and equipment situation right and I decided that until I could persuade the Sultan to change his mind, it was up to me to solve my problems using what resources we had available.

If I couldn't be allowed to raise more infantry for operations in Dhofar then I must consider what infantry I could remove from North Oman where there had been incursions before, and where more could be expected at that time from Iraq and Saudi Arabia. The Sultan had ordered that no troops were to be moved south to Dhofar from North Oman.

Having looked carefully at the position I decided that we could spare one company of infantry from one up-country battalion. I also relieved the infantry battalion in Dhofar of certain defensive and static tasks by sending a company of the Baluch-manned Guard Regiment to Dhofar. I would further augment the numbers of infantry on the ground by attaching a troop of Oman Gendarmerie from North Oman to the theatre of operations. These sub-units would serve for four months in Dhofar and then return to Northern Oman, being relieved in turn in a regular roulement by further companies and troops supplied from their parent units. I also decided to move the remainder of the artillery less one troop to the Dhofar area. Finally, in order to increase our fire-power there, having discovered in the Fort at Bait-al-Falaj a number of Vickers machine guns and ascertained that there was plenty of ammunition for them, I put in motion a programme to set up, equip and train a Medium Machine Gun Platoon from the Guard Regiment for service in Dhofar. This would have the additional advantage of getting more of the Guard Regiment on operations which would be good for them professionally and morale-wise. The Vickers would be splendid in certain areas of Dhofar because of their long range and their capacity for sustained indirect fire. Pat Waterfield was going to Salalah shortly and he undertook to support my ideas to the Sultan. I felt that as I was so new at that stage, I could not expect the Sultan to have sufficient confidence in my judgement to overcome his preconceived ideas as to the disposition of troops and the disbursement of funds. Crossing my fingers for Pat's success, I set out on a programme of visits to get to know the rest of the officers and men under my command, together with the terrain in which they operated and trained, and to meet the personalities in Government whom I had not hitherto seen. I also made my overall plan for the security of the Sultanate as well as for the prosecution of operations in Dhofar, and issued my first training directive.

Oman is such a photogenic country that no matter how hot or humid the weather, every visit I made was, for me, full of excitement and ever-changing scenery. I made it my practice to visit units every other day so that I had alternately one day at Headquarters and the next spent with a unit or sub-unit of the Armed Forces. When I arrived in Oman the Northern Frontier Regiment, less two companies, was based at Nizwa, the old Imamate capital of Oman. One company was stationed further north at the delightful, palm-fringed town of Ibri and the other was on top of the Jebal Akhdar at Saiq. The force at Nizwa detached one platoon permanently as garrison for the towering, drum-shaped fort in Nizwa itself (the battalion's lines were several miles south of the town) and a further platoon was located at Bilaad Sait, the home of Ghalib and Talib, two of the three leaders of the opposition in the Jebal Akhdar Campaign. My usual routine for visits was to fly by Beaver from Bait-al-Falaj, taking my IN basket so that I saved time in paperwork. I found it easy to work in a Beaver and later, easier still to work in Dakotas when they arrived. During my return trips from visits I would write up my notes together with chits for executive action to those members of my staff who would have to carry them out. I discovered later that these were referred to in my Headquarters as 'the White Man's Purdon'!

On my initial trips I spent much of the time looking out of the aircraft getting to know the lie of the land, thereafter airborne office work occupied most of my time. The Beaver would take off, flying low past my house, where Patricia and Angela both of whom had by then joined me, would be standing by the verandah waving to me. Then the aircraft would climb steeply up over the sea lying sparkling blue below us, and head off for the day's destination.

For this trip to Nizwa, we followed the Wadi Sumail which almost always held water and was punctuated by oases of palm trees, dark green against the greys and light reds of the surrounding arid valley and rocky hills, with oleander-fringed pools of water reflecting the blue of the sky. To our left our first landmark was Bid Bid, headquarters at that time of the Desert Regiment. This was also situated on a wadi the length of which was interspersed with water pools. The neat lines of huts in the cantonment, and the shale airstrip were clearly visible. The nearby village of Fanjah was a joy to walk in under the cool shade of the date palms and alongside its bubbling, sparkling, flowing 'falajs' (water channels).

Sumail came next, dominated by a large terra-cotta coloured castle-fort set on an eminence in the middle of the village above thickly-clustered palms and a wide stretch of reed-fringed water. Then on to Izki, where a detached company from the Bid Bid battalion lived inside a wire-surrounded little camp beside a dusty airstrip. The pilot swung right with an increased roar of the powerful radial engine and climbed up to cross the mighty Jebal Akhdar, that vast rock mass, its great slab sides violet, purple and grey, the colours changing in the different lights of day, with black chasms where huge precipices dropped dizzily to clusters of palm-surrounded tiny houses at the foot of the narrow wadis far below. The top of the mountain was dotted with bushes and on its sides terraced slopes were planted with fruit trees – pomegranates, oranges and peaches – and with vegetables of various sorts; I could see why the Omanis called it the Green Mountain.

We flew over Saiq where NFR had a detached company and looked down on the gravel airstrip and little cantonment, then dived steeply towards the NFR camp, the old town of Nizwa to our right dominated by the great fort set among palms and other greenery, the wadi water reflecting the sunlight. At last we straightened out and glided over one end of the battalion airstrip, bumped onto its flattened, stony surface and rolled to a halt beside some open sided barusti-roofed sheds where three Landrovers waited behind a group of dark green bereted figures in khaki drill, and some bare-headed, overalled mechanics with burmails of fuel and a hand-pump with which to replenish the Beaver's fuel tanks.

Three officers came forward to greet us, Hugh Sanders the CO, John Clarke the Second-in-Command and Patrick Hibbert-Foy the Adjutant. They escorted me, Mike Legg and Jules Brett, the pilot, to the Mess for breakfast. We drove to the Battalion Guardroom first where I inspected an immaculate Quarter Guard dressed in starched khaki drill uniforms. The men had polished brown leather chapplis on their feet and were wearing dark green NFR berets, their bugler blowing a clipped General Salute as the soldiers presented arms.

In the cool anteroom of the Mess I met those officers who were stationed in Nizwa; among them the thin, spare, ascetic-looking, charming Colin McLean, a former priest and, as I write, a priest again. Anwar, the Senior Mess Steward, like his waiters dressed in white with a green cummerbund, came in to say that breakfast was ready and as we seated ourselves on either side of the long, polished, mahogany table, I looked at the officers of the battalion and considered their histories.

The battalion had recently completed a tour of operations in Dhofar during which an attempt had been made on the life of the Sultan whilst he was inspecting the Dhofar Force. Dhofar Force was a unit of Dhofari soldiers officered by Pakistanis, and was the Sultan's own 'private army'. This he had lavishly equipped with weapons and various items of equipment, including American Cadillac armoured troop carriers, which we could have done with in SAF. The Sultan would not allow Dhofar Force to be part of SAF and we were not supposed to liaise with them. However, he had at last given me permission to do so and I wanted to use this unit, in however small a way, to our advantage. During my stay in Dhofar I had visited them and called on the CO, Lieutenant Colonel Saki Raja, a brave and pleasant Pakistani who had been bayonetted several times while trying to protect the Sultan from those of his men who were concerned in the assassination attempt, before they escaped to the jebel. The soldiers were mainly negroid slave stock although there were, I was told, pure Dhofaris among them. I had already met a number of the Dhofar Force soldiers and was sure that we could make good fighting men out of them if only the Sultan would put them under SAF command. (He never did!)

Hugh Sanders sat on one side of me at the breakfast table and John Clarke on the other. Hugh was about to leave the battalion having finished his tenure of command, and to return to England. He was an experienced infantryman and would be relieved by another one who had already hit the headlines in the national press during the Korean War. Mike Harvey – the only Gloucestershire Regiment officer, I gathered, to successfully fight his command out of the fierce battle of the Imjin. I had not yet met him but I had heard how, having noticed the Chinese were going for the high ground and encircling the rear of the Gloucesters, Mike had led his men towards the low ground, straight for the Chinese and then circled round behind them, getting his men back into our own lines. The only casualties incurred were inflicted by United Nations tanks whose crews did not initially recognise Mike's men as friendly forces. For this deed he was awarded the Military Cross. He had also received a Kenyan decoration for his part in putting down a mutiny in East Africa. He sounded a cool, thinking leader. John Clarke, the Second-in-Command was a tall, lean, deeply sunburnt man who had started life in the Blues, had made a name for himself in the Jebel Akhdar Campaign and had proved to be a sound and reliable Second-in-Command in Dhofar. He was a shy, reserved, taciturn man with the kindest of hearts, a dry sense of humour, and was much loved in SAF. He was said to keep a veritable library of diaries filled with copious entries in tiny writing which everyone longed to read!

After breakfast I walked round the lines and visited the barrack rooms, showers, ablutions and cookhouses. In those days there were no punkah fans or air-conditioning in the other ranks' accommodation, but the long, dark, high-ceilinged barrack rooms with large, wide-opened windows were reasonably cool and airy, and we knew that there was not yet sufficient money for such improvements, much though we wished for them. I spoke to as many men as I could. Then I was taken off in an open Landrover to visit the town of Nizwa itself, to call on the Wali in the great fort and the garrison platoon. We went off in a whirl of dust. A wide wadi lay on our left fringed with reeds and full of water. On arrival at the fort we walked through the narrow souk, its tiny shops full of stalls selling bales of cloth, trinkets, pots and pans and aromatic spices of all sorts. Red lumps of raw camel meat and goat flesh hung under a throbbing covering of flies; brightly-coloured piles of fruit were heaped in adjoining shops all with their attendant swarms of flies. The male citizens of Nizwa, in off-white disha dashas and coloured turbans, stalked along. Martini-Henry rifles and filled cartridge belts slung over their shoulders, with khanjars at their midriffs on ornate belts. Black-shrouded Omani women-folk chattered by the shops, their faces covered by the unsightly, visored, burkha masks worn so that no male could see their countenances. In contrast were the unveiled, coffee-skinned Baluch women, gay in strikingly coloured fluttering silk or cotton robes – bright oranges splashed with cobalt blues, brilliant yellows, vivid greens, indigos and fluorescent scarlets, all the colours of the rainbow in attractive contrast.

The fort had a huge, faded painting of a Portuguese sailing ship still discernible on the surface of its cream and ochre-coloured rounded wall; and, after the sentry under his awning had presented arms we shook hands with him and passed the time of day. By now half a dozen elderly askars had pressed forward, with wrinkled, brown faces, straggly grey beards, near-toothless grins, eager to shake our hands and conduct us to the presence of the Wali. On the way some prisoners shuffled forward, legs shackled together at the ankles with logs, to shake their manacled hands with ours. They were surprisingly cheerful and friendly.

Having crossed an upwards-inclined, polished log some forty feet long, with footslots hacked in its surface, we ascended a series of crumbling, earthen-and-stone steps until we arrived at the entrance to the Wali's majlis, or reception room, where again retainers came forward to shake hands, greet us and lead us inside. We kicked off our chapplis and walked in. The Wali, a thin man in his late 40s, advanced, shook hands and, at his invitation, we sat on cushions positioned along a series of Oriental carpets, our backs against the earthen walls of the majlis. We then took some five minutes exchanging Arabic greetings *'Kayf Haalak?'* ('How is your health?'); *'Bikhayr, Al hamdulillah!'* ('Well, thanks be to God!') and then enquired after each others' families, male relatives, the Sultan, and various personalities. Then came a pause which I found almost embarrassingly long, and then some more *'Kayf Haalaks?'* and *'Al Hamdulillah's'*.

After this a khaddim entered bearing a beautiful silver coffee pot which had a graceful, long curved spout and a knobbed, ornate lid. In his other hand he carried a cluster of tiny cups one of which he handed to each of us. With a swooping movement of the coffee pot he unerringly directed a stream of coffee into our minute cups. We sat and sipped the black, acrid, aromatic coffee and chatted. *'Shay Khabbar?'* ('What's the news?') we asked, and the Wali gave us the local Nizwa gossip.

I in my turn told how the Sultan was, and how I hoped to meet the Sultan's son, on my next visit to Salalah. I told him about the war in Dhofar and of general news in Bait-al-Falaj and Muscat. By now halwa was being served, that delicious sweet, reminiscent of a softer, stickier, more spicy Turkish Delight. I always considered the Nizwa variety the best I ever tasted, a delicious and fitting complement to the bitter Arab coffee, but having a phobia about fat officers I have always had to restrain myself from eating as much as I would have liked!

After three cups of coffee and having waggled our cups to indicate that we required no more, a servant came round with a jug of water in one hand and a towel in the other. In turn we washed the fingers of our right hand under a jet of rose water and dried them on the towel he offered. Another servant followed with a smoking incense burner. This was supposed to be wafted with your hand over and under your beard. Rather embarrassed because I am clean-shaven I waved this cloud of sharply-scented smoke under my bare chin.

Then it was time to take our leave, so putting on our chapplis outside, thanking the Wali and saying goodbye, we made our way down from his quarters across the courtyard below and into the Fort. This was entered over another large, long, inclined log and then through a huge heavy black iron-covered wooden door, whence we climbed up dark, narrow flights of winding stairs. The ceilings above were perforated with grilles through which in bygone days boiling oil or water could be poured on hapless attackers as they climbed their tortuous way from below. Each flight of steps was lit by a hurricane butty, or oil lantern, placed on the ground. We emerged from the gloom through a large door onto the roof, into blinding white, hot sunlight.

The NFR garrison platoon was drawn up on the roof of the fort for inspection and after I had walked round, chatted to everyone and shaken hands, the men went to their action stations. Although we were on the roof of the fort, its curved walls still towered around and above us. Huge embrasures faced over the town, most of them housing ancient Portuguese cannon. Above my head, some thirty feet up, a narrow, railless ledge went round the inside of the Fort's wall. The soldiers swarmed rapidly up some narrow steps which led to it and took up their alarm positions, light machine guns dominating the approaches leading to the Fort from the town below. Other riflemen manned the lower, gaping gun-embrasures which covered all roads and lanes in Nizwa, and the reserve section was grouped centrally together with Platoon Headquarters, ready to reinforce or move to wherever or whatever was necessary.

I quickly climbed the steep steps and ran along the ledge from one post to the next, thinking how easy it would be in the dark to trip or overbalance and fall some thirty feet to the flat roof below. I checked each field of fire, then descended and visited the rest of the posts and sections.

We said goodbye to the platoon, smart in their starched khaki drill shirts, slacks and polished brown leather chapplis, and wearing their dark, rifle-green NFR berets. I noticed two trap doors in the floor and having enquired what they were, these were raised and I gazed into two dark pit shafts, fifteen or more feet deep and about 8 feet by 6 feet in area. Some time before my arrival in Oman it was normal for a prisoner to be lodged in each. They were let down on a rope which was then hauled up. Whatever food and water was allowed was lowered by rope and the trap door was otherwise kept closed. So the unfortunate prisoner existed in this small, deep, rectangular pit in utter darkness and with little air. He had the earth floor as a bed and as he had to urinate and defecate on the floor (human excreta was still in evidence in one cell as I looked down) his conditions would not have please Amnesty International, poor soul.

After a light snack in the Mess, Hugh took me to see another platoon. This was based at Bilaad Sait, the village where Ghalib and Talib had lived, the two brothers who with Suleman bin Himyar, Ruler of the Green Mountain, had waged the Jebal Akhdar Campaign against the Sultan. Because of this the Sultan had decreed that a platoon would be stationed there until further notice.

We drove along the bumpy road through Nizwa stopping en route to examine some of the falajs which had been constructed with such ingenuity and skill by the Persians when they had occupied the country a thousand years before. It was cool down the flights of steps leading to the flowing water below where tiny fish darted in the water's clear depths. On we went, amid the dust, the scrub bushes, palms and cacti, until we reached the village of Bilaad Sait, with the NFR platoon encamped nearby. A wire perimeter ran round the tents and a fortified stone sangar perched on a steep hill within the wire, dominated village and camp alike.

It was warm climbing the steep path up to the sangar in the hot afternoon sun and we were glad of a drink of loomi in the platoon commander's tent on our return. To me the existence of a platoon in that location for punitive reasons was a waste of manpower. I determined to get it moved back to the remainder of its company but it took me nearly two years to achieve this move as the Sultan was implacably determined to hold down the village of his enemies!

Next morning I flew to Ibri to see the company of the Northern Frontier Regiment which was stationed there, its lines being about a mile from the town. Ibri was a lovely place overlooked by the massif of the Hajar Range and surrounded by an earthen wall and groves of luxuriant palm trees. It had plenty of water, a fort where the Wali lived and a space outside where grunting camels rested on folded legs. We flew there in the early morning and Mike Legg, Mick Webb the excellent pilot (who had been at prep school with my two sons) and I got out of the Beaver and walked over to a sand-coloured, open Landrover whose occupants were hurrying towards us. A tanned young Captain introduced himself as Ewan Tailyour. Ewan was one of the Royal Marine officers seconded to SAF and the son of a former Royal Marine Commandant General, the late General Sir Norman Tailyour. We motored into the camp, inspected the smart Quarter Guard, went round the lines, visited the cookhouse and then, sitting on a vine-covered patio outside a delightful little Officers' Mess surrounded by a pleasing garden with a fish pond and flowering shrubs, we had breakfast. Afterwards we strolled across to the next bungalow, where lived Rex King of Shell, a staunch friend to so many of us in the Sultan's Armed Forces, and a generous and thoughtful host. We spent the morning on the range shooting with the men of Ewan's Company, after which we called on the Wali, a nice old man, father of the Wali of Buraimi. He seemed a sound, dependable person and easy to talk to.

In the afternoon we toured the town and surrounding countryside to give me an idea of the terrain and in the evening the Wali laid on a display of racing for us. The small Arab horses were a splendid sight. They had no saddles or stirrups, and the riders careered up and down outside the palm-overhung mud walls of the town. The show ended with a display of camel racing, riders sitting cross-legged shrilly encouraging their ungainly mounts.

That evening I went round talking to the soldiers and was impressed with their high morale and spirit; I was sure they would be a great success on operations in Dhofar and I was to find out just how staunch and brave they were during the months ahead.

My next visit was to the Desert Regiment. At that time this was the most recently formed infantry battalion. Its senior company was called Red Company as a reminder that the battalion had been formed from men of the Muscat Regiment whose regimental colour was red. The Desert Regiment whose men wore sand-coloured berets was stationed at Bid Bid with a detached company at Izki and another at Rostaq. It was commanded by Lieutenant Colonel Brian Barnes, Irish Guards. Its Second-in-Command was Major Ivor MacEwan, a large Scot who spoke fluent Baluch. Major Micky Boyd, MBE, another experienced Irish Guardsman, commanded Headquarter Company and the rifle companies were commanded by Paul Mangin (Red Company), solid, pipe-smoking, reliable and loved by his men. Jonathan Nason, a charming Queen's Own Highlander and expert rifle shot, and capable Dick Edwards of the Queen's, both big men like Paul, commanded the other two rifle companies. I had been practising hard at my Arabic and, having inspected the smart Quarter Guard on my arrival, I made them a short speech of congratulations in Arabic. I could almost see my words rebounding off their foreheads as they stood stiff and uncomprehending before me, dressed in starched KD, white blancoed web belts and sand-coloured berets! Having shaken hands all round as was the custom, I moved away accompanied by the burly figure of the Second-in-Command. 'Do you know, Ivor,' I said, 'I am really worried about my dreadful Arabic. I don't believe any of those men understood a single word I said!' 'They didn't, Sir,' replied Ivor consolingly, adding as an after-thought, 'You see, they are all Baluch and that's the only tongue they understand just now!' I then discovered that all Baluch had to receive training in the Arabic language and that these recent arrivals had not yet mastered it!

Desert Regiment was the next unit due for operations in Dhofar and Brian Barnes and his battalion were working flat out to be ready in time. I accompanied Brian as he visited training and was pleased to see how fit all ranks were. The battalion camp was situated off the Wadi Sumail in the Wadi Bid Bid from which it derived its name. The wadi was a succession of sparkling pools of clear water, bordered by the inevitable, pink-flowered oleanders and clumps of dark green rushes. The men were able to bathe in these pools and above the Officers' Mess was another deep pool where we went for a refreshing swim that afternoon.

We discussed tactics for Dhofar; Paul Mangin's Red Company was to be the first of the detached companies to go there, where they would operate initially under the command of the Muscat Regiment. Brian would fly there once Paul was established and get to know the terrain and the enemy's *modus operandi*. He would also arrange for the officers and senior NCOs of the remainder of the battalion to carry out attachments to Red Company in order to acquire familiarity with the task ahead, with the terrain, and to acquire the necessary tactical expertise.

With Brian at the wheel of the Landrover we motored up the Wadi Sumail to Izki, and the next company. On the way I reflected on the very different conditions prevailing on the day I had first seen Brian. Today the towering mass of the Jebal Akhdar hung over us, vast slabs of rock glaring white, grey, purple and indigo in the fierce sunlight, with perpendicular chasms of black shadow where the cliffs fell sheer in great sombre gorges to ground level. Beside us was the stony Wadi Sumail with its wide, shallow stretches of blue water and behind us hung a cloud of white dust. The previous occasion on which I had seen Brian Barnes had been a summer's day in London. My younger son Tim and I had been about to cross the Mall when we heard the steady thumping of drums and the crash of martial music. Looking towards Admiralty Arch along the wide roadway lined with trees cool in their summer greenery, we could see a solitary mounted Metropolitan policeman riding towards us on his bay horse, and following behind him, the brass of their instruments flashing in the morning sun, came the bearskin-topped, scarlet and blue of a Guards Band.

We waited to watch the band pass, followed by a company of guards-men swinging along with that swagger peculiar to the Irish Guards. Then came the rest of the 'Micks' led by a spare, dark, hatchet-faced major with a black moustache. We waited until Brian Barnes and his men had passed, their Colour borne by a tall ensign, and the crash of music died away. I little thought then that that same company commander would command one of my battalions in Oman.

Dick Edwards and Philip Carte were supervising a field-firing exercise in the nearby foothills where the men were running up and down with the agility of mountain goats and engaging various targets. I noted some capable platoon commanders in particular Staff Sergeants Charshambe and Pattan, both of whom were Baluchs. The former had won the Gallantry Medal (Oman's equivalent to the Victoria Cross) and the latter would be awarded the Bravery Medal, the next highest decoration. 'Well,' I thought, 'They will just about be ready in time and, provided they have a week or two to settle in when they get to Dhofar, they should give a good account of themselves.'

Except in Dhofar where operations went on unbroken day in, day out, Friday (or as it was called in Arabic, Juma'a, the Muslim equivalent of our Sunday) was our day off. As we worked very hard during the other six days of the week it was pleasant to have a lazy start to the day, write our weekly letters home and have an undisturbed breakfast. Then the bearers would load up our Safari Landrover with beach umbrellas, towels, rush mats, ice boxes, food and drink and off we would go to swim. Usually we went to 'Blackpool', SAF's own beach given to us by the Sultan. This was located in the camp of the local oil company. PDO – Petroleum Development Oman – a subsidiary of Shell, at Mina al Fahal some half hour's drive from our house. When we got bored with going to 'Blackpool' we would swim and picnic at Qurum beach a little further on. This was a great expanse of sand which we normally had all to ourselves save for the occasional Omani fisherman and one inevitable SAF Landrover with Malcolm Denison and Bob Warner, both of whom used to spend their day sitting up to their waists in the sea, reading in wicker armchairs!

The sea here was shallow and you had to wade out a long way to get sufficient depth in which to swim. Shells of all sorts of lovely shapes and colours were on the beach in abundance and we have a fine collection of these at home. Occasionally there were sea snakes swimming in the water or stranded on the beach. I remember touching with my rubber sandal, an apparently dead sea snake lying on the sand and being galvanised when it suddenly came to life and struck at me. Bill Carden with his charming wife Anne and their daughter Claire, would often join us on these occasions, Bill being HBM's Consul General in Oman at that time. Later, sadly for us, the Cardens left when Bill became Director of the Middle East College of Arabic Studies at Shemlan in Lebanon. He continued his distinguished career becoming British Ambassador in Sana'a to the Yemen Arab Republic, and later in Khartoum to the Sudan. Bill had started his career in the Sudan Civil Service and the Sultan used to say that he spoke classical Arabic, quite the best of any expatriate in Oman. The Cardens became close friends of ours and sometimes we would cook a holiday breakfast together on Qurum beach in the cool of a winter's early morning over a fire of myrrh, after which we would go for a walk with our dogs, Hebe the Great Dane and Cho San the Peke and collect shells. Then, while Anne and Patricia chatted, and Claire and Angela played, Bill and I would wade out into the sea and discuss matters of state. He and I worked closely together and these weekly chats would keep Bill in the picture as to our doings and plans in SAF and brief me as to the thoughts and possibilities in the minds of the British Government. Bill was a very good friend to the Sultan and to Oman. In the final outcome he naturally had to be the mouthpiece of the British Government. I, on the other hand, was the servant of the Sultan, the Commander of his Armed Forces, and my loyalty was to him and to Oman, tempered always by the fact that my ultimate loyalty lay with my Queen and Country in the event of there being a conflict between what I felt was right and wrong. There were a few occasions when I felt I should not immediately tell Bill certain plans for the future because I felt that HMG might not approve of them, yet I as the man on the spot believed they were right. An instance of this was after the British pull-out from Aden when I advised the Sultan that his Forces should occupy the Kuria Muria Islands lest they fall into the hands of an unfriendly neighbour. There seemed to be a certain amount of political uncertainty in UK on this subject. I knew that we had not the time to wait about even if the British Government's ultimate decision agreed with ours, so we acted immediately. Of course we informed Bill as soon as operations were in train as I hated not telling him in advance, but he might have had to convey to me HMG's advice, which perhaps would be contrary, and it was best not to risk that! As events turned out, we were right and occupation by the unfriendly Marxist South Yemenis of a base from which they could operate near Omani coasts was avoided.

As lunchtime approached, our two families would move to the shade of the cliffs at one end of Qurum beach and with glasses of Chablis in our hands we would chip off and eat rock oysters while standing up to our waists in the sea.

Once every six weeks or so I would fly down to Dhofar for anything from four days to a fortnight or longer, during which time I would go out on operations and have Audiences with the Sultan. Life was therefore exciting and full of variety and interest. I was lucky in my staff, all of whom were volunteers and most of whom were young and active. The more elderly were well worth their places, as these were men who knew the Arab or the Baluch well and loved them, and Oman. Their fund of knowledge, experience and compassion was invaluable to SAF.

We had a hospital next door to our Headquarters in the Fort, in which were housed the Forces' sick and injured as well as wounded soldiers from Dhofar. I had gone over to visit the hospital the day after I took command and was appalled. Men were lying in hot, dark, stuffy rooms, there were no trained nurses, no patients' diets, and a generally depressing atmosphere of neglect and disinterest prevailed. This was a situation that could clearly not be tolerated and I sent for the doctor responsible and gave him two weeks in which to show a marked improvement. This he failed to achieve. I thereupon removed him from office and incurred my Sultan's displeasure. Pat Waterfield told me that the doctor concerned had been recruited personally by the Sultan who would be angry at my action. However I knew I was right and I flew down for an Audience at which I respectfully put it to the Sultan, having apologised first for having unknowingly acted without his agreement in an appointment he himself had made, that if he did not trust my judgement and experience it would be far better that he should ask HMG to remove me from command forthwith and have me replaced by someone else. I asserted that on professional matters such as this, as his Commander, I must be allowed to run my command as seemed right to me, whilst continuing to refer matters of major policy to him. He was very cross initially but in the end he agreed and from then on allowed me to run the Force my own way, save when it came to spending money! So I brought in Ian Hynd, until then Regimental Medical Officer of Muscat Regiment, to be the Force Senior Medical Officer, having first replaced him with an excellent Indian MO on deputation from the Indian Army, Captain Habeeb Ashruf. I never regretted this decision. Iain, a Scot, could speak both Baluch and Arabic and had a wonderful way of winning the confidence of us all, especially the soldiers, a deep compassion and a sense of humour which he needed a lot! Nothing deterred him and he was a fine doctor. From that moment our Force Medical Service was born and never looked back, although we had some difficult times ahead.

I brought Jim Dolphin-Rowlands in from Midway to be the Administrative Officer and Joyce Sanderson, the wife of Louis Sanderson, Pat Waterfield's Deputy, volunteered to be Matron as she was a trained nurse. Joyce was loved by her patients because of her motherly, kindly attitude and for her confidence-inspiring knowledge and efficiency. Jim Dolphin-Rowland quietly got on with helping Iain to set up a sound and progressive administrative back-up.

First we had the entire hospital thoroughly disinfected, washed, cleaned out and repainted. Then we had a large refrigerator purchased and installed for the safe holding of vaccines and medicines. Ceiling punkah fans were put into all wards and a programme was initiated for each ward to be equipped with air-conditioning. Proper flush WCs and running water, showers and basins were put in, an area was set apart for convalescents, with a sitting-out place and garden at the back of the hospital buildings. Isolation wards were built on the flat hospital roof, games, magazines, journals and newspapers were provided, also fruit, soft drinks and special diets. Orderlies were trained by Iain Hynd, and two British male staff-nurses came out on contract, engaged by Brigadier Pat Waterfield. The shortage of accommodation and money was so great (the British subsidy was discontinued shortly after I became CSAF, even though the money from oil had not begun to come in at this stage) that those who were being trained for hospital work at Bait-al-Falaj and Salalah and as company medical orderlies, had to receive their instruction in the old donkey lines which we converted into classrooms because they were conveniently situated close by the Fort and the hospital.

Pat Waterfield had by now succeeded in arranging the secondment of sufficient military doctors from the Indian Army Medical Services for each battalion to have its own Regimental Medical Officer, as well as for a Resident Medical Officer and a dentist to be stationed at the Force Hospital at Bait-al-Falaj. These officers were an immediate success and a morale booster. The badly wounded from Dhofar were flown to Bahrain for treatment at the Royal Air Force Hospital as we still did not have the surgical facilities required to cope with them. The less severely injured and cases of sickness from there were dealt with either on the spot in Salalah where we had a Medical Centre or in Bait-al-Falaj Hospital. I asked again for the secondment of field surgical teams from the British services in order to save lives which might otherwise be lost by delay in urgent treatment but these were not to materialise until shortly after I left.

Casualty evacuation in Dhofar was another problem, lives being lost and injuries aggravated by wounded men having to be carried long distances on donkey back or on stretchers. Additionally, of course, this impeded the successful prosecution of operations and, indeed, endangered the lives of the rest of the troops concerned. Sometimes the ground could be cleared to allow a Beaver to land to take off casualties, but in Dhofar this was fairly rare and of course ground clearance took time. The obvious answer was helicopters but despite my urgent representations the Sultan did not consider them of sufficient importance to purchase at that stage.

My requests for the secondment of a detachment of helicopters from the Royal Navy, Army Air Corps or Royal Air Force, for a Field Surgical

Team, and a detachment of SAS, made to the Director of Military Operations, and other senior officers during my UK leaves, and during their visits to the Sultanate, supported by requests through and backed by the British Consul General, were turned down. I imagine the reason for this refusal was political, but failure to support our requests prolonged the Dhofar War by years and resulted in needless deaths and woundings. It was ironic that after Sultan Said bin Taimur had been deposed, all such assistance materialised with alacrity. I persisted and, eventually, the purchase of helicopters was approved during my last six months as CSAF, thanks to the support of General Roly Gibbs and of Hugh Oldman, Pat Waterfield's successor but they together with a Field Surgical Team, and some SAS, did not arrive until after I had handed over command.

CHAPTER TWENTY-THREE

COMPONENTS AND PERSONALITIES

In addition to the Army and the Air Force, CSAF commanded the Sultan of Oman's Navy, or, as it was then called, the Coastal Patrol. The Coastal Patrol in April 1967 consisted of a solitary, large, motorised dhow, capable of carrying two companies of infantry. Her name was *Nasr al Bahr, Victor of the Sea*, and I boarded her in Muscat harbour where she was moored alongside the quay. The crew who manned the deck as I came aboard were local coastal Omanis for the most part and clad in navy blue drill uniforms. Their headgear was a blue, Indian Congress-style cap, and they wore blue singlets with quarter sleeves, blue trousers and had bare feet.

They were commanded by a tall, barrel-chested, powerfully built European. 'The original Viking', I thought, looking at this large, golden-haired man with his yellow beard. 'Jeremy Raybould, Sir,' he introduced himself, shaking hands with a grip like a clamp. and thus began my association with one of the bravest and most natural leaders I have served with. We were to be under fire together on a number of future occasions and he was to be decorated more than once for his gallantry, not only in the face of the enemy, but for saving the lives of his men in the deadly danger of a violent tropical storm at sea.

I went along the drawn-up ranks of men, shaking hands and talking to each one of them, ending up with the cook. One or two looked very old indeed but there were a number of young men too. I thought they looked a good lot and felt at home with them. My confidence in them was to be justified over and over again. We were to carry out a number of operations together and their staunch behaviour under fire, loyalty, cheerfulness and professionalism were beyond praise. We always seemed to have some

223

excitement when we sailed together and I used to really look forward to these trips.

That morning we cast off and Jeremy showed me round the ship. In a rather shy, diffident way he told me that he was afraid he was breaking orders because he slept on top of the bulk of the ship's ammunition, explosives and pyrotechnics and he hoped that I didn't mind! He showed me that there simply was no suitable place for them other than below his bunk. I could see that he was not in the slightest bit worried for his safety; however I now was! I had long kicked against red tape and bureaucracy in the enforcement of unrealistic rules and regulations so I told him that until he or I could think of a better place for them he had better continue to sleep on it! I confess that from then on I had the uneasy knowledge that I should have been able to think out a better alternative but I never did!

Two months later we acquired a second, large, motor dhow, the *Muntasir*, which like *Nasr al Bahr* could also carry two companies of infantry, so that we were then able to move a battalion by sea, which was to prove very valuable operationally.

We went out of Muscat harbour under power, round a huge oil tanker lying off the P.D.O. oil installations, the great ship's black sides towering above us, past Fahal Island which was shimmering in the furnace-like morning heat. Jeremy ordered the engines to be stopped and for *Nasr al Bahr* to come under sail. We glided along by Qurum beach past a large grounded ship which had been gutted by fire, the burnt-out skeletons of the vehicles she had been carrying as deck cargo standing black on her decks. The cargo of paint in her holds was said to have been set alight by terrorists several years earlier. We watched sea snakes swimming near the hulk, writhing along with their heads on top of the water.

We returned to Muscat with the dhow's engines throbbing powerfully and Jeremy invited me to present himself and his crew with their medals for the Dhofar Campaign. Before my three years in command were up I would have pinned decorations for gallantry on several of his crew and Jeremy would have received the Bravery Medal from the Sultan.

As I have said, SOAF also came under CSAF's command. At that time it was a small air force, consisting of piston-engined Provost ground-attack aircraft armed with cannons and fitted for rockets, and for bombs of up to 500 lbs. The other aircraft in those early days were single-engined Beavers which had four seats and quite a bit of space behind them for cargo. As some of the piston Provosts were two-seaters, I decided I would fly with the Air Force as soon as possible.

SOAF was commanded by Brian Entwhistle, a very capable, regular Squadron Leader. He and his pretty wife, Jill, were the only married Service pair permitted to live in the Sultanate other than CSAF and his wife.

I had already flown several times in our Beavers and was impressed by the way in which our generally extrovert, cheerful, tearaway young pilots underwent a seeming change of character directly they were at the controls of an aircraft. Gone were the laughing young men I had seen yesterday splashing the few young European girls on 'Blackpool beach'. In their places were mature, serious-minded pilots who inspired confidence. We got into the Provost. Brian saw I had my helmet on, and that I was properly strapped into the seat beside his. The engine roared into life and he taxied out onto the runway. We took off over the fort and swung left and inland, still climbing.

Brian did some aerobatics first of all, having advised me to press down with my feet on the floor of the cockpit to avoid 'greying out' from the pull of gravity during manoeuvres. I found that this worked admirably. We then made for the bombing range for practice so that I would get the idea of the assault capabilities of this aircraft and also see the pilot's eye view of ground targets. Brian pointed out to me, from several thousand feet above the ground, the targets which he would bomb, cannon and machine gun. I was surprised how difficult I personally found it to locate them, even such large ones as the hulks of Army 4 ton lorries. This was a useful lesson, and made me admire the accuracy of our SOAF pilots when they supported us in action in Dhofar. We carried out a series of attacks and I returned having had a most instructive and valuable morning that was to prove of great value to me in the three years that lay ahead. Royal Air Force training had done us well in producing these fine men, both regular and contract officers, and every one of them made a valuable contribution to our war in Dhofar. Furthermore, after the pull-out from Aden they were to be the only pilots in the Royal Air Force with up-to-date ground attack battle experience until the Falklands Campaign. They fired their rockets, guns and cannons and dropped their bombs under enemy fire which increased in intensity and accuracy as the adoo were equipped by the Communist Bloc with sophisticated weapons. Few of our pilots did not have bullet holes in their aircraft at some time on their return from operational missions. The Beavers also had to fly with the possibility of enemy ground fire and to land on strips, some of which were very short indeed, and rocky and well into enemy terrain so I had given orders that the pristine white Beavers were to be properly camouflaged to lessen the chances of their being seen and hit.

I was informed by Pat Waterfield that two Dakotas would shortly arrive, as well as Strikemasters (an attack version of the Jet Provost) to replace the piston-engined aircraft. The morale of the pilots was excellent as was that of the non-flying officers, and they endeared themselves to the soldiers by going out on land operations in Dhofar and learning from first-hand experience what the ground troops' problems were.

I was also struck with the quiet efficiency of the Airwork personnel who maintained our aircraft. They were completely integrated into SOAF, each one of them was 'one of us', and they did their stint in Dhofar based at RAF Salalah. There were some who never wanted to leave 'the sharp end', such as Jack Mahood, and who were a tremendous help by their devotion to their work in keeping these vital aircraft airworthy. I was delighted when we obtained permission for Airwork personnel to be eligible for the Dhofar General Service Medal, which all of us agreed they fully earned.

Obviously we had to build up SOAF in strength and in sophistication, including setting up a training programme to eventually hand over to Omani aircrews and ground crews. I had complete confidence that Omanis would prove worthy successors as the Air Force expanded, as indeed they have done.

After visiting the Coastal Patrol and the Air Force my next visit was to another of our regiments, the Oman Gendarmerie. This unit was almost entirely composed of Arab soldiers. Its British Officers were generally older than those in the other battalions, and were mainly former officers of colonial police forces. The OG, as the unit was usually called, manned border posts on the frontier where the soldiers lived in Beau Geste type forts whence they patrolled their areas of responsibility. OG Headquarters was at Sib on the Batinah Coast, in those days about forty minutes drive from Bait-al-Falaj. Sib was green and lush, tall trees abounded, mangoes, palms, peepuls and acacias gave cool shade to gardens, and brightly-coloured birds filled the early morning with the rich notes of their song. Wealthy Muscat Indian and Arab merchants had built houses there with gardens bright with dahlias, bougainvillea and lantana.

The camp with its fort and cantonment was situated on rising ground to the south of the long, wide, shallow, gravelly, usually dry wadi which led to the sea a few hundred yards away. The garden of the Officers' Mess was lovingly planted and tended and had a green, thick lawn, kept short by 'the lawnmower', a sheep.

There was also a small swimming pool, in those days unusual and much appreciated by its users, who, in the hot, humid summer of the Batinah coast, often sat in its cool blue water in wicker armchairs, reading, chatting and sipping iced drinks.

On my first visit to the OG I flew to Sohar further up the coast. This was a place I grew to love. Sohar, even more humid than Sib during the hot weather, was an area of green trees, cultivated fields and little narrow lanes fringed with bushes and cacti. The surrounding countryside was red earth from which grew trees up to fifteen feet high among which grazed herds of goats and camels. Sohar was a small place and the OG post was in Kashmir Lodge, a two-storey whitewashed building, with a garden and a cantonment of barrack huts, cookhouses and ablutions which were also painted white. The action of the humidity and of the sea air was such that the walls of the barrack huts inside and out were in constant need of repainting. The parade ground was sandy, soft and dusty. Graceful palm trees grew in profusion, there were brown, mud brick walls between the perimeter and the sea, and on the beach outside was a small mosque near which the shallow boats of fishermen were dragged up.

As the Beaver came in to land I could see a small group of figures waiting by the edge of the red airstrip, two Landrovers parked nearly behind them, with four more figures standing by the vehicles.

The Beaver rolled to a halt, turned in a swirl of fine red dust and taxied back to the group awaiting my arrival. Two deeply sunburnt men, each with a moustache, advanced towards me. Tony Best was the Commandant (OG had been originally formed by Gurkha officers, and the CO was known as 'the Commandant'). We shook hands and Tony introduced me to Bill Aucutt. They reminded me of those Empire-building, pith-helmeted types in pre-war Barney's Punchbowl Tobacco advertisements pictured strolling through exotic-looking bazaars. They wore dark blue berets, with the SAF badge (common to all units in those days) blue, pre-war British Indian Army-type mazri shirts, web belts, neatly pressed khaki slacks and sand-coloured suede desert boots. We moved over to the Landrovers, where I shook hands with the two Arab drivers and the other two soldiers, all of whom were very smartly dressed. Instead of blue berets they wore blue and white checked shemaghs. The pilot handed over some mail and various sacks and parcels. The two OG gendarmes remained to guard the Beaver and the rest of us got into the Landrovers and bumped off through the trees and thorn bushes past herds of goats, grazing near low-slung, black Bedu tents and the occasional camel. We followed a track fringed by hedges towards Kashmir Lodge which I could see white against the vivid blue background of the sea. We drove through the entrance gates to the courtyard where a smart Quarter Guard was drawn up for my inspection. The lean, dark Arab soldiers looked, and were, excellent fighting material. The Arab is never subservient. He knows he is just as good a man as you are, and, whilst splendidly disciplined and respectful, talks to you very much 'man to man'.

Having shaken hands with the Sergeant Major and the members of the guard, complimented them on their smartness and had a chat, I was conducted round the lines and made various notes on things that required doing to improve living conditions. The barrack rooms were spotless, the kits a model of neatness, the men fit-looking, cheerful and happy. We then went over to Kashmir Lodge for breakfast. Here I met two Force 'characters', Sandy Gordon, the OC, who was just back from a visit to one of his sections, and Carl Seton-Brown, the Sultan's Intelligence Officer. Sandy, lean, tall, bony and cadaverous, was a former parachutist, who had later served as a police lieutenant during the Malayan Emergency. He had a wonderful rapport with his men.

Carl Seton-Brown was a very experienced and successful Intelligence Officer and a lover of country pursuits, especially shooting. Carl introduced me to his venerable-looking headman, Omar, who was a valuable source of information and was to play a useful part in the Wadi Jizzi incursion later on.

Kashmir Lodge reminded me of an English country house. Downstairs it was cool with large bedrooms opening from a dark, wide stone passage. Upstairs was a dining room, a living room, more bedrooms, and a roof-cum-balcony overlooking the garden whose main path passed through an arch formed by two huge, inward-curving whale ribs which looked like giant white-grey tusks.

The living room smelt of furniture polish and leather, the walls were lined with bookcases filled with sporting volumes, while copies of 'The Field', 'Shooting Times', 'Fishing Gazette' and 'Country Life' were scattered round the various tables, chairs and sofas. Breakfast was brought into the dining room. The talk was mainly about the local intelligence situation and of possible threats to the Sultanate through the Trucial States, at that time mainly from Iraq, and from Saudi Arabia where the rebel leaders from the Jebal Akhdar uprising were living in the Dammam area. Carl also spoke about local personalities and I began to get the picture of affairs in this, the northern seaboard of the Sultan's domain. Afterwards Tony Best and Bill Aucutt, each wreathed in aromatic clouds of pipe smoke, and Sandy, took me for a conducted tour of the garden which had a graceful group of tall, slender palms by the western wall near the house. We viewed the fruit, vegetables and flowers, and made the acquaintance of the Kashmir Lodge flock of domestic geese, beautiful white birds in wonderful condition and dog-like in their friendliness.

After a stroll along the adjoining beach over the soft sand, past native fishing boats, some of which were made of rushes, and where wiry, muscly, smiling fishermen wearing only loincloths, greeted us, it was time to return to the Beaver to visit the two posts in the Sohar Sector at Assuad and Khatma Milaha. We took our leave of Carl and Sandy and bumped off in the Landrovers down the pleasant lanes and out among the scattered trees to the airstrip where the guards, standing under the shade of the Beaver's wings greeted us with wide smiles and vigorous handshakes. Two camels were shooed off the airstrip, we climbed into the aircraft, strapped ourselves into our seats, rolled down to the seaward end of the runway and turned.

The Beaver shook as the powerful radial engine roared, and then we were running down the strip, were airborne, climbing and circling to look down on Sohar Camp, Kashmir Lodge, the mosque, the fishing boats on the beach, and as we turned away to follow the verdant Batinah coast up to Assuad on the border our last sight was of three uniformed figures looking up from the parade ground and waving, the Sergeant Major and two gendarmes. Kashmir Lodge would always be a favourite place to return to: the officer team there was a strong one and the Arab soldiers were first-class.

We droned on over the Batinah coastline which, thanks to the presence of fresh-water springs, was abundantly green, with date palms, mangoes, and fields of vegetables among which stood little barusti huts and white-washed, flat-roofed houses. Tony Best leant over and pointed downwards when we crossed a stretch of sea and I saw the huge, black, bat-like shape of a giant manta ray, apparently motionless just below the surface. Then the aircraft turned in to the land and below us I could see the rough road that led from the Sultanate into the Trucial States. There was a cluster of small buildings by the frontier gate, and across the road two OG soldiers were looking upwards. Some former British Army Bedford 4 ton lorries loaded with goods were parked beside the road with a group of local Arabs. Then we were coming into land on yet another dirt and gravel strip.

The Beaver rolled to a stop, where two Landrovers, with smart gendarmes were waiting for us. After introductions, handshakes and greetings, we drove off in a thick cloud of dust towards the frontier post we had just flown over. Assuad was the main entry point into Oman through the adjoining Trucial State of Fujairah (whose Ruler, at that time, was affectionately known as Fudge!). All incomers to Oman were closely scrutinised and their belongings searched to make sure no rebels, weapons or ammunition entered the Sultanate.

On our arrival the guards on duty dashed forward to shake our hands but I noticed that one man remained keeping an eye on the civilians whilst greetings were exchanged and that he only came forward himself when his place was taken by another watchful gendarme. We were also greeted by every other person present and there ensued the lengthy process of enquiring after each individual's health and that of his family before we looked round the area. Then, climbing into our open-sided Landrovers we bumped off towards the nearby OG fort at Assuad itself. This was a small, white-washed building with a crenellated square tower at the entrance. On top of the tower was mounted a searchlight beside which stood an armed OG sentry who looked down keenly at us as we approached.

Outside the fort was drawn up the customary smart Quarter Guard, heads up, shoulders back with rifles at the present as I got out of the

Landrover, their blue and white shemaghs fluttering in a sudden zephyr of hot wind. The staff sergeant saluted briskly and I inspected the lean, fine-looking, upright men, their eyes looking straight into mine, each soldier answering loudly and proudly the questions I put to him. I congratulated them on their bearing, drill and turnout, shook hands all round and we entered the fort together. This was built to enclose a square. I visited the high-ceilinged, shady, cool barrack room in which the beds were widely spaced, each bearing a neatly-laid kit for me to look at and I noticed that the floor was spotless. Then we visited the store, office, and cookhouse. The Post Commander and I climbed up the steps to the tower to chat to the sentry on duty, to see the surrounding area from his point of view, and to switch on his searchlight, to ensure it was working – its lit bulb was just discernible despite the white glare of the Omani sunlight.

Then down we trooped to a room containing a trestle table and benches where we and all the gendarmes other than the duty sentry, sat down, plates of biscuits, pineapple chunks and peach slices were put before us and we were offered halwa and Arab coffee. Afterwards we washed our fingers in a large china mug of water. The SOAF pilot, new to Oman and to Arab customs, was engrossed in conversation with the Staff Sergeant and had not noticed what the rest of us were doing. On being handed the mug he put it to his lips and drained the contents. This convulsed everyone and some of the gendarmes nearly fell off the benches in their mirth. The poor pilot was never allowed to forget this, but he was not the only new officer to make a similar mistake!

As we moved off to look at the frontier area, patrolled from the Assuad post, I thought what happy, humorous, manly personalities the Arab gendarmes had. They were natural soldiers who, after some intensive training, would do well in Dhofar.

We stood on the small foothills looking into Fujairah and after Tony Best had indicated to me the main approach routes into the Sultanate, we returned to our Landrovers, drove to the airstrip and took leave of our hosts. Then we climbed back into the Beaver and roared up into the sky, waving down at the guards below at the frontier post and headed inland for Khatma Milaha, another Beau Geste fort. Here we repeated the same process except that the pilot did not drink from the washing-water mug! By the end of the day I had a far better idea of the ground and the problems and also had a 'feel' as to the morale and efficiency of the Oman Gendarmerie. We landed at Sohar to drop Tony Best and Bill Aucutt and replaced them with two heavy ice boxes containing local fish destined for upcountry units and Bait-al-Falaj and flew back along the coast to our Headquarters.

CHAPTER TWENTY-FOUR

NORTH OMAN

My next trip to the OG was to the troop at Buraimi (scene of the Saudi invasion incident in 1955), and the frontier posts at Sumaini and Qabil, each post manned by a section of a sergeant and nine gendarmes.

Buraimi was commanded by Major Grahame Vivian, MC, whom I had last seen when he was commanding a company in his battalion of the 2nd Gurkha Rifles in Malaya. Serving with him was the Sultan's Intelligence Officer for that Sector, kindly Tom Lomas, a former colonial policeman loved by everyone. To reach Buraimi on this occasion we flew up towards Sohar and then inland along the boulder-strewn Wadi Jizzi. The Wadi Jizzi was one of the main access routes into Oman from the Trucial States and I and my family were to grow to know it well, as we bumped along it by Landrover when we toured all our posts in northern Oman (and were thoroughly spoilt by our hosts). This we did *en famille* twice every year.

As we came to the far end of the wadi we saw before us a large whale-shaped feature which dominated the surrounding ground; this was Jebal Haffif in the Trucial States. We then swung right towards the Buraimi oasis, part of which was in the Sultanate and part in the Trucial States. My eye was caught by a great crenellated white 'sugar cake' fort to our left, a most attractive and impressive building. This was Fort Jahli, Headquarters of the local Trucial Oman Scouts squadron, commanded at that time by an enormous Highlander, David Severn of the Black Watch.

We flew over the wreck of an aircraft and landed smoothly on a long, gravel runway on which much larger aircraft than ours could land. The small, sunburnt, fit-looking figure of Grahame Vivian came forward, accompanied by tall, silver-haired Tom Lomas. We drove off after the

231

usual greetings all round, through masses of tall palm trees along a wide sandy track, the sides of which were littered with the decomposing heads of cows, goats and sheep, past two-storey earth houses, up an incline and through the perimeter fence which surrounded a neat compound of huts with a guardroom on the left of the entrance.

Having inspected the Quarter Guard and met all the men, we went into Tom Lomas's office where, over a cup of tea, he briefed me on the local intelligence situation, after which Grahame put me in the operational picture and gave me a rundown of local personalities. I learnt that after a tour of the lines and breakfast we would call on the Wali of Buraimi, and then on the T.O.S. at Fort Jahli where Colonel Pat Ive, OBE, Commandant of the Scouts, would receive us. Before that we toured the OG lines in Buraimi Camp, visiting the cookhouse and the spotless, immaculate barrack rooms with some of the smartest kit layouts I had seen until coming to SAF. It was a tonic to chat with the cheerful, alert soldiers. Tom then showed me the well which had needed a pump for some time, and on my return to Bait-al-Falaj I got the Defence Department to supply and install one. Then we went on to view Tom's remarkable vegetable and flower garden which was always being added to and improved and which supplied a much appreciated supplement to the diet of all ranks at the post.

After a wash, and a tour through the Officers' Mess rooms, we went through fly-meshed swing-doors into the comfortably furnished little anteroom for a pint of iced loomi and a chat. Then Raji, the Pakistani cook, came smilingly in to serve us a breakfast of melon, papaya and bananas, followed by fish from the Batinah coast and 'egg rumble tumble with chillies'.

Breakfast over, we congratulated Raji on his cooking and set off to call on the Wali of Buraimi. Once again we bumped past the array of smelly, decomposing, severed animal heads (I resolved to mention this eyesore to the Wali when we met) and through the cool shade of tall palms before arriving at his ochre-coloured fort. Here we were welcomed by a group of askars whose apparent ages ranged from 19 to 90. Having shaken hands all round we were escorted inside amid a babble of excited voices and up a flight of earth stairs to where the Wali awaited us. It was surprisingly cool inside the fort and we kicked off our shoes outside the majlis, where he received us.

The Wali was a young man, sensible, friendly and intelligent. I had already met his father, the Wali of Ibri. We had a chat about local affairs seated on rugs on the floor, backed by plump cushions, regaled with delicious halwa (the Wali told me that Nizwa halwa was the best in Oman, and that his halwa had come from there), and Arab coffee. He was clearly a trier at his job and Grahame and Tom told me that he was helpful and cooperative. (He never did do anything about the animals heads, though!)

We took our leave of the Wali, said goodbye to his askars and headed towards Fort Jahli.

It only took us a few minutes to reach the Trucial Oman Scouts' imposing fort. Happy atmosphere and cleanliness prevailed at Fort Jahli and the burly figure of Pat Ive, clad in red and white checked shemagh with Scouts' badge in the agal, long blue mazri blouse, khaki-drill slacks and suede desert boots came forward, accompanied by the towering figure of David Severn.

The Trucial Oman Scouts, a fine, smart and disciplined force, patrolled and policed the desert wastes, mountains, towns and villages of the seven Trucial States. (The Trucial States are now called the United Arab Emirates): Abu Dhabi, Dubai, Sharjah, Ras al Khaima, Fujairah, Ajman and Umm al Qawain. The Scouts were officered by both British and Arabs. All British officers were volunteers. I got to know them well and I am sure they envied us the operational service we enjoyed in Dhofar and that they would have done well there. However, the Scouts' Dhofari squadron would surely have complicated matters had they been involved in our campaign!

This was a first-class sub-unit, commanded by Ken Wilson who had a great way with his Dhofaris. The Dhofari officers and men were natural soldiers, intelligent, excellent at weapon training and fieldcraft, and it was rumoured that when they were on leave in Dhofar, they fought against SAF.

I would certainly not underestimate our enemy in that rebellious province. Pat Ive invited me to inspect a smart Quarter Guard, then took me up the steps and into the Fort where I was introduced to two of his Arab officers. The fort was comfortably furnished and the British Army, which administered the TOS, had done them well. Pat, with his friendly, straightforward manner, inspired confidence and was determined that there would be the best possible relationship between the Scouts and ourselves and that we would work together as closely as possible.

It was not easy to obtain permission from the Sultan for Intelligence Officers of the TOS to enter Oman to consult with their opposite numbers in SAF. Shortly after this visit to Fort Jahli I had an Audience with the Sultan at which I explained the importance to both TOS and SAF for this liaison after which things were easier. Pat and Jeanette, his wife and their children became great friends of ours and we used to drive over the desert to stay with each other at our respective homes. I wanted to find ways of releasing SAF troops from being tied down to garrison duties in the Sultanate and Pat Ive agreed to 'sit on' certain possible incursion routes into the Sultanate, should I wish to remove those of our sub-units who were responsible for that task for limited periods. We did this on several occasions, for which I was very grateful to Pat and his Scouts.

Pat arranged for me to meet his Squadron Commanders in their own areas of responsibility so that I might appreciate the ground over which they operated. After our visit Pat and David joined us in our Buraimi mess for drinks, lunch and more chats. I felt confident that the relationship between our two commands would be a happy one, which it was.

My next two ports of call were on our Oman Gendarmerie frontier posts at Qabil and Sumaini and we drove to both of these in Landrovers (although each post had an airstrip) because I wanted a closer look at the ground. Both posts consisted of 'barusti' (palm leaf) huts which, although cool enough, were fragile and liable to damage in the event of very strong winds. They were also unpleasant in sandstorms and during our rare downpours of rain. I knew that money was terribly tight in Government but having seen the state of some of the accommodation, I was determined to get new barusti huts erected and this was done within a few days by our Defence Department.

After the inspection of smart Quarter Guards there was the usual 'fadal' where these generous men plied us with biscuits, pineapple and peach slices from their own meagre resources, and with Arab coffee. At these and subsequent sessions I grew to know them. Later, they took me off to their frontier posts where I met the gendarmes on duty and the Government Customs officials. In those days caravans of camels passed into and out of Oman and the posts had dozens of kneeling, grunting, belching camels 'parked' beside them, while their loads were being examined. We were particularly concerned that no weapons or ammunition should be smuggled into the Sultanate.

I found a great fascination in these desert outposts and also with the famed Rub' al Khali, the Empty Quarter, into which I would later travel with our Oman Gendarmerie patrols, on some occasions accompanied by Patricia and Angela.

In charge of the Sultan's Armed Forces Pay and Records was Major Bob Warner, whom I had known in Egypt when he had been the Liaison Officer to the British Military Mission to Saudi Arabia. Bob had begun his career as a boy in the Duke of Wellington's Regiment and had a fund of experience. Having served with Arabs since the early 1940s he knew them well, and had not only established a good relationship with our own Omanis, but also with our Baluchis whom he used to recruit at Assuad on the frontier, via the Trucial States. The original Baluch soldiers in SAF were enlisted in Gwadur which was at that time an Omani enclave in Pakistan, but the Sultan later sold it back to Pakistan. I consider that our mixture of Arab and Baluch was a good one. I am not sure what the original reason for mixing the Regiments was but I suspect it was 'divide and rule' with British officers commanding both Arab and Baluch soldiers.

To me the Arab was akin to the Irish or to the Highland soldier, fiery, gallant, impetuous and with tremendous dash in attack. The brave but more stolid Baluch I compared to the good old English country regiment soldier, determined in the assault and resolute and imperturbable in defence. I learnt from first-hand experience in Dhofar what gallant soldiers both races made and I greatly admired the splendid young British officers who led them from the front.

Bob used to go up to the frontier whenever we required Baluch recruits, having 'put the word out' beforehand, and a vast throng would be awaiting him when he arrived with his recruiting staff at Assuad. These potential recruits would be squatting in the early morning light with enviable oriental patience. Bob usually had far too large a number to choose from and hundreds were turned away, but he picked good men. Whilst on the subject of Baluch, they had one side to them that had to be catered for. If one of them felt himself aggrieved and did not have his grievance quickly dealt with, he tended first to hug it to himself and brood on it, after which he would communicate it to his fellow Baluchis. These might take a joint oath with him to refuse to carry out some particular task or duty until the real or imagined injury had been put right. Of course with good NCOs and officers who bothered about their men and who kept in constant touch with them this never arose, but with inexperienced officers it could happen and trouble would then ensue. It happened twice very early in my time as CSAF as I shall recount later.

There tended to be an underlying rivalry between Arab and Baluch soldiers, but once they had been in action together they were welded by shared experience into a close-knit team of friends with mutual confidence, trust and respect.

On the Pay side, Bob Warner was assisted by some grand old Pakistani lieutenants and senior NCOs, most of whom had served in the former British Indian Army. SAF was still influenced by its close previous links with the Indian Army and Arabic ranks were not then used. Commissioned ranks were British with 'Sahib' after them, so that Bob was 'The Major Sahib', and so on. The Pay and Records Office was on the upper floor of the Fort at Bait-al-Falaj. The Fort itself had been built some 250 years earlier and in my time was not air-conditioned. However, because of its very thick walls it was not too hot to work in, despite the intense heat and humidity at the height of summer. The Fort was built around a large square 'well', in the bottom of which the Force Ordnance Depot kept some of their stores. The first floor was about 20 feet above the ground floor and from it you looked down onto this wide, square 'well' area over the carved, wooden balustrade surrounding it.

There was a guardroom on the ground floor, from which winding stone steps, polished and worn with age, led up to the first-floor and emerged through a doorway near the Operations Room which led to my office in one of the turrets of the Fort. On the left of the steps was the 'G' Clerks' office. I also had my own flight of outside steps up to my office from the hospital side via a verandah which ran the length of the building.

I used to spend an hour with Bob and his staff about once a fortnight, discussing personnel and Force problems, and Pay and Recruiting matters. Thanks to Bob and his staff our Pay and Records were on a very sound basis and the Force owed a great deal to their expertise and hard, steady work. Bob was a wise and knowledgeable person with 'his ear to the ground' as to what was going on and any undercurrents.

My Chief Clerk, Niaz Ahmed Khan, was a Pakistani with service in the old Indian Army and under his firm and kindly rule the Force clerical staff, all of whom were Pakistanis at that time, worked happily and contentedly. Niaz, when I last saw him in 1964, was a captain, still working at Force Headquarters, cheerful and charming as ever.

Next door to Pay and Records were the AQ offices where the DAA & QMG, (first Tony Adams and then John Moore) and his staff worked. They were first-class officers, keen, cheerful and competent. They worked hard and enjoyed their spare time too.

When I first arrived the Confidential clerk was the excellent Bombardier Davis who also delivered the UK mail to us all, bumping around the various messes and bungalows in his open Landrover; we eagerly awaited the sound of its engine about an hour after the thrice-weekly mail plane returning to Bahrain had taken off.

Also on this floor were the Intelligence Offices. My GS02 Intelligence was Michael Aris, of the Royal Anglian Regiment. Michael proved a strong right arm. He had won a Mention in Despatches when serving as a subaltern with the Lincolns in Malaya during the Emergency, and was a down-to-earth, well-trained officer. GS02 Intelligence was a tricky job because the incumbent had to serve two masters, CSAF and the British Consul General. As I have said, there were one or two occasions when the views of Her Majesty's Government and those of the Sultan did not wholly coincide and it required a wise judgement to steer the right course. Michael, and later on his successor, the excellent John MacFrederick of the Royal Irish Rangers, never put a foot wrong.

In the same office was the Force Intelligence Officer, the charming, good-looking Malcolm Denison. Malcolm, who walked with a slight limp caused by a wound he had received during the Jebel Akhdar campaign, had an amazing rapport with the Omani Arabs. I believe he even thought like one of them and he certainly spoke Arabic like one. His bungalow was rarely free of mysterious figures with whom he would drink coffee and hold long conversations. He was a fund of information with his finger on the pulse of Oman and its neighbouring Arab States. I grew to have great confidence in him and his judgement and to rely on him and Michael Aris as to what was going on in Oman.

Dhofar was a different matter, and there we had another first-class man in Major Bob Brown, MBE, of the Cameronians, a dark, thin, saturnine Scot, usually dressed in plain clothes, an Arab head-dress worn turban-wise and with a pistol at his hip. Bob was one of the very few British who knew what was going on in Dhofar and he had an uncanny 'nose' for intelligence. Sadly, the Sultan mistrusted Bob because he did not approve of Bob's important contacts in Dhofar, and eventually Bob left SAF for the Trucial States, tragically to SAF's and Oman's disadvantage. Bob had been at Sandhurst with the Sultan's son, who served in the Cameronians, Bob's regiment, on leaving Sandhurst. After Bob left, although we had some keen and hard-working officers to succeed him, we never had worthwhile intelligence in Dhofar, not even from Bob's good headman, the Dhofari Said bin Gheer, during my three years as CSAF.

In addition to moving a troop of the Oman Gendarmerie to Dhofar on rotation and to putting a company of one of the up-country battalions, and one from the Guard Regiment under command of the Dhofar battalion, I moved all the strike aircraft there, less one remaining to show the flag in Oman, and all save three Beavers, plus both the armed dhows. In that way we had considerably increased the striking power of our original Force in Dhofar by nearly a battalion, and I had managed to convince the Sultan that all this was necessary.

Before I went back to Dhofar for another spell of operations I visited the Oil Installation Police (OIP), a unit administered by the Oman Gendarmerie but paid for by PDO, the Oil Company. Its task was the defence and security of the PDO camps and oil fields. The OIP had two main camps: one, which included their Headquarters, was at Mina al Fahal, the main PDO camp on the coast near Bait-al-Falaj, and the other was out at the oilfields in the desert wastes of Fahud. Their commander at that time was Major Kingsley Gray, MC, a veteran of the Second World War and of the post-war campaign in Malaya. Unlike the all-Arab Oman Gendarmerie, the OIP was an all-Baluch unit, its other British officers being the dependable David Thompson and the friendly, huge-moustached Geoff Williams, the latter being in command at Fahud. I drove out to see the OIP in their neat camp at Mina al Fahal, met all the men and saw their accommodation which, having been recently built by PDO was in very good condition. I walked through the clean and airy barrack rooms and then set out to tour the Oil Company camp with Kingsley and the Sergeant Major and visit the men on duty at the entry gates and various vulnerable points, such as the oil tanks and the generating plant. The men seemed happy and content and I watched some of them firing rifles on the 25 metre open range nearby.

The Oil Installation Police were trained first as infantrymen at the Sultan's Armed Forces Training Regiment at Ghalla. In order to give them a bit of interest in life I decided to allow volunteers from OIP to serve in the SAF Infantry battalions or indeed any SAF unit, after completing their requisite basic training. Older Baluchis from those units replaced them in OIP, because its duties mainly involved static or camp perimeter guards.

OIP wore the same uniform as the OG, except that they wore a red and white checked shemagh instead of the blue and white one. When I left they had changed out of uniform and were playing volleyball, their favourite game. I was pleased to see that Kingsley had laid out several courts for this sport at which the Baluch were masters. They used to play for hours on end, entirely absorbed in it.

The officers at Headquarters SAF had a Mess, and a club called the Musketeer. Each had his own little house (or 'bayt'). Conditions were fairly spartan, and recreational activities were mainly running, swimming, water ski-ing and sailing. An embryo golf course existed. The British NCOs had their own Mess and quarters and their own spare time interests, also mainly sailing from Blackpool Beach, sea fishing and swimming.

What I did notice when I arrived was a lack of team spirit between the battalions who were fighting the war in Dhofar, and the Headquarters Staff. This was because neither knew each other properly and I suspected that there might be people in Headquarters who did not fully appreciate the problems of the fighting men in Dhofar. I therefore decided that, without exception, all my British staff officers and NCOs would serve spells on operations in Dhofar and that they would spend all that time on the jebal and not back in base camp. When they got to Dhofar they were each allocated to a rifle company, given a rifle and ammunition, and wholly integrated into their sub-unit. They ate goat and chappatties, drank strong sweet tea or Arab coffee and discovered that their fresh rations were on the hoof. When they went out in search of the enemy they lived on tinned 'hillalled' mutton (sheep killed in accordance with Muslim custom), canned fruit and dry biscuits, suffered from thirst, and appreciated the need for a high standard of physical fitness in order to operate in the steep, rugged country. They experienced how the rough terrain, the jagged, twisted lava rocks underfoot, cut to pieces the plimsolls worn by the soldiers and how shirts and trousers were torn and ripped by the cruelly sharp thorn bushes they passed through, and which made the need for frequent unit requests for replacement of clothing all too obvious.

In their turn, the infantry battalions got to know their staff officers and NCOs, and appreciated their being with them to learn their problems. The staff relished the active service, the excitement and the comradeship of the

Dhofar War, and I had a terrific job getting them back to Headquarters! This brought a refreshing change to SAF Headquarters at Bait-al-Falaj where the problems of war were better appreciated and where the staff now really strove to serve their friends in Dhofar.

I made sure that all who served there from my staff did so long enough to qualify for the Dhofar Campaign Medal as an outward and visible sign of their participation in, and knowledge of, the war we were all determined to win. They qualified for it as fighting men on the jebal, and the award marked them out as part of the SAF team, who knew the problems and conditions from first-hand experience, having shared the dangers and discomforts at 'the sharp end'.

Next morning I was airborne on my way to see the rest of the OIP at Fahud. We followed the oil pipe-line along the Wadi Sumail. On our left was Bid Bid, the tiny, white shoe-box-like huts of the battalion camp standing in regular lines, and directly below us were the lush date palms and shining falaj water channels of the village of Fanjah, ever a likely hotbed of intrigue and treachery despite its beauty and seemingly friendly inhabitants. On-wards we travelled over Sumail, then Izki was below us, with on our right the towering, menacing, rocky mass of Jebal Akhdar. Jules Brett, the pilot, who had recently won the Sultan's Commendation for his gallantry in Dhofar, grinned over his shoulder and bawled at me over the roar of the Beaver's engine, 'Peaches and pomegranates now ripe at Saiq!' From Saiq, NFR's resident company dominated the surrounding area on top of the Jebal Akhdar, its formerly rebellious inhabitants now very friendly. I would be able to collect much appreciated fresh fruit for the various Messes and for Patricia and Angela and our guests, on my next trip. Away to our right we could see the round fort of Nizwa, surrounded by palm trees, looming over the former capital of Oman as it had done for centuries, while the great Jebal Akhdar dwarfed it in turn. Then we were heading out into the desert, the gravel road and the oil pipeline clearly visible below us. Soon we could make out small features in the distance, low hills, straight black plumes of smoke rising vertically into the air and the orange glow from the tops of slender pipes where flames of escaping gas were being burnt. This was Fahud, with its oil rigs, temporary, buildings and portable huts, each one of which was air-conditioned, as I noted with envy. The Oil Company had more money for the comfort of its men than had the Sultan.

Then we were down on the airstrip and trundling along the runway to where red-faced, beaming Geoff Williams awaited us, his fierce, bootbrush moustache belying his friendly, open personality. We got into his Landrover and drove off in a cloud of dust towards the little oil township. We went straight to the neat, modern-looking OIP camp, leaving some of Geoff's men to guard the Beaver.

Having inspected the smart Quarter Guard, I met the soldiers in the lines, then had a tour in Geoff's Landrover round all the oilfield Vulnerable Points where I spoke to the OIP soldiers on guard or patrol duty. After a quick breakfast in Geoff's quarters of egg banjo and sweet Baluch tea, we drove off to cover the entire area of the oilfields. We visited the dominant nearby features, the various oil wells, oil rigs and other installations and met the main personalities – who all seemed to come from Texas that day, huge, slow-speaking, sunburnt giants in Stetson hats, with friendly smiles and bone-crushing handshakes. 'Do you know what the outside temperature is?' asked Geoff. '126°,' he answered his own question. Although scorchingly hot it was a dry and not unpleasant heat, there being no humidity out in the desert at Fahud.

The whole trip fascinated me, the mystical, open desert, the vibrant oil fields, the feel of future prosperity in the air, the sense of physical well-being from the clear, dry air and the fact that our men were clearly happy, smart and efficient. They had volleyball, football and indoor games for their off-duty hours, good food and good living conditions and a complimentary report from the local Oil Company Manager who said he was delighted with them. Geoff told me he got on very well with the Oil Company people. This was apparent as we went round the camp and oilfields.

My next visit was to SAF Training Regiment at Ghalla, and I went off on my own in my Safari Landrover driven by my local Baluch driver, Corporal Haider Bahram. Corporal Haider was my driver throughout my time as CSAF and I could not have asked for a better driver or a more loyal, cheerful and reliable friend. He was very jealous of my position as CSAF and allowed no vehicle to overtake my Landrover! For anyone to try to do so was apparently *lese majesté* as far as he was concerned, and once when we actually were passed I lost my name badly with him for not hauling back the offender, a 'taxi' 4 tonner from Al Ain in the Trucial States, which had unwittingly committed the cardinal sin, in Cpl. Haider's eyes, of overtaking the 'Commander Sahib' (and, I suspect, of showing a clean or rather, dusty, pair of heels to the furiously affronted Haider, who thereupon gave me a long lecture as to what I must do in the future!)

On this occasion no one passed us and we travelled peacefully along the road, which was lined in places with dust-covered trees, the occasional ramshackle building and more often than not, by just sand and boulders. We turned off the main road which led on towards the interior, and, after forking left away from the coast, churned up a track seemingly composed entirely of round loose stones. This eventually led onto a neat straight, gravelled drive. We passed through a wooden-framed gate with a guard room alongside and into the place where all our recruits were trained. A sunburnt, wide-shouldered, moustached, squarely-built figure saluted, and that grand Irish soldier Jim Sheridan, an old friend of mine, stepped forward to welcome me in his soft Irish brogue. Jim, formerly of the Royal Irish Fusiliers, had been in the wartime SAS, whose wings he wore on his shoulder, and had three rows of medal ribbons on his broad chest. He was another Force character, a very experienced soldier and a good trainer who ran a happy and purposeful unit. Jim and I, so far as I know, are the only two British officers whose sons have followed in their fathers' footsteps by serving in SAF. Jim's son, Guy, a Royal Marine, served with distinction during my time, in the Muscat Regiment, winning the Sultan's Commendation Medal for his bravery in Dhofar, and then went on to be decorated with the OBE for his distinguished service in the Falklands Islands Campaign. My son Tim arrived straight after an operational tour in Northern Ireland and served for nearly two years in Dhofar in the Southern Oman Regiment of which he became the Adjutant, before going on to serve in the Cease Fire Monitoring Force in Rhodesia, under Major General Sir John Acland, and be decorated with the MBE.

Jim took me on a tour of the offices and lines after which, having breakfasted in the Officers' Mess, we went off to visit training. We watched recruits at drill, physical training, fieldcraft, map reading, shooting on the ranges and negotiating the assault course with its inevitable 'death slide', on which we had a go. I told Jim Sheridan that I wanted him to fly to Salalah and base himself in Dhofar for a month in order to go out on operations there to get the feel of the place, to learn the enemy's techniques, and then to come back and tailor his tactical and weapon training accordingly.

He was overjoyed, quickly handed over, and was on the next aircraft for Salalah! I managed to prise him out after he had been there seemingly for ages, certainly long over a month, where he was revelling in the operational side and he returned reluctantly, having qualified for yet another medal, and only partly mollified when I said I wanted him and his senior staff to visit Dhofar regularly to continue to keep in touch! We agreed that we would relieve his non-Dhofar-trained instructors with selected men with recent battle experience in Dhofar and the ability to put over what they had learnt there to the recruits.

SAF Training Regiment was a bustling, happy, well-motivated organisation and would be even more effective when we had injected new blood from among our bright, Dhofar-experienced officers and NCOs. It continued to be a first-class training unit after Jim eventually retired and was succeeded by another experienced 'father figure', John Clarke, beloved by all ranks. John brought with him, from his appointment as Second-in-Command of the Northern Frontier Regiment, his riding camel. After his successful tour in command, John was followed by another John, the former second-in-command of the Muscat Regiment, that swashbuckling soldier of fortune John Cooper, MBE, DCM.

We had many larger than life characters serving in the Sultan's Armed Forces at that time, and they all put their stamp on it, and contributed to the tremendous pride and bond that all who have served in SAF will always feel.

Most countries with armed forces have a Ministry of Defence or equivalent. I have mentioned that our equivalent was called the Defence Department, and the Minister of Defence, then quaintly styled the Military Secretary, was Brigadier Pat Waterfield, MBE. Here was another living Omani legend, another character who was larger than life. Pat, a former Regular Gunner officer, was an experienced wartime soldier with pre-war service in British India. He claimed, if I remember rightly, to have sunk an Iranian warship during the Second World War! Pat originally came out to Oman to command the Muscat Infantry. He understood so well the Arab and the Indian minds and was a devoted and loyal servant of the Sultan, who trusted Pat's judgement in everything.

I liked Pat from the moment I met him and we got on well. We used to meet at least once a week in the bungalow which housed the offices of the Defence Department and discuss the present and the future. He was a big man in every way, and held himself like a Guardsman. He never flapped, never, and I admired him for his calmness and ability. He had a tremendous, occasionally acerbic, sense of humour and I found him great company and a most amusing friend. He was very tight on the purse strings though, and whilst he had wisely planned far ahead for the re-equipment of SAF, I did wish that he could have persuaded the Sultan to agree to the purchase of the helicopters we so badly needed and to allow me to recruit yet more infantry as a matter of urgency.

We now had two Dakotas which made a vast improvement on the 7 hour Beaver flight with its refuelling halt at Masirah Island. Also, should the vital Midway Road across the operational stretch of jebal between that camp and Salalah be cut, urgently required troops and equipment could be ferried down by air even during the months of the 'Khareef' when the jebal was covered in blinding mists and drenching rain. Pat had arranged for the Shorts' sales team to bring out one of their Skyvans to give us demonstrations, and we had flights in the capable, short take-off and landing, capacious little transport aircraft. As a result, Pat put in an order for a number of Skyvans. These later came into service in SOAF and proved their worth operationally in Dhofar.

Pat's reputation inside the Sultanate was very high and his prestige among the Omani Royal Family, the Walis and the Sheikhs was unrivalled.

He usually seemed to be smoking a cheroot and was very much the image of a senior official of the pre-war Raj. Madeleine, his wife, was a darling, a real soldier's wife and we enjoyed it when she was living in their big rambling bungalow once she returned from running their house in England and seeing their grown-up children.

The Deputy Military Secretary, Colonel Louis Sanderson, was a Lowland Scot. Known in the Army by the nickname of 'Fuzzy' because of his thick, wavy hair, Louis had won his first Military Cross in Palestine before the War with his parent regiment, the King's Own Scottish Borderers. He had been ADC to General Montgomery who was GOC of 8th Division there. He later earned a Bar to his MC whilst commanding a company in an Argyll and Sutherland Highlanders battalion. He then returned to serve Monty again, this time as one of his renowned band of hand-picked Liaison Officers, that team of brilliant young men who, on the Field Marshal's behalf, 'Smelt the battlefield' for him, and through whose eyes he saw the picture when planning his tactical moves.

After the war Louis had commanded the Sierra Leone Regiment, receiving HM The Queen on her visit to it and being decorated with the OBE. He came to Oman as Pat's No. 2 and he and Joyce, his wife, were living in a bungalow a few hundred yards from ours. The Defence Department, which consisted of British, Indians, Pakistanis, Baluch and Arabs, worked hard and I found them friendly and helpful.

I was in the happy position of being totally independent. I had no boss, other than the Sultan, who was Commander-in-Chief of his Armed Forces. I had found a tremendous rapport with him and I and my family grew to love the old man. Of course I didn't think he should isolate himself down in Salalah where, away from the majority of his people, he was a target for anti-Sultanic propaganda which charged him with being remote, with being out of touch, and with living in a much earlier age. People just did not know him. When I got to know him better I used to beg him to return to Muscat City and from there to travel throughout his Kingdom, but he wouldn't. He cared not one whit for world or public opinion. He thought he was doing what was right for his people and he was determined that there would be no sudden change to modernity and to possible decadent ways. He had made plans for the future of Oman, for education, for hospitals, for new ports, for radio and television, and for new roads. But he wanted to make haste slowly – alas, too slowly, as it turned out, for he could not galvanise himself into the 'Great Leap Forward' when he should have done. I remember when he and I were discussing the future of education in Oman, his saying to me, 'We must train plenty of artisans and technicians, and not too many officials. The country needs the former in quantity, but if we produce too many Government officials for the jobs that will be available, we will breed many discontented young men.'

On the few occasions when the Sultan did go out among his people in Salalah they cheered him to the echo, while the women gave their shrill ululating cries of greeting. You could almost touch his royal dignity and presence, and had he gone to Muscat and got around among his people, he would surely have been a terrific success. I think he also could shut his mind to unpleasant things, as well as being very hard and tough, and he had little time for the inmates of Jellali. He had no time for his Dhofari subjects and used to quote an Omani proverb to me, 'If you are out walking and meet a Dhofari and a snake, tread on the Dhofari.' I don't believe he trusted Baraik, the son of the Wali of Salalah; and certainly he did not trust the excellent Bob Brown. Sadly for SAF he gave the order that Bob was to go and we lost our vital source of local intelligence. Because Bob of necessity had to deal with Dhofaris in order to get information and, like all of us, wanted to see their conditions improved, he became suspect in the eyes of the Sultan. Bob went off to Abu Dhabi to the service of Sheikh Zayd, Ruler of Abu Dhabi, and did not return to Oman until the accession of the present Sultan. The lack of good intelligence was to be prevalent during my time and I often wonder if we would have seized an early victory had Bob remained; I believe we could have.

As well as encouraging SOAF officers to serve on the jebal we encouraged Army officers to fly on operational missions. This proved valuable in appreciating each other's angle operationally and resulted in sensible appreciation and action in support of each other. Jeremy Raybould and his two ships came in on this combined operations aspect, too, as I stationed one of his vessels permanently off the Dhofar coast and the other there most of the time (save during the monsoon when the seas were well-nigh impossible for dhows). As both *Nasr al Bahr* and *Muntasir* could carry two companies of infantry, we were able to mount battalion-sized, amphibious operations to our tactical advantage. Jeremy flew on missions and SOAF officers were frequently carried in these ships, too, so we all grew accustomed to the strengths, weaknesses and foibles of ground, sea and air to our mutual advantage and to enhancing the successful prosecution of the War.

We were woefully short of fire support. We needed a full regiment of artillery. It seemed to me that the new British light gun was what we required for Dhofar, especially as it was air transportable. Its purchase was eventually approved before I left. Because of his constant mistrust of the loyalty of his people in Northern Oman as well as the possibility of incursions, the Sultan continued to insist that a certain number of units must be kept there including artillery.

Whilst appreciating the need for having an immediate readiness force quickly available for internal security in the north, it was plain that unless we finished the War in Dhofar quickly, it would escalate with the most unfortunate results for the future integrity and stability of the whole country. One of my major tasks was to persuade the Sultan of the seriousness of the situation. Gradually I won his confidence and gradually I managed to get more soldiers to where they were urgently required. Eventually I moved the entire battery less one troop to Dhofar. Of course this was not enough but it meant that we still had gunner support in the north should it be needed. We also used this sub-unit as a training troop to prepare gunners for Dhofar and it enabled us to carry out a *roulement* of gunners so that they could return to North Oman for rest and retraining.

Mohammed Ashraf, John Lewis's Second-in-Command, was a strong right arm and later I used to *roule* him and the battery commander so each could get a well-earned break in North Oman as well as to instil up-to-date operational training into those of our gunners stationed up country. At that time the battery was largely Baluch so, looking ahead to the future, we decided to bring in and train up Arab soldiers as well, which we did with success. We also trained both Baluch and Arab officers for this keen and efficient unit.

Our Force Signals Officer, David Ingham, and later David Cook, was assisted by a number of Pakistani Contract Officers. Our Signals School was in Bait-al-Falaj and it was a pleasure to visit the intelligent young recruits under training. Many of those young signallers became senior officers of the modern SAF after the present Sultan, His Majesty Qabus bin Said, succeeded as Ruler and his Armed Forces were Omanised.

The Force Mechanised Transport Unit was commanded by Keith May, another enthusiastic and able officer. Keith was strongly supported by a team of local officers and senior NCOs and they did fine work in training drivers for the Force. Never have I seen drivers take such care of their vehicles as they did in SAF, and they had to operate over some incredibly rough country. In Oman we had every difficulty for vehicles to contend with, the red, soft, shifting sand sea of the Empty Quarter with its sharp-tipped dunes rising to 500 feet; the gravel desert of North Oman; the boulder-strewn, twisted and sharp lava outcrop terrain of Southern Dhofar and the 'moon country' to its north. It was an education to see our drivers negotiating this sometimes excruciatingly bad going, nursing their vehicles along like loved, living creatures.

I have mentioned how during my first visit I noticed that our vehicles were inclined to be 'bulled up' with shiny paint and gleaming windows and windscreens, all of which reflected the rays of the sun and the moon, and betrayed our presence. Flying glass presented an additional potential hazard. As there was no matt paint available and no money to buy it anyway, I think it was Mike Harvey who initiated repainting vehicles with the existing ample stock of shiny paint and then, whilst the paint was still wet, flinging different colours of sand on to it. This proved effective camouflage. We took out the windscreens and driving mirrors and did without them, windows were wound down or removed. Headlights on operations were covered with hessian, as were rearlights. We were becoming adept at improvisation – we had to!

The fact that we managed to keep so many vehicles operational was not only due to our devoted drivers but in a large part to our Force EME Workshops and to the drive and leadership qualities of the extrovert, ebullient ex-REME Contract officer who commanded them – Major Jim Hill, MBE. Visiting Jim's workshop was like having a blood transfusion or a glass of good, chilled champagne – you simply couldn't help feeling the better for it! I used to look forward to my visits there, and would arrive at the workshops at about 7am as they were only about 5 minutes walk from my office in the Fort. I'd be met by a beaming Jim and we would go into his office for a few minutes talk after which we would visit every bay and vehicle in the area, and chat with each individual.

We were terribly short of money and spares but Jim and his men did mechanical marvels, rebuilding complete lorries and Landrovers and keeping our aged Ferret scout cars going. Jim used to go out to wrecks and accidents and tow in vehicles if possible, and if it was not possible to tow them, he would remove every sound working part. He wasted nothing and if it had not been for his cannibalising and imaginative improvisation SAF transport would really have been in a bad way. The NCOs, men and the apprentices under training were inspired by his infectious good humour and enthusiasm; they loved working for him and the Force Workshops were full of happy, smiling faces and feverish activity. SAF owes a great debt to this burly, cheerful, energetic personality and his work was recognized by the award of the Sultan's Distinguished Service Medal when, sadly, Jim left us to work in Kuwait.

SAF was fortunate, however, in his successor Major Len Mallet and the atmosphere and tempo in Force Workshops remained excellent.

The Force Ordnance Depot was commanded by Major Dick Hopper, with Charles Fisher as his Second-in-Command supported by a team of Pakistani officers and NCOs who, despite the quite inadequate accommodation, performed an excellent job of receiving, holding and issuing the vast quantity and multifarious types of stores, rations, weapons, ammunition, clothing and equipment required by the ever-growing SAF. We had an advanced Ordnance Sub Depot in Dhofar located at our camp at Midway to serve our troops on the jebal. This was commanded first by Jim Dolphin-Rowland and, after I had translated Jim to Administrative Officer of the Force Medical services, by Captain Charles Butt. We had a dedicated service from all these officers and their staff. Dick Hopper was succeeded in due course by John Martyn-Fisher, who remained with the Force on contract, and I was to meet him again in 1975 at a vastly different Midway, by then called Thumrait, where a huge operational aerodrome had been constructed and the Imperial Iranian Air Force was based to support the Iranian Brigade in Dhofar.

Also located at Bait-al-Falaj with detachments in Muscat in the old Portuguese forts of Murani and Jellali, was the Guard Regiment. This was the all-Baluch unit commanded by Lieutenant Colonel Richard Anderson, who was also the Commander Muscat Garrison, with as his Second-in-Command, Captain Aziz-ur-Rahman. The Guard Regiment spoke Urdu which Richard, formerly a Green Howard, but afterwards a Rajputana Rifleman, spoke fluently.

The soldiers in the Guard regiment wore a little, round, khaki headdress rather like a pillbox, immaculately starched khaki shirts, shorts, scarlet hosetops and polished brown leather chapplies. They were very smart and the NCOs tended to favour fierce black moustaches.

I regularly visited the company guarding the Fort at Bait-al-Falaj with Richard and Aziz-ur-Rahman, when I would turn out the Quarter Guard, visit the lines and cookhouses and watch the company shoot on the nearby open range. Accompanied by Richard, I would visit those Guard Regiment soldiers who were stationed at Fort Murani and Fort Jellali. Fort Murani overlooked what the Sultan used to call his 'visiting book', the rocky cliffs on which the crews of visiting HM ships had painted the names of their men-of-war. Legend has it that the young Nelson had led a painting party from his warship when a very junior officer. Seemingly interminable steps had to be climbed to reach the top of both forts where the guards were quartered.

Muscat City, other than in the winter months, was extremely humid and hot, and was rather like a bowl which trapped and held this stifling, wet, enervating heat. Richard and I would arrive there by Landrover at about 6am, dressed smartly in red berets, khaki shirts and slacks, red stable belts and sand-coloured suede desert boots. The heavy, dark, wooden, iron-studded doors would be opened by a smart Guard Regiment soldier and we would begin our upward climb. I can't remember how many steps we surmounted and no doubt I would exaggerate if I attempted a guess, but there seemed to be an awful lot! By the time we reached the top, dripping with perspiration in the humid heat, our initially smart turnout would be reduced to a wet, clinging shirt and slacks! Meanwhile the Guard had turned out and were standing immovable in perfectly starched shirts and shorts, scarlet hosetops and gleaming leather chapplies, putting our own turnout to shame!

I enjoyed walking round Fort Murani with its huge, ancient cannon, each bearing its old coat of arms and pointing threateningly over the capital below, through the wide, open embrasures of the fort. The floors were kept spotlessly clean, the great, lofty barrack-rooms likewise but they were spartan in their lack of luxuries. After a hospitable drink of loomi or tea and having had a chat with everyone we would make our way down again, enter our Landrover and head through the narrow streets of Muscat for Fort Jellali.

Apart from the pleasure of seeing our soldiers this was one visit I never enjoyed. At that time Fort Jellali was a prison, housing political prisoners and ordinary criminals, the former including a number of Dhofaris. I hate seeing people and animals deprived of their freedom and I suspected that there were people in Fort Jellali who should not have been there. Having seen my own soldiers on my first visit I walked round the cells with Richard, accompanied by the head jailer to whom I took an instant dislike. The accommodation was grossly overcrowded, I remember counting fourteen men in one small cell, each wearing manacles on hands and ankles. Some of the poor people tried to shake hands with me through the bars and enquired after my health and that of my family.

Out of earshot, I remonstrated with the sullen, evil-looking jailer and later on that morning had an Audience with the Governor of Muscat, Saiyyid Shihab, uncle of the Sultan. I told him that the conditions of the prisoners were quite uncivilised. The dignified old gentleman listened to me courteously and then virtually said 'You get on with commanding the Armed Forces and leave me to execute the Sultan's commands, including the running of Fort Jellali prison!' However, I spoke very strongly to the Sultan about it at my next Audience and matters did improve a bit. But I loathed visits to Fort Jellali thereafter.

The Guard Regiment also manned a little post at Mughshin away out in the desert on the Dhofar-Saudi Arabian border, and I used to visit our detachment there in their barusti camp and sampled their strange-tasting drinking water. I questioned the tactical value of stationing them there, but the Sultan was immovable as to its importance at that time and there they had to stay – for the moment anyway. However, I now had a company of the Guard Regiment trained for operations in Dhofar, including a large Vickers medium machine gun platoon.

Thus was born Z Company which proved itself, under the command of the redoubtable Spike Powell to be a great asset in Dhofar. This brings me to Spike, a Rhodesian officer who had recently joined us on contract and was to become another legendary figure in a Force full of vivid personalities. Spike was a rough, tough, highly experienced fighting soldier, warm-hearted, a golden man. Inevitably he teamed up with Jeremy Raybould who often accompanied him during armed forays on the Dhofar jebal, sometimes in Spike's Landrover with its mounted Vickers and other paraphernalia of war. Spike's fire-breathing personality, his steadiness under fire, his selfless bravery and his sound, cool leadership won the trust and affection of his Baluch soldiers, who adored him and fought magnificently under his inspired example. Tragically, Spike was to be killed after he left SAF and returned to fight for his native Rhodesia. The Viscount aircraft in which he was flying was brought down by a SAM 7 missile between Kariba and Salisbury. He will never be forgotten by us, his comrades.

CHAPTER TWENTY-FIVE

PERSONALITIES AND PROGRESS

About six months after I had taken over as CSAF, two officers who were to have a great impact on SAF arrived in the Sultanate. Lieutenant Colonel Peter Thwaites, Grenadier Guards, took over command of the Muscat Regiment and Lieutenant Colonel Mike Harvey, MC, Gloucestershire Regiment, took command of the Northern Frontier Regiment. Trevor Alexander had departed for the Ministry of Defence having received a well-earned OBE, to serve in the Military Intelligence Department dealing with the area of the Middle East which included Oman. Trevor had enjoyed a considerable influence with the Sultan and had been of great help to me, particularly during my early days in getting the Sultan's agreement to a number of innovations I wished to introduce, and which the Sultan was chary of assenting to because at that time he had not yet given me his full confidence.

Hugh Sanders left too and sadly I have lost all contact with him, nor have I seen him at any of the SAF Association Lunches or Dinners. I believe he left the Army fairly soon after departing from SAF. Peter Thwaites and I had met before when he was staying with Trevor during a break from the Arabic Course which he was attending in Aden. After Peter retired from the British Army as a brigadier, he became the Chairman of the Chiefs of Staff Committee at the Ministry of Defence in Oman. He had all the charm and ability I have grown to expect from Guardsmen and proved himself a brave and resolute commander in action, participating in all his battalion's many operations in Dhofar, even if only a company went out. He was a most amusing companion, full of fun and good stories, witty and intelligent and a writer of a number of plays which have been well

251

received in the West End. He loved polo and had played in teams which included members of the Royal Family.

He was no stranger to active service. Having joined the Army towards the end of the War, he served in Egypt, in the Cameroons, and with the Federation Army in Malaya during the Emergency. Peter quickly stamped his personality on all ranks of the Muscat Regiment and they would have done anything for him because of his kindliness, sense of humour and his gallant and personal style of leadership. A short time was left of Muscat Regiment's tour in Dhofar before MR returned to North Oman. Peter used those weeks to get to know the Dhofar operational area so he could train his battalion to take the war to the enemy on his Regiment's return from Northern Oman about a year later, for its next operational tour.

The other new CO, Mike Harvey, had been commissioned during the War and served in a number of post-war campaigns all over the world. His breakout in Korea typified his ability to think clearly and act coolly under stress, and he was to demonstrate this attribute again and again during his battalion's highly successful operational tour in Dhofar.

In appearance Mike's looks belie him. He wears horn-rimmed glasses, has a heavy moustache and thick, wavy, dark hair. His voice is quiet. He is about six-foot tall, powerfully built, and is one of Britain's leading experts, and authors, in the Martial Arts, particularly Judo, Akido and Karate. He proved to be a brilliant trainer who really knew his stuff from the basics. Like Peter Thwaites, he spent a preliminary period in Dhofar to thoroughly get to know the ground and to find out all he could about the enemy. He then went up to Nizwa and took over command of the Northern Frontier Regiment. His battalion's British officers at first did not know quite what to make of this deceptively mild new commander, a non-smoking teetotaller who appeared to talk big about physical strength and agility, until at his welcoming mess night they found he actually could tear up telephone directories, smash wood blocks and bricks with his bare hands and throw enormous rugger forward types effortlessly over his shoulder! They also admired his skill as an artist, he used to illustrate his papers on tactics. Indeed, Mike has drawn all the pictures for the various books he has written on Martial Arts.

I left my two new COs to settle in to their commands, confident in their ability to train, lead and administer their battalions and that both MR and NFR would give an increasingly effective account of themselves when they next served in Dhofar.

We had a fairly steady flow of senior visitors to Oman from the British Army. All requests for them to enter the Sultanate had to be 'vetted' by the Sultan and it was by no means certain that he would give the necessary permission. This was excellent because we could ensure that only those whom we felt could really help us were allowed in, and the 'swanners' and 'rubberneckers' could be excluded. I think we only had one 'dud' during my three years as CSAF. He was very much in a position to help but was obviously not interested in us and he made that clear. The help for which we asked him would have made a vital contribution towards the speedy and effective prosecution of the Dhofar War. To preserve the anonymity of the visitor I am not revealing his appointment nor what help I requested, but after he had drunk a large number of gin and tonics at my bungalow in Bait-al-Falaj and eaten a big lunch, he departed. My next contact with him was a Thank-you letter in which he said, 'I will never forget my day with you in Sharjah!' As Sharjah was the Headquarters of the Trucial Oman Scouts his degree of interest in our problems becomes apparent!

After the British withdrawal from Aden a new, two star command was established in Bahrain and its commanders during my time as CSAF were, in turn, provided by the Royal Navy, the Royal Air Force and the Army. We had excellent relationships with all three – Rear Admiral John Martin, Air Vice Marshal Stanley Grant and Major General Roland Gibbs.

Roly Gibbs and I had been at Sandhurst together before the war and he had been commissioned into the 60th Rifles. He had had a brilliantly successful career as a fighting officer, earning a DSO and an MC, serving with distinction in North Africa, Italy, France and Germany, and in many post-war campaigns. He was a superb infantryman who really knew – and remembered – his 'basics' and we loved it when he and Davina, his very attractive, vivacious wife, visited us. They were so generous, too, and would arrive laden with all sorts of delicious foods and drink, at that time unobtainable in Oman.

While Peter Thwaites and his reinforced command were completing the last few weeks of their current operational tour in Dhofar I turned my attention to the next battalion due to go there, the Northern Frontier Regiment, where Mike Harvey was now firmly in the saddle, having already made his quiet but very strong personality felt throughout this fine Regiment. I flew up to Nizwa to spend several days with him to see how his battalion training was progressing.

The material in NFR was excellent and most of the officers and men had served in Dhofar already. Mike Harvey knew exactly what was required for their forthcoming operational tour and proved to be a superb trainer, organiser and leader of men. He taught each man to take his place as an effective member of his section, his platoon, his company and his battalion. His officers and men shot by day and by night, at long ranges, at short ranges, from standing, kneeling, sitting and lying positions; they practised the deliberate shot at a target in sight for some time, and the quick one or two shots at the fleeting target. They relearnt the arts of patrolling, of ambushing, of silent signals, of judging distance, of fire and manoeuvre, of use of ground, and of locating the position of the enemy by his fire. The latter art had been too long neglected and was not at all easy in Oman where the mountains and steep-sided, rocky wadis distorted the echo of a shot and made it seem to have come from somewhere other than the actual position of the firer, but constant practice helped greatly. Mike had acquired a number of captured Soviet-bloc weapons and his officers and men learnt to tell the difference between the sounds of the enemy AK47s, Simonovs and Shpagins and those of our own weapons.

We had light-coloured khaki uniforms which did not meld into the Dhofar landscape and, as no camouflaged kit was forthcoming for financial reasons, we decided to camouflage the shirts and trousers with which we were issued. Mike was the initiator of this and produced the Force's first 'Flower Pot Men' from home-made camouflage, his men having cut out their own dies and stamped dark green and brown paints onto shirts and slacks. The paint lasted for quite a time and was easily renewed. I would not let anyone wear dark glasses because of the reflection and consequent give-away of position but I was quite happy for my officers to grow and wear beards on the Jebal in Dhofar where water, other than in the Khareef season, was always scarce and where, as a large number of our soldiers were bearded, the chance was lessened of British soldiers being picked out as targets because of their clean-shaven faces. After a bit they all got tanned almost to the deepness of Arab and Baluch. Fair-haired, fair-skinned officers had to take their chance but they, including the gallant David Shillinglaw, who had been under aimed enemy fire on over ninety occasions by the time I left SAF, survived miraculously, even though their nationality was so apparent.

Mike Harvey was a mine of information on Communist tactics, and his training directives were liberally interspersed with the maxims and tenets of Chairman Mao and his Russian friends. I had decreed that all NFR officers should carry out familiarisation tours with the Dhofar battalion, going out on operations, getting accustomed to the terrain and to enemy methods and tactics. This increased confidence and, throughout my visits to NFR as training progressed from individual, through section, platoon and company to battalion training, I could see this unit become an increasingly highly-tempered weapon. Officers and NCOs grew adept at controlling the fire of mortars, artillery and ground-attack aircraft.

Mike found some thickly-wooded country between Nizwa and Fahud to simulate the conditions of the wooded areas in Dhofar and to practise and confirm direction-finding skills in map reading and with the compass. I expected, and was to get, tremendous results from Northern Frontier Regiment. I accompanied them on a number of operations of varying size and duration from company level upwards including amphibious ones, and Mike and his men earned my complete trust, confidence and admiration. His team of officers, particularly in the rifle companies, was a young one, but war is a young man's art at that level.

The Royal Marines invariably sent first-class officers to SAF, who arrived properly trained in their infantry skills. I think in my time that every Royal Marine officer was decorated for gallantry. Royal Marines serving in the battalion at that time were Ewan Tailyour, whom I have already mentioned, Jeremy Lee, who commanded 'A' Company with skill and dash, and the huge, dark, good-looking Adrian Wray, who broke the hearts of all the single European girls in Oman. Among the non-Royal Marines, I have mentioned David Shillinglaw, flaxen-haired, vibrating with enthusiasm and energy, and brave as a lion. David being Royal Tank Regiment, cheerfully served as a company officer whilst learning his trade as an infantryman. It was not long before Mike Harvey said David was ready for command of a rifle company and he then proved himself a fine leader and tactician. David and I were old friends from his time as a student on the All Arms Battle Group Course which I had been running at Warminster. When he heard that I was going to Oman where there was a war on, David lost no time nor opportunity in pressing his wish to join SAF, including nobbling me at a Royal Tank Regiment Dance before I left England, and following this up by letter!

Meanwhile Desert Regiment was about to move to Dhofar to succeed Muscat Regiment. MR had had a long, tough year of active service and I was anxious to get them back to Oman for leave, retraining and reinforcing. They had done well earning a number of decorations as well as the praise of the Sultan. They would be stationed at Bid Bid with companies at Izki and at Rostaq. They were a happy battalion and Peter had already shown himself to be a fine, brave CO, while the battalion exuded the confidence of one that had proved itself under fire and in arduous conditions. As part of my 'beefing up' of the troops on the ground in Dhofar, Desert Regiment already had a rifle company there – Paul Mangin's Red Company – serving under the command of Muscat Regiment.

All officers and senior NCOs in the remainder of Desert Regiment had by now been to Dhofar for a minimum of a fortnight and had been on operations with Red Company. They had returned with an insight into techniques, tactics and terrain in Dhofar, which had resulted in a feeling of confidence within the battalion, and Brian Barnes was already down in Umm al Ghawarif Camp with his key staff living with MR and getting the feel of operations. I planned to visit the battalion once they had moved into their operational bases and drawn breath.

At about this time, to keep us busy in Northern Oman, we had a small incident which was dealt with successfully by the Oman Gendarmerie and perhaps shows how on-the-spot decision can gain its maker a wholly undeserved reputation for prescience! I was contacted early one morning by Pat Waterfield to be told that two political prisoners had escaped from Fort Jellali and that the Sultan himself was taking the closest personal interest in their recapture. I alerted Tony Best by radio and went to his Headquarters at Sib to brief him. Together we selected a number of defiles through any of which the escaped prisoners might pass on their way to freedom. Their shortest and likeliest route would be towards the Trucial States. I selected one particular place that Tony had not earmarked and I remember him looking at me rather strangely at the time. However, somehow I *knew* that this was where an ambush would catch them, and it did.

Tony put his men out like lightning and the soldiers who made the capture did so without causing any injury to the escapees. I was very pleased with the OGs efficiency in deploying so swiftly and in the confidence that the professionalism of this unit gave me. My small share in their success was a stroke of luck, Irish second sight, or an inspired guess, but it made my name with the Sultan! Had the prisoners gone by any other route they would have been collected by OG in any case so I could hardly lose! The Sultan was delighted with the Oman Gendarmerie and now welcomed the presence of their troop in Dhofar and its removal from North Oman.

About this time Alan Bridges came out to take over as CSOAF and Brian, who had done splendidly, and Jill Entwistle departed with their two children. Alan, Lilian his wife, and their children took up residence in their bungalow next to the Waterfields. About the same time SOAF received three reinforcements of very experienced vintage: Flight Lieutenants (at that time) Lek Mintout-Czycz, a Pole, Mac MacDonald and Jack Winn. All had been RAF bomber pilots in the Second World War. They were to fly our transport aircraft. A confidence-inspiring trio, they proved themselves a great asset to SOAF. Lek had all the charm of his race, was married to a Scots lassie, and one of his boys at that time was a captain in the RAMC. Lek later commanded the Royal Flight in Oman.

Mac and Jack were tragically killed on operations in Dhofar after I had left SAF, when the airstrip on which they had just landed their Caribou came under fire. They had been bringing in heavy burmails filled with drinking water. Unknown to them the loadmaster, in a natural rush to speed unloading procedures, had unfastened the restraining straps that held the burmails secure. Suddenly the airstrip came under enemy fire and the aircraft was ordered to take off. The load of heavy, water-filled oil drums shifted and destroyed the balance of the aircraft which crashed in a wadi nearby, killing its occupants, depriving the Force of two splendid pilots and a first-rate loadmaster, and tragically bereaving their families.

Our two Dakotas were a great help. The first to arrive was said to have been the personal aircraft in Europe of General of the Army Dwight D Eisenhower, and its next owner had been another president, Konrad Adenauer of West Germany. Shortly after the second Dakota arrived. Flights to Salalah were put on a regular twice a week basis, with extra trips should operations so demand. We could now airtroop platoons at a time, with flying time reduced, and movement of personnel, animals and stores in quantity was at last possible throughout the Khareef period. Civilian dignitaries were also able to visit Salalah to see the Sultan or to attend to government business in Dhofar. Speedy movement of wounded and sick was also enhanced with a reduction of our dependence on the Royal Air Force. Previously we had to call for RAF aircraft based in either Sharjah or Muharraq in order to get our seriously wounded or very ill men to British hospitals. Loadmasters were trained from among our Arab soldiers; the one I remember best is Gunpowder Joe who had already made himself famous during the Jebal Akhdar Campaign.

About this time, too, Gulf Air changed from Dakotas to Fokker Friend-ships which gave a swifter, more pleasant, service between Muscat and Bahrain whence the UK flight connections were made. We all looked forward so much to those days when we really were in touch with the outside world and mail and visitors arrived. Letters and airmail copies of *The Times, The Daily Telegraph* and other papers and magazines were read again and again.

Originally Patricia and I were looked after by two rather puritanical bearers. Their upbringing made them frown on the alcohol that we infidels drank or offered to our friends, and they also watered down our loomi. Our first cook was a surly, unpleasant Goanese nicknamed 'Diaz the Poisoner' but all three had now been moved on and in their places we had recently acquired a dear old North West Frontier Pakistani called Said Ali, and a rather too nice, too servile Indian Christian. One day Said Ali went for the Christian with a knife, fortunately harmlessly, but as a result Said Ali had to depart. The Indian was then discovered with a bottle of our gin in his quarters so he too departed!

In a clean sweep, I had replaced Diaz by another Goanese, Gaspar Fernandez who became a great ally and family friend and who, under Patricia's supervision, developed into a superb cook. I also acquired a man as No. 1 Bearer who remained to look after all my British successors, the peerless, upright, devoted Sharif, a former Havildar in the Baluch Regi-ment, who was conscientious, smart, kindly and efficient. I could never fault him and he was a true friend and helper to my family. Under him was a very decent No. 2 Bearer, Bashir. We now had a happy, contented and hardworking staff. Those who have not been lucky enough to serve in SAF or in our old Indian Army may find it hard to believe what devoted and wholehearted service these simple people give, and how little are their demands. The main reward they ask is to be appreciated.

Operational service in Dhofar changed the young and immature into men very quickly, and Patricia used to remark on this to me when these enthusiastic, hardened young veterans came to see us before departing for England on leave. I was very proud of our fine young men and indeed of their senior officers. And the men we commanded had our complete loyalty and affection, too. The soldiers, Arab and Baluch, responded magnificently to leadership, proving themselves keen, stoical and brave, and those of us who have had the honour of commanding them will never forget them. Somehow we all felt that we officers had to prove ourselves better than we really were to deserve such loyalty and such friendship.

After duty many of us went down to the SAF beach at 'Blackpool' to swim, sunbathe, snorkel, sail, water ski or fish and our little yacht club provided cool drinks. Some Juma'as (Fridays) instead of taking our Landrover and a picnic lunch to Qurum or Blackpool Beach, we would go on an expedition to the Hajar Bowl, driving along boulder-strewn wadis, through occasional lush palm groves irrigated by channels of cool water beneath the shade of the trees. Often we would go *en famille* with the Cardens, taking any visitors with us. I remember one occasion when we came to a deep, long pool in a wadi filled with invitingly clear water, we decided to swim in it and to picnic beside it afterwards. Bill Carden's preliminaries consisted of tossing in large rocks to roust out any snakes or nasties, followed by throwing in his daughter, Clare, followed by Anne! I seem to remember that when he explained to me the reason fro all these preliminaries I was the last entrant!

Our bungalow had its resident poisonous snakes which lived in the roots of a jasmine bush in the front of our verandah, although we could never find their nest. They had caused the death of two Jack Russell terriers belonging to our predecessors, but fortunately Patricia's Peke and my Harlequin Great Dane survived them. We had a very lucky escape one day when driving back from the beach. After I had parked our Safari Landrover under its barusti shelter Angela got out and dashed to the back of the bungalow to where her menagerie of pet animals was housed. As she ran, I saw a snake directly in her path and roared at her to come back. Heedless of my bellows she ran right over it. I saw the snake raise its head off the dusty ground but it did not strike – it couldn't; quite unknowingly, I had already driven over it in my heavy vehicle and broken its back. Surely an Act of God.

On another occasion we were having our local (Pakistani, Arab and Baluch) officers to tea and these dignified gentlemen, in their flowing, laundered robes, wearing turbans or skull-caps, were walking along the verandah with us. Local officers' teas were always a bit sticky to get going owing to the innate shyness and good manners of the guests and I used to ask along British officers who spoke fluent Urdu, Baluch and Arabic to help make our friends feel more at ease. On this occasion Colin Maxwell, Malcolm Denison and Richard Anderson, I think, were helping us out when a snake suddenly fell off the verandah roof onto Malcolm's shoulder and then down onto the verandah, along which it swiftly glided and swayed its way with its head up. I was near a pyramid of old cannon balls which were stacked by a large ship's gun which stood at one end of our patio and on impulse picked up a heavy cannon ball and tossed it at the snake. To my amazement it struck the snake on the head, crushing it flat against the stone verandah floor! Of course our guests accredited me with being a fantastic marksman and the ice was well and truly broken for a most successful and animated tea party!

Our daughter Angela had a large number of pets which were constantly reinforced or replenished by the kindness of the British officers who looked on her as a small sister. People would arrive with gazelles, rabbits, pigeons, hens, ducks and guineapigs. I think there were 64 pigeons in the lofts behind the bungalow. Muscat Regiment's Pioneer Platoon came unbeknownst to me one day while I was in Dhofar and put up a high wire stockade divided into two. In one side they housed the gazelles, rabbits and an Abyssinian Cavy, and in the other Daniela the donkey and her foal Arish. A duck shared this space and swam happily in a half burmail of water but, one day, Patricia, rushing out in response to an anguished cry from one of the bearers of 'Memsahib, donkey fighting duck,' discovered that the uncertain tempered donkey Daniela had bitten the poor bird and killed it. There were also bantam hens and a rooster and I remember one dreadful night when Patricia and I watched helplessly as a Fenec fox suddenly bounded from the flat roof of the bungalow, an errant hen in its jaws. The bird had not been cooped up because it had sneaked off to roost up there. Corporal Haider had installed its double by next morning but Angela was undeceived, demanding to be told where the original was and refusing to believe that this was she because, she said, 'Her eyes are different!'

The Local officers' Mess were kindly hosts and we enjoyed going to supper there. Sometimes this would be followed by an outdoor cinema show. Instead of the usual western habit of drinks about an hour before dinner, then coffee and liqueurs or brandy after the meal, I found the local officers' way of entertaining greatly to my liking. This consisted of about twenty minutes drinking orange squash or Vimto beforehand, after which we would sit down to a delicious curry followed by fresh fruit. Immediately the meal was over the custom was to get up, shake hands all round to say goodbye and depart! As we rose for work at five in the morning this practice ensured an early night and yet we had all had an enjoyable evening.

On the occasions of the two Eids (Feast Days) after the great Mohammadan religious occasions whose periods of fasting culminated in Feasts, the British officers would go down to the lines to greet the men at their meal and to partake of it. The food was mainly goat and rice followed by fruit, and the men ate in groups of about ten, squatting round great communal trays of food and exchanging with us shouted greetings of *'Mubarrak al Eid'* ('Feast Day Greetings') followed by much handshaking.

Handshaking is a great thing in the Arab world. I remember one occasion when a Landrover of the Desert Regiment bearing the then MTO, Lieutenant Said Salim and some soldiers stopped on the road to Nizwa. Patricia, Angela and I were returning from an up-country visit and were shaking hands all round, including with the passengers in the back of the vehicle. I discovered that a pair of hands vigorously pumping mine were manacled, and on asking Said Salim who it was, he told me in his Etonian accented English that they belonged to a convicted murderer en route for execution in Muscat! (I am glad to say his sentence was remitted; he seemed such a nice chap!)

I was told of one man who was convicted of murder and, as was the custom at that time, the victim's family were given the option of blood money and letting the murderer go free, or of deciding his method of execution and carrying it out themselves. In this case the family refused blood money and sentenced the murderer to be blindfolded and to walk backwards into a deep pit into which sharp, upward-pointing stakes had been driven. The murderer, not showing any fear at the prospect of a ghastly death by impalement, told the next of kin how much he regretted murdering their relation, shook hands all round and stepped boldly backwards to his fate – only to be caught by members of the victim's family! They told him that in view of his bravery he deserved to live. They accepted the proffered blood money and the reprieved murderer eventually became a respected member of society.

On the subject of murder, while I was in Oman we had a quite unexpected and out-of-character event when a doctor at the American Mission was murdered. He was called at night and went to the gate of his house, where his assailant killed him. The Mission played such a vital and much appreciated medical role in a country so badly in need of its help that the point of the murder of this fine doctor was mystifying. So far as I am aware the murderer was never discovered.

Pat Waterfield decided – whether because of this I do not know – to restart the Omani Police from scratch as, beyond traffic control at the entrance to Muscat's main gate, they were not in great evidence, and the policemen themselves were low-calibre individuals. He asked me to provide the initial batch of recruits from our latest intakes to SAF and to give them their basic training at the SAF Training Centre. We picked a fine body of young men and Bill Aucutt, Second-in-Command of the Oman Gendarmerie was appointed Commissioner of Police. Bill prepared the police training syllabus which these new constables underwent after passing out from army recruit training. The Royal Omani Police is now a very large, efficient and well-equipped Force and a credit to the Sultanate.

Crime was rare and it used to be said that you could safely leave a purse full of gold coins beside the road leading up country and find it intact three weeks later in the same place. Certainly in 1967 no children in any of the souks ever asked for *baksheesh*. Alas, well meaning people from the oil company were wont to distribute largesse during visits and by 1970 the cry of *'Baksheesh'* was becoming prevalent.

At the behest of the Sultan, certain decorations had been initiated in addition to the Gallantry Medal which already existed. The conditions for earning the Gallantry Medal were laid down on lines similar to those for the Victoria Cross. I should say here that while British officers were serving on secondment (later called Loan Service) to SAF, they were not entitled to receive British honours and awards. However, Her Majesty the Queen had graciously permitted the acceptance and unrestricted wearing of all Omani orders, decorations and medals, which of course was a real boost to morale. Two new decorations had been instituted, the Bravery Medal (W.B.) ranking second only to the Gallantry Medal, and the Distinguished Service Medal (W.Kh.M.), which could be won either for gallantry or for meritorious service. The post-nominal letters of the various Omani awards are normally only used by British Officers when on service in the Sultanate. I have always disliked the idea that there should be separate gallantry awards for officers and other ranks so I asked the Sultan to make all our gallantry awards open to All Ranks and to this he agreed.

We also had the Sultan's Commendation, which equated to the British Mention in Despatches but instead of the Oakleaf worn on the British campaign medal ribbon a miniature khanjar (Omani dagger), was worn. His Majesty, Sultan Qabus replaced this by a Commendation Medal, an excellent idea. I maintain that by not differentiating between the ranks of those who receive decorations, not only is it fair but that they mean more to the recipients.

I particularly remember one occasion after an operation in Dhofar when I had been out with Northern Frontier Regiment. Whilst we were snatching a couple of hours sleep among some thorn bushes, I lay on the rocky ground under my lightweight half-blanket and listened to the quiet murmur of voices around me. From the other side of the thorn bush I overheard two

Arab soldiers discussing the latest list of gallantry awards for the campaign. Said one to the other, 'Sergeant Said, Corporal Obeid, the Brigadier Sahib and Colonel Harvey Sahib have all been awarded the Bravery Medal,' and another voice said, 'Yes, and Staff Sergeant Hamad Mana and Colonel Thwaites have been awarded it also.' I felt we were true comrades in arms.

During this time our clothing and equipment had begun to improve and better rations had been introduced, with more meat, more fish and more fruit. No longer did I see my men in torn shirts and trousers (except during an operation in the thorny scrub, when this was inevitable) as we now had plenty of replacements for clothing and footwear. I had obtained an agreement for All Ranks to wear suede chukka boots instead of plimsolls, as the latter tore so easily and failed to give the necessary ankle support. In addition, better quality sweaters were being obtained to wear in cold weather.

CHAPTER TWENTY-SIX

RUBSHAS, AN INCURSION IN OMAN, AND DHOFAR AGAIN

One morning when I was in my office in the turret of the Fort at Bait-al-Falaj I was contacted by the second-in-command of an up-country battalion to ask me to come as quickly as I could, as one of his companies which was destined for Dhofar had refused to go there under its present British officers. Taking Tony Adams my DAA & QMG with me, I flew up and landed on Izki airstrip. The second-in-command was there to meet us and informed me that the company, which was an all-Baluch one, had taken a brotherhood oath not to soldier under certain of their present British officers who, so they said, swore at them, treated them like dirt and had deprived them of their rightful rations. The NCOs were unable to do anything with them, although they themselves were staunch and loyal. The distrust and dislike by the men for these two British officers was obviously immense.

There were three or four ringleaders, or spokesmen, while the rest reminded me of a flock of sheep led by the bell-wether. They were determined to stick together and were completely under the sway of their spokesmen. I sat down with them and slowly and carefully by question and answer arrived at the true story. The rations had not been deliberately fiddled I discovered, but the CQMS had, on behalf of the company, bartered Army biscuits with the villages for eggs, fruit and vegetables for the men in an effort to vary their diet. Technically he had been wrong to do so, which was easy to explain, and the men accepted it. Regarding the officers, it did appear that the men had a grievance and the officers admitted that they had indeed sworn at them from time to time and this had earned their men's resentment. However, in the best interests of discipline and of the officer corps in general, and because I believed that the ringleaders were real troublemakers, I was determined that the men must be made to go to Dhofar under their officers.

I explained to the men that they must go to Dhofar under their present leaders but that meanwhile I would have a full investigation made into their complaints. They seemed quite content with this until once again the ringleaders started haranguing them, after which the men again flatly refused to move. By this time it was getting dark so I told the men that they had had my final word and that I would return next morning. Whilst my talks with the men were going on I had had the armoury and all weapons quietly secured with a guard from another battalion which had just returned from Dhofar, a platoon of which was already scheduled to take over the camp and the remainder of whose company would have arrived by next morning. I had previously spoken with one of its company officers, Lieutenant Jan Mohammad, and given him certain additional orders.

Next morning, early, I flew back and found the soldiers, about a hundred strong, lined up in an orderly and disciplined way on the edge of the airstrip. When I spoke to them I was answered defiantly by the ringleaders. However, I now had confirmation that it was only on account of their 'Brotherhood Oath' that the men would not desert their spokesmen and I took a tough line. I told them that either they all went down to Dhofar with their officers to serve in the campaign, and await the results of my official enquiry, or I would disband their company and send them all back to Pakistan that very day. I had actually provisionally hired the necessary launches to do so and these were waiting in Muttrah Harbour. Furthermore, I would shame them by having them escorted under armed guard to the launches by the men of another regiment.

A number of men called out that they would follow my orders, after which the whole company said they would do the same. Then up spoke the ringleaders again reminding them of their oath, and back we were to where we began! As this was repeated several times I ordered the arrest of the troublemakers by the NCOs. This order was clearly a surprise to the NCOs but they obeyed and the ringleaders, shouting at their comrades to support them, were physically removed. This was a fairly tense period and it certainly strained the rest of the company to see their spokesmen to whom they had sworn the oath of 'togetherness' being taken away, still shouting!

Facing the remaining men, I told them that I wanted their word that I, and all SAF, could rely implicitly on their loyalty and that if they gave it, I myself would accompany them on their first operation against the enemy as a mark of my confidence in them. I reminded them that there were proper ways to bring real or imagined grievances to notice which, should they ever occur again, must be followed.

There was a silence. I stood there facing them, Tony Adams behind me with the Battalion second-in-command, plus Jan Mohammad who had been talking to the men the previous night after his chat with me. Then various voices yelled out at me. I could not catch what they said but suddenly the ranks broke and the company charged straight at me and our small group of officers. It looked as if my exhortations had failed and we stood there awaiting the next stage of this unhappy affair. Pounding feet, white eyeballs, white teeth in brown faces, and I was surrounded by a mob of soldiers shaking my hand, smiling, patting my back and vowing eternal loyalty! The 'rubsha' was over! I dealt with the two officers, the company went to Dhofar on time and did well under its existing leadership. Both British officers proved good operational soldiers, earned their men's respect and liking, and learnt their lesson. The 'spokesmen' had departed that very day, discharged from SAF, and it was not long before members of this company were being cited for bravery and devotion to duty. The old lesson was the importance of keeping the closest touch with your men and always being accessible and well-informed, as well as dealing without delay with real or imagined grievances, and not letting them fester, to grow and erupt.

About this time we had news of an incursion by an armed group said to number about thirty men, allegedly trained and equipped in Iraq. They were reported to be moving down the Wadi Jizzi into the Batinah Coast area where they apparently hoped to spread disaffection. I happened to be visiting Dhofar at the time and had just returned from an operation on the jebal. I had had an Audience with the Sultan the night before I was due to fly back to Bait al Falaj when, having briefed him on the conduct and result of the operation in which I had just participated, I told him about the incursion in the North. He leant forward in his armchair, listening intently. I said to him, 'I can handle this in two ways, Sir.' 'Yes, what are they?' 'Well, Sir, the British Army way, which is to use minimum force. At the most we might even have to hit them over the head with a rifle butt if they are aggressive and capture them.' 'I see. What is the other way?' 'Shoot the lot, Sir, and I recommend this as a deterrent to future such attempts.' 'Yes, this course seems to us the correct one, please give instructions accordingly.'

I did, and so it came about that John (Noddy) Edward-Collins and an all-Arab force from the Oman Gendarmerie met the invaders and defeated them in a skilfully conducted fire-fight. The survivors of the gun battle still believing that the 'opposed' population only awaited their arrival to rise against the Sultan, got lifts in 'taxis' – old, ex-British Army 4-tonners carrying overloads of passengers – and arrived in Sohar. Here a group of alert Oman Gendarmerie noticed some travellers who looked 'different' and from the ground below, ordered them to get out of the vehicle. They did, and one drew a dagger on the Gendarmes. But, remember, we weren't doing it 'the British way'! The knife drawer was immediately shot dead. This was the last of the incursions. The leader, after the initial sharp action with the OG In the Wadi Jizzi turned tail and fled back whence he came, to tell his story, which was just what was needed.

The operations to round up the enemy lasted about a month in gruelling heat. Tim Landon, although suffering from jaundice, did splendid work on the Intelligence side. For their gallant and distinguished conduct, Corporal (later Sergeant) Said Ali received the Bravery Medal, John Edward-Collins, who commanded so skilfully, and Staff Sergeant Humaid, the Distinguished Service Medal (Gallantry) and Malcolm Denison, Grahame Vivian, Tim Landon, Lance Corporal Said Ali and Headman Omar Mohammed, now wear the Commendation Medal.

Desert Regiment were now installed in Dhofar, holding a position high on the jebal, dominating the seaward approach route, and based on a craggy eminence called 'Everest'. They had another company based at an airstrip called Januk on the edge of the monsoon area, and a third company on the Midway Road. Brian Barnes was an energetic commander and earned the respect of all ranks in his battalion by his professionalism. His battalion soon came into contact with the enemy and fought a number of successful minor engagements in one of which Staff Sergeant Charshambe, a platoon commander who already held the coveted Gallantry Medal, was rewarded for his bravery by being commissioned in the field.

Jonathan Nason, Paul Mangin and Dick Edwards all proved successful company commanders, the two former earning Distinguished Service Medals. Jonathan, commanding 3 Company, walked the jebal like a true laird and grew a ferocious beard. I remember when I was on a patrol with him one day we passed a group of young Dhofari women. The women invariably gave the alarm when security forces were detected by calling out or knocking together cooking pots. 'Did you notice them, Sir?' asked Jonathan. 'Not particularly,' I replied, but stopped this time and had a good look. 'If they were given a really good bath and dressed by Pierre Cardin, there is not a model in Paris could touch them,' declared the expert Highlander!

I also spent some time with Paul Mangin who commanded Red Company. Paul was a true countryman, a deep thinker and tactically and administratively sound. He spoke fluent Arabic and his men were devoted to him. Dick Edwards, large and cheerful, I also accompanied on patrols and found him an able and enthusiastic leader. His place in No. 2 Company, when his secondment ended, was taken by Tony Holman of the Gloucestershire Regiment, who had another Gloster, Dick James, as his second-in-command. Tony was the typical rugger forward and tended to lead his company in action in that spirit. He and Dick were both imperturbable under fire, had had enemy medium mortar bombs explode extremely close to them and were apparently impervious to their effect!

One fine young officer who, sadly, was wounded by enemy mortar fire, was a young Cambridge engineering honours graduate, Dick Peters, who came to SAF on contract because, as he informed me, he wanted the adventure out of his system before he settled down to being an engineer. I am happy to say that his tour of duty included being awarded a Commendation Medal for his bravery. A tragedy which struck DR was the death by drowning of its very experienced Headquarter Company Commander, Major Micky Boyd, MBE. Micky, an Irish Guardsman, having already had a distinguished regimental career, left the Regular Army and came to SAF on contract. He was brimful of experience and wisdom and his death was a cruel blow to us all.

The Adjutant was Captain Tim Reid, Queen's Lancashire Regiment and it did not surprise me to hear that he had later served with that élite corps, the Special Air Service Regiment, returning with them to Dhofar on operations. Major Jimmy Parsons was the Quartermaster, a great humorist and the battalion owed much to his administrative acumen and long years of experience.

Desert Regiment had a year of tough, tiring work with many encounters during which they suffered casualties and also inflicted a number on the enemy. Serving with them was another of our Royal Marines, Captain Hugh Affleck-Graves, known to his men as 'Captain Toweel' because of his great height. ('Toweel' means long, tall.) Hugh, too, was decorated for bravery in action and later graduated to the Staff College at Camberley where what he learned in Dhofar no doubt served him in good stead. The MTO, Lieutenant Said Salim, whose English was learnt from a former Etonian company commander was to become a colonel, and His Excellency, Minister for Diwan Affairs at the Palace. He was the present Sultan's first ADC after his accession.

Brian Barnes brought his battalion back to North Oman, leaving Jonathan's company behind. Brian had been awarded the Distinguished Service Medal for his leadership, and now it was the turn of Northern Frontier Regiment under the redoubtable Lieutenant Colonel Mike Harvey. Mike's preparation for battle had been masterly and no detail had escaped him.

It was a confident, highly trained and fit NFR that took over from Desert Regiment in Dhofar and Mike immediately began to carry the war to the enemy. I sent 'Nasr al Bahr' down for seaborne operations under the fire-eating Jeremy Raybould. Spike Powell and Z Company of the Guard

Regiment equipped with Vickers and .50 Brownings were well settled in there, plus a troop of Oman Gendarmerie, supported by Strikemasters and Beavers of SOAF. I gave Mike a couple of weeks to settle in after which I flew down to Dhofar to take part in one of his early operations which was designed to accentuate SAF's dominance of the jebel. Our destination was Darbat. Mike met me when I arrived by Dakota at RAF Salalah and took me by Landrover along that dreadful, dusty, corrugated, spine-jarring road, marked and flanked by concrete-filled burmails which led from the airfield to Umm-al-Ghawarif Camp.

We looked into the Operations Room to see Colin McLean, the Second-in-Command and Sandy Dawson, the Adjutant, both Scots, and to get the latest battalion situation report. After breakfast, escorted by the Recce Platoon we roared up in a cloud of dust to the jebal plateau, along the Midway Road which was picquetted by Mike's men, his picquets and positions dominating the area. All seemed to be quiet, no sign of adoo, but the usual herds of cattle and goats attended by jebali women and children were moving between the beehive-shaped huts of the little jebali villages above which the smoke of cooking fires hung in the still air.

Mike's officers and men were fit, alert, full of enthusiasm and exuding professionalism. After a cup of tea at Ambush Corner we drove back down the Midway Road, waved at by smiling Arab and Baluch soldiers from their picquet positions but I noticed that the sentries on duty in each sangar never took their eyes from their arcs of responsibility and were ready for immediate action. Down the winding hairpins of the steep descent to the Salalah Plain we drove, with before us the wide, shimmering expanse of the sea shining brilliantly in the midday sun. There was the Sultan's Palace on the sea's edge, the deep green of the lofty, graceful palms that grew in profusion in the verdant soil and, in places, I could make out the white of the ceaseless surf, endlessly thundering onto the white beaches of the Frankincense Coast.

Mike and I had an Audience at the Palace ahead of us that evening and I wondered how he had gone down with the Ruler. We turned west along the plain to look up the vast and forbidding Wadi Jarsees and Wadi Jardoom, both enemy access routes to the plain and the scenes of previous actions. We agreed that NFR would 'do' both of these wadis in the near future in order to fully establish our dominance over these troublesome and difficult areas. Next we had a session with Andrew Fuller, the SIO (Sultan's Intelligence Officer), regarding NFR's forthcoming operation in the Darbat area. Afterwards we walked round the lines chatting to the Baluch and Arab gun crews manning the 5.5 inch howitzers and 25 pounders, and to the NFR men who were busy preparing to move out with us on the first leg to Darbat. Morale was clearly tremendously high and I felt exhilarated at the prospect of going on operations with this fine battle group next morning.

After we had each showered, Mike and I changed into civilian clothes for our Audience with the Sultan and drove off with an escort past RAF Salalah, in through Salalah's perimeter fence, past the gates manned by armed askars, through the lush fields of sugar cane, vegetables and fruit trees, past the groves of tall coconut palms, their leaves whispering in the evening breeze, and into the narrow streets of Salalah itself. The sturdy, negroid, slave-stock women walked gracefully along, clad in their flowing, brilliantly coloured, gaudy garments. Grunting camels swayed along as usual, bearing loads of firewood cut on the jebal and escorted by matt-haired, dark, wiry jebalis who wore nothing but a sarong-type cloth, called a futta.

The gates of the Palace were dragged open by askars and the two Landrovers stopped by steps which led up to the doorway in the side of the great building. Saiyyid Hamid, charming as ever, met us and politely ushered us up the stairway, through the door and down the long, wide, cool passage into the small audience room with its padded armchairs and its model of the oil rig in its glass case. Then the Sultan walked in, erect as a ramrod, a purple and red almost spherical turban on his head, wearing a snow white disha dasha. Round his waist was an embroidered belt with a silver khanjar and his bare feet were clad in leather sandals. In his quiet, courteous voice he bade us be seated and pressed a bell beside him for tea. A tray was brought in by a negroid slave with the usual three plates of thinly-cut sandwiches, made from delicious soft, fresh, very slightly sweet homemade bread. There were two cakes, one iced, the other fruit and nut. The Sultan poured tea and soon we were engaged in an animated discussion.

I saw with pleasure the attention he paid to Mike's laconic opinions on the best way to win the war and wondered if through Mike SAF might yet get the extra infantry, artillery and helicopters we so urgently needed. Mike described his forthcoming operation, the Sultan nodding his turbaned head at intervals, saying 'I see'. I gave him news of the rest of the Force and a bit of local gossip at which he grinned, and he then said he would like to see us both when the operation was over. He pressed the bell beside his table again and a khaddim entered and took away the tray. The Sultan stood up, the audience was over, and we took our leave.

We drove back through the black, velvety Arabian night, the air heavy with the scent of spices and of woodsmoke. Great bright stars hung above us, holes in Heaven's floor as the ancients used to say. The surf thundered on the beaches behind us and ahead and above us loomed the faint mass of the jebal with Darbat over to our right, our destination tomorrow. I wondered how we would fare on NFR's first operation and if we would meet the adoo. We had drinks on the Officers' Mess verandah, supper, and an early night. There was a lot of walking and climbing ahead of us over the next few days and we wanted to start the operation felling rested and fresh.

At 5am I drank several cups of early morning tea, showered, dressed in camouflaged K.D. and suede chukka boots and ate a sustaining breakfast in the mess. Then, wearing our shemaghs and having put some magazines of ammunition into our pouches and drawn our rifles, Mike and I were off, moving easily along behind Bill Prince's rifle company. Our party consisted of Mike Harvey, myself, Suleiman who was Mike's signaller, RSM Marhoun, John Lewis the battery commander, John's signaller, and bringing up the rear, Andrew Fuller the SIO. Then followed another rifle company. We passed the gun lines at the end of the camp. The Baluch and Arab gunners would be moving out when we got to Samrhan, our first base, in order to support us for our operation. Reliable, experienced Mohammad Ashraf would be bringing out the 5.5s and 25 pounders with an infantry protective escort. The early morning air was crisp and the men looked fit, lithe and alert as they swung along towards the jebal, the Reconnaissance Platoon moving ahead followed by Arthur Brocklehurst's company. Their task was to seize the commanding features en route, and to guard the progress of the column.

Two Ferret scout cars moved at the rear of the column, red-brown dust rising as they progressed. We passed Dhofar Force's camp at Ain Arzat and hoped that enemy sympathisers, if any, in the ranks, would not signal our move to the adoo. We had to either pass their camp or go up into the jebal and then east and the latter would certainly have betrayed our coming to the adoo.

We reached our first base near the ancient site of Samrhan without incident, and the battalion settled down, vantage points were occupied, and reconnaissance of the route for the night march was then all-important. Leaving the preparations to the officer responsible, Mike, Andrew and I went off with a small escort to look round the ruins of Samrhan. When I look back now and think that I could have possessed the almost ageless pestle and mortar that I discovered there and which could have been put in a Landrover with no trouble I almost regret my single-mindedness at the time! After a fascinating dig around we returned in time for an evening snack. The column then moved off and it grew dark.

We now began to relearn some lessons. First, it transpired that the officer responsible for reconnoitring the route had decided to 'cuff it' and had remained in base, so there was confusion as to which track should be followed. Next, that same officer lost his head and started bawling at Lieutenant Ali, holder of the Gallantry Medal and the Military Medal, both won during the campaign in the Jebal Akhdar. Ali commanded the leading platoon and was following the correct route, but his NCOs found the British officer's example contagious and they in turn started shouting at their men. However, Mike quickly established an enormous grip of all concerned and there was no more sound of human voices!

The British officer concerned learnt from his mistakes and later did well. To give us immediate fire support we had a section of 81mm medium mortars and a supply of bombs for them. These were carried on donkeys. Each battalion had a platoon of donkeys in those days and very strong, willing and useful they were, attended by their wild-looking Omani mountain-men handlers. Recently the head vet from Cyprus had come to operate on the donkey's vocal chords as nothing would have given surprise away more than the sounds of braying. However, we were all a little concerned because we suspected that one particular animal, known as 'the sergeant major' had not been operated on successfully and we hoped, if this proved to be true, that his handler could grip his muzzle in time to smother any noises he might make. These great little animals moved sure-footedly behind us, and the mortar section I knew could get their tubes into crash action very quickly and put their bombs on target with considerable accuracy.

We halted at intervals to listen and to check direction. Soon we were climbing fairly steeply upwards, the only sound being the muffled clink of a mortar barrel striking a thorn bush, the rustle of feet padding along the rough path and the occasional cry of some night bird. The still air was scented by the bruised stems of shrubs and bushes trodden underfoot, and by the heavy perfume of night-flowering plants.

Dawn broke as we reached Darbat. The huts and general area were swiftly and silently surrounded by Mike's men and all approaches occupied to ensure against surprise attack by the enemy. Alas, there was no enemy on this occasion.

Sunrise, and we looked back and down across the broad crescent-shaped Salalah Plain out to the blue sparkling sea. Darbat was a village with lofty, graceful palms bearing great round green coconuts. There was a calm river, in and around which were well-nourished cattle. The river was fringed by pastures of tall, green grass and its waters disappeared in a breathtaking drop of hundreds of feet over what, during the khareef, must have been a dramatic and vertiginous waterfall, overhung by a single, gnarled and ancient tree. We were already hot and sweating and the heat of the sun on our backs was increasing as it rose in the heavens.

The headman and some elders crowded around us proffering green coconuts to the soldiers and ourselves. These they slashed the tops off with blows from sharp, machete-like knives, and we gratefully drank the cool, sweet, slightly fizzy, refreshing coconut milk. I refused a large bowl of warm camel's milk but Andrew Fuller manfully gulped it down to my admiration! We searched the surrounding area throughout that morning, including all caves and likely lying-up places but had no contacts. At least we now had a good idea of the ground.

We came back by a different route to minimise the chance of being ambushed on our return journey, exhorting everyone not to cease their alertness so that in the event of any action we could react like lightning, seize the initiative and inflict casualties on the opposition. My first operation with NFR had ended bloodlessly but we had been allowed to learn painlessly from mistakes that could have cost us dear. They were not made again and we hoped that next time we would have something tangible with which to mark our success.

After this Mike Harvey embarked successfully on a series of aggressive operations designed to dominate the Dhofar jebal and its inhabitants. No area was to prove beyond the reach of his battalion and this included the very border between Dhofar and the Marxist People's Republic of Yemen, the country which provided sanctuary and succour increasingly for the Dhofari rebels, particularly from its base town of Hauf. The so-called peace loving communist countries who delighted in fishing in other people's troubled waters in furtherance of their own interests were pouring in Soviet block weapons to the adoo and providing them with instructors and advisers.

The Dhofaris have magnificent natural qualities as soldiers and proved a formidable enemy. They naturally knew their own country intimately and used this knowledge together with their skills of fieldcraft and marksmanship to advantage, if allowed the element of surprise. Thanks to Mike's tactics, NFR were also getting to know their operational terrain and were dominating it by strong patrols and skilful ambushes. Small actions were fought and NFR began to inflict casualties on the adoo. In order to protect the rather exposed RAF airfield in the Salalah Plain, posts, round which rock sangars were built, were established on the routes which led to the airfield from the jebal and manned by soldiers of the Guard Regiment. Patrols operated from these bases, which were called 'hedgehogs', and offensively dominated all approaches. Artillery SOS tasks were registered to deal with any attempts by the adoo to attack RAF Salalah with Katyusha rockets which we now knew they possessed and which might be slipped through one of the many jebal tracks by night on camelback.

By day the plain was scoured by Ferret scout cars as well as by foot patrols. The strong perimeter fence with its entrance gates dominated by tall, stone-built watch towers denied the approaches to the town of Salalah itself. Mike promised to let me know when he was next mounting a sizeable operation and I returned to Bait al Falaj in a Dakota piloted by Lek Mintout, with 'Gunpowder Joe' as loadmaster-cum-steward. The aircraft was full of soldiers going on leave as well as a sprinkling of Omani Government officials and tradesmen returning from Salalah. Orange juice in cardboard cups, and sandwiches, were handed round to everyone on board and, thus sustained, I looked to see what John Crompton, my efficient Brigade Major, had sent me in my IN tray. Among the correspondence were requests for visits from a variety of senior officers from the Ministry of Defence and from the Gulf. The Sultan now allowed me to bring certain visitors to Dhofar in order to get the feel of the operational area. General Roly Gibbs who was due to visit us shortly was a tremendous favourite with all ranks. He walked round the sangars and operational positions, inevitably in terrific form and inspiring us all by his presence.

I quickly worked out whom we wanted from the next batch of would-be visitors and made appropriate recommendations for Pat Waterfield to convey to the Sultan who never failed to support them. I was glad also to see that two padres were coming to spend a few days with us from Headquarters British Forces Gulf to conduct Church of England and Roman Catholic services for us expatriates. Richard Anderson organised these visits and we looked forward to them. Another batch of new officers were on their way, both seconded and contract, and these would have to be 'broken in' before being given command of soldiers in action.

The rest of the paperwork was fairly routine and I had completed it all by the time the Dakota dipped down to land on the airstrip at Bait al Falaj. The Staff Captain 'A', tall, capable Tim Herbert advanced to receive what was now my OUT basket. John Crompton and John Moore, who had by now succeeded Tony Adams as DAA and QMG, quickly brought me up to date with events which had taken place whilst I had been away in Dhofar, while Corporal Haider Bahram loaded my kit into my Safari Landrover.

Alan Bridges the commander of SOAF briefed me as to the air side of things and then Cpl Haider drove me away from the airfield. We went along the tarmac road through the gates of the Headquarters, past saluting sentries, along the rough earth and stone track by the old donkey lines, the Fort and the Hospital. We continued past Alan's and Pat's bungalows and then swung left up the drive to our home where the two women in my life were already awaiting me at the end of the verandah, with Sharif and Bashir, Nos. 1 and 2 bearers, in attendance.

CHAPTER TWENTY-SEVEN

NORTH OMAN AND DHOFAR

By now Muscat Regiment was back from post-Dhofar leave. Its Arab soldiers had not had far to go, but some of the Baluch had been faced with enormous journeys to their homes, after their aircraft had landed them in Karachi. These could involve up to a fortnight's walk or camel ride each way.

Peter Thwaites had got down to retraining the Muscat Regiment. This began with individual training for each officer and soldier and progressed through section, platoon and company, up to battalion training. We all knew what we were up against and how to prepare ourselves. Muscat Regiment had settled into their battalion camp at Bid Bid with the usual detached companies at Izki and at Rostaq.

One of MR's first major events was a ceremonial parade at Bid Bid at which Peter invited me to present decorations awarded for bravery and distinguished service in Dhofar to a number of officers and men of his battalion. The parade took place very early in the morning to avoid the worst of the heat of the day and I flew up in a Beaver, skimming over the reed-fringed pools of the wadi to touch down on Bid Bid airstrip. Here the much-bemedalled John Cooper, the Second-in-Command, resplendent in Sam Browne and wearing Muscat Regiment distinctive scarlet tam-o'shanter bonnet, starched KD uniform and suede chukka boots met me. Peter, with the battalion drawn up behind him, against a backdrop of the dinosaur-back, serrated ridge of stark mountain range in rear of the camp, received me with a General Salute after which he invited me to present the decorations.

All ranks were already wearing their Dhofar Campaign Medals and I now presented Bravery Medals to Peter Thwaites, Peter Raven and Simon Sloane, and the Distinguished Service Medal (Gallantry) to Patrick Brook. Daddy Lawrence the Quartermaster; Lieutenants Jan Mohamed and Khalfan received Distinguished Service Medals. The final recipient was the small, very dark, tough Private Obeid, on whom I pinned the Bravery Medal. I was to present him with a second Bravery Medal shortly before I left SAF, by which time he was a sergeant. As befits a battalion commanded by a Grenadier the parade was extremely smart and the turnout immaculate.

Everyone then fell out for breakfast and I was taken round the gardens afterwards, where the influence and enthusiasm of Richard John was already in evidence, and a splash pool had been made. After a walk through the palm-shaded lanes of nearby Fanjah, along the clear, water-filled falajs which irrigated the crops, Peter and some of his officers took me to a deep pool in the wadi near the end of the airstrip for a refreshing, cool swim before lunch.

After lunch I departed by road for Bait al Falaj. I had great confidence in Peter and his fine battalion and they were to do splendidly when they returned to Dhofar on roulement, nine months later.

Threats of incursions inspired by the old gang of Suleiman bin Himyar, Ghalib and Talib were ever-present and entry routes from Saudi Arabia or by sea-mounted forays from Iraq through the Trucial States were always a possibility. So the Oman-based battalions, in addition to training for the war in Dhofar had to be alert to possible attempts to raise a revolt in Northern Oman.

In addition to our friendship with the Trucial Oman Scouts, we got on well with the Abu Dhabi Defence Force, which was also under British command. Brigadier John Paley and his staff were very pleasant and cooperative. I had enjoyed knowing Tug Wilson who, before John Paley took over, was Commander Abu Dhabi Defence Force and he and his staff had had a good liaison with mine. How we envied them the seemingly bottomless well of money from which they drew to equip and pay the ADDF! Thanks to Abu Dhabi's great oil wealth, their pay scale was higher than ours and attracted, inevitably, not only many good Omani soldiers but British officers, both seconded and contract, a number of whom had previous SAF service. We longed to be able to have the financial support that Sheikh Zayd so unstintingly gave the ADDF and wished that we too could have the helicopters and fast patrol craft with which they were provided, also their excellent weapons, equipment and uniforms.

In an effort to get every possible advantage out of other nearby armed forces we tried to tap the Royal Navy and Royal Air Force. However, although Her Majesty's Government were quite prepared for seconded and contract British officers to fight against the undoubted threat to Western interests posed by the rebels (the initials under which the Dhofari rebels fought, PFLOAG, stood for People's Front for the Liberation of the Occupied Arabian Gulf) they were not prepared to openly support their old and loyal ally, Sultan Said bin Taimur any further than that.

The most we could hope for were reports of sightings of dhows that could be serving the cause of the rebels near the Aden borders sent from the one patrolling RAF Shackleton that daily droned down our coast and back on its slow, long-range reconnaissance, and the possibly deterrent effect of the presence of a Royal Navy frigate or minesweeper during one of their occasional visits to the Dhofar coast. We simply could not convince the British Directorate of Military Operations, nor the Defence Staff, that if they gave us what we asked for straight away – very little at that time – we could crush the rebellion. They had to support SAF with far more aid and consequent expense later. The old principle of 'Firm and Timely Action' had to be learned yet again at the expense, as always, of lives and limbs.

So we had to do the best we could with our very slim resources, operating over terrain that could swallow up several divisions of infantry. We denuded Northern Oman as much as the Sultan would countenance, although every reduction had to be fought for because of his near-phobia in connection with the past Jebal Akhdar rising and his insistence on a physical SAF presence in certain areas connected with the rebellion's three leaders. Still, by now we had a roulement of nine months' duration in full swing, with our artillery, less one section, deployed in Dhofar (I never did seek his permission for that!), an extra rifle company supplied by an up-country battalion plus Z Company of the Guard Regiment under Spike Powell, and a troop of the Oman Gendarmerie. Furthermore, I had now located all possible strike aircraft in RAF Salalah, and all the Beavers we could spare, only retaining a couple of Strikemasters in North Oman for 'showing the flag' flights and pilot training. We had to keep some Beavers based in Bait al Falaj for casualty evacuation and for regular up-country supply and liaison flights. Should an operation so demand it, we were able to reinforce Dhofar with all our aircraft but we obviously had to remember the possible threat to the North, where we had already had one recent incursion.

By now, Desert Regiment had completed its tour of duty in Dhofar and its commanding officers had changed, Teddy Turnill of the Royal Anglian Regiment having taken over from Brian Barnes.

We had built up Midway as a base also and the kindly, loquacious and hard-working Charles Butt was in command. Under him we managed to improve living conditions, the camp was properly defended by a Guard Regiment detachment and the airstrip was lengthened so that the Dakotas could land and take off.

Desert Regiment Headquarters was at Nizwa, less its two detached companies. One of these was at Saiq, where it enjoyed a reasonably cool summer at some 10,000 feet above sea level, surrounded by terraces where crops and fruit were grown including peaches and pomegranates. The other company was based at Ibri to the north, that delightful walled town abundant in tall, shade-giving, green palm trees and flowing watercourses. DR's seasoned officers and men were training hard after their post-Dhofar leave and incorporating the lessons learned from their previous tour of operations.

The Guard Regiment, since we had instituted the rotation of its soldiers for duty in Dhofar, now had enhanced self-confidence and morale. They, too, had had the opportunity of proving themselves fighting soldiers, received recognition in the form of decorations and, sadly, had suffered their share of casualties. They were fine-looking Urdu-speaking Baluch, mostly heavily moustached and very smart. I was to see for myself their stoicism under fire and their cheerful acceptance of danger.

The Oman Gendarmerie too, were delighted to be in on the act in the Dhofar War and Tony Best, their commander, had lost no time in getting out with them into the jebal there. I met him one morning walking down the Midway Road with the inevitable pipe between his teeth and a large grin on his face. I think it was Geoff Williams who actually took the first OG troop down to Dhofar. Geoff who was serving with the Oil Installation Police at that time had somehow wangled himself an early operational tour, as did his CO, Kingsley Gray!

A month later Tony Best, who had returned from his spell in Dhofar, and his men were doing some interesting patrolling in the sand sea of the Empty Quarter and I accompanied him and his Landrover crews. We drove up the steep slopes of red sand, some of which rose to crests about five hundred feet high. Often these crests were knife-edged, and the vehicles would plunge almost vertically down the other side, with the gendarmes in the rear of our Landrover occasionally joining Tony and me precipitately and painfully in the front seat! At other times we balanced on the base of the vehicle, both front and rear pairs of wheels unsupported in the air! But this normally only happened when the onslaught on the summit was insufficiently determined. The OG drivers soon became skilled and the car commanders were good at direction finding.

Patricia and Angela were invited to join us on one expedition and having spent the previous night at OG's Mess in Buraimi, we left before dawn for the Rub'al Khali, entering the red-gold, wind-corrugated dunes of the vast rolling sand sea just as it was growing light. We stopped for breakfast cooked by smiling gendarmes and soon, seated on rush mats on the smooth sand, we all enjoyed 'hubs and dhal', soft, flat, round portions of unleavened bread with which we scooped up curried lentils from a communal cooking pot, and drank Arab coffee. We ventured a considerable distance south and then turned west, following the great, shifting, Arabian sands as they marched onwards towards Saudi Arabia. There must have been few European women up to then who had been in the Empty Quarter. When the sun was high and the dry heat intense we turned homewards, eventually emerging from the red sand onto the harder, lighter, sandy-coloured Oman desert and steered for Jebal Haffif whose whale-back shape indicated that the border between Oman and the Trucial States was near. We called in at the two little OG encampments at Sumaini and Qabil before driving, pleasantly tired and very sunburnt, along the track that led into Buraimi itself, a track still regrettably bordered by the ever-present odorous, severed heads of cattle and goats!

Tom Lomas was a golden man and his death in a Landrover accident, the fault entirely of a rogue Arab taxi driver from Al Ain, was a tragedy that shattered all of us who were his friends, and his friends were many indeed. He and Sandy Gordon were irrepressible together, very much 'the terrible twins', their red letter day each year being the annual Scouts' Ball, a most enjoyable affair which was held in Sharjah by the TOS, and to which invitations were greatly prized. We had been invited, as had Tom and Sandy, and were looking forward to it.

John MacFrederick in my Regiment, who had by now taken over from Michael Aris as my GS02 Intelligence, had also been invited and he, Sandy, Patricia and I set off in our respective Landrovers from Sohar across the desert tracks for Sharjah. We called in for a cooling soft drink at a desert rest house and then continued on our final stage to Sharjah. We drove up to Pat Ive's house and hardly had we been greeted by Pat and Jeanette with their customary, kindly warmth than Patricia was hit by the most virulent tummy upset and had to take to her bed. Shortly afterwards, Pat informed us that John and Sandy had also been struck by the same bug – all three of them had had similar orange drinks at the little desert café. I had drunk Coca Cola and thus escaped. Pat Ive's senior doctor came up with a miraculous remedy that put all three of the tummy complainants back on their feet in good time for the evening ahead.

We joined the crowd of guests who were watching the smart Scouts Pipe Band as it played a selection of Scottish tunes, resplendent in scarlet and white shemaghs and white uniforms. The Ball itself was the greatest fun. Plane-loads of girls had been flown in from Aden and Bahrain, dancebands played and a delicious buffet dinner had been provided. Among the couples circling round the dance floor was Tom Lomas, looking the picture of avuncular respectability with his well-groomed silver hair, crisp white dinner jacket and a gorgeous girl in his arms. He gave us a great grin as he went by and made a mock leer at his partner.

Not far away was the tall, emaciated figure of Sandy Gordon, a wide grin on his cadaverous face, both arms raised in a sort of mad Highland fling – I could see no sign of his partner. Clearly here was a man bent on enjoyment!

And so the evening progressed in the happiest way until in the small hours of the morning I was drawn aside to be told that Sandy Gordon had suddenly been taken seriously ill and admitted to hospital. Excusing myself from our party I explained to Patricia where I was going and made for the Scout's sick bay. I was shown into a freezingly-cold, air-conditioned room in which stood a single, white-painted, clinical-looking metal bed, a chair and little else. Beneath a sheet with not even one blanket, lay the long, shuddering figure of Sandy Gordon, his facial expression like a death's head, his dentures having been removed. 'What's wrong, Sandy?' I asked, horrified by his appearance. 'I feel dreadful, Sir,' replied Sandy, 'my head is splitting, and I am unable to stop shivering.' 'Who put you here, Sandy?' I asked. 'A doctor ordered me out of the marquee and straight into bed. He told me that I was incurably ill,' replied the shivering, white-faced, near-corpse of the former, robust, wartime member of the Parachute Regiment and erstwhile bandit-hunting lieutenant of the Malayan Police. Feeling very worried, I told him to try to rest and assured him that I would be back shortly. As I made my way back to my party I passed a bar at which sat one of the TOS junior doctors and I paused to ask him if he knew what could be wrong with Sandy. He informed me curtly that it was he who had ordered him to bed and that Sandy was seriously ill. He added that he knew Sandy of old and indicated that he had been present on other appearances by Sandy at the Scouts' Ball. It became apparent to me that this particular doctor was very, very drunk and aggressive, too. Light dawned on me and happily Pat Ive arrived. I asked him to accompany me to see Sandy and my mood of worry vanished. I said to the doctor that I believed he was only pulling Sandy's leg and that the joke was over. In his drunken state he flatly refused to discuss the matter. Fortunately Pat Ive who had meanwhile visited Sandy and reached the same conclusion as I had, rejoined us. With a livid face Pat made it quite clear to the drunken, truculent MO that Sandy was to be discharged from the sick bay forthwith. Sandy rose from his bed with alacrity and I understand the doctor concerned left the Scouts next day, this particular performance having been the most recent of a series of previous 'blacks'. In no time a beaming, dinner-jacketed Sandy was back on the floor quickly regaining his party spirit and the black cloud had passed from our evening. However, Tom Lomas, John MacFrederick, Patricia and I did not let Sandy forget his 'illness' for a long time!

Tony Best, COG, had an infectious sense of humour; he was a sound, experienced soldier and a most amusing companion. He prided himself on his skill as a Landrover driver and I remember the day he took me by his own special route to Buraimi. Fortunately an OG patrol eventually collected us from where we were utterly stuck and took us to the camp, after which 'Bog with COG' became the 'in' phrase with the Oman Gendarmerie! I must say I handed it to Tony for determination. He tried every conceivable way to free the Landrover from the soft sand and several inconceivable ones!

I usually arrived with units an hour or two before breakfast and when, for example, I would visit Sib, I would be driven there by Corporal Haider, arriving at this picturesque, little Batinah Coast village by 7am. Early on I had ordered that quarter guards to greet me would be discontinued as they were an unnecessary embellishment and only involved extra 'bulling' for my benefit. I still don't know if it was Tony or the rest of OG, or both, but this was the one and only unit which invariably flatly ignored my orders on the subject! Whichever station of the OG I visited, there drawn up, despite my orders to the contrary, would be a smart Quarter Guard of gendarmes, a picture in pressed blue mazri shirts tucked into light KD starched slacks, wearing polished, brown leather chapplies, their blue and white checked shemaghs fluttering in the breeze, their silver SAF badges set in the centre of their black aguls reflecting the rays of the early morning sun. I had to inspect them!

The post commander and I would then walk round the camp, climb to the top of the battlemented watchtower by the gate, shake hands with the sentry beside the mounted searchlight, and look across the gardens of Sib to the azure blue, crinkled water of the Arabian Sea sparkling beyond the deep green of the mango trees, and the great splashes of magenta, scarlet, purple and orange bougainvilleas in the rich merchants' gardens. Then would follow a tour of the cool, stone-floored, whitewashed barrack huts, the larder storeroom with its sacks of rice and its variety of aromatic spices. Next we would go into the cookhouse for a chat with the cooks, and to inspect the meal; cross the parade ground perhaps, to listen in to a squad carrying out judging distance under the shade of grey-green gum trees, and after that to watch another squad drilling, clouds of white dust spurting up under the gendarmes' stamping feet.

A session with the Orderly Room staff and the Adjutant followed then by a visit to Captain Guy Simonds, MBE, the Quartermaster – were there any OG officers without moustaches?! – and his helpers. What an immaculate QM's store and Guy assured me that kit really was issued from it! By now it would be time to move over to the Mess for breakfast.

Charles Holdaway had by now arrived in OG, a tall, extrovert man – yes, moustached also! – full of good humour and personality. He, Guy

Simonds and John Bennett the Adjutant, would join us for breakfast and soon I would be having my leg pulled because I had said all officers must be fit and those who were overweight were to slim down. On one occasion I was handed a large sheet of paper with illustrations, if I remember rightly, drawn by Guy, depicting OG officers in various attitudes of violent exercise, appropriate comments emerging from their mouths in 'balloons'. They were a happy team and great fun to be with. They had a deserved name for hospitality and Patricia and Angela particularly enjoyed the superb teas these kindly hosts provided.

After breakfast Tony and I would drive off to visit isolated posts on the Batinah Coast, motoring through lush crop-filled fields irrigated by an abundant supply of the fresh water that bubbled up from springs – some springs could even be found out on the sea shore. The last stages of our journey would be along the beach, the large-clawed crabs scuttling in crowds before the wheels of the Landrover as we made our way quickly over the firm sand, past fishermen, some with reed boats and some with larger wooden craft which they had pulled up the sand. We would then come on a group of little barusti huts with a white flagpole from which flew the Sultanate flag. Here lived the section of gendarmes whose task it was both to watch the coast in case of unauthorised landings, and to patrol the nearby villages.

The Arabs' hospitality is such that even if they are down to their last rations and drop of water they will press you to eat and drink and imply that they have both in abundance. We used to bring them tins of peaches and pineapple chunks and perhaps some biscuits so as not to impose on them, and we would all sit round in the shade discussing local and SAF affairs, eating fruit and drinking cups of coffee. There was always a great handshaking send-off when we left and we would be escorted to visit the local dignitaries in nearby villages and to call in at village schools to watch the small groups of children seated in a circle on the ground intoning their lessons in chorus after the teacher.

On other days I would fly to Sohar where Sandy Gordon would meet my Beaver at the airstrip and his driver would collect the mail in its sandbag and the fresh food in its icebox, together with cartons of drinks and cigarettes. Sandy, the pilot and I would drive off in Sandy's open Landrover through the flat, tree-covered area adjoining the airstrip, past the inevitable tents among the bushes, outside which goats and chickens foraged, where little children played in the dust and where women were busy tidying their little camps, their menfolk shouting greetings to us as we passed. On we would go, up the lane fringed by low hedges on either side, and there would be Kashmir Lodge ahead of us, white-washed and two-storied, its distinctive clump of graceful palms at the western end. In through the gateway pausing to dismount and shake hands with the sentry, and then a group of men would come forward to greet us. Tim Landon, formerly 10th Hussars, had succeeded Carl Seton-Brown and was an outstandingly good successor. Young, eager, with a shy smile, he was a sensitive person who felt very keenly about the poverty and rigidity of the Sultanate, and loved Oman and its people deeply. Later, when Tim was in Dhofar leading a half company of MR under command of NFR, he was to show his personal bravery and bold initiative in an action in which I was participating. I was happy to recommend him for a decoration and to be able to write its citation from what I personally saw at close hand. I was worried that Tim was becoming too emotionally involved and whereas I was always ready to hear his views and opinions, I did not want him to antagonise the Sultan, who had already got rid of that splendid Intelligence Officer Bob Brown because he felt he was getting close to the wrong sort of people – according to the Sultan – in Dhofar.

Tim had been at Sandhurst with the Sultan's charming and cultured son, and this again the Sultan appeared to hold against Tim. Tim had with him his headman, Omar, the knowledgeable and experienced old Omani who had been with Carl Seton-Brown.

After I had inspected the Quarter Guard, we would look at Sandy's resident flock of geese, while his dear little, brave Jack Russell, Wadeeb, would quarter around and we'd make our tour of the lines. Then we would go to the beach past the little mosque where the soldiers prayed and talk with a group training near the sea's edge. A discussion about the fresh water might well follow, after which we would go into Tim Landon's office to hear the latest local intelligence. After breakfast, we would return to the airstrip down the same attractive lane and after the gendarmes had shooed any camels from the airstrip we would take off, circling round as we gained height, the Beaver's engine roaring and the figure of the Sergeant Major waving up at us growing tinier as we ascended and continued on our trip to visit other OG locations.

There were not many Europeans living in Muscat at that time and those who did so knew each other well and used to enjoy each other's company at lunches, dinners and the very occasional dance. Bill and Ann Carden, and David and Nancy Crawford, their successors, gave cocktail parties, lunch and dinner parties whenever interesting or important visitors came to Muscat. Going into Muscat town after dark was always fun as you had to go through the arched city gates which had a guardroom inside. From this askars emerged to swing open the great wooden gates which were shut after 'dum-dum', the name for the time when cannon had once fired at dusk from the gaping gunports high up on Fort Murani. This gunfire, sadly, had been replaced by a small explosive charge being detonated instead. Those who walked through the narrow, winding streets after dark were required by law to carry lit lanterns which added to the sense of mystery and of the picturesque as you passed through the silent passage ways (no transistors in those days!) and crossed pools of orange light spilled from windows and open doorways.

At the Embassy, dinner guests would foregather on the wide, airy verandah overlooking Muscat harbour. It was hard not to think of the poor wretches incarcerated in nearby Fort Jellali's grim cells and to wonder what sentences, if any, they would have merited in England under British justice. Women guests wore long dresses of light material; the men, Gulf Rig. We would go into the dining room for dinner, during which the guests would be listened to with interest as they gave us the news of where they came from and what they did. Afterwards, if it was a small party, we would move to the comfortably furnished, air-conditioned study, or to the pleasant drawing room if it was a large gathering, to chat and drink coffee followed by liquors or loomi before making our respective ways home. Or we might be sitting on the roof of John Shebbeare's house drinking chilled champagne in the warm, humid darkness, with the lights of other houses softly glowing around us.

At other times friends in PDO invited us to their well-appointed, comfortable, air-conditioned homes in the Mina al Fahal compound. Francis Hughes, the head of PDO, and Brenda his wife entertained generously in their large house set on a rocky bluff overlooking the sea; here we would meet visiting dignitaries of the oil world. Francis was held in high regard by Sultan Said bin Taimur, with whom he was said to have considerable influence. For his distinguished work in bringing oil to Oman, Francis was awarded a well-deserved OBE.

We enjoyed entertaining at home. Our house had a wide covered verandah in front, outside which was an expanse of gravel leading to, at one end, a roundish, smooth, concrete patio which had electric plugs installed for standard lamps. In front of the patio was a garden which had been made and planted by the Smileys, to whom I feel sure all successive CSAFs and their wives must have been most grateful.

Sharif and Bashir would be waiting at the end of the verandah by the patio, from where they could see the approach of our guests' Landrovers. Gaspar Fernandez would be bent over his cooking pots in the kitchen which was situated at the end of the house and Fakir, the cookboy-cum-sweeper would be in attendance ready to run errands and wash up. The guests would be met on arrival and escorted to the patio where we would sit out in wicker armchairs in the soft light of the standard lamps, under the Arabian moon and a profusion of stars for pre-dinner drinks. I remember one dreadful occasion when I was exhorting a female guest of whom we were particularly fond, to finish what remained of her drink and to have another, and I urged her to 'put it in your hollow tooth'. Later, when entering the lit dining room I was appalled to find that one of her front teeth had come out that evening and she was naturally feeling highly sensitive about my references to 'hollow teeth'! My family have never let me forget my performance on that occasion as 'the charming Irishman'!

Patricia had made our house so attractive and comfortable, and we loved it. We would walk through the drawing room with its white Pakistani carpet, its chintz-covered sofas and armchairs, rugs scattered on the carpet, into the dining room, cool with its air-conditioning, where silver and glass gleamed on the polished table. Sharif and Bashir, wearing white, with dark green cummerbunds bearing the silver crest of my Regiment, the Royal Ulster Rifles, would be awaiting us. We gave dinner parties once or twice a week, and always when we had house guests, of which we had a fairly endless stream. Parties tended to end early as most of us began our day at dawn.

I loved the early mornings in Oman. I would get up and stand on the verandah in my sarong and flip-flops, the air would be still and reasonably cool. Over the lines in the cantonment the smoke of the cooking fires would rise pencil-straight into the still air as the first meal of the day was prepared. This consisted of sweet, pancake-like, greasy piratas and a pint of hot sweet tea per man; and I could smell the woodsmoke from where I stood. Looking to my right, towards the garden, beyond the gun which had been taken from a ship sunk during the war by a Japanese submarine and over the pyramid of 18th century cannon balls incongruously piled beside it, I usually saw a string of camels pacing along on their way to Muttrah or Muscat for market, some with comatose riders rocking to their motion, and some with loads of fruit, vegetables or other merchandise on their humped backs.

After drinking early morning tea and eating some papaya or mango, I would shave, shower and put on my uniform in my dressing-room, where everything was neatly laid out for me by the bearers. There would be a cough on the verandah, Corporal Haider signalling his presence, generally bearing some gift, a hen or a duck for Angela, or flowers or scented branches off some shrub for Patricia. He would then drive me to the airstrip on visit days or to the Fort on office days. On office days I would get out of the Landrover by the flight of age-polished stone steps which led steeply up to the verandah above, and go into my office which was situated on the first floor of the circular turret at that end of the building. I would normally be left in peace for the first half hour to go through my IN tray, after which I and the Staff Officers concerned would assemble in the map-covered Operations Room which led off my office, for the day's briefing by the

Brigade Major, DAA & QMG, and GS02 Intelligence. Necessary decisions would be given and perhaps several hours would be spent in planning operations or large scale training exercises. From 9am to 10am we all went off to breakfast. Visitors from SAF and from outside the Sultanate would join us at our house for the meal. Afterwards there would be more office work, a stroll to the nearby Defence Office for a discussion with Pat Waterfield or his senior staff and then my morning walk round the hospital wards. On office days I usually visited one of the Headquarters units such as Force MT, Force Workshops, Force Signals, Force Ordnance Depot, the up-country artillery troop, one of the schools or the Guard Company. Or it might be a visit to SOAF Headquarters to chat to the pilots or to go around the hangars and workshops where the devoted Airwork ground crews would be maintaining and repairing our aircraft. Here, a jet Strikemaster would be having some of its intricate electrical wiring circuits replaced; there, another would be having bullet holes repaired. Or I would walk round the offices and talk about pay or recruiting to Bob Warner, or chat to the clerks in the various offices.

It was British MOD policy that the infantry battalions and SOAF should be commanded by regular seconded officers, so we arranged that the other three major Army units – Oman Gendarmerie, Guard Regiment and Training Regiment, (and also the Navy Coastal Patrol) would be commanded by contract officers. Within the regiments, companies and their equivalent were commanded by the best man for the job, whether contract or seconded. Battalion seconds-in-command were all contract officers, and any rivalry that had existed between contract and seconded officers was removed. SAF needed both types of commission, the valuable experience and continuity provided by the contract officers, and the new ideas and 'up-to-datedness' of the seconded, and I was determined that both elements would be welded into one team, with fair opportunities for promotion for both.

CHAPTER TWENTY-EIGHT

OPERATION 'GRANITE', AND SOME AMPHIBIOUS OPERATIONS

My time as CSAF comes to an end.

Richard John's company of Muscat Regiment was currently detached to Dhofar under command of Northern Frontier Regiment. I had received a signal to tell me that Richard had been seriously wounded in the Wadi Hinna, well out in enemy territory in Western Dhofar. The story was going round that the adoo had used a silver bullet to 'get' him. Richard was to go into Hedley Court for many months but the splendid doctors and staff there put things right and turned him out in great order. Mike Harvey felt that this incident might have an adverse effect on morale and, worse still, elate the adoo, so he resolved to go to the site of action to bring the adoo to battle and give them a bloody nose. I decided to go with him and flew down to Salalah. The operation was given the codename 'Granite'. I did not want to get in Mike's way but I did want the chance to share what could be a 'punch up' with him and his men and help avenge Richard's wounding.

I quote from Mike Harvey's Report. 'This is a notorious area of sheer escarpments and narrow, precipitous tracks in mountainous jungle. Trails winding and zig-zagging through near impenetrable and almost inaccessible mist-swept crags. It can only be reached by a gruelling seven hour stalk through terrain completely suited to ambush tactics. The nature of the terrain dictating movement in most places to a single track. A classic guerilla base. This base camp is used as a temporary staging post for rebels moving through the tree line between the jebal and their safe base at Hauf. It is an active adoo area in which there have been two recent encounter

287

battles, with casualties both to SAF and to the adoo.' The operation was mounted through a base called Januk and the area of 'Everest' was to be secured as a preliminary phase.

As usual RSM Marhoun attached himself to me, and Mike Harvey, myself, the RSM, Mike's signaller Suleiman, and Nick Cameron, the wiry, young, Kenya-born Major who had succeeded John Lewis as our senior gunner, plus his own signaller completed our group. Mike took with him A Company commanded by 23 years old Jeremy Lee, a Royal Marine. Jeremy was to prove himself cool, decisive, brave and mature, on this and subsequent operations. He was a natural leader with great charm as well as professional ability. Mike also took the attached company of Muscat Regiment, Richard John's boys, under another Marine, stocky, efficient Mark Murray, ready to avenge their commander, with Tim Landon, the other company officer.

We moved off from the area of Januk at last light and I remember the pleasant scent of herbs and shrubs on the night air, the clicking noise made by some sort of insect and the sight of glow worms in the dark which appeared as small phosphorescent points of light on the branches of bushes. We lay down for a couple of hours sleep before dawn, having posted sentries, covering ourselves with the half of a lightweight blanket each of us carried. We were so tired that we hardly noticed the sharp rocky ground and the spiky thorns. Next morning, before first light, we were up and moving quietly and by this stage, well opened out, towards Shershitti, a known enemy haunt.

At times the going was across knife-edged, twisted lava rock, and we padded through dense, sword-pointed thorn bushes that slashed our clothing while their barbs sometimes remained embedded in our skin. Soon the hot sun beat down on us and I had a strong feeling that we were being watched from the higher ground ahead. We emerged onto a flat escarpment and continued westwards in the general direction of the border with South Yemen, with Jeremy Lee's Scouts moving carefully ahead followed by their point section, then by the rest of the leading platoon. After them came Jeremy with company headquarters, followed by two more platoons extended to either side of him, with his fourth platoon in reserve in rear ready to move wherever he wished. Our command group moved after them, and behind us came the donkeys, some carrying 81mm mortars and ammunition, others carrying water. Behind them came one of Mark Murray's half-companies under Tim Landon, followed by the other half company under Mark. They were the rear guard covering us from threat of attack from behind.

We were by now in a vast saucer circled by higher, broken ground at the rim. Again I had this strong feeling of being watched – we all sensed it –

but no one was in sight, no flocks, no women or children. We had to cross this wide, open expanse and covered each other forward tactically, ready to fire should a target present itself. 'Perfect killing ground!' muttered Mike to me. 'Richard John was wounded over there.'

The sun increased its heat, we reached the saucer's rim and moved right round it clearing any cover, but still there was no sign of, or move from, the enemy. Yet we were convinced that they were about. Mike pressed on for several more miles and we searched caves, likely hiding places and observation positions. It seemed utterly deserted. The silence was oppressive and, if it had been a film, I felt that the background music would have been that thin, growing, high-pitched, drawn-out note on the violin that denotes tension and impending violence! Still no signs, so we moved back following a different route. We would not, even if we had no hold-ups, reach our nearest forward base, where our artillery was located, before the next afternoon. We were within range of our guns however, which would be comforting if we met the adoo, which we still hoped to do.

At last we saw signs of habitation, conical-shaped huts and cattle enclosures fenced with massive slabs of stone, but no humans or animals. About four hundred yards away was a large expanse of thick cover and Mike gave orders for it to be searched. I saw the soldiers moving into it, weapons at the ready, the men wary and alert. No one. Mike suggested breakfast and gave orders for protection of the area while everyone ate and for sentries to be relieved in their turn so that they, too, might eat. At that moment (as so often seems to happen!) there was an earsplitting sound as of canvas being ripped by a giant and a hail of bullets swept us as the enemy opened fire with a number of Soviet automatic weapons! Like flashes we dived for cover then looked for targets to shoot back at. Our soldiers where shooting towards where the enemy firing came from and I looked for a suitable target to engage. I could see nothing, absolutely no one, although our constant practice in locating the enemy by his fire certainly indicated to each of us the general area of his positions. I noticed someone firing purposefully and rapidly. Feeling annoyed with myself at my inability to spot any adoo but determined not to waste a round until I could see a target, I asked the firer to indicate to me his target. Shamefacedly he confessed he could see nothing and I told him to stop wasting his ammunition. We had not yet won the firefight nor had we succeeded in pinning the enemy down. Jeremy Lee could be heard roaring orders to his mortars but still the enemy kept up their deafeningly loud and close hail of intensive fire.

Nicol Cameron who, with his signaller, had been pinned down near a bush, brought artillery fire on to and behind the enemy position and while this was going on Mike Harvey moved Tim Landon and his half company round the enemy's flank. Directly the artillery fire stopped, Mike launched Tim's half company which was led personally by Tim into a spirited and irresistible assault. The noise of exploding shells and bombs was now replaced by that of hand-held automatics as our Sterling sub-machine guns and SLRs ripped into the opposition. This sound died away in a very few minutes and was replaced by the shouts of sub-unit commanders during the mopping-up and consolidation phases.

I had witnessed the major part of this action after the initial torrent of fire standing up, not because I was feeling particularly brave but because RSM Marhoun who was beside me had stood up fully exposed to the enemy fire, and I couldn't possibly look him in the face if I had been using cover while he had not! To make matters worse I noticed that under his now open shirt he was wearing a white singlet which was far from my idea of good camouflage! His great nostrils flaring in his black, negroid face, he pointed out enemy positions to me which I had not previously seen. He had fantastic eyesight as I was to note on numerous future occasions.

We joined Tim's men on the objective where enemy corpses were being searched and their AK47 rifles taken. Mohammad Omar, one of Tim's submachine gunners proudly showed me the dead man he had despatched, a neat pattern of bullet holes stitched vertically down the body of the corpse. After we had thoroughly searched the immediate area, the dead were collected and the prisoners whom Jeremy Lee had captured were made to carry them. We took the corpses back to Salalah with us 'pour décourager' any of 'les autres' or sympathisers who might be inside the town perimeter.

My younger son, Tim, who served later with SAF in Southern Oman Regiment told me that he met a Dhofari officer of the Firqat forces who had taken part as an enemy in this particular action. He told Tim that he had known who I was and had actually fired at me. Although I am indeed grateful to him for having missed me, I hope he is a better shot now that he is a soldier of the Sultan!

The Sultan was delighted at Mike Harvey's successful action. Mike carried out a further series of skilfully planned and effective operations, some of which were amphibious when, backed by the intrepid Jeremy Raybould and the crews of *Nasr al Bahr* and *Muntasir*; and supported by our increasingly accurate, bold SOAF pilots, he established a real dominance throughout the jebal and the plain.

I accompanied NFR on a number of these amphibious operations. They were invariably meticulously planned by Mike, every eventuality seemed to have been catered for and he always seemed to catch the adoo flat-footed. His operations were sound tactically, his training beforehand, and his comprehensive administration were a model, and among the Principles of War he used with such effect were Offensive Action, Surprise and Concentration of Force. His plans were simple and crystal clear and all who served with him had utter faith in his leadership. To join NFR on these forays I would fly down to Salalah by Beaver or Dakota, or, occasionally, by Strikemaster if time was short. Mike would meet me at the airfield. At the camp I would change into my camouflaged kit, take a rifle and ammunition, have a cup of tea while Mike briefed me, and then we would be off to Raysut to board either *Nasr al Bahr* or *Muntasir*.

Jeremy Raybould would be waiting on the jetty to greet us, usually accompanied by his twin warrior Spike Powell who invariably joined in if any action was imminent. The soldiers were always so welcoming and would crowd round to shake hands. This was in the days of integrated battalions when Arab and Baluch mingled happily and effectively, both races being grand fighting men.

On one occasion we landed at night on a beach well beyond Rakhyut and after the Geminis had ferried us all ashore, we moved silently inland climbing steeply up a narrow, twisting path until we reached the more open, rolling country above. We paused frequently to listen, and during one of these pauses the moon came out, bathing the countryside in its white light. As we crouched among the thorn bushes and boulders, RSM Marhoun, that splendid, fearless soldier, snuffed his great nostrils like a horse and whispered 'Hurma' (women). He could smell the Dhofari women and in five minutes we saw above us on the hillside the round, conical huts that the jebalis lived in.

Mike moved the main body around to the high ground above the huts with enough stops elsewhere on the ground to surround the village, and we then moved downhill, clearing each hut in turn. The women, once over their surprise, made their usual noise to alert their menfolk but one young man was taken whom Andrew Fuller recognised and arrested as a known adoo. We continued our search operation and although we heard warning shots we encountered no more enemy on this occasion. Having reached Mike's objectives in daylight we moved along westwards further up the coast along the high ground, taking a different route and keeping alert throughout. We were then ferried back out to *Nasr al Bahr* and *Muntasir* at about 11am.

After we had put to sea we had a radio message reporting a concentration of pilgrims near a khor (inlet) further up the coast towards the PRSY border. This group was thought to consist of some unfortunate Pakistanis on a Haj pilgrimage, dumped there by one of the many villainous dhow captains who exploited these pilgrims. He had probably told them to walk inland and over the hill where they would see Mecca before them! *Nasr al Bahr* and *Muntasir* headed westwards. Mike, Jeremy Lee, Adrian Wray and myself were aboard *Muntasir* commanded by Jeremy Raybould. Two Vickers guns were mounted on each dhow, manned by Baluch soldiers from the Guard Regiment.

Sailing under engines up the coast through a sea of glorious blue accentuated by our white wake creaming behind, and looking upwards at the towering cliffs of the Dhofar Jebal to our right it was difficult to believe that we were probably being watched by hostile eyes and that fire could be opened on us at any moment. Jeremy Raybould kept his two ships outside enemy mortar range until we came to the khor where, on the beach, we could see the figures of a crowd of people moving rather aimlessly about. We closed the shore and, when we were within a fairly short distance of it, a storm of small-arms fire broke out. A Baluch Vickers gunner fell dead beside his weapon and the helmsman, standing between Mike Harvey and myself, fell wounded to the deck. Jeremy Raybould, moving like a panther, leapt to the wheel and signalling to *Nasr al Bahr* to conform, took both vessels outside the range of enemy small-arms fire. Meanwhile Jeremy Lee and Adrian Wray had got just about every Bren gun on board mounted on the rails and were returning a withering fire against the adoo who, having originally infiltrated the crowd of pilgrims, were now on higher ground.

Mike and I took over a Vickers whose gunner lay dead and, with Mike firing and myself as No. 2, we soon had a stream of effective fire pouring back at the enemy. RSM Marhoun, as ever when the action was hot, stood beside us, conspicuous with his white vest showing and, thanks to his amazingly keen eyesight, indicated the enemy positions. We silenced the enemy fire completely, sailing in again to confirm that we had done so. We later heard that we had inflicted heavy casualties on them including several killed and a number wounded. Our casualties were one fine Baluch Vickers gunner killed, the helmsman wounded and one or two scratches. I had my arm grazed by a bullet about which no amount of eloquence on my part could deceive Patricia on my return! When we got back to Raysut that evening and made arrangements for the pilgrims to be collected, we were saddened to learn that one of our 4 tonners had been blown up on an enemy mine and that two soldiers who were travelling in it had been killed. The enemy use of mines meant that, where time did not permit us to sweep the existing motorable tracks and their verges to detect these deadly weapons, we had to drive alongside them on virgin soil.

I was to go on further amphibious operations, some with NFR and some later on with Muscat Regiment under Peter Thwaites, and when he left, his successor, Fergus McKain-Bremner.

I have mentioned that our platoons were commanded by staff sergeants. I was unable to persuade the Sultan to make platoon commanders a commissioned appointment but he was quite prepared for outstanding staff sergeants to be commissioned in the field, such as that fine warrior Charshambe who had won the Gallantry Medal.

I tried to get our only local captain, Aziz-ur-Rahman his majority but this had to wait until the present Sultan had succeeded his father. The old Sultan never could see why anyone should be raised in rank and paid more for doing the same job – and there is logic in that point of view! Also, the old Sultan used to tell me to look at what happened to those other monarchs and heads of state who promoted their officers: the colonels then got rid of their rulers!

Our medical arrangements were now much better, and besides each battalion having its own medical officer, there was a trained medical orderly in every rifle company. At Salalah we had a small advanced hospital, staffed by the battalion MO and a team of trained assistants which included a staff sergeant British male state registered nurse on contract. In North Oman at Bait al Falaj Hospital we had Lieutenant Colonel Iain Hynd, his administrative officer Jim Dolphin-Rowland, matron Joyce Sanderson and the Indian Army Medical Officer on deputation, Captain Habeeb Ashruf plus Major Seifi Vasi, our dentist. There was also a full staff of trained medical assistants under our second British male SRN, and a kitchen producing decent hospital diets as well as ordinary meals. However, we still had to evacuate our seriously wounded to the RAF hospital in Bahrain because of our lack of field surgical capacity.

By now we were a hard, fit, combat-experienced, tactically sound and confident Force. But we would not win the Dhofar war unless we had helicopters, more infantry, transport aircraft, the SAS, a field surgical team, and more artillery, especially the new British light gun. I wrote yet another impassioned paper for the Sultan with copies to Pat Waterfield and his successor, Hugh Oldman, and to General Roly Gibbs. In this, I asked again and even more strongly for all these vital necessities which we had to have if we were to bring hostilities in Oman successfully to a close. In Pat Waterfield's successor I had an instant and enthusiastic supporter, because Hugh Oldman had been my predecessor but one, and knew and appreciated my problems from first-hand experience both in Oman, and in South Arabia, where he had commanded a battalion of Aden Protectorate Levies. Hugh had commanded an infantry battalion in the War in France and Germany, knew his stuff and fully agreed with and supported my paper. He went down to Salalah, saw Sultan Said bin Taimur and convinced him that what we had been asking for for two and a half years was indeed vital.

So at long last we were able to start planning to raise our next battalion of infantry which is now called the Jebal Regiment. We also knew, thanks mainly to General Roly Gibbs, that our application to the British Ministry of Defence for teams from the Special Air Service Regiment to increase our expertise in ambushing and other skills and to help us with in the battle for the 'hearts and minds' of the Dhofaris, had at last been agreed, together with the provision of a field surgical team in Salalah. John Watts commanding 22 SAS came to visit us to see Dhofar for himself and I went out with him on a night patrol on the Salalah Plain.

Colonel the Viscount Slim, OBE, commanding Special Air Service Regiment, had already visited us with the experienced Lord Patrick Beresford, a friend from my Borneo days, and was well aware of our problems. Hugh Oldman told me that he would be placing an order for both Iroquois and Jetranger helicopters, and for the new British light gun! It had taken two and a half of my three years as CSAF to succeed in my battle for these essentials! Meanwhile the enemy had not only received skilled instruction and quantity supply of modern weapons from the Iron Curtain countries but had greatly increased in numbers. A year earlier and we might have militarily won the War but it took Sultan Qabus bin Said's sincerity and approach to win the battle for the 'hearts and minds' of his Dhofari subjects. Final victory was not to come until 1974.

I was able to see a lot of the next battalion for Dhofar duty whilst it was in North Oman. This was the oldest and most senior regiment in SAF, Muscat Regiment. The regimental headgear was, as I have mentioned, a scarlet Balmoral bonnet, 'toorie' and all. I was told that Sultan Said bin Taimur had been so impressed with the battalion of the Cameronians (Scottish Rifles) which formed part of the British Force that came to his assistance during the Jebal Akhdar campaign that he had ordered that MR should wear similar headgear in Sultanate red.

The gallant Simon Sloane had now become Peter Thwaites's Adjutant, but this did not stop him going on operations.

Among Muscat Regiments' officers were a number of cavalrymen, Patrick Brook and Richard John I have already introduced. Richard Kinsella-Bevan of 5th Royal Inniskilling Dragoon Guards, a keen regular soldier would later return as a lieutenant colonel to command an armoured regiment, and Sir Ranulph Fiennes, Royal Scots Greys, commanded the Reconnaissance Platoon. Before he came to SAF I was told what a handful Ran was! I think the adoo may have found him such, but I was indeed glad and fortunate to have him in SAF. A charming young man and another natural leader, he earned a richly deserved Bravery Medal in Dhofar.

Peter had good local officers and NCOs. One of his staff sergeants (later Brigadier) Hamad Mana won the Gallantry Medal, the Distinguished Service Medal and the Bravery Medal, all three as a platoon commander. One of his section commanders was Corporal Obeid with two Bravery Medals, and so it went on.

NFR was back in North Oman, Lieutenant Colonel Karl Beale, MC, ex-SAS, had succeeded Mike Harvey, and Muscat Regiment moved down to Dhofar again. Peter Thwaites was due to take UK leave and John Cooper would take over command in his absence. Shortly after Peter Thwaites went home on leave, the Midway Road was opened to allow a southbound convoy through from North Oman to Salalah. MR had a very difficult time during this operation, as the adoo had used the mists of the Khareef to considerably reinforce their strength astride the Midway road, and had blown up the Ramp, the steep, sleeper-based rise in the road from Midway Camp to Salalah. The convoy had had a number of casualties and a gunner detachment, which had been under command of Hugh Affleck-Graves, had been badly shot up. Receiving his first baptism of concentrated fire as a SAF officer was John Westing of the Queen's Regiment who was to prove to be another fine leader. John Cooper flew up for a conference at Bait al Falaj after which he came over to our house for drinks and told me about the road opening. I felt I should take part in the next one and told him so out of earshot of Patricia and Angela!

Peter Thwaites had come back by then and I proposed myself for a week's visit which Peter manfully accepted. He had decided to use his entire battalion less the camp guard, plus the attached company from NFR commanded by David Shillinglaw. I flew down to Salalah by Dakota with a number of soldiers of MR returning from leave and Peter Thwaites met me at the airfield. We drove to his battalion camp at Umm al Ghawarif where I attended Peter's operational briefing for the road opening. This was a very clear exposition and everyone knew exactly what was required on the morrow.

Peter Thwaites had invented his latest drink, a potent mixture of rum and loomi. We all sat outside the Officers' Mess in the garden amid the sound of crickets, the whirring of bats' wings and the deep croaking of bullfrogs from the pond in the mess garden, and drank some of these delicious concoctions. After supper we all had an early night and next morning were up before first light. For the road-opening operation Peter had two companies, each commanded by a fire-eater, driving down from the north from the direction of Midway, consisting of Roger Brown, with his MR Company and David Shillinglaw with his NFR Company.

Peter and I drove out before first light to the Plain to where the gun lines were situated ready to support the road opening. I was accompanied by the battery commander, Nicol Cameron, and wise old Mohammad Ashraf commanded the gun position. While our leading troops were moving up in the dark to occupy the picquet positions which had to be held in order to safely use the road, Peter and I walked round the gun lines chatting to the crews who were standing ready by their 5.5 inch howitzers and 25 pounders.

Suddenly there was the sound of small-arms fire and enemy bullets struck the ground around us in the gun lines. Fortunately they caused no casualties but one of the leading platoons had been anticipated in occupying its picquet and the adoo had got there first and engaged our gun lines. A small fire fight took place before the enemy firing ceased and all MR picquets had firmly occupied their positions. We were up on the plateau when dawn broke, the sea a shield of glimmering, grey-blue behind and below us. We advanced on foot with a company on either side of the road and one moving behind in reserve. As always, Peter was well forward, moving between his two leading companies and I accompanied him. As it got light enough for men to see, they picked us out and I will never forget the lump it brought to my throat as they clapped and cheered even though the enemy had already opened up and we were advancing under aimed fire. As far as I remember, we carried out no less than five battalion attacks that day with Peter imperturbable as ever, handling his battalion most professionally. Twice, when the opposition had hardened and progress was difficult, Peter deployed Roger Brown's and David Shillinglaw's companies from the north behind the opposition, and this had the desired loosening effect on the adoo.

By late afternoon enemy opposition had been overcome, firing had ceased and Peter and the main body of the battalion had joined hands with the two northern companies. He and I went up with some Landrovers to collect Roger's and David's casualties and met both these splendid warriors near Aqabat Jasmin, Ambush Corner, in a deep, grassy wadi. The sun had not yet gone down and we waded hip high through the tall, lush grass. Birds were calling melodiously and vividly-coloured butterflies flitted among exotic flowers. In these surroundings it was difficult to remember the need to be ever alert, to recall how excellent the adoo were at fieldcraft and also what a dangerous and unpredictable enemy they were. David and Roger, of course, both exuded enthusiasm and it was better than drinking a glass of chilled vintage champagne to be with those two exhilarating warriors among their brave, beaming soldiers.

We heard later that the enemy had suffered heavy casualties and as a result of this crushing defeat by Muscat Regiment, never again in my time as CSAF did we have trouble on the Midway Road, or indeed on the jebal in its proximity. Muscat Regiment had given the enemy a really bloody nose and showed them who called the tune. A memory to carry with me is of the tough, resilient Ranulph Fiennes, moving towards the enemy with his Reconnaissance Platoon, effortlessly carrying a GPMG, a rifle and a scout telescope! With officers and men like these the successful outcome of the Dhofar War could surely never be in doubt.

On another occasion Peter Thwaites decided on a seaborne operation.

By then, because of the number of troops we had to keep on the jebal to counter increased enemy strength, and our consequent decrease in numbers to the west, the adoo had overcome its askar garrison and occupied Rakhyut on the coast. Rakhyut was a small fishing village and although tactically this was no loss, psychologically it was a most regrettable victory for the rebels. The Sultan was very good and philosophical about it. I asked him if he would like us to take it back but he realised that had we done so, and we easily could have, we would have then had to garrison and supply it from our already insufficient strength as we could not rely on askars based so far away. So Peter, who knew that the enemy had at least two heavy Shpagin machine guns covering Rakhyut harbour entrance, decided to trail his coat there in an armed dhow and force the heavy machine guns to reveal their positions by opening fire on us. As soon as they did he planned to call in SOAF Strikemasters to annihilate them.

I went with Peter and Jeremy Raybould on this operation and we sailed at dusk in *Muntasir* heading for the PRSY border. *Muntasir* had powerful engines and throbbed along through calm seas under the lowering mass of the Dhofar mountains which were clearly outlined against a night sky in which a myriad of stars hung like orange lights. We could smell the scent of herbs and grass from the land and at times woodsmoke from jebali fires. The naukhodar (ship's master) was at the wheel and Peter, Jeremy and I sat with a drink discussing the operation. After we reached our territorial limit and had had a look at 'the other side' we would turn, come back and enter Rakhyut at first light.

All would depend on radio, as it was considered unwise to predetermine our time of arrival at Rakhyut in view of the vagaries of the weather. Ideally, the SOAF strike aircraft should arrive immediately the enemy revealed their positions by opening fire on us. In case the wind or the sea, or both, got up and delayed or advanced our timing the pilots would be scrambled by radio. After completing our mission at Rakhyut we would sail on round the coast past Salalah and then visit the Muscat Regiment garrison in the little seaside town of Taqa where, after a recent enemy attack on the town, our people were bolstering up and re-training the askar garrison of the fort. Afterwards, we would ambush the tracks leading to Taqa throughout the night in order to deal with any adoo coming in either to reconnoitre or to attack the fort again. We would return to base the following morning. I turned in early, and after a couple of hours, sleep came up on deck on being called by one of the crew because we were nearing Ras Darbat Ali, the Oman border with the People's Democratic Republic of South Yemen.

Jeremy Raybould was on deck and I could see his bearded profile silhouetted against the bright night sky. He told me that he had heard over our radio that the *Ghazal*, a PDRSY former Royal Navy minesweeper was said to be at sea and he wondered if our approach was known to the South Yemeni regime. However, we never met the minesweeper and turned homewards under the lee of Ras Darbat Ali having seen no vessels, and thudded back towards the little fishing village of Rakhyut.

As it began to get light – Jeremy had timed it admirably – there lay Rakhyut on our port bow and he, Peter and I stood on deck as *Muntasir* moved in towards it. SOAF had been called up on the radio and strike aircraft armed with cannon, rockets and bombs should be overhead any minute. We could make out the fort and little houses as we slowly came in. Someone said, 'For what we are about to receive…' Our guns were manned and suddenly a Shpagin opened up with one round, the sound unnaturally loud. We expected this to be followed by a hail of fire directed at us but presumably the enemy gun had jammed and either no one else was awake, or they did not recognise our ship with its Sultanate flag fluttering bravely, for what it was. We searched the skies for our aircraft but none appeared – we then discovered that the radio operator had not been able to get through to SOAF after all! He had passed his message, had received no acknowledgement, but had failed to tell us this! Happily for us we were not left in a hornet's nest and were able to come home to tell the tale.

As no other weapons opened fire, and no enemy posts revealed their positions, Jeremy turned *Muntasir* round and we glided out of the harbour mouth unscathed. This emphasized the need for officer-to-officer radio contact on such important occasions. Still, we felt we had at least shown that the Sultan's warships could go where they chose, but with a strong feeling of anti-climax we went below for a sustaining breakfast.

Later, having arrived off Taqa, we went ashore in a Gemini powered by an outboard motor, skimming across a shimmering sunlit sea of dazzling blue. Spike Barker-Schofield awaited us with some of his men and to-gether we walked up to the fort through the little village. The temporary presence of a stiffening of Muscat Regiment regulars in this little town to supplement the askar garrison had done wonders for local morale. Spike and his men were improving the soldier-like qualities of the askars who were a very mixed bag, ranging from youths to ancients, and armed with flintlocks, Martini-Henrys and Lee Enfields.

Our men could only be there on a very temporary basis as no one in his senses would dissipate his already insufficient infantry force in penny packets tied down as local garrisons. Intelligence reports had stated that the adoo might visit Taqa again that night, so Peter, Spike and I went off on a recce to get the layout of the little town and its approaches in our minds. Peter planned the disposition of his ambush parties accordingly and briefed his men. With great difficulty – I had eventually to resort to giving him a direct order! – we dissuaded Jeremy Raybould from joining us for the night ambush phase and sent him off to resume his patrol along the coast! As there were insufficient numbers, Peter and I formed one of the two-man ambushes and took up our positions on the beach near where an inland track came in.

Sited among palm trees about 150 yards behind us was a Bren group with orders to fire without challenge at anything that moved. Before the moon rose we were all lying in our chosen positions, camouflaged, and with every approach to Taqa covered by fire. The moon rose, bathing the beaches, palm trees and surrounding countryside in a brilliant white light and we could see for miles. The members of the ambushes were silent, motionless and well hidden. The only sounds were the beat of surf on the beach, the rustle of the palm leaves, the barking of the local dogs and the occasional sharp cry of a night bird. The latter could have been adoo signals, and everywhere men sharpened their alertness straining their eyes and ears for sight or sound of enemy movement. But war consists mainly of boredom and this was one of those nights. The moonlight faded, a breeze got up, cocks crew, and the sky paled as another day dawned. Stiff and with our tired eyeballs feeling as if they had been taken out and dipped in the sand of the sea shore, on Peter's command we got to our feet, RV'd and breakfasted in the fort.

By the time we had finished breakfast *Muntasir* was at anchor and a Gemini was creaming towards us to collect Peter and me. Saying goodbye to Spike and his men and leaving them with a fresh radio, extra batteries, rations and ammunition, we set off to *Muntasir* on our way back to Raysut and on to Umm al Ghawarif camp. Peter and I had an Audience with the Sultan that evening. Peter got on marvellously with him and the Sultan clearly liked and trusted Peter. Peter had interesting anecdotes to tell of life on public duties in London and of polo at Smith's Lawn at Windsor which the Sultan loved. He also liked Peter's aggressive instincts and listened avidly to future operational plans.

At each Audience I was granted I never failed to be impressed with the kindness shown to me personally by the Sultan, yet he was always the Ruler, regal and dignified. He invariably wore a rather large, almost top heavy, rounded turban on his head, the main colour motifs being purple and crimson. Otherwise he wore a single spotlessly white, flowing jellaba with a belt round his waist into which, in the centre front, was placed a silver khanjar. On his bare feet he wore either plastic or leather sandals. He had a spreading, grizzled, mainly grey beard, his nose was large and fleshy and his eyes were large and liquid-brown. These normally had a kind, indeed, polite expression but when something annoyed him they clouded and could become extremely angry looking. His English was perfect, almost unaccented, his voice soft and his whole manner utterly dignified and courteous. I and my family had grown very fond of him and of his charming son, the present Sultan, and he was invariably kindness itself to us. He had a great sense of humour and was very shrewd. If only his sense of public relations had been modern and he had gone among his people, as does his son, His Majesty Sultan Qabus bin Said, he would have had them eating out of his hand. Perhaps he felt it would be courting popularity, and therefore showing weakness if he did so. The Sultan therefore lost the chance of impressing his charismatic personality on those he ruled.

I always used to tell him respectfully exactly what I thought and what I believed he should do, even though occasionally I clearly angered him in so doing. But he knew of my liking and respect and my loyalty to him, so he was never cross for long. After we had exchanged greeting and pleasantries he would lean forward in his padded armchair, press the bell in the wall of the little study, then a palace servant would bring in the tea tray and the Sultan would pour out. Whenever Patricia and Angela were with me there would be fresh milk for Angela from the Sultan's own herd of cattle. It was tricky ground when raising sensitive subjects with the Ruler, and I used to look upon myself as someone walking down a corridor lined by opened doors, each keyless and with automatic locks, so that once a door closed it could not be opened again. My aim was never to have one of these doors closed! Once Said bin Taimur had said 'No!' he would never, never change his mind. Peter and I had an enjoyable Audience. The Sultan agreed to all our requests, and, tea having been removed, we took our leave.

Outside the night had fallen and as the Palace Askars swung open the heavy, iron-studded doors from the Palace compound the road lay white before us under a bright full moon. We drove back to Umm al Ghawarif Camp between the avenues of tall coconut palms, their round fruit clearly visible in the rays of the moon. And so to the Officers' Mess for a drink and a chat in the garden before going in to dinner.

What happy times those were, and what splendid teams of officers and men there were in the regiments, in SOAF and in the Coastal Patrol. Other than commanding my beloved Battalion of Royal Ulster Rifles, I don't think I have ever had three such happy years as my time in Oman.

John Crompton had departed for the Ministry of Defence and promotion, and his successor was Andrew Shelley, of the Royal Green Jackets. Again, I was lucky. Andrew was a fellow Rifleman who loved Active Service soldiering, and proved to be an energetic, cheerful, enthusiastic and effective BM. Mike Legg, my smiling, jolly GSO3 had gone also, to be promoted and to command a company of his regiment on operations in Northern Ireland. His successor was the very capable Dan Baily, a Royal

Anglian. At the end of Dan's Secondment he was relieved by Peter Walton, RAOC, another excellent officer. The able John Moore, who was Tony Adams' successor as DAA & QMG had Tim Herbert and James Vickers as his staff captains, and these two blades created havoc among the presentable females in PDO! David Thompson who had come into the Headquarters from the Oil Installation Police was full of solid commonsense as Staff Captain (Movements).

John MacFrederick was still GS02 (Intelligence) and Malcolm Denison also remained, fortunately, in view of his incredible rapport with the locals. Bob Warner, that wise old statesman, was still the strong right arm as OIC Pay and Records. Colin Maxwell, promoted to colonel and decorated with the Distinguished Service Medal (W.Kh.M) had come back from England with a new hip joint and was active and agile, and of course beloved throughout SAF and indeed the Sultanate.

Sadly, Peter Thwaites left us at the end of his secondment, his gallant and distinguished service having resulted in his being decorated with the Bravery Medal, the Distinguished Service Medal and the Commendation Medal. As with Mike Harvey, I was very sad to see Peter go. We had built the new SAF together and shared the excitements, the frustrations and setbacks and also the satisfaction of serving under the Sultan. In Peter's place came Fergus MacKain-Bremner with whom I had served at the School of Infantry. Fergus was another proper infantryman and lost no time in getting out on operations and settling himself firmly in to command. Muscat Regiment did not have long to do in Dhofar before being relieved by Desert Regiment and so I went down to what proved to be my last operation as CSAF, having given Fergus time to settle in. By then the strength of the enemy had increased still further and their equipping with Communist-bloc weapons had gone apace. They had occupied the little seaport village of Sudh on the east coast of Dhofar so we decided to chuck them out with B Company, Muscat Regiment in a seaborne operation. B Company was commanded by tough Peter Bennett, a large, fair haired ex-SAS soldier.

Hugh Oldman had come down to Salalah to see the Sultan, and Fergus invited him to dinner in Mess on the night following the operation. There had somehow been leaks of information after the Sultan had been briefed on recent operations, so it was decided not to let him know about the proposed reoccupation of Sudh until it had been successfully accomplished. Fergus needed all available men for a road-opening operation immediately afterwards so he would be unable to spare any soldiers to garrison Sudh when we pulled out of it, even temporarily. We hoped that the Sultan would send some of his askars – of whom he had an abundance – to occupy Sudh after MR departed and I decided to signal him accordingly as soon as the place was back in our hands. Unlike Rakhyut, Sudh would not have been difficult for askars to hold and supply, and reinforcement other than during the Khareef would have presented comparatively little problem, as it was relatively accessible.

Accompanying B Company were Corporal Brown of the Queen's Own Highlanders, who was attached to the battalion as a GPMG instructor, and Sergeant Sexton of the Cheshire Regiment who had come to us to instruct on the 81mm medium mortar. Both were the very best type of British NCO: they emanated calm confidence and thirsted to fire their weapons in anger.

Jeremy Raybould had carried out a reconnaissance of the proposed landing area and had returned to say there were no snags from the amphibious side. A Royal Navy minesweeper happened to be off Dhofar and although the Royal Navy was forbidden to join hostilities or to fire unless fired on, the very presence of this small warship in the vicinity could be helpful. We sailed on the eve of St Patrick's Day and Fergus and I went over by Gemini with Jeremy Raybould and called on the captain of the minesweeper, Captain Gunning, an impressive young Ulsterman with considerable presence and the capacity of making decisions. He was later to command the Sultan of Oman's Navy. He readily agreed to my request that at first light he should be off Sudh with his Bofors gun trained on the fort, although he was not permitted (to his regret and obvious disappointment) to fire. The sight of the gun pointing at them would give no comfort to the opposition.

Fergus had planned that SOAF Strikemasters would start the assault by screaming in low over the town at first light while Geminis took in our leading elements. *Nasr al Bahr* and *Muntasir*, having transferred the initial wave of soldiers to the Geminis out of sight of Sudh would follow with the remainder and sail right into the harbour with every available Vickers, Browning and GPMG mounted and manned, and with 81mm mortars ready to fire from steel base plates on the decks. We left Raysut in glorious weather and I have a photograph of myself sleeping on a hatchcover. Solicitous Muscat Regiment officers, ever-mindful of my reputation, had carefully placed a quantity of empty bottles of wine, beer and whisky around my recumbent form! I have never really convinced my family that the photograph which Fergus thoughtfully sent Patricia was a 'frame up'!

We were all up well before first light and had something hot to eat and drink. St Patrick's Day dawned bright and clear. By now, our leading wave was surging forward in their Geminis and we were gliding swiftly after them in the two armed dhows. At the same time the Strikemasters of SOAF shrieked and whistled low over our heads close to the low, flat roof tops of Sudh then soared upwards, round and back again to repeat the performance. Our leading infantry were already systematically clearing each house in turn. By then Fergus, Corporal Brown and I had landed and, having made our way to the fort had climbed up to its roof. Here we were joined by the cigar-smoking Peter Bennett and Corporal Brown opened up on a fleeing adoo who was disappearing over the rim of a nearby rocky hilltop.

Within a very short time Sudh was in our hands and I radioed to the Sultan to tell him so. I asked him to send us a garrison of askars, told him we would continue to occupy Sudh until their arrival and that meanwhile we would put the little town in a state of defence and bring ashore rations for the askars. Alas, he refused to send the askars! Whether or not it was because I had failed to inform him previously about this operation (later, when I explained my reason he accepted it completely) or whether such a sudden and unexpected request was too much, I shall never know. We hung on hopefully for a further twenty-four hours and then pulled out, feeling very sad that an operation achieving complete surprise and carried out with such élan and precision, had not been completed as it should have been by the installation of a permanent askar garrison.

The night we returned, Hugh Oldman had dined with us full of congratulations and said that he had been with the Sultan when my radio request came through. He said the Sultan had been delighted but nothing Hugh could do or say would persuade him to release the askars we needed, even though he had enough and to spare!

Muscat Regiment were nearing the end of their operational tour and already advance parties were arriving from their successors, Desert Regiment. The square, ebullient Teddy Turnill arrived, promising to 'Zap!' and 'Pow!' the enemy. His hardened veterans like Dick James, Mike Kane, Tony Holman and Paul Mangin were out on the jebal already, in the areas they would take over from Muscat Regiment.

Desert Regiment badly missed their splendid former SAS soldier, Captain Eddie Vutirakis, who had won the Bravery Medal by calmly walking into an unmarked enemy anti-personnel minefield and carrying out a badly-wounded soldier who was thrashing about in agony and liable to set off other mines. Eddie had been tragically murdered by a disaffected, unhinged soldier who had then fled to the rebels. Eddie Vutirakis was quite one of our finest officers and we all mourned his passing.

Before Muscat Regiment left, decorations for brave and distinguished service were announced and the Sultan gave each soldier in the battalion a gift of money, as he had done to NFR, to mark his appreciation of their devoted service. The regiment then looked forward to well-earned and well-deserved post-operational leave before starting retraining in North Oman prior to yet another tour in Dhofar.

My own time as Commander Sultan Armed Forces was nearly up. I was the last CSAF to serve a full tour of three years' secondment, as it was found that our contemporaries who had commanded brigades in UK and BAOR were already six months or more into their next brigadier's staff jobs by then, and therefore at least six months ahead in the promotion stakes. John Graham, my successor only did two and a half years as CSAF and I think I am correct in saying that Tim Creasey and after him Ken Perkins did tours of only two years in command to compete on fair terms in the military rat race. Despite this I would hate to have forgone my three years. I loved every minute of serving with such splendid comrades – Arab, Baluch, Indian, Pakistani and British – and what other brigadier in the British Army was commanding a comparably-sized force of all three services with a war to run and the opportunity to get out on operations at grass-root level?

For my next appointment, I had been selected to command the School of Infantry, the pinnacle of any infantryman's ambition in his own trade, and I felt that I had amassed quite a bit of first-hand, down-to-earth, up-to-date, practical operational experience which would be of use to the Infantry.

As the time for our leaving Oman approached I found that more and more I dreaded saying goodbye to my comrades-in-arms. Visiting the battalions and other components of the Force, SOAF and the Coastal Patrol, I hated the thought of not serving with these men any more. The leave-taking ceremonies were harrowing; such kind, warm things were said, presentations made, and after each farewell visit the route out of each unit would be lined by soldiers firing their rifles in the air in farewell salute. There was a memorable evening in our Headquarters Mess which Patricia and I will never forget. Colin Maxwell made the kindest of speeches and the officers gave us a large, solid silver Omani coffee pot and two ashtrays, made entirely of melted down Maria Theresa dollars. We learnt later that the maker of these articles had had to be taken out from Nizwa gaol to work on them as he was the only craftsman of sufficient expertise to be entrusted with the task! I do hope he was not put back inside again, as we treasure them!

Then John Graham, my successor, flew in. He had obviously had a detailed briefing beforehand and did not require much information from me. He was looking forward to it all and Rosemary his wife and their two children joined him a few days before we left. We said goodbye to Desert Regiment in Dhofar where they had just taken over from MR and took our leave of the Sultan. Patricia and Angela flew down with me in a Dakota and we were collected from Umm al Ghawarif Camp in one of the Sultan's cars. Desert Regiment provided an escort and for the last time we were ushered up the Palace steps by the charming Court Chamberlain. The

Sultan came in and we all had tea which he poured out as usual. He said the nicest possible things.

It was with a heavy heart that I took my leave of Sultan Said bin Taimur. He had been my Commander-in-Chief for three years, had given me his confidence and support and, I like to think, his friendship. I had become devoted to him. He had had a most unfair press, partly because he was anxious that the worst of Western influences should not erode the fine people of his country, for which he had made detailed and far reaching plans for the future. Having brought his Sultanate from bankruptcy to solvency he was not going to risk the former again by spending too much too fast. Yes, he did live the life of a seeming recluse in Salalah but he had a good intelligence network – although it was not good enough to prevent the coup which deposed him four months after my departure – and was kept informed as to what was going on, certainly in North Oman. Perhaps some of his advisers could have been younger, more up-to-date and more dynamic, but their disinterested loyalty to him could not be faulted. Also, once people had proved themselves to him the Sultan never forgot, and his loyalty towards them was as great as theirs was to him and he found it incredibly hard to retire them.

Yes, he was a hard man with political prisoners, but when he had come so near to losing his throne less than ten years before in the Jebal Akhdar, and to losing his life in the Dhofar Force assassination attempt, is his attitude to the Dhofari rebel leaders so difficult to understand? Of course, he should have moved amongst his people far more, but I think that perhaps an innate shyness played a considerable part in his reluctance to do so. Certainly on the one public occasion when I saw him among his people in Dhofar he was received with rapture.

Our visit ended, and the Sultan accompanied us to the top of the steps which led down to the Palace courtyard, something he had never done before. I found it hard to speak. We looked back as the car took us out through the Palace gates and he was still standing there looking after us, waving. We were never to see him again.

On the day of our departure Andrew Shelley, my Brigade Major, told me that the men wanted to tow the Landrover to the airport and that I was requested to stop outside the Fort al Bait al Falaj, my Headquarters for three years, to say goodbye to my staff. I am ashamed to say that I refused. I simply could not face it. I knew that, stupidly, I would have been unable to say a word and that I would break down. So, for the last time my Baluch driver, dear old Corporal Haider Bahram, brought round our Safari Landrover to the front of our bungalow. Our kit had already been loaded into an Andover kindly sent for us by the RAF for our journey to Sharjah where we were to spend the night with Pat and Jeanette Ive. Sharif, that fine, loyal man, Bashir, Fakir the sweeper, and Gaspar Fernandez our Goanese cook, were all there, all crying as they shook our hands. Then we were off, looking back at our devoted staff waving from the bougainvillea and jasmine-covered verandah of our home for three unforgettably wonderful years. Down past the Defence Department bungalows to the Fort with all the staff assembled outside waving and clapping, and on through the main gate, acknowledging my last 'Present Arms' from the ferociously-moustached Baluch Guard Regiment sentry.

On to the airfield where we said goodbyes all round to David and Nancy Crawford, to Pickles and Hugh Oldman, to Alan Bridges, Lilian his wife, and their children, and to many other friends, including Saiyyid Turki, Director of Customs, a member of the Royal Family. Andrew Shelley, John Moore, Peter Walton and Alan Bridges walked over to the steps of the aircraft with us and there, lined up, were my commanding officers, all tried and trusted friends. Tony Best of the Oman Gendarmerie, Fergus McKain-Bremner of Muscat Regiment, Karl Beale of NFR, Nicol Cameron ... by now I really was beyond speech and could only silently grasp their hands and bolt up the steps into the aircraft. The aircraft taxied down the runway, turned and took off.

The captain of the aircraft said, 'Would you like to beat up the airfield, Sir?' and without waiting for my reply, proceeded to turn round the Andover and sweep low over a row of upturned faces and waving hands. I have never forgotten what it was to be a soldier of the Sultan, and never will.

After a happy stay with the Ives at Sharjah and with the Gibbs at Bahrain, we flew to Beirut, and were met by Anne and Bill Carden with whom we stayed for five enjoyable days before we returned to England. Bill was then Director of the Middle East College of Arabic Studies at Shemlan. We saw a lot of lovely Lebanon, its greenery, its clear rushing streams and French-looking towns, all of which was in marked change to the arid yet breathtaking scenery of Oman. We visited the Bekaa Valley and later marvelled at the glory of Baalbek. We also met a number of delightful Lebanese, but the presence of the unhappy Palestinians in their refugee camps near Beirut airport was a sad, uneasy forerunner of the cancer that entered and grew in the body of that gem of a country, ravaging it and almost killing it in the years that were to come.

May lasting peace come to Lebanon and to its people.

I was to return to Oman again in 1974 when I marvelled at the progress made under the enlightened rule of the present Sultan, the Sandhurst-trained, cultured His Majesty Sultan Qabus bin Said.

CHAPTER TWENTY-NINE

COMMANDANT, SCHOOL OF INFANTRY, WARMINSTER

On my return from Lebanon we had a short leave in my native Ireland, saw my mother, Biddy my sister and her husband Colán MacArthur at their home in Marble Hill, Co. Donegal, and visited other relatives and friends in the north and south of that lovely country.

We then visited Patricia's relatives in England, after which I moved down to Warminster leaving Patricia and Angela at the cottage we owned in Reigate. I moved into the comfortable Infantry Mess at the School of Infantry while I took over from my good friend Glyn Gilbert, who was about to be promoted major general and appointed General Officer Commanding 3rd Division. I enjoyed my few days in the Mess, renewed my friendship with the Staff, and experienced for myself the high standards that prevailed there. In those days we still had a number remaining of our ex-wartime Free Polish, Free Czech and Yugoslav Mess Staff. Some of them during the War had held commissions; for example Ziggi the barman had been a squadron leader bomber pilot in a Polish-crewed Wellington.

I had an excellent handover from Glyn and then moved into Battlesbury House, the comfortable quarter allotted to the Commandant. The Director of Infantry who had his headquarters at the school Major General Michael Forrester, was a much decorated infantryman, having a CB, two DSOs and two MCs, and years of wartime battle experience.

My staff were a distinguished, operationally experienced group of officers. Colonel Frankie Boshell, DSO, OBE, who had been with me at Sandhurst, was later succeeded by Colonel Tod Sweeney, OBE, MC. The Officers' Wing was commanded by Colonel Peter Downard, CB, DSO, DFC, now a major general, the Support Weapons Wing by, successively,

Colonels Mike Dauntsey, DSO, and Mike Harvey, CBE, MC, both retired as brigadiers. Johnnie Clements, OBE, MC, who also retired as a brigadier, commanded the NCOs' Wing, handing over to Cyril Morgan, OBE.

The Officer Commanding the Company Commanders' Division, ended his career as General Sir David Mostyn, KCB, CBE, and his successor is now Brigadier Joe Starling, CBE, MC, Colonel Peter Walter, MBE, MC, a particularly tough and able soldier commanded the Battle School at Brecon, and three of my instructors in the Platoon Commanders' Division are now Major Generals – Hew Pike, CB, DSO, MBE, Jack Deverell, OBE, and Brian Dutton, CBE. We had the cream of the British Infantry to teach our students. It was a happy place blessed with a delightful civilian staff and had an exciting, dynamic air about it.

We also had excellent specialist officers from our supporting arms – Gunners, Sappers and Signals, as well as liaison officers from various Commonwealth countries – India, Australia, Canada, sometimes New Zealand, and from France and the United States of America. The School was also the Headquarters of the Small Arms School Corps, that small and select body of high-calibre specialists in Infantry Weapons. The Commandant of the School of Infantry was ex-officio Commandant of the SASC, so I got to know the Corps members well and became very fond of it. Naturally the Corps had some superb shots. When I took over, I noticed that a fair number of the SASC had no recent active service experience and I was anxious that we should not produce a Corps of theorists. So, to make sure that as many as possible underwent practical operational experience we got them out in rotation to Northern Ireland, (where one earned a decoration) where they were attached to Infantry battalions, and to the Sultan's Armed Forces in Oman where the Dhofar War was still in full swing. All this proved valuable from both a practical and a psychological point of view. In future, they and those whom they instructed would know that what was put over was based on recent practical experience of what the infantryman encountered under active service conditions.

We also changed the SASC headgear from peaked hats to green berets, and got their career structure on the right line. The lowest rank in the Corps is sergeant, and the rank structure includes a high proportion of officers, including lieutenant colonel. I was delighted when during my time as Commandant, Sergeant (now Major) Tony Harveson won The Queen's Medal at Bisley, and I was proud to be Patron of the SASC Comrades Association for several years.

The Demonstration Battalion during most of my time as Commandant was the 1st Worcestershire and Sherwood Foresters, commanded by Lieutenant Colonel Richard Leman. They were an efficient, dependable and very well-behaved battalion on whom I could rely completely. In my last two or three months the 2nd Battalion of The Royal Irish Rangers took over from them, under Lieutenant Colonel Harry Howard and proved dashing, cheerful successors.

I had an outstanding Regimental Sergeant Major at the School, WOI Laidlaw DCM of the King's Own Scottish Borderers. RSM Laidlaw had won his Distinguished Conduct Medal for great gallantry in Korea, I believe it was in the same action in which Sergeant William Speakman won his Victoria Cross. Mr Laidlaw was a most impressive soldierly figure of a man and ran an excellent and comfortable Sergeants' Mess. I always used to have him with me when our VIP visitors arrived so that they could see the best type of British warrant officer. During my twenty months as Commandant we had visits from the Commanders in Chief of the Imperial Iranian Ground Forces and of the Greek Army, the Defence Minister of the Philippines, and high-ranking officers from the USA, France, Holland, Turkey, Yugoslavia, Egypt, Iraq, Saudi Arabia, Nigeria, India, Pakistan and Jordan.

Practically every member of the Army Board visited the School as well as the Commandant of the Staff College and the GOC-in-C Southern Command. The Commander 1st British Corps and all the BAOR Divisional Commanders came to see us prior to taking up their appointments in Germany. Life was very full and very busy, and it was good for the morale of the School, both students and permanent Staff alike, to be so much in the public eye.

General Forrester left on retirement, and in his place came Major General Charles Dunbar, CB, CBE, a fine Scottish soldier in every way and great fun to work with. Like his predecessor, Charles Dunbar fell over backwards not to interfere in the running of the School, but we knew he was always there ready to help in any way if need be. Each year the Director of Infantry held, and the School ran, the Infantry Commanders' Conference. This was attended by all infantry battalion, brigade and divisional commanders and by a number of other senior officers.

We had a keen PT staff, and produced teams at all sports. I played for the School basketball team and I remember how, during the match against the Royal School of Artillery, Larkhill, commanded by my friend Brigadier Geoffrey Collin, his senior APTC instructor appeared to take a real aversion to me! I don't think he knew who I was but he decided that I was a natural trouble-maker and I was specially called over by him to have my fingernails examined, and he warned me on a number of occasions for rough play; several instances were probably justified as I am essentially a rugger player. Even when I was sitting silent on the side lines with some other team members waiting to go on and two of them were talking, I was warned that if I went on talking my team would be penalised! The junior members of our team loved it! I have never understood how I antagonised him unless there was some secret bet between the two School Sergeants' Messes – mine strongly denied this! Anyway, we won!

At Christmas 1970, I had given my staff an extra day off for pre-Christmas shopping, and had gone for a run on the training area. On my return I was told that the C-in-C Southern Command wished to speak to me on the telephone. At that time this was General Sir Michael Carver, and having served under him before, I knew only too well that he is the sort of man who sees and knows everything! And I had a guilty conscience because I had given my School a day off and had not informed anyone. So when I heard the C-in-C's voice I thought I was for it! General Mike said, 'Corran, you've knocked around the Middle East a bit.' 'Yes, Sir,' I replied cautiously. 'Well, I want you to fly out to Baghdad on the 2nd January for a week to represent the British Army at the Jubilee of the Iraqi Army.' 'Grand, Sir,' I replied, relieved that my sins were not to be discussed.

So it came about that I found myself with Air Commodore Robbie Robertson, CBE, en route to Iraq travelling by Lufthansa to Munich, and by Swissair from Munich to Baghdad. We were travelling first-class and were plied with champagne and delicious food by pretty hostesses. We had a little bit of trouble at Munich because we were carrying our swords and had quite a difficult time persuading a German official that we really did have to wear them in Iraq. We compromised, he insisting that the two weapons be held in the captain's compartment despite our assurances that we did not plan to hijack the aircraft.

On arrival at Baghdad the champagne treatment had given me great confidence in my Arabic and I appeared on the local television programme speaking entirely in that language. Normally my standard is pedestrian but I had a nice interviewer and scored good marks because I said (which is true) that the Arab is a brave soldier, quoting instances from my three years' experience of the War in Dhofar of acts of gallantry by the Omani Arabs in the Sultan's Armed Forces.

At that time Great Britain was none too popular in Iraq, top of the favourites' league being the USSR. The Russians had sent a delegation commanded by a powerful looking colonel general but their only Arabic speakers were their Defence Attaché and his assistant. There were Communist bloc delegations from Poland, East Germany, China, Vietnam and others. The West, so far as I remember, was only represented by France, Greece and the United Kingdom. There were a number of Third World Countries including most of the Arab States, India, Pakistan and Sudan.

Robbie and I were quartered in a very nice hotel on the banks of the River Tigris, right in the middle of the city. Before we got off the Swissair jet at the airport the wife of our Air Attaché who had kindly come to meet us, whispered to me, 'Your rooms will be bugged and the telephone will be tapped,' a weird sensation as I had never experienced that sort of regime before. Because of the incredibly bad winter weather in London our flight had been delayed for a day and we missed a religious ceremony and wreath-laying at a memorial to national heroes. Some sections of the local press had represented this, before our arrival, as a deliberate avoidance of the occasion by Great Britain but my champagne-lubricated TV interview had apparently squared the situation!

Robbie and I were determined to put up a good show for Great Britain. My Arabic held up and we chatted to the other Arab delegations and got to know them. We noticed that the Communist bloc kept themselves to themselves, only their Defence Attachés appearing to know Arabic. So gradually we found ourselves rising in the popularity stakes and whereas we used to be ushered into our places last, we were now being shown in first! Various demonstrations, such as the assault course carried out under live fire were impressive, instructors standing over soldiers who were crawling through low wire entanglements, and firing sub-machine gun bullets into the ground just inches from their bodies.

When we visited the Air Force Base at Habbaniyah, again we got on well with the Iraqis and Robbie came into his own because of his professional ability as an airman, and his friendliness and charm.

The big event was the Jubilee Parade held on a large airfield, which was a most impressive and well-staged performance. We sat there in warm winter sunlight, while massed armour, rank upon rank of heavy Russian tanks, Soviet artillery and vehicles rumbled past the saluting base, and MiG's and other, mainly Soviet, jets, screamed overhead. Then came the marching infantry. First a battalion of tough-looking Rangers, wearing camouflaged kit and parachute boots doubled by chanting rhythmically; they looked a formidable unit. From then on it was pure British Army! The massed bands with their highly-polished brass instruments flashing in the morning sun strode past to such tunes as *Colonel Bogey*, *Daughter of the Regiment* and *The Sound of the Guns*, while following them, preceded by officers carrying their drawn swords as if on a Sandhurst Sovereign's Parade and wearing service dress, peaked caps, Sam Browne belts and all, came thousands of smartly marching Iraqi infantry, their ranks beautifully dressed and covered off. I had a delightful Egyptian General on my right who later became Defence Minister and he said to me with a smile, 'The British Heritage, you see!' Noticing that he was wearing a British ribbon, I asked where he had got it. 'My MBE? With the Long Range Desert Group!' he replied.

On my left, next door but one to me, was a small, wiry Arab lieutenant colonel who looked at me with what seemed a passable imitation of hatred.

I understood why when, on asking my immediate left-hand neighbour, a Colonel in the Yemen Arab Republic Army who the man was, he replied 'He is People's Democratic Republic of South Yemen' and of course his country at that time was giving succour and sanctuary to the Dhofari rebels who were waging war against His Majesty Sultan Qabus bin Said. One night we all attended a concert in a cinema with 'turns' by acrobats, dancers and jugglers, and on another we went to watch Iraq's national wrestling champion defeat an enormous French wrestler, a colossus of a man.

On our last night we all went to the Embassy Club in Baghdad where there was a terrific floor show. The Russians, East Germans and other Soviet-bloc delegations sat together at one long table at which I did not notice an Arab present. They rose in turn and drank toasts to each other. Their behaviour was impeccable, but there seemed to be no intermingling with their hosts or with any non-Communists. Robbie and I had now become very much 'two of the boys' and found ourselves sitting at a central table with our own delightful Iraqi Army lieutenant colonel aide, the anglophile Egyptian general, a Sudanese general, a Jordanian brigadier general, the Libyan Chargé d'affaires, a Syrian diplomat (most amusing) and a very senior Japanese diplomat. We had an incredibly jolly evening. Each one of us found a bottle of whiskey placed before him on the table and the wine flowed also. A bevy of pretty French dancers stole the show. The Iraqis adored them. 'Which do you like best, Corran?' asked the Sudanese general. 'At taweela,' I replied immediately ('the tall one') indicating a six foot-plus smasher with a marvellous figure and a mane of tawny hair. This reply was received rapturously as she was just the sort of woman Arabs admire – as did the Japanese diplomat, who made some rather undiplomatic advances!

Suddenly it was 5am and we just had time to catch our aircraft – Robbie and I had wisely done our packing in advance. We reached Baghdad airport in the cool early morning January sunlight. An immaculate guard of honour was drawn up, wearing white helmets, scarlet jackets, white pipeclayed belts, black trousers and gleaming black boots. The men had their bayonets fixed and the officer in front carried a drawn sword. To my great surprise we were asked to inspect the guard before entering the Lufthansa jet. They were a credit to the Iraqi Army.

Soon we were seated in comfortable first-class armchairs, with early morning glasses of chilled champagne in our hands. However, I knew my mission was not over because before we left, the CGS of the Iraqi Army had sent for me to ask me to persuade the British Government to allow Iraqi officer cadets to attend our courses at Dartmouth, Sandhurst and Cranwell and to let their selected officers attend our Royal Navy, Army and Royal Air Force Staff Colleges. 'You see,' he said to me, 'if you Western Governments will not sell us your arms and equipment and refuse our best officer cadets and officers permission to attend your courses, you force us to turn to the Communist bloc for armaments and training. Many of us served with the British and have a great affection for your country and your Armed Forces.' I promised the General that I would represent his views in the right quarter and I wrote a paper for the then VCGS, General Sir Cecil 'Monkey' Blacker, and sent a copy to my C-in-C.

General Monkey is not only a very hard man physically (he used to have wrestling matches with my toughest APTC instructors whenever and wherever he visited me!) but he is very down-to-earth. He considered the Iraqis' request carefully and I appeared before a number of senior people including Foreign Office officials. As a result of it all I understand that Iraqi officer cadets and officers were once again welcomed on our courses.

As Commandant of the School of Infantry I carried out several other interesting visits. One visit accompanied by Malcolm Cubiss, my excellent GS01, was to attend the annual autumn exercise in Rhine Army. I am not sure how it happened but I was met at Gutersloh by a Landrover driven by my old friend and former batman, Sergeant Larry Gains in my Regiment, who announced that he would be with me for the duration of my time in Germany. I became the driver, Malcolm the map reader and Larry took over as radio operator. We stayed overnight in German inns and managed to see a great deal of the exercise and to benefit from it.

On another occasion, with my 'DQ', Major Robert Sullivan-Tailyour of the Worcestershire and Sherwood Foresters, himself a fluent German speaker, I spent ten days at the German Army Infantry School in Bavaria. We were most kindly received by the Commandant, Brigadier General Kurt von Witzendorf, a holder of the Knight's Cross of the Iron Cross. His staff were most kind and welcoming and we were shown their mechanised infantry weapons and vehicles. Their Rangers would be a credit to any Army and we saw some of their very tough – at times hair-raising – training. Perhaps I was most impressed by the demonstration of house clearing and village fighting which was supervised by a veteran of the 'Ost Front', and which I found most instructive. On one evening the Commandant and his charming wife had us to dinner. We also dined with other officers and their families, and were taken round the beautiful city of Würzburg where we sampled some delicious German wines in the famed Burghospitalkeller below the ground in the city, where we were personally entertained by its Direktor. This was followed by supper and a tremendous singing session in a Weinkeller. Our final treat was a visit to the Bundesgrenzschutzpolizei, that crack force of Border police who took us round the East Zone Border by vehicle and later in one of their helicopters.

What a very impressive paramilitary organisation they were with grand officers and men. We met one policeman who had just been decorated for rescuing under fire a wounded East German who was escaping through the mined wire fence.

Towards the end of my time as Commandant at Warminster the School took over the British portion of the Jungle Warfare School at Kota Tinggi, as the School of Infantry's Jungle Warfare Wing. Malcolm Cubiss and I flew out for this and stayed at a hotel in Singapore on the Bukit Timah Road. Its air-conditioning was simply freezing! We had a good staff at the Jungle Warfare School including, to my surprise and pleasure, some of my dear old battalion charwallahs whom I had last seen when shaking their hands to say goodbye at Serian in Borneo on the day I handed over command. One of them still proudly wore the Indian North West Frontier Medal he had been awarded whilst serving in our Indian Army.

I indoctrinated Malcolm into 'Singapore Slings' and we swam with the Staff of the School in the warm rollers off the East Coast of Malaysia one Saturday afternoon. I spent a couple of nights staying with Peter Thwaites who had commanded Muscat Regiment with such élan in Oman. Peter was the perfect host and just before I was going out to dinner with the commander of 28 Commonwealth Brigade and his wife, Michael and Angela Walsh, I went into Peter's drawing room for a quick drink and a Beecham's powder as I had contracted a dreadful cold from the hotel's arctic air-conditioning.

I was talking hard to a charming New Zealand wife and my drink was handed to me from a silver salver. Seconds later I thought 'that was never handed to me by Peter's Chinese houseboy, surely it was by an Arab?' Had my streaming, feverish cold made me delirious? I asked for another drink and this time I was waiting to see who brought it. Sure enough, in came a large, powerful, bearded man wearing an Arab shemagh! He halted in front of me and, indicating the pretty New Zealand girl, said, 'I understand you have already met my wife, Sir!' And so I met again that gallant, powerful, swash-buckling commander of our little Omani Navy – Captain Jeremy Raybould – who was just passing through with his wife on their way home to New Zealand!

Whilst in Nee Soon and staying in Peter Thwaites' quarter, Wentworth Lodge, I visited 1st Royal Highland Fusiliers commanded by Lieutenant Colonel David Anderson of which Regiment Major General Charles Dunbar was Colonel. David and I were old friends and our two battalions had got on famously in Iserlohn in the days when our units had shared the service of that paragon of NAAFI managers and friend to all ranks, George Newlove. George was now in Singapore continuing to win golden opinions. I found the battalion in its usual excellent state.

One of the two brigadiers in the Military Secretary's Department at that time came and spent the night with us at Warminster. He told me that I would go no further in the Army and that I would not be promoted. Although this depressed me, in life there is always something nice round the corner and one day Charles Dunbar sent for me and told me that I was to be promoted to major general and appointed General Officer Commanding North West District which had its Headquarters at Cuerden Hall near Preston, Lancashire. Charles himself had been a previous GOC there and told me how much he had enjoyed it. So even MS get it wrong sometimes, which can be comforting! I was to hand over the School to that brilliant officer, Frank Kitson, and to take over from Jim Wilson, a good friend and a versatile and able extrovert who, incidentally, had been the Association Football Correspondent of the Sunday Times since 1958!

CHAPTER THIRTY

GOC NORTH WEST DISTRICT

I took command of North West District on my birthday, after an extremely kind and thoughtful handover from Jim and Jean Wilson. Cuerden Hall is a lovely Lancashire home made of red brick and set in beautiful grounds with splendid views over the adjoining countryside. It had a walled garden beyond its lawns and trees. The house was divided into three parts. In one wing lived the GOC, his family and staff, in the central portion was the Officers' Mess and the remainder of the building housed the Headquarters. North West District covered Lancashire, the Isle of Man, Cheshire, Cumberland and Westmorland, so it contained not only some of Britain's major industrial towns but some of its most beautiful countryside, in particular the Lake District and the valley of the River Lune. The District also had a small enclave across the Border in Scotland where a Royal Army Ordnance Corps installation was located at East Riggs.

From the moment we arrived, we loved the Lancashire people among whom we lived, and found them the kindest and warmest folk we have met in England. A sign at the entrance to our drive which said 'GOC's House' always reminded me of a story told by Charles Dunbar. He and Jean his wife were working in the herbaceous border in front of the house when Charles had the feeling that he was being looked at. Turning round he found himself being regarded by a small boy who asked, 'Is this Gock's House?' 'Yes,' replied Charles, 'and I'm Gock!'

The two regular battalions in the District were stationed at Saighton Camp near Chester and at Weedon Camp near Blackpool. At the start of my time 1st Green Howards were at Saighton Camp, later to be relieved by 1st King's Own Royal Border Regiment. At Weedon was 1st King's

Regiment, later succeeded by 1st Cheshire Regiment. These battalions were well commanded and administered and a pleasure to have in the District. We had a large number of units of the Territorial Army, keen and well recruited. There were two battalions of Lancastrian Volunteers as they were then styled, with Colonel The Earl of Derby, MC, as their enthusiastic Honorary Colonel. One of these battalions had a war role in BAOR and the other was for Home Defence. The Duke of Lancaster's Own Yeomanry at that time had an infantry role. Although this must have been a disappointment to these yeoman cavalrymen, it did keep the Regiment in existence and they did well as infantrymen.

A number of detached companies of TA battalions were also located in the District. These had their other components in various parts of the United Kingdom and included companies from 4th Parachute Regiment, the Royal Regiment of Fusiliers, the King's Own Royal Border Regiment and the Mercian Volunteers. We had a fine Territorial Royal Engineer Regiment commanded by a keen Territorial officer, a Civil Engineer, Colonel John Timmins, OBE. A TA Royal Artillery brigade had its Headquarters in Chester and regiments dispersed in the north of England, Scotland and Northern Ireland. It was commanded by a regular Brigade Commander, an old and close friend, Brigadier George Arnold, MBE, whom I had first met when he commanded Imjin Battery, 45 Regiment Royal Artillery. Colonel Frank Masters, CBE, TD, his deputy commander, was the epitome of the very best type of Territorial officer. We had a first class TA Royal Corps of Transport regiment which had a major role in BAOR and a Royal Signals Brigade Headquarters. When I first became GOC the brigade commander was the former Scottish rugby international, Brigadier Graham Jackson, OBE. His successor was another distinguished Signaller, Brigadier Derek Baynham, OBE, GM.

There were two TA general hospitals, each with a BAOR wartime role, one based in Liverpool and the other in Manchester, the only regular officers on their establishments being their respective PSAOs (Permanent Staff Administrative Officers). There was a regular Royal Artillery testing range on the coast and a large Royal Army Ordnance Corps unit at Longtown in Cumbria. There were various other small units, both Regular and Territorial, Liverpool and Manchester University Officer Training Corps (both good) and a number of Army Cadet Force and Combined Cadet Force contingents.

We had well appointed hutted camps in the Isle of Man, a Regular Army Junior Soldiers Unit at Fulwood Barracks, Preston and a number of Army Careers Information Offices in the most important towns in the North West. The Regimental Headquarters of several local regiments were located there, the Lancashire Fusiliers at Bury and the Cheshire Regiment at

Chester Castle, for example. Everyone trained hard and with enthusiasm. Territorial units regularly went over to BAOR to participate in large-scale, realistic and practical exercises and the regular battalions served in Northern Ireland on operational tours. We ran District exercises, some of which were physically tough and demanding. On one, my ADC at that time, Captain Charles Linford, Royal Irish Rangers, was awarded the UKLF Commander-in-Chief's Commendation for saving a Territorial soldier from hypothermia during a bleak, icy, blizzard-swept cross-mountain operation.

The late Brigadier Sir Douglas Crawford, CB, DSO, TD, was our greatest Territorial. He was Honorary Colonel of our local Light Anti-Aircraft Regiment and had such a powerful, humorous, extrovert personality. His regiment had a Pipe Band which I suspect he financed and I think they wore the Crawford Tartan. He used to visit his regiment regularly in UK and BAOR and they loved him. The Territorial Army Association was particularly well served and strong. The Chairman had served throughout the war in the Manchester Regiment and after the war had commanded a Territorial battalion of his regiment, eventually becoming Colonel TAVR for North West District. He was Colonel Sir Richard Martin-Bird, CBE, TD and a more charming, helpful and delightful person I have seldom met. Sir Richard was most ably supported by the Secretary of the Association, a retired Regular Carabinier, Brigadier Hugh Ley, CBE, who would surely have risen to considerable heights had he not retired early. Hugh was a powerful personality, outstandingly efficient and did a tremendous amount for the TAVR in the North West of England. Colonel Donald Gibbs, CBE, TD, was the senior Territorial Officer at my Headquarters, and I will always be grateful for his wise advice and enthusiastic, loyal support.

I inherited two excellent staff officers from Jim Wilson. Colonel Sir Geoffrey Errington, Bt was Colonel GS, and Colonel David Ranft who had been with me in the All Arms Division at Warminster was Colonel AQ. They had a good staff to support them, including some ROs (Retired Officers) who were worth their weight in gold. My PA, Miss Marie Halliwell, was a wonderful help to me, as indeed she had been to a number of my predecessors. Marie knew everything, never flapped and ran the office like clockwork.

I tried to get around my District as much as possible and spend the minimum of time in my Headquarters. For long distances I travelled by helicopter, taking off from and landing on the lawn outside my drawing room window. Otherwise I was driven by Sergeant Forbes RCT, a quiet-spoken Highlander from Morayshire, a charming man. My first ADC was Captain Jerry Steele of the Royal Anglian Regiment whom I inherited from Jim Wilson. After him came Charles Linford, of my regiment, a keen, hard professional soldier. Then for my last year came Willie White, also of my regiment, a real character with a twinkle in his eye, very good at his job and with a sweet wife, Olivia, whom we regard as one of our daughters. We were fortunate in our house staff. Corporal Cruse of the Army Catering Corps produced delicious food, as did his successor, Corporal Carter. Corporal Adams of the King's Own Border Regiment, as House Corporal, made everyone welcome and many will remember his habit of whispering in their ear, 'Another little drop of wine, Sir (or Madam)?' Lance Corporal Storey of the King's Regiment was my orderly, a fit, slight young man. He taught our parrot a few things I shan't forget – sadly the parrot won't either!

I had hardly arrived at my Headquarters when I had to attend a Royal occasion. By that time the orders to disband Commands had gone out and the lieutenant generals' appointments and Headquarters at Northern, Western, Eastern and Southern Commands had disappeared. Headquarters Western Command, which used to be based in Chester, had officially disbanded but the GOC in C, Lieutenant General Sir Napier Crookenden, had remained in post for a few more days to tidy things up.

So when I paraded myself in full dress at Runcorn Railway Station one morning to await the arrival of the Royal train bringing the Queen and Prince Philip to visit Runcorn New Town, I stood beside General Crookenden on the railway platform. The train arrived and Her Majesty stepped down on to the red carpet. Sir Napier and I, left hands on the hilts of our ceremonial swords, raised our white-gloved right hands to gold-embroidered, peaked caps in salute as the Monarch passed, bowing and smilingly acknowledging our salutes. Prince Philip, who was following, paused and asked sharply, 'Why are there two generals here?' The GOC in C quickly explained the reason but it was yet another instance of how very well-informed, up-to-date and alert is our Duke of Edinburgh.

Another memory of that day is of travelling to Runcorn in the motorcade of official cars seated beside Patricia. The cheering of the crowds was incredibly loud and approving. It occurred to me that as we were about number twelve in the motorcade it might not be the Royal Car that was pleasing the crowd so uproariously but perhaps one somewhat nearer. I stuck my head out of the window and I think I got the answer – surely that was a lieutenant general's shirt-sleeved arm protruding from the preceding car window, and surely it was brandishing a General Officer's sword to the delight of the onlookers!

We had several bishops in our District and we got to know two of them in particular for whom my wife and I have much affection and respect. Eric Mercer who became Lord Bishop of Exeter had served in the war in the Sherwood Foresters in Italy, where he was Mentioned in Despatches,

DAA and QMG of a brigade in Palestine, and a GS02 in GHQ Middle East Forces, Rosemary, his wife, had captained either Oxford or Cambridge Ladies Athletics Team. They were a great pair and we very much enjoyed their company. The other pair we knew and liked was John and Rosemary Bickersteth. John had been a captain in the Buffs and later in the Gunners during the war. He became Bishop of Bath and Wells.

The first night the Bickersteths came to dinner with us we had the then Chaplain General, staying with us. We had not met the Bickersteths before and as John Youens had been held up on his trip we had been showing him to his room and had not been in time to meet the Bickersteths when they arrived. We were perturbed to find them standing in the large, lofty drawing room being entertained by Iago, our parrot, with what my mother used to call 'bathroom noises'! I have often wondered what they must have thought!

We cooperated closely with all our local police forces and especially we grew to know our County Force, the Lancashire Constabulary. I used to give a regular talk on the Army to the Inspectors' Courses at Hutton Hall, their Police College, and we held joint study periods there during my years as GOC.

We had the usual round of VIP visitors and did a lot of entertaining, but of course it goes with the job and Patricia and I were used to it.

North West District and the North East District in York produced, between them, by far the largest percentage of recruits for the British Army and I enjoyed going round our Careers Information Offices to see our cheerful staff. I invariably came away invigorated by their enthusiasm. In Preston Army Careers Information Office, I was happy to have an old St Nazaire Raid Comrade-in-Arms, Major Jack Aspden.

I, and all the officers and men at my Headquarters, used to go to Fulwood Barracks one day a week to shoot rifle and sub-machine gun, as I have always felt we do not shoot enough in the Army and that consequently our marksmanship suffers. We also ran a circuit training room in an old Nissen hut in Cuerden Hall grounds where my staff and I worked out. News of this latter activity got to the press and one day, Major Ken Russell, my Public Relations Officer, asked me if I minded some journalists and photographers coming along when we were using the place. I was not keen but as I had always found the press helpful, courteous and friendly, and because they have a job to do, I said they could visit us. We continued exercising while they were in the circuit training room. What I had not bargained for was that everyone else who was exercising would be cut out of the pictures they took and that I alone was to be featured! So it was with horror one morning that I opened a famous national newspaper to find a photograph of myself, stripped to the waist, squatting like a toad and holding a drill anti-tank round behind my neck! Another famous paper printed a kinder picture where I was using a pulley apparatus on a wall, but still no sign of any of my henchmen of whom at least six were present during the press visit! However, the wording was definitely kind and, I thought, approving – 'General leads fight against flab ...' What I did dread was the reaction of my friends to that terrible squatting picture and sure enough I found out! Major General Charles Dunbar was holding his annual Infantry Conference at Warminster and I attended it. It seemed to me that on each of the four days it lasted, whenever something was needed to break the monotony a slide of that dreadful picture was flashed on to the screen in the Blenheim Hall to thunderous applause and raucous cheers. That put an end to any further press visits to what one paper had called the 'General's Torture Room'!

When the then CGS General Sir Peter Hunt had been staying with us about a year before, I told him that, much as I was enjoying myself, I longed for an active job overseas and asked him to bear me in mind should one come up. When he stayed with us again he told me – typical of his kindness – that Patricia and I would be going to Cyprus where I was to be appointed General Officer Commanding Near East Land Forces. We were thrilled. Before we left we gave a party for all the Lord Mayors, Mayors and Chairmen of cities, towns and boroughs situated in the District, on the lawns of Cuerden Hall. The summer evening was a lovely one and we had two military bands, one being the 2nd Royal Irish Rangers, my own Regiment, together with the Corps of Drums of a third Regiment. We had huge, two-coloured pavilions where drinks and supper were served and the sun shone on all six hundred of us.

I paid farewell visits to those of our Territorials who were taking part in various exercises in Belgium and in Germany and said good-bye to our regular battalions at Saighton and Weedon.

They are a great lot in the North West, perhaps my Scouse grandmother's blood accounted for my enjoyment in serving there.

During this time I was appointed Honorary Colonel of the Queen's University Belfast Officers' Training Corps (Territorial Army). The officers, Permanent Staff and men and women cadets were a joy to be with. The OTC had all the intelligence, enthusiasm and special flair that I associate with that great Belfast University. A number of my family have been graduates of Queens including my father, my eldest son, Patrick, various cousins, and my godfather, Air Vice Marshal Sir William Tyrell who had been in the OTC himself. I greatly enjoyed visiting them at camp and at their Headquarters in Belfast, they were such a tonic. I look back on my time as their Honorary Colonel with pride and happiness.

CHAPTER THIRTY-ONE

GOC NEAR EAST LAND FORCES, CYPRUS

I flew from Brize Norton in a VC10 on 16 January 1975 at 8am and arrived at Royal Air Force Akrotiri that evening. I was met by the Station Commander, Air Commodore Don Hall and his attractive wife Joyce and, to my delight, as I had not seen him since April 1945 when we were both released from Colditz, by Sir Martin Gilliatt, Private Secretary to HM Queen Elizabeth The Queen Mother. Col David Woodford, the Colonel GS, was also there as was my ADC, Captain (later Major) David Emsley, Green Howards.

On the way to Flagstaff House, Episkopi, which was to be my home, David Woodford briefed me on the local situation. Since the Turkish invasion of Cyprus a few months before, the Greek Cypriots had become incensed that Britain had taken no physical action to eject the invaders. At that very moment there was a crowd of six hundred people staging an anti-British demonstration in nearby Limassol and schoolchildren were blocking the bypass to stop British cars.

We arrived at Flagstaff House, a beautiful place set in lovely grounds on a glorious site overlooking the sea. Hardly had I arrived, than I found I was programmed to depart! By 8.30am the very next morning I was on my way, with my ADC, back to RAF Akrotiri en route for those parts of Near East Land Forces remaining in the Gulf that were under command of, or the concern of, the GOC. These were Sharjah, where we had a Military Assistance team which was sadly on the point of closing down, and Oman where the British non-seconded element taking part in the Dhofar War, although under operational command of the Commander Sultan's Armed Forces, was the responsibility in certain matters of GOC Near East Land

Forces. There was also the British Army Element stationed at RAF Masirah, the island off the Omani mainland. This consisted mainly of men of the Royal Signals and of the Royal Engineers Postal Service who were a Near East Land Forces responsibility in various ways.

We took off in a Royal Air Force Hercules carrying some Army Postal Service couriers, several Royal Signals personnel who were due for a nine months' unaccompanied tour in Masirah and some stores for RAF Salalah. On the way we heard on the radio of two bombs exploding on British property in Limassol and of anti-British demonstrations in Nicosia, the capital of Cyprus. These incidents were because of the British Government's decision to allow the Turkish Cypriot refugees to be resettled in the Turkish-occupied north of Cyprus.

We flew over Luxor and along the Nile, then across miles and miles of yellow desert after which we passed Bahrain and finally after descending over a fleet of moored oil tankers, landed at Sharjah at 5pm. Here I was met by Lieutenant Colonel Derek Carson, OBE, of the Queen's Own Highlanders, and stayed with him and Pauline, his talented wife, for three happy days. During this time I visited the Military Assistance Team in their excellent, spacious accommodation which was large enough to house an infantry battalion, an armoured squadron and a gunner battery or its equivalent and which was sited near good desert training areas.

The Ruler of Sharjah was most upset that the British were pulling out of the Gulf and had said that our presence could not have been more tactful, nor could he have had more polite guests. Military training exercises avoided going near the town of Sharjah and no organised units in uniform entered it. British personnel kept a low profile to avoid offending nationalism. I spent a morning with the Guards Parachute Company, seeing them on exercise. This was an excellent company commanded by tough, enthusiastic Robert Corbett of the Irish Guards. Also training nearby were men of a logistic regiment including three Territorials, all of whom were thoroughly interested in and enjoying the exercise.

I met some old friends from SAF days, one of whom Lieutenant Colonel Ken Wilson, an experienced Gulf soldier, told me that he had eight lieutenant colonels serving under him, one seconded British and seven Arabs! This was part of a cosmetic promotion exercise for locals!

After my stay in Sharjah I flew to Oman as I wanted to pay my respects to His Majesty Sultan Qabus, to HH Sayyid Faher, who was the Minister of the Interior and Assistant Minister of Defence, and to the Commander Sultan's Armed Forces, Major General Tim Creasey. I also wanted to see as many as possible of my old comrades-in-arms who were still serving in the Sultan's Armed Forces. I found that SAF, like the country, had changed greatly. Whereas in my day money was so very difficult to come by and the

British Government reluctant to provide military assistance, now that the Communist threat to a major source of oil had at last been recognised, all necessary military help had been provided by Britain and this, together with bountiful injections of money from the Omani oil revenue, from Saudi Arabia and from Iran, had transformed the Armed Forces. The Air Force had been expanded threefold, a modern Navy had been formed and the Army had the extra infantry, modern artillery, armour, helicopters and transport aircraft so necessary to support it. One thing had not changed and that was the Omani people. I found them as unspoilt, warm, friendly and hospitable as they had been when I first went there in 1967.

Fergie and Olivia Semple very kindly had me to stay and my first bearer, Noor Mohammad looked after me. I flew to the top of the Jebal Akhdar in a Defender aircraft of SOAF and landed at Saiq in the glorious, cool air of the mountaintop, ten thousand feet up. Here I was met by Major Grahame Vivian, Major Alan Fearnley of the Small Arms School Corps, and Rais (Captain) Pattan, whom I had last seen in 1970 when he was a staff sergeant in Desert Regiment. Alan and Pattan took me round the Battle Camp where I saw soldiers shooting on various ranges and using the most up-to-date mechanical targets. From Saiq we flew down to Nizwa to lunch with Muscat Regiment, where I met more old friends.

After lunch we flew back to Seeb where a member of the Omani Royal family took me to see the well appointed Royal Stables and their lovely horses. We went next to the Royal Gardens which hold wild animals and birds, where I sampled honey from the bees which fed from the flowers and shrubs which grew there. The Royal beekeeper was a very calm man and showed me some queen bees in the hives. Then, taking my hand he put my finger in among a swarm of bees to taste their honey. His calmness transferred itself to me and the bees, although they walked softly over my hand, never stung me.

That night Saiyyid Faher gave a buffet supper to which he had asked many of my old friends including members of the Government. He presented me with a magnificent silver khanjar. I was distressed to find that in my absence Major Mohammed Ashraf, who had been one of our key Gunner officers in the Dhofar War, had driven in from Rostaq just on the off chance of seeing me and had waited one and a half hours in the driving rain. He had left me such a kind note and I was particularly upset not to have seen him.

I visited the Sultan of Oman's Air Force and the Sultan of Oman's Navy and was impressed by their modern equipment and increase in size. I had a chat with Tim Creasey in the 250 year old white-painted fort where my office used to be, and met a number of my old clerical staff, before lunching with Tim and Annette in my old bungalow. There I saw our dear old bearer, Sharif, who had two of his male family working with him for the Creaseys. My corporal driver, another old comrade-in-arms, was in tears when he said good-bye.

I was then flown by RAF Andover to RAF Masirah. After attending a party that night for all ranks I flew off early next morning to RAF Salalah where I was met by the Station Commander, Wing Commander Peter Gillett, OBE, and by OC 'Cracker' Battery, Major Richard Denyer, RA. Having joined the British officers and NCOs for soft drinks I visited Headquarters Dhofar Brigade and met two more old friends, Major Jim Parsons, now QM of the Oman Artillery Regiment, and Lieutenant Colonel Bob Brown, MBE, of the Intelligence Staff, now happily restored to the Sultanate.

I then visited an impressive field surgical team under Lieutenant Colonel John Iffland RAMC. There were a number of wounded in hospital from a recent severe battle in which Jebal Regiment had suffered heavy casualties but they were cheerful and comfortable.

Then I flew to a Gunner OP of 'Cracker' Battery guarded by men of Southern Regiment, all Baluchis, amongst whom were several with whom I had served previously. I watched some good shooting by the 25 pounder 'pistol gun' of 'Cracker' Battery, then flew to the gun position to meet the Omani gun crews and their British instructors. Next, David Emsley and I were flown to a position called Hammer 2 where we went on patrol with Southern Regiment, accompanied by their barrel-chested CO, John Gordon-Taylor.

Escorted by a group of firqas, we descended a steep, rocky track which wound along the side of a gorge past occasional bushes of pink, wild frangipani. The aim of the patrol was to visit a place where water, dripping from the rocks, had been channelled into two cement tanks which led into each other and whose construction had been supervised by a British Royal Engineer NCO. We heard afterwards from the SAS that we were observed throughout by the adoo, who were too far away to open fire on us.

We flew back in the twilight and met Brigadier John Akehurst, Commander of Dhofar Brigade, whose tactical opportunism and brilliance was to win the victory that was instrumental in successfully ending the Dhofar War. John, a charming, relaxed man, has the happy knack of effortlessly winning the devotion of those who serve under his command. He has written a good book about his Dhofar days called 'We Won a War'. I also met an old friend from my time as CSAF, the gallant Lieutenant Colonel Patrick Brook, MBE. John and Shirley Akehurst had me to stay in their pleasant bungalow.

Next morning, I visited Salalah to see its changes after the five years since I had left it. Afterwards we drove along a tarmac road to Umm al

Ghawarif Camp which made a pleasant change from the dreadful track that had existed during my days as CSAF. I visited the British and Indian staff of the Department of the Environment in the Indian Club, and then saw the British non-seconded NCOs and private soldiers for tea and a chat in the NAAFI.

David Emsley and I flew back to Cyprus via Teheran in a Royal Air Force Hercules. We had a dramatic view of the lofty, white cone-shaped summit of Mount Ararat rearing up through the cloud layer. The mountain's height is over 18,000 feet, I believe.

On arrival at Akrotiri David Woodford met me and briefed me in the staff car en route to Flagstaff House. It appeared that the British Government's decision (announced with no previous warning to us in Cyprus) to allow the Turkish refugees to leave Greek-occupied Cyprus for Turkey en route for Turkish-occupied Cyprus, had really soured Anglo-Greek relations and had caused the recent disturbances. Archbishop Makarios had said that this act must have serious effects on the future of the Sovereign Base Areas. Politicians! The British Government could hardly have chosen a more sensitive moment to give its decision, just when it looked as if Turkish-Greek talks had a chance of beginning.

What a lovely house Flagstaff House is! It is set in extensive grounds, with trees, bushes and flowerbeds bordering the drive, and a wooden sentry box at the gate. At the back are green lawns and flowerbeds filled with roses and scented shrubs. On the far side of the house was a vegetable garden, and beyond it fruit trees – oranges, lemons, grapefruit, figs and ugli fruit. From the back of the house the blue sea can be seen and birdlife was prolific. Great Egyptian vultures wheeled and soared on thermals and nested on the sides of the cliffs. By the time we left that lovely island we had seen ninety-six different species of birds, as Cyprus is on the edge of the main migration routes. The bachelor household staff had their own quarters, including a club, with bar, cookhouse, dining room, bedrooms, bathrooms and loos, and their own two Greek-Cypriot cooks. Here lived our three Sudanese bearers, Osman, Awad (who was to be awarded the British Empire Medal) and Sami; with them I was able to keep up my Arabic; here also lived Lance Corporal Long, my driver, and later his successor Lance Corporal Wilks, both grand young men, also my tremendous character of an Orderly, Lance Corporal Gilsenan of my Regiment. The Khartoum Club, as it was called, was also for the use of my married staff and families, and of my Greek-Cypriot staff. The latter included two gardeners, two maids, two cooks, a kitchen man, and six Sovereign Base Area policemen. A very important member of my staff was my peerless Personal Assistant, Sergeant Diana Driscoll. They were all such charming, delightful people, we grew to love them, and were heartbroken to have to say goodbye to them, fifteen short months later, when we left, our tour cut short by yet more Defence Cuts.

I found Cyprus still bleeding from the Turkish invasion and one of my aims was to restore confidence and friendship between ourselves and the Greek-Cypriots in their portion of the war-torn and divided island.

The Commander-in-Chief, Air Marshal Sir John Aiken, KCB, was determined to get things back to normal and on 28 January 1975, four days after my return from the Gulf, he asked me to reoccupy an evacuated British Camp called Berengaria, situated between Episkopi and Limassol. We decided to put 300 men in by convoy that afternoon having cleared with Colonel Rossos of the Greek National Guard that there would be no trouble from his men. I was informed that this would be the first time since the coup that the British would have moved out *en masse* from the Sovereign Base Areas and as I had not yet seen Berengaria I decided to go there to test the water immediately prior to our servicemen moving in. Dressed in Service Dress, and accompanied by David Emsley, we set off in my gleaming black staff car, flag flying, driven by Corporal Hawley.

We passed through a slightly started Vehicle Check Point of 1st Royal Scots and took the rather bumpy road into Berengaria. En route we had some catcalls and baleful looks from men in a roadside cafe before we entered the camp which was being guarded by the Greek National Guard (GNG). The GNG seemed nice lads and they surprised me by turning out and giving me a smart present arms. After a chat with them I saw round the camp which had been looted and despoiled by Greek-Cypriot refugees who had been stripping the quarters of carpets, refrigerators and even of double beds. We re-equipped the huts, put a section of Royal Air Force Regiment into the camp for security and stood by a platoon of 1st Royal Scots to be lifted in by Puma helicopters if need be.

Once I had seen for myself that there were proper facilities for our 300 men, I drove out via Limassol where little notice was taken of us other than the odd scowl, and we re-entered the Western Sovereign Base Area through Episkopi village – which was then officially Out of Bounds – via another Royal Scots road block finding them as always smart, alert and cheerful. They were a fine battalion.

The move in to Berengaria Camp went well and soon relations with the local Greek-Cypriots in the area were back to normal.

For the first part of my time in Cyprus, 1st Battalion Welsh Guards was stationed on the Island. Half, under their tough and able Commanding Officer, Lieutenant Colonel Peter Williams, formed part of the United Nations contingent, and the other half, commanded by Lieutenant Colonel Charles Guthrie, were under my command, and stationed in Dhekelia, from where they operationally patrolled the borders of the Sovereign Base

Areas. Charles Guthrie is a brilliant and charming officer, and a fine leader, and it is not surprising that he has risen to the highest positions in the Army. It was a very great honour to me to take their St David's Day Parade, and to present the Leeks.

One of my first visits as GOC was to RAF Akrotiri commanded by Air Commodore Donald Hall, a high calibre, relaxed officer. I was fascinated to see the American U2 aircraft which was based there and to meet its impressive pilot, a USAF colonel and his supporting ground crew. I met the members of incoming and outgoing RAF Hercules crews, and had explained to me the amazing 360° radar cover which is given from the top of Mt Olympus.

Turkish refugees who had stayed in a temporary camp at Happy Valley Sports Complex had left behind a lot of domestic farm animals and on my way to and from Flagstaff House I kept seeing one very dejected pair, a huge mule and a small, elderly donkey. One Saturday lunchtime David Emsley and I were returning from GHQ and it had been pouring with rain for several days non-stop. By now all the beasts had been removed from Happy Valley save the mule and the donkey. There they stood, fetlock deep in water, heads hanging, their bones outlined against their poor, emaciated skins. David and I got out of the car, moved the two poor, docile, shivering beasts to higher ground out of the water and by that afternoon had them installed in a lean-to shed at Flagstaff House, washed, dried, blanketed, fed and watered. The mule, who was over 17 hands high, although very tame at first, sadly became most aggressive after a few days of good feeding and went for anyone approaching him, biting and kicking.

After a bit longer, during which time he became even more aggressive, I reluctantly gave him to a Greek-Cypriot farmer at Fassouri on the way to Akrotiri, where he would be worked hard but looked after decently. Poor old mule, he escaped from his new owner and somehow made his way back to Flagstaff House where he was found, standing patiently in his old lean-to stall, over 10 miles away from the farm. Sadly, he once again attacked everyone who approached him so we had to send him back to the farmer where, I am glad to say, he settled down. The donkey, who the vet assessed as being over 20 years old, we christened Asphodel after the masses of asphodel growing on the headland by our house and he was greatly loved. He always whickered when he saw any of us and was very affectionate and gentle. My wife and I were very sad to leave him behind when we eventually had to depart from Cyprus but, happily, my successor, Major General Sir John Acland, KBE, promised to keep him and care for him and to ensure he ended his days at Flagstaff House.

The border (called the Green Line) between Turkish-occupied and Greek-Cypriot areas was held by a multi-national United Nations Force.

At that time UNFICYP was commanded by Lieutenant General Prem Chand PVSM, one of my great friends. Prem, a distinguished soldier with much UN Peacekeeping experience particularly in the Congo is a charming man, and a fine leader. He later commanded UNTAG in Namibia. He had a very happy HQ in Nicosia, located in Blue Beret Camp. His Force consisted of contingents from Austria, Australia (Police), Canada, Denmark, Finland, Sweden and the United Kingdom with some Republic of Ireland soldiers, the senior of whom was Colonel Gerald O'Sullivan, an able and delightful person who later became a general, and Chief of Staff, Irish Army. The UN Force had a tricky job, especially in dealing with the Turks who were generally aggressive and uncooperative. The British contingent was commanded by a determined parachute soldier, Colonel Peter Chiswell, who was also Prem's Chief of Staff.

During my visit I called on the British High Commissioner, Sir Stephen Olver, a clever, good-looking diplomat, who was very helpful. Sir Stephen took me to call on Mr Chris Veniamin the Greek Cypriot Defence Minister. Patricia joined us for lunch at the Olver's, where we met various members of the foreign Diplomatic Corps stationed in Nicosia, and General Prem Chand and his beautiful wife, Lota.

The next day as I was attending a buffet dinner party in the Officers' Mess Episkopi to say farewell to the Royal Scots and to welcome the Royal Irish Rangers, I and my senior staff officers were summoned to Headquarters Near East and informed that there was likelihood of an immediate Turkish attack on Nicosia airfield. I and two senior staff officers, David Woodford and John Groom had no time to change, and remained wearing our dinner jackets throughout the night in our operations room, which helped us to feel suitably relaxed, although the Air Force rather put us to shame by changing into uniform. General Prem Chand asked me for an armoured squadron so that he could augment a show of force on the airfield and throughout the night Peter Chiswell kept us fully in the picture about Turkish Army moves.

Sir John Aiken managed to get agreement from Mr Callaghan, who was Foreign Secretary, to our sending our armoured squadron to the United Nations Force, and I am glad to say Mr Wilson the Prime Minister sent a tough signal to the Turks stating that he hoped that they would NOT attack Nicosia airfield. Meanwhile, I gave instructions for the armoured squadron vehicles in their camp at Dhekelia to be painted United Nations white and asked Peter Chiswell to fly eighty UN blue berets and badges, plus blue UN flags for the vehicles, to Perghamos Camp Dhekelia, for wear by Major Jeremy Blacker and his B Squadron, 1st Royal Tanks. These were duly flown in by helicopter in time for Jeremy and his squadron (who had worked all night to get ready) to motor in their now white-painted vehicles that morning on to Nicosia airfield, each one of them wearing size 7 blue UN berets!

As a result of the UN show of force the Turks did not invade the airfield. This was the first chance I had had of seeing my staff under conditions having an operational flavour and I was delighted with them.

In February 1975 the Ministry of Defence, on behalf of the Government, began to make noises about reducing our numbers of civilian staff. The morale effect on our numerous locally-enlisted civilians, Greek-Cypriot and Turkish-Cypriot, many of whom had fought for Britain in the war (one was a holder of the DFM and one had the MM) and who were dependent on our employment for their livelihood, can be imagined. They also decided to cut the Royal Air Force.

At that time we had a strong Royal Air Force presence on the island based on the airfield at Akrotiri. This force of aircraft, working in conjunction with the Royal Navy and Royal Air Force at Gibraltar and at Malta, enabled the movement of all Soviet warships in and around the Mediterranean to be constantly and accurately monitored. This powerful Near East Air Force ensured considerable British prestige in the area, including the Arabian Gulf. Now, at the stroke of a pen, the Government removed all the fighting and transport squadrons from Akrotiri, all the Lightning, Vulcan and Hercules Squadrons, and left the RAF with four ageing air sea rescue Whirlwind helicopters!

Pressure was also exerted on the Army to reduce to below a viable strength even though the political situation in the Near East had not improved. However, such is the lot of the Services when dealing with politicians, most of whom never learn from the lessons of history, and leave it to the Armed Forces to pay later in lives and limbs for their own vote-catching political expediency. History repeats itself fairly monotonously, but it was sad and frustrating to see so many fine and loyal people having their lives and happiness adversely affected and our military capacity dangerously weakened. From now until I left the island my staff was forever involved in correspondence on force reductions and with visits on the same subject from the Ministry of Defence. Life became one perpetual uncertainty and a continuous battle with the theoretically-minded, penny-pinching establishment-slashers of Whitehall. Defence cuts are a popular and easy option to the British Treasury.

Nicosia was never settled during my time as GOC. A typical incident would be an exchange of small-arms fire lasting throughout the night, perhaps set off because EOKA gunmen fired into the air. The Turks would retaliate with light machine-gun fire, whereupon a Greek National Guard post might open up with a recoilless anti-tank gun (often misrepresented by the media as heavy mortars). One night a married captain in the

Canadian contingent was shot dead in a sudden exchange of fire which broke out whilst he was standing on the balcony outside his room in the Ledra Palace Hotel where he was billetted. The previous night (31 March 1975) there had been over twenty explosions in Limassol, and burst after burst of small-arms fire but fortunately on that occasion there were no casualties.

On 3 April I was flown up to Blue Beret Camp, Nicosia by my usual pilot, Staff Sergeant Scott, BEM. Here I visited those doughty veterans of many United Nations Peace Keeping Operations, 1st Royal Canadian Regiment and was given a briefing as to their dispositions and those of the Greek and Turk warrior elements. Tough, experienced Major Bob Thompson took me on a fascinating tour of the Green Line which separated Greek from Turk in the Old City of Nicosia where I had not been since I was a company commander during the EOKA Campaign in 1958.

Bob Thompson had been in the Canadian Guards, was five years in Canada's airborne forces and appeared highly 'switched-on' and on top of his job. We drove along the narrow, winding streets flanked by Greek National Guard positions on one side, faced by Turkish Army and Turkish-Cypriot Fighters from the other. Every now and then we stopped at strategically-placed observation posts manned by intelligent, alert young Canadian soldiers. I was impressed at how well briefed they were, all ready and able to speak lucidly and enthusiastically about what they knew of the local situation – which was considerable. There is no doubt that when it comes to UN soldiering the Canadians are the experts in every way.

Bob Thompson had been shot at with a Bren and, fortunately, missed from a Greek National Guard OP on the night that the fine young captain had been killed. He told me that the Canadian captain, who was 29 years old, had served in Vietnam with the UN, where he had been captured and escaped. What a dreadful waste of a brave young life. I visited the Ledra Palace Hotel which was then used as a barrack block and noted the numerous pretty, young chambermaids who must have gladdened the hearts of the Canadian contingent!

It was practice in the UN that the sentries in United Nations OPs must come out and salute every UN vehicle that passed. This was obviously an irksome chore to those OPs overlooking a busy road. I am a great admirer of the Royal Marine Commandos and I was amused to hear from my ADC that the RM Commandos who occupied one particular OP on a hill overlooking the Episkopi-Paphos road had made a life-size model UN soldier complete with blue UN beret, mounted it on a trolley and had made the model a hinged arm. Directly a UN vehicle was spotted, the Commando sentry in the OP would pull a cable and out would trundle the UN 'sentry'. Another cord would be tugged and the hinged arm would snap smartly to the salute. Far below, the driver of the UN truck or car would acknowledge this courtesy. Another tug on the cable, down would come the arm, after which back would trundle the trolley and the 'sentry' to the OP!

Patricia and I often used to visit Paphos at weekends and got very fond of Theo's Restaurant on the harbour front. In those days Paphos was unspoilt and people sat at tables on the waterfront, with native craft floating in the sea close beside them as they ate. We usually had Saturday or Sunday lunch there and sometimes we dined there when the moon and stars were reflected in the water of the little harbour dominated by its old Turkish fort.

Early one morning, Captain James McCarthy-Morrough, 2nd Royal Irish Rangers and Sergeant Davis, his Reconnaissance Platoon sergeant, were checking the car park beside Episkopi airstrip where the possessions of Turkish-Cypriot refugees were being held. On hearing a noise, James looked over the boundary fence and saw a man who failed to see him. Leaving Sergeant Davis on the gate to observe the intruder with a Starlightscope night-viewing device, James ran back to 2nd Royal Irish and returned with the Rangers' Immediate Readiness Section and two Royal Air Force policemen.

Posting a cut-off group under Sergeant Davis at the main gate where he found the hasp of the padlock had been sawn through, James swept the car park with the remainder. They surprised and captured a group of five men, one of whom (the look-out) was lying on his back! The group leader offered to show James the location of the rest of his group who, he said, were outside the wire. Sending back the remaining four prisoners under Sergeant Davis to the main gate, James crawled under the wire with the captured leader. As they were going down the hill the man tried to make a break for it, turning and firing two shots at James from a 9mm pistol. James McCarthy-Morrough sprang at him, knocked up his arm and overpowered him. During the struggle the man managed to fire two more shots at James, but missed again. By now some of James's Rangers had come up and the man was disarmed. In his pocket they found a full 9mm pistol magazine and a primed Czech hand grenade. The Royal Irish Rangers guarding the original four captives had had to 'restrain' one of them with a pick helve when he made a run for it! They also discovered a loaded pistol dropped by the gang in the car park and in addition found that the group had coupled-up two pairs of Turkish-Cypriot-owned cars that were in the car park and had loaded them with kit which they had intended to drive away. The leader of the armed thieves was said to be a hard-line EOKA B leader. For this exploit James McCarthy-Morrough and Sergeant Davis each received the Commander-in-Chief Near East's Commendation.

Sir Stephen and Lady Olver left, but fortunately, in their place came Donald Gordon, CMG, as High Commissioner, a very wise and supportive Scot, and his sweet wife, Molly. Donald went on to become the British Ambassador to Austria.

About this time, the United Nations were anxious to get Nicosia airport into use again and had persuaded the Turks to allow the UN to remove three Cyprus Airways Trident aircraft that were marooned on the runway, together with various trolleys and trucks placed there to block it. They had also agreed that we could fill in the numerous bomb craters, rocket holes and cannonshell scabs in the surface of the airfield. For this we attached to the United Nations 62 (Near East) Field Squadron, Royal Engineers, commanded by Major John Farmborough, as well as an Engineer Field Troop from 48 Field Squadron which was out on a training visit from Ripon, together with the Assault Pioneer Platoon of 1st Devon and Dorset Regiment. For this task they were all now wearing the blue beret of the United Nations as they were temporarily part of UNFICYP.

I visited them several times and always found them in terrific form, keenly interested, working very long hours, hard and efficiently. It was estimated that the task would take about four months to complete but these wonderful lads finished it in six weeks. The sad and disappointing thing was that, because of their efficiency and speed of completion, they were then returned to British Army command two and a half months earlier than expected, which meant that they failed to qualify for the United Nations Cyprus Medal which was only awarded after a minimum of four months in UNFICYP. On each of my visits a number of the officers and sappers would ask me to try to get them this medal. However, I had to sadly point out that because of their very enthusiasm and professional ability they had finished their task long before the qualifying period was up. The British Serviceman has few opportunities nowadays to earn a medal which is the outward and visible sign that he has been on operational service. I sympathised with the wish of these men to have the UN Medal to further denote their time as effective, professional soldiers playing their part in the United Nations Force in Cyprus.

9 Signals Regiment, Royal Signals was permanently stationed in the Eastern Sovereign Base Area at Ayios Nikolaos. This was a Communications Unit and a first-class one. At that time it was commanded by Lieutenant Colonel David Milton and was a happy, hardworking and dedicated regiment. It included Royal Navy, Army, Royal Air Force and civilians in its ranks, its accommodation and its sporting and recreational amenities were excellent and I always enjoyed visiting it.

By now we were making friends with the Greek-Cypriot population including the then Mayor and Mayoress of Limassol, Fotis and Aloi

Kolakides, a charming couple. Throughout the Armed Forces the old friendships and relationships were being re-established and life was getting back to normal. We allowed the local sportsmen to shoot again inside our Sovereign Base Areas which was greatly appreciated by them.

Cyprus is such a beautiful island; in the winter it was possible to waterski off the lovely beaches and to ski on the snowy slopes of Troodos on the same day. The spring flowers are glorious and, because Cyprus is on the edge of the bird migration routes between Europe and Africa, a great variety of birds can be seen. There was so much to do in the way of sports and recreation. In addition to rugger, soccer, cricket, basketball, squash, badminton, swimming, cross-country running, boxing and waterpolo, there was freefall parachuting, gliding, a flying club, scuba diving, sailing, polo, riding, karting and a pack of draghounds! The whipper-in was my helicopter pilot Staff Sergeant Scott, BEM, and his wife, a physiotherapist, was Master. One of my Retired Officers Lieutenant Colonel Bob Ambrose was Field Master and the Hunt was widely supported by all ranks. Skiing, waterskiing, rock climbing and gymnastics were also popular. Other activities included such hobbies as war-gaming, stamp collecting, archaeology (such fascinating 'digs' on the island), the martial arts and painting.

As can be imagined, Flagstaff House and Cyprus attracted a seemingly endless stream of visitors, and Patricia had to run a sort of Five-Star military hotel. We rarely had the house to ourselves and most days we gave either a lunch or a dinner party. Few non-military people realise the planning and supervisory work this causes GOC's wives.

The Signal Officer in Chief Major General Tony Tighe was due to arrive one night, and I told Corporal Gilsenan to be sure to be at the door to meet him. Thinking he had time he went upstairs to close the curtains and, of course, our guest arrived. I dashed out and welcomed him. Looking round I saw Corporal Gilsenan calmly descending the stairs. 'Corporal Gilsenan,' I gritted out, 'You never met General Tighe!' 'Indeed and I never have sorr,' smiled the red-haired Irishman, advancing hand outstretched, 'How are you, Sorr?!'

The battalion controlling the Eastern Sovereign Base Area during my first few months was 10th Gurkha Rifles. I had last soldiered alongside them during the Borneo Campaign. I have, like all British soldiers, always greatly admired those superlative fighting men, the Gurkhas. The 10th were commanded by Lieutenant Colonel Chris Pike, who had been awarded his DSO in Borneo in the same action during which one of his men, Sergeant Rambahadur Limbu won his Victoria Cross. Chris and his Gurkhas had the Eastern Sovereign Base Area under firm control and exuded calm confidence. He took me round his area and showed me various Turkish Army and Turkish-Cypriot Fighter positions and a large number of Turkish soldiers who were patrolling, observing and manning trenches.

Chris Pike took a firm and friendly line with the Turks and it paid off as the Turks treat acquiescence as weakness. The Greek-Cypriots were fond of and respected the Gurkhas who stood up for them and protected them. Greek-Cypriots love to talk politics but as they cannot speak Gurkhali and in any case the Gurkhas would probably not have been interested, there was little room for possible disagreement!

Force level reductions and redundancies were to continue to occupy my time until I ceased to be GOC. MOD were again putting pressure on us, this time to reduce the strength of the British contingent in UNFICYP. General Prem Chand and Peter Chiswell opposed this on operational grounds and I supported them because the situation in Cyprus showed no signs of improving and the Turks were being particularly aggressive. Fortunately an excellent Mr Jackson of the Foreign and Commonwealth Office was visiting Dhekelia and I flew up to have a chat with him. He was as sharp as a needle and pleasant with it. I told him that neither we nor the United Nations Force in Cyprus would be able to reduce our Internal Security Forces in strength in the foreseeable future and gave him the reasons why.

Regarding the terms for redundancy, I pointed out that we had large numbers of loyal, conscientious Greek and Turkish-Cypriots who had served the British Empire faithfully for years – some of them for thirty years or more – a number among whom had served operationally and with distinction in the war. I stressed that redundancy terms for these employees must be good, not only in well-earned recognition of their devoted and faithful service but also, realistically because if (as so often in the past) HMG was niggardly, and soured them off, the British Government could be forced to spend far more than the amount of money they would save by having to deal with a resultant 'difficult situation' caused by former employees who had become unfriendly overnight. He took all my points and I must say here that of all the senior civilians who visited us from England I felt the greatest confidence in him, and certainly the redundancy terms that followed my chat with him were not mean.

The GOC Near East Land Forces had a bungalow on Mount Troodos overlooking Pine Tree Leave Camp, with a sitting-cum-dining room, three bedrooms, a bathroom-cum-loo and a front and a back verandah. It is built of wood, has a corrugated iron roof, and is furnished simply but comfortably. This bungalow was an oasis of peace from the occasional 'fraughtness' at Episkopi, and a haven of coolness and clear, pine-scented air, away from the summer heat of the Sovereign Base Areas. We made it available to my officers and their friends when we were not occupying it so it got a lot of appreciative use in all seasons. In summer, when we stayed there, we would go for long mountain walks in the pine woods, and have buffet Sunday lunches at the friendly Forest Park Hotel at Platres several hundred feet below. Our bungalow helper was called Orpheus, a charming Greek-Cypriot and he always had a welcoming fire going in the cold weather and the beds made for our arrival. At night Scops owls used to call in the woods around us and you could feel the peace of the place. The charming, tiny, stone-built garrison church was about a hundred yards away and its foundation stone was inscribed with the fact that it had been laid by Sir Ronald Storrs, KT, CMG, CBE, Governor of Cyprus in 1928. The church is called St George-in-the-Forest, and has wooden beams, white-washed inside walls and a nice altar and altar cross. It would seat a hundred people comfortably, being about 30 yards long and say 15 yards wide. Not far away, on the Nicosia Road is the British Military Cemetery. The earliest graves include those of Guardsmen who died of enteric after being evacuated to Cyprus from Field Marshal Lord Wolseley's Gordon Relief Expedition in the Sudan. Many of the headstones were in poor condition, and we asked the Commonwealth War Graves Commission to restore them.

As GOC Near East Land Forces, I was responsible for the logistic support of UNFICYP and saw a great deal of that multi-national force. As part of our supporting task our RAOC Bakery in Dhekelia baked over forty different sorts of bread for our UN comrades-in-arms!

The British Armed Forces are adept at winning the 'Hearts and Minds' of the inhabitants of whatever country in which they serve. Cyprus was no exception. I had a particularly good Commander Royal Engineers in Lieutenant Colonel 'Miff' Tuck. Miff had all sorts of projects going to help the local Greek-Cypriots, ranging from building piers for their fishing boats, to making concrete tanks in which to dip their sheep. One of his projects was the Kambos Track high in the Troodos Mountains. This was a project in which our sappers of Major John Farmborough's 62 Squadron operated in co-operation with Cyprus Forestry Commission workers in clearing a track through the Kambos Forest to save millions of pounds worth of valuable timber before it could be attacked by beetles and fungus. The locals were delighted with the track and in Kambos village itself where our team lived, our sappers told me that they used to be dragged into the cafes each evening and plied with coffee, wine or beer.

The Battle for the 'Hearts and Minds' of the Greek Cypriots, as taught by Field Marshal Sir Gerald Templer in Malaya and by General Sir Walter Walker in Borneo, was being won in Cyprus. However, we were not out of the wood yet. A few days later, on 26 June, I discovered this while waiting on the Flagstaff House helipad for my Sioux helicopter piloted by Major Peter Child to arrive. The aircraft arrived late and instead of Peter, it was flown by his co-pilot, Captain Tony Hayhurst. Peter Child had been shot at and wounded as he flew over a Greek National Guard (GNG) defensive position which had just been constructed on high ground astride the Nicosia to Limassol Road not far from the place called Halfway House. The 'chopper' had been flying at a height of about 600 feet and after being hit it landed immediately beside the GNG position. A GNG officer and about twenty men came out and offered medical attention to Peter Child who had been hit in the leg and was bleeding badly. However Tony Hayhurst, sensibly wanted to get him to the Princess Margaret's Royal Air Force Hospital, Akrotiri, for the best medical attention, so he refused their aid, took off and flew Peter to the hospital. The Greek National Guard denied that anyone had shot at the aircraft. I then took off and, having a suspicious nature, I looked for a bullet hole. Sure enough, I found it in the lower part of the perspex bubble in the Sioux. Having been at the receiving end of SKS rounds in Dhofar I recognised it as such and registered a strong protest with HQ Greek National Guard who were equipped with that weapon, pointing out how easily Peter Child could have been killed. Tony Hayhurst could also have died in the probable crash. Later we received a full apology and an admission that an ill-disciplined soldier had fired at the helicopter.

The time now came when the 2nd Battalion of my Regiment was to leave Cyprus, and on 30 June, at 6.30am the Band, Bugles and Pipes, dressed in No.3 Dress and looking extremely smart marched into the grounds of Flagstaff House. The pipes played 'Going Home' and the Band played 'Auf Wiedersehen' after which WOI Gilpin, the Bandmaster, came up, saluted and said, 'Just came to say Cheerio, Sir.' I thanked him and wished them all good luck. Off they marched to the tune of 'Killaloo' with its Ranger yell and I looked sadly after them as they disappeared from my view. They had done so well in Cyprus and I was proud of them. When they arrived on the island they had handed me a Royal Irish Rangers' Regimental flag to fly alongside my Near East Land Forces' flag from the flagpole in the grounds of Flagstaff House.

We were still not free from incidents and on 20 July 1975 some yobbo of a Greek-Cypriot youth fired four shots over the heads of Major Patrick Wood, MBE, and his family while they were on Pissouri Beach. Another clot, apparently a Turkish-Cypriot fighter, fired his rifle in the little village of Pyla and one round found its way into the roof of a married quarter in Richmond Village, Dhekelia, fortunately injuring no one.

I called on the Turkish Army commander towards the end of July and we agreed the importance of mutual avoidance of incidents. I found him a disappointment as I had been told that he had fought in the splendid Turkish Brigade in Korea. Instead, it appeared that he had never had operational experience until the recent Turkish invasion of Cyprus. Dressed in US Army-type fatigues he gave an impression of arrogance and his disparaging remarks about the fighting ability of the Greek and Greek-Cypriot soldiers did not endear him to me. I remember wishing I had not initially been so polite and friendly.

On 11 August I flew off for another visit to the Sultanate of Oman as I wanted to see how our people serving on Masirah Island were faring. I had brought David Emsley and Lance Corporal Williams who was one of my drivers with me to give them a break and a chance to see Masirah Island.

On arrival I was taken to the Royal Air Force Mess for a drink followed by dinner. After dinner Squadron Leader John Stirzaker drove us to the beach to see the turtles who were laying their eggs. Each of us was armed with a torch and, seated in a white Landrover, we hurtled along the wet, glistening beach. We came on a turtle who had just laid her eggs and was covering them over with sand before returning to the sea. Another turtle was digging a deep, narrow, round hole with her back flippers, reaching down with one, bringing it up semi-curled round a handful of sand. While one back leg was delving, the free one gave a flick, ridding itself of sand. Then the great turtle laid masses of soft-shelled eggs in the hole it had scooped out. We saw a hatch of tiny young turtles appear from a hole in the ground from which they struggled up and onto the gently sloping beach. We carried some of them down to the edge of the surf when apparently the feel of wet sea water, perhaps less warm than the proximity of their fellows in the hole in the sand, caused them to turn back to the dry sand.

We pushed them back into the sea. Someone had a large, unpleasant looking crab under which he had found two more baby turtles unharmed as yet. Meanwhile the crab had grabbed a torch that had been put down and held it in its solitary huge claw until relieved of its burden! We drove back along the very edge of the ocean which seethed forward in flat rushes often under the Landrover's wheels. To our right, the sea was discernible by three lines of white foam and a perpetual roar. Over it hung a slight mist and the warm, moist, humid air was redolent of the ocean's smell. We raced along the wet sand. The large, rounded shapes of turtles appeared in our headlights as they dragged themselves up out of the water to lay their eggs or, returning, entered the wavelets. The smaller forms of the sand crabs, white in the headlights' glare, skittered sideways as they tried to avoid our crunching tyres whilst the occasional hermit crab dragged his heavy shell along, dropping motionless at any movement it saw.

I wondered how many of the baby turtles would survive the menacing line of crabs, and when daylight came, escape the attacks of the seagulls as well as the hungry predators within the ocean itself in order to return later as adults to lay their own eggs on Masirah's beaches.

During the next two days I visited all our people at RAF Masirah and found everyone in great heart. Afterwards Group Captain Keith Hepburn, the Station Commander, drove me to see the monument erected in memory of the ten crew members of the SS *Ennerdale* who were massacred by the locals when they were shipwrecked on the point in 1904. As a result of his sorrow and anger at this murderous act the then Sultan decreed that no islander should leave Masirah for ten decades, nor might anyone build, nor own, a permanent dwelling. The present Sultan rescinded this decree in 1971 and a permanent mosque, a hospital and a desalination unit were under construction. At that time the village of Ras Hilf was still almost entirely composed of squalid huts made from beaten-flat oil drums and corrugated iron, but it has now been thoroughly modernised.

We flew back by RAF Hercules over the Red Sea, Egypt – along the Nile – and then, having skirted Sinai and Israel, landed smoothly at night at Akrotiri in a rectangle of landing lights.

A couple of days later the first of a number of convoys of Turkish refugees from Paphos passed through the Western Sovereign Base Area and I watched their progress past Episkopi. The convoy travelled at about 35 mph, headed by a white Sovereign Base Area Police car with flashing blue lights, followed by a white UNFICYP police car, and then by a blue Cyprus Police Landrover. After these vehicles came several white UN Landrovers and then a procession of coaches drive by Turkish Cypriots each with a UN soldier seated beside him, bearing impassive or melancholy looking Turkish-Cypriots, each vehicle piled high with beds and bedding, bundles and furniture. The procession was completed by Turkish-Cypriots driving their own cars with, in the rear, a UN medical detachment and a UN recovery vehicle (both British).

Overhead in a white-painted UN helicopter flew the UN Deputy Chief of Staff, Peter Chiswell. How sad it was to see these people who, until the interference of Greece and, later, of Turkey, had lived happily with their Greek-Cypriot fellow countrymen and were now displaced as a result of the acts of those two countries, and Great Britain's inaction.

On 29 August we had news of a bomb placed in a garage next to Alexander Barracks, Dhekelia. Major Ken Norsworthy our redoubtable RAOC bomb disposal expert made it harmless and destroyed it. Ken did excellent work throughout my time in Near East Land Forces and it was pleasing to see his gallant and dedicated efforts recognised by a well-earned MBE.

General Prem Chand used to hold periodic parades on the airfield at Nicosia to present United Nations Peace Keeping Medals. I remember one excellent parade, commanded by the CO 1st Royal Tank Regiment, Lieutenant Colonel Tony Walker. It was beautifully organised, on a cool evening and the sun went down like a red ball in a cloudless sky, silhouetting the reeds and long grass beyond the far end of the airfield. 1st Royal Tanks, in white-painted Scout cars and 1st Duke of Wellington's Regiment, including their Band, were extremely smart. Prem made a charming speech and the medals were handed out to everyone on parade.

One of the sad things in Cyprus was seeing British casualties from Dhofar when they were evacuated to the RAF Hospital at Akrotiri. One man whose courage in adversity shone like the sunrise was WOII Fleming, a Liverpuddlian in the Special Air Service Regiment who, while serving his fifth tour in Dhofar, was shot near Defaa and paralysed from the waist down. His brave little wife had been flown out to be with him, such a grand Scots girls from Selkirk. They had three children and life must have looked uncertain to the Flemings. However, he went off to Stoke Mandeville Hospital and I know he will have made a success of life. Just meeting WOII Fleming and his wife was an inspiration.

By now it was May 1975, and we British had completely re-established cordial links with the Greek-Cypriots and we entertained and were asked out by many of them. We got little opportunity to meet Turkish-Cypriots socially but were fond of the Muftizades who lived nearby. Faik Muftizade, whom I had first met during the EOKA Campaign, had had a distinguished career in the Colonial Service, having been awarded the OBE and later, in what were obviously harrowing and difficult circumstances for him after the Turkish invasion of Cyprus, his bravery won him the Queen's Gallantry Medal.

In January 1976 I paid my farewell visit as GOC Near East Land Forces to Oman. Having been flown in a Royal Air Force VC10 to Masirah accompanied by my ADC, Captain Ewing Grimshaw, Royal Irish Rangers, we were met by the new Station Commander, Group Captain Jim Bayard, and Squadron Leader George Aylitt, OC No. 1 Squadron, Sultan of Oman's Air Force. George informed me that he was flying me to Salalah in a Strikemaster jet ground attack aircraft and gave me just enough time to change into a flying suit. Ewing was to follow with our kit in a SOAF Defender. We flew through the night and George did a beat-up of Salalah to announce our arrival.

Shirley and John Akehurst kindly had me to stay. I spent the next two days in Dhofar visiting those non-seconded British officers and other ranks for whom I had responsibility, and the Headquarters and units of Dhofar Brigade and SOAF. I saw an armoury of captured enemy weapons, Soviet, of course. I visited Rakhyut Village by Iroquois helicopter and saw below me Baluch soldiers of the Southern Regiment bathing in the sea close to the shore while, about thirty yards out to sea, I counted over sixty sharks swimming!

I went on to another coastal village, Dalkhut, where I chatted to a four-man SAS Training Team under a Fijian Sergeant and then on to Muscat Regiment's position at Sarfait, which then consisted of a pillbox made of sandbags, perched on the side of a sheer cliff 600 feet high. I had last been there with Mike Harvey and Northern Frontier Regiment in 1969. On this occasion we had three 'incomers' fired by heavy artillery from the People's Republic of South Yemen across the border, the shells exploding with loud bangs just below us. I was interested to see that SAF were still using donkeys in that rugged terrain and spoke to several of the handlers who had served with me in Dhofar earlier on. A brigade of Iranians was in Dhofar and a sizeable component of their air force was at Thumrait when I called in there.

In Northern Oman I stayed with Ken Perkins, who was now CSAF, and paid my farewell visits to his headquarters, to H.H. Saiyyid Faher at the Ministry of Defence, to HQ North Oman Brigade and to various battalions. Everyone I met was kindness itself and I will always have the happiest memories of Oman and the Omani people.

I had a grand team in Cyprus of all ranks and had loved my time with them. Although I had lost David Woodford and John Groom, both of whom became Major Generals, I had acquired two splendid supporters in John Pownall, late 16th/5th Lancers and Thomas McMicking, Black Watch. That most loyal of men, Godfrey Curl, had taken over from Brigadier Jim Holden as Commander of the Eastern Sovereign Base Area. However, thanks to the Wilson Government's Defence cuts the RAF C-in-C's job was downgraded to 2-star, and the GOC's to 1-star. This meant I unexpectedly had to retire early, and my post was filled by John Acland, a Scots Guardsman who was later to be knighted as a major general for his distinguished work as Commander of the Cease Fire Monitoring Force in the transition of Rhodesia to Zimbabwe.

The Army had been my life for thirty-seven years. I had never wished to be anything but a soldier and I hated the prospect of leaving it and its comradeship; the splendid men and women of all ranks of its regiments and corps, together with the excitement and the immense satisfaction of doing the thing you liked best in the world. It was sad also to leave Cyprus and the men and women of my command there. Sergeant Diana Driscoll, my invaluable and delightful Personal Assistant, had touched me so much by refusing the opportunity of going home when her overseas tour was up to join her fiancé and get married. Instead she informed my ADC 'I'll stay till the General goes.' Bless you for that Diana! We had a number of kind farewells throughout Cyprus and on our last night Patricia and I took my senior officers and their wives to Theo's at Paphos for a last farewell party.

It was terribly sad saying goodbye to our staff at Flagstaff House and then we were on our way for the last time, to the airfield at Royal Air Force

Akrotiri. As it was Wednesday, a sports afternoon, I had given an order that no one would come to see us off as we just wanted to slip away. Ewing Grimshaw, like the good ADC he was, had tried to persuade me to wear a suit, but I wanted to be comfortable and despite his and Patricia's pleas I wore a sports jacket and cord trousers. As we drove off I found he had put my hat in the car, and I said, 'Ewing, you know I hate hats!' All was revealed when we reached Akrotiri, and then I wished I'd listened to advice!

Ewing had been sworn to secrecy so could not tell me that Michael Aris, once my GS02 Intelligence in Oman and now commanding his battalion 'The Pompadours' in Cyprus, had mounted a Guard of Honour on the airfield complete with the Regimental Colour, Regimental Band and Corps of Drums. Feeling grossly under-dressed but very moved, I was received with a General Salute, inspected the smart Guard and turned towards the aircraft. There, in spite of my orders, stood my staff! I found it very difficult indeed to say anything as I shook the hands of these people of whom I had become so fond.

A smiling man in Royal Air Force uniform stepped out from behind them, 'So you thought you'd slip away without giving us the chance to say goodbye, Corran!' said my Commander-in-Chief, Air Chief Marshal Sir John Aiken! On entering the VC10 I was cheered to see the smiling face of Diana Driscoll, looking up at us from her seat directly behind ours. We were just about to sit down where there were three seats side by side, when a Royal Air Force crew member came up and said apologetically, 'We tried to keep all the seats clear, Sir, but that officer there refused to move, and said that you would want him with you.'

A huge, dark, craggy, good-looking young Royal Marine Commando captain stood up, smiling. 'He is quite right,' I said, 'we do want him with us.' Adrian Wray who had won his Sultan's Bravery Medal on an operation with me in Dhofar, had become a close friend and, knowing how I would be feeling at this particular time, had engineered it to sit with us on our homeward flight. Patricia told me afterwards that Adrian and Ewing were determined not to let us think about leaving and they kept up a flow of non-stop amusing conversation until we had landed at Royal Air Force Brize Norton. I will always remember Adrian's and Ewing's kind thoughtfulness. And so my career in the Regular Army came to an end. I would not change one moment of it.

I believe there will always be excitement and challenge ahead for our Armed Forces and that they will meet whatever is in store, cheerfully and successfully. But whatever Government is in power must always ensure that the Defence Services are sufficiently strong and given the best possible equipment, training facilities and conditions of service, and never neglect the defence of our country. Freedom, of all things, is worth paying for, and the peerless men and women of our Armed Forces deserve only the best. As I write, our Armed Forces, especially the Guards and Infantry in the Army, have been, in my opinion, far too savagely slashed. I pray that in the light of the inflammatory situation in Europe, the Middle East and Africa, wiser counsels may yet prevail.

INDEX OF NAMES

A

Andersen, Maj. Gen. Hans, OBE
Anderson, Brig. David, CBE
Anderson, Gen. Sir John, GBE, KCB, DSO
Anderson, Lt. Col. Richard
Angus, Flt. Lt. D.D.
Anwar, Mess Steward
Archdale, Lt. Micky
Aris, Brig. MA
Arengo-Jones, Brig. ARA, OBE
Armitage, Flt. Lt. John
Arnold, Brig. George, MBE
Ashraf, Maj. Mohammed
Ashruf, Capt. Habeeb
Aslam Khattak, Dr. KM
Aspden, Maj. Jack
Aucutt, Maj. Bill
Auchinleck, FM Sir Claude, GCB, GCIE, CSI, DSO, OBE
Awad, Bearer, BEM
Aylitt, Sqn. Ldr George
Aziz-ur-Rehman, Maj. MBE, OBI, Sardar Bahadur

B

Bader, Gp Capt. Sir Douglas, CBE, DSO*, DFC*
Bailey, Mr. Eddie
Baily, Lt. Col. Dan
Ballantrae, Brigadier Lord, GCMG, GCVO, DSO, OBE
Bamford, Brig. Geoffrey, DSO
Barker-Schofield, Maj. "Spike"
Barnes, Lt. Col. Brian
Barnes, Lt. Bob, RNR
Barrow, Col.
Bashir, Bearer
Bassett-Wilson, Capt. Paul, MC*
Battersby, Mr
Baudains, Maj. Billy, MM
Baxter, Brig. Harry, OBE, GM
Baynham, Brig, Derek, OBE, GM
Baynham, Maj. Derek
Beale, Lt. Col. KS, MC
Beattie, Capt. SH, VC, RN

Brooke, Maj. Gen. Frank, CB, CBE, DSO
Brooke, Brig. Oliver, CBE, DSO
Brookeborough, Viscount, KG, CBE, MC
Brooks, Col. WE, MC*
Brooks, Mrs Elizabeth
Brown, Lt. Col. Bob, MBE
Brown, Judge, James, TD, QC
Brown, Capt. MG
Brown, Lt. Col. RVC
Brown, Maj. "Topper"
Brown, Cpl.
Browne, Brig. HWL, OBE
Bruce, Maj. Hugh, RM
Bruce, Flt. Lt. Dominic, MC, DFM
Bruford-Davies, Maj. ER
Buchanan-Dunlop, Brig. AI, CBE, DSO
Burke, Brig. W. DSO
Burn, Capt. Michael, MC
Burney, Lt. Christopher
Burtonshaw, Lt. Bertie
Butler, Gen. Sir Mervyn, KCB, CBE, DSO, MC
Butler, Sgt. RH, MM
Butt, Maj. Charles
Byrne, Maj. SA, MBE

C

Cairns, Col. Tom, DSO
Cairns, Maj. Willie, MBE
Callaghan, Lord, of Cardiff, KG, PC
Callaway, Cpl. T. "Cab"
Cameron, Maj. Nicol
Campbell of Alloway, Lord QC
Campbell, Capt. Alexander, CIE, DSO, RIM
Campbell, Brig. AP, OBE
Campbell, Lt. Col. Arthur, MC
Campbell, Mrs Ellinore
Campbell, Col. MJA, OBE, MC
Campbell, Michael
Cantopher, Col. JK, OBE, GM, TD
Carbery, L. Cpl.

Cooke, Lt. Col. David
Cooke-Collis, Lt. Gen. Sir James, KBE, CB, CMG, DSO
Cooley, Rfn
Cooper, Sir Ernest
Cooper, Lt. Col. John, MBE, DCM
Cooper, John, CMG
Cooper, Mrs Jan
Cooper-Key, Maj. Caryll
Copland, Maj. W. DSO
Corran, Miss Maud (Mrs Richard Purdon)
Corbett, Maj. Gen. Robert, CB
Cortis, C. Sgt. Bruce
Cosgrave, Sgt, Palestine Police
Courtown, Earl of, OBE, TD
Cowley, Lt. Col. VLS, DSO, MC
Cowley, Mrs "Doss"
Cox, Maj. Gen. WR, CB, DSO
Cracknell, Maj. Martin
Craddock, Lt. Gen. Sir Richard, KBE, CB, DSO
Craddock, Lady
Craig, Canon
Crawford, David CMG
Crawford, Brig. Sir Douglas, CB, DSO, TD
Crawford, Maj. Gen. Patrick, GM, QHP
Crawford, Mrs Nancy
Creasey, Gen. Sir Timothy, KCB, CBE
Creighton-Williamson, Lt. Col. Donald
Crennell, Superintendent Bill
Crocker, Gen. Sir John, GCB, KBE, DSO
Crookenden, Lt. Gen. Sir Napier, KCB, DSO, OBE, DL
Crookshank, Lt. Col. RFA
Crookshank, Mrs Babs
Crompton, Lt. Col. John
Cross, Col. John, OBE
Crowther, Capt, W.
Cruse, W01, ACC
Cubiss, Brig. Malcolm, CBE, MC
Cummins, Lt. Col. ML
Cunningham, Lt. Col. Freddie OBE
Curl, Brig. GJ, CBE
Curl, Mrs Valerie
Curtis, Cdr. Dunstan, DSO, RNVR

D

Deverell, Maj. Gen. Jack, OBE
Diaz, "The Poisoner"
Dockerill, Sgt. AH, DCM
Dolphin-Rowland, Capt. Jim
Donaldson, Flt. Lt. Don
Donnelly, Maj. DH
Dougan, Sgt.
Douglas-Withers, Maj. Gen, John CBE, MC
Downey, Sgt.
Downey, L/Cpl.
Downward, Maj. Gen. PA, CB, DSO, DFC
Dowse, Maj. PA, MBE
Dowse, Mrs Margaret
Doyle, Lt. Col. Paddy
Driscoll, Sgt. Diana, (Mrs Murtagh)
Drummond, Brig. John, CB, DSO
Du Boulay, Lt. Col. MHH, MC
Dumas, Maj. Hugh
Dunbar, Maj. Gen. CW, CB, CBE
Dunbar, Mrs Jean
Dundas, Field Marshal Sir David, KB
Dundas, Admiral, Sir James, GCB
Dundas, Mrs Ethel
Dundas, Kenneth
Dundas, Miss Mary
Dundas Petrie, CH
Dunseath, Maj. DR, MC
Dunseath, Col. Patrick
Durrant, Sgt. Tom, VC
Dutton, Maj. Gen. Brian, CBE
Dyball, Maj. Gen. CBE, MC, TD

E

Eaglestone, Rfn
Eastwood, Lt. Gen. Sir Ralph, KCB, DSO, MC
Eckersley, Rfn. Bill
Edward-Collins, Lieut. Col. J.R.
Edwards, Asst. Commr. of Police, Roger, MBE, QPM, CPM
Edwardes, Maj. Dick

F

Freeborn, Supt. Paddy, RUC
Friend, Mrs Helen
Friend, Paul
Frost, Maj. Gen. John, CB, DSO, MC
Fullaerton, Flt. Lt. B.M.
Fuller, Capt. ABI
Fynn, Lt. Col. FW, MC

G

Gabriel, Capt. RC, RE
Gage, Capt. R.
Gains, Sgt. Larry
Gallagher, Maj. Brian
Gallwey, Maj. Denis
Gamblin, Flt. Lt. RW
Gardiner, Lt. Col. Colin
Garland, Maj. Al
Garrett, Lt. Dicky
Gavin, Maj. Gen. JM, CB, CBE
Gerrard, Capt. J.J. BEM
Ghalib
Gibbs, Field Marshal Sir Roland, GCB, CBE, DSO, MC, HML
Gibbs, Lady
Gibbs, Col. Donald, CBE, TD
Gilbert, Maj. Gen. Glyn, CB, MC
Gillett, Wing Commander Peter, OBE
Gilliatt, Lt. Col. Sir Martin, GCVO, MBE, DL
Gilsenan, L/Cpl
Gilpin, Bandmaster
Giraud, General
Glennie, Brig. Jack, CBE, DSO
Going, Maj. Gerald
Goldfinch, Flt. Lt. Bill
Good, Brig. IH, DSO
Goodfellow, Flt. Lt. W.
Goodwin, Lt. Col. Jock
Gordon, Lt. Col. ACG
Gordon, Maj. Gen. DS, CB, CBE, DSO
Gordon, Donald MacD, CMG
Gordon, Mrs Molly

H

Harrington, Lt. Col. W
Harknett, Sgt
Harvey, Brig. Mike, CBE, MC
Harvey, Capt. Mike, RN
Harverson, Maj. Tony
Haveron, L/Cpl
Hawley, Sgt
Heelis, Col. Brian, OBE
Henry, Rfn. Hugh
Henry, Maj. Michael
Henry, CSM "Sam", MM
Henry, Miss Vera
Hepburn, Gp. Capt. Keith, OBE
Hepworth, Brig. C.F.
Herbert, Gen. Sir Otway, KCB, DSO
Herbert, Maj. Tim
Hibbert-Foy, Maj. Patrick
Higson, Col. Alex, RM
Hill, Maj. AE
Hill, Maj. Jim, MBE
Hodges, Cpl.
Holdaway, Major CRS
Hollis, Maj. Frank
Holloway, Stanley
Holman, Maj. Tony
Holworthy, Col. Richard
Hood, Col. WC
Hopetoun, Capt. The Earl of, MC (See Marquis of Linlithgow)
Hopper, Maj. R
House, Lt. Gen. Sir David, GCB, KCVO, CBE, MC
Houston, Maj. Gen. David, CBE, JP
How, Maj. Dick, MBE, MC
Howard, Brig. Harry
Hoyle, Cpl. Bob
Huddleston, Rfn.
Hughes, Mrs Brenda
Hughes, Lt. Colin
Hughes, Francis, OBE
Hughes, Capt. Norman
Hulme, Squu. Ldr. P.S.
Humaid, CSM
Hunt, Gen. Sir Peter, GCB, DSO, OBE

Kane, Major Mike
Keating, Cpl.
Keats, Lt. Jack, DSC*, RNVR
Kedward, Rev. Ned
Kelly, Lt. Tony
Kelly, Flt. Lt. Mike
Kelly, CSM
Kendrew, Maj. Gen. Sir Douglas, KCVO, CB, CBE, DSO**
Kennedy, President John F
Kennedy, RSM "Scrape"
Kenny, CSM, BEM
Kerans, Cdr. DSO, RN
Khalfan, Lt
Kines, Cpl W.
King, "Kitchener"
King, Sgt
King, Sqn. Ldr. Pat
Kinsella-Bevan, Col. R.D.
Kitchener of Khartoum, Field Marshal Earl, KG, KP, GCB, OM, GCSI,
    GCMG, GCIE
Kitson, Gen. Sir Frank, GCB, CBE, MC
Knox, Brig. FYC, DSO*
Knox, Lt. Col. RJ
Kolakides, Mrs Aloi
Kolakides, Fotis
Kostas
Kramer, Sir D.

L

Laidlaw, RSM, DCM
Laird, Maj. Fred
Laister, Col. Tom, OBE, TD
Lamb, Col. TBL, OBE
Lancaster, Colonel, Julian
Landon, Brig. JTW, KCVO
Langford, Lt. Col. Patrick
Lawrence, Maj. "Daddy"
Lawton, Sir Frederick, PC, QC
Lawton, Capt. "LULU"
Lee, Maj. Jeremy, RM

Mac/Mc

MacDonald, Flt. Lt. "Mac"
McDowell, Maj. TB
MacEwan, Maj. Ivor
MacFrederick. Lt. Col. JJ
McGonigal, Maj. Sir Ambrose, MC
McGonigal, Lt. Eoin
McGonigal, Maj. Bob
McGregor, RSM. W.
McGregor, Mrs
McGuinness, Maj. Mike
McGuinness, Rfn.
McHugh, Cpl.
McIlhagga, Mrs
MacIntyre, Brig. AD, MBE
MacKenzie, Capt. George
McLean, Lt. Col (now Father Colin) C.
McLeod, Lt. Col. Bentley
MacMaster, "Footie"
MacMaster, Mrs Vera
MacMicking, Brig. Thomas

M

Mackain-Bremner, Col. Fergus, OBE
Mackworth-Praed, Capt.
Madocks, Col. R.G. CBE, TD, DL
Magee, Cpl.
Magee, Rfn.
Mahood, Jack
Majury, Maj. Gen. JHS, CB, MBE
Makarios, Archbishop
Mallett, Lt. Col. Len
Mangin, Maj. Paul
Mans, Maj. Gen, RSN, CBE
Margerison, Cpl
Marhoun, RSM
Marios
Martin, Mrs Doreen
Martin, Vice Admiral Sir John, KCB, DSC
Martin, Cdr., RP, DSC
Martin-Bird, Col. Sir Richard, CBE, TD, DL

Muftizade, Faik, OBE, QGM
Muir, Maj. Gordon, MBE
Mulholland, Lt. Michael
Muller, Maj.
Müller, Maj.
Mulligan, Maj. JWH
Munden, Maj. Herbert
Murphy, Major JC
Murphy, Canon JGMW, LVO
Murray, Lt. Col. Mark, RM
Murtagh, Mrs D (Diana Driscoll)
Myatt, Maj. Frederick, MC
Myers, Capt. Peter

N

Nahas Pasha
Napier, Maj. Gen. LHS, CB, OBE, MC, DL
Napier, Brig. Jack, CBE
Napier, Mrs Muriel
"Nark" The
Nason, Maj. Jonathan
Neave, Lt. Col. Airey, DSO, OBE, MC
Neely, Brig. K. MBE
Neill, Col. DF, OBE, MC
Neill, The Very Rev. Ivan, CB, OBE
Neill, Mrs Pat
Nelson, Admiral Viscount, KB, Duke of Brontë
Newborough, Lord, DSC, ERD (See Micky Wynn, DSC)
Newlove, George
Newman, Col. AC., VC, TD
Newport, Capt. GPG
Niaz Ahmed Khan, Capt.
Nicholson, Brig. Claude
Niven, David
Nixon, Maj. Sir Christopher, Bt., MC
Nixon, Maj. CDHJ., MC
Nixon Rfn.
Noor Mohammed, bearer
Norsworthy, Maj. Ken., MBE
Northcott, Rev. John, RAChD.

O

Obeid, RSM
O'Cahan
Oldman, Col. Sir Hugh, KBE, MC
Olive, Mr
Oliver, Lt. Gen. Sir William, GBE, KCB, KCMG
Olivier, Lord
Olver, Sir Stephen, KBE, CMG
Olver, Lady
O'Leary, Col. Denis., OBE, MC
Omar, Headman
Omar, Jundee
Orpheus
Osman, Bearer
O'Sullivan, Gen. Gerry, DSM

P

Packard, Lt. Gen. Sir Douglas, KCB, CBE, DSO
Paddy, Lt. Col. D
Painter, Brig. JLA
Paley, Brig. John, CBE
Paley, Maj. Gen. Sir Victor, KCB, DSO, OBE
Parker, Flt. Lt. Vincent ("Bush")
Parr, Stanley, CBE, QPM
Parsons, Maj. Jimmy
Parsons, Lt. Col. R.
Passaportis, Maj. Gen. Theo
Pattan, Rais
Patterson, RSM Alec
Patterson, Maj. Gen. AGW., CB, DSO, MC
Pearson, Maj. Gen. Sandy, CB, DSO, MC
Peele, Maj. Mike, MC
Penn, Lt. Col. Sir Eric, GCVO, OBE, MC
Pennington, Lt. Harry
Pepple, King
Perkins, Maj. Gen. Ken., CB, MBE, DFC
Peters, Capt Dick
Petrie, CH Dundas (see Dundas Petrie)
Petrie, Maj. JF
Petrie, Patricia (Mrs Patricia Purdon)

Pickard, Wing Cdr, DSO, OBE, MC
Pinckney, Capt. Philip
Philip, HRH Prince, Duke of Edinburgh, KG, KT, OM, GBE, PC
Pike, Brig. Christopher, DSO, OBE
Pike, Maj. Gen. Hew, CB., DSO, MBE
Pike, Lt. Gen. Sir William, KCB, CBE, DSO
Ponsonby, Maj. Gen. Sir John, KCB, CMG, DSO
Pope, Lance, CMG, CVO, OBE
Pope, Brig. Philip,DSO, MC
Porter, Mrs
Powell, Maj. "Spike" MBE
Pownall, Brig. John, OBE
Prem Chand, Gen. Dewan, PVSM
Preston, Capt. AE
Price, Brig. Rollo, CBE, DSO
Priest, Maj. Tim
Prince, Maj. WTT
Pritchard, Capt. Bill, (WH)., MC
Prittie, Lt. The Hon Terence
Proctor, Lt. Col. John
Profumo, Brig. John, CBE
Püpke, Hauptmann
Purdon, Angela (Mme Zerrouck)
Purdon, Mrs Angela (Mrs TCRB Purdon)
Purdon, Charlie
Purdon, Capt. Denis
Purdon, Col. Sir Edward
Purdon, Dr. Henry
Purdon, Mrs Myrtle
Purdon, Col. Sir Nicholas
Purdon, Mrs Patricia
Purdon, Patrick HB
Purdon, R Patrick de Lacherois
Purdon, Lt. Col. TCRB., MBE
Purdon, Maj. Gen. W Brooke, DSO, OBE, MC
Purdon, Dr. Richard
Purdon, Flt. Lt. Richard, RCAF
Purdon, RHF

Q

Qabus Bin Taimur Al Said, His Majesty The Sultan of Oman

R

Ryan, Lt. Niall
Ryder, Capt. RED., VC., RN

S

Said Bin Taimur Al Said, His Highness Sultan
Said, Ali, Bearer
Said, Sgt
Said Bin Gheer
Said, Salim, Col.
Saint, Paul
Saki Raja, Lt. Col.
Saltonstall, Lt. Col. John, OBE
Sami, Bearer
Sanders, Lt. Col. Hugh
Sanderson, Lt. Col. LGS., OBE, MC*
Sanderson, Mrs Joyce
Savage, AB., WA, VC
Scott, Family, Crumlin
Scott, S/Sgt. BEM
Scott, Mrs
Scott, Brig. John, OBE
Scott, Mrs Jan
Scott, JM
Scott, Maj. Gen., TPD., CB, CBE, DSO
Semple, Brig. Fergie, OBE, MC
Semple, Mrs Olivia
Seton-Browne, Maj. Carl
Severn, Maj. David
Sexton, Sgt
Shaharim, Maj.
Shannon, JW
Shannon, Mrs Felicité
Shannon, Mrs Gwendoline
Sharif, Mohammed, Havildar
Sharpe, Brig. AK., OBE
Shaw, Lt. Hamish
Shaw, Maj. John, DSO, MC
Shebbeare, John
Shelley, Maj. Andrew
Sherman, Rfn

Stockwell, Gen. Sir Hugh, GCB, KBE, DSO*
Storey, L/Cpl
Stopford, Col. Viscount, OBE, TD, (See Courtown, Earl of)
Stone, Mrs Georgina
Storrs, Sir Ronald, KCMG, CBE
Sturgeon, Col. WES, OBE
Sturgeon, Mrs Milly
Stutchbury, Lt. John
Stuttard, Capt. Darrell
Suleiman, Jundee
Suleiman, Signaller
Suleiman Bin Himyaar
Swayne, Sir Ronald, MC
Sweeney, Col. "Tod", OBE, MC
Swinburn, Maj. Gen. Hugh, CB, OBE, MC
Swinburne, Lt. Col "Chatty"
Swiney, Col. David
Sykes, Capt.

T

Taggart, Brig. AB, MC
Taggart, Capt. Nigel
Tailyour, Gen. Sir Norman, KCB, DSO
Tailyour, Col. Ewan, Southby, OBE, RM
Talib
Taylor, Col. Hugh
Taylor, Major Maurice
Taylor Mrs Ruth
Templer, Field Marshal Sir Gerald, KG, GCB, GCMG, KBE, DSO
Terrey, Maj. FAL ("Badger")
Terrey, Mrs Alma
Theo. (Platres)
Thom, Flt. Lt. Don
Thomas, Gen. Sir Noel, GCB, DSO, MC
Thomas, Lady
Thompson, Brig. Gen. Harry
Thompson, Capt. David
Thompson, Major Robert
Thompson, Capt. TD, RM
Thorne, S.Sgt.

U

V

W

Wadsworth, Capt. Brian
Walker, Gen. Sir Anthony, KCB
Walker, Lady (Beryl)
Walker, Lt. Stewart
Walker, Gen. Sir Walter, KCB, CBE, DSO**
Wallerstein, Col. A.
Wall, Rev. Clifford
Wall, Denys
Wall, Mrs Molly
Wall, Richard, OBE
Walsh, Maj. Gen. Michael, CB, DSO
Walsh, Mrs Angela
Walter, Lt. Col. Peter, MBE, MC
Walton, Col. Peter
Ward, Miss, FE (Mrs W Coates)
Ward, Col. James, CB, VRD
Wardle, Flt. Lt. HD "Hank", MC
Warner, Maj. Bob
Warton, Flt. Lt. K.F.
Watchman, my dog
Waterfield, Brig. Patrick, MBE
Waterfield, Mrs Madeleine
Waters, Maj. A.
Waters, Capt. Mary
Watkins, The Rt. Hon. Lord Justice Sir Tasker, VC, GBE, DL
Watton, JF
Watson, Dr WH, MC
Watts, Lt. Gen. Sir John, KBE, CB, MC
Webb, W. Cdr, Michael
Weir, Maj. Gen. Sir John
Weir, Maj. JFF, MBE
Wellington, Duke of KG, GCB (First Duke)
West, Gen. Sir Michael Alston-Roberts, GCB, DSO
Westing, Lt. Col. John
Wheeler, Capt. Jack
Wheeler, Lt. Gen. Sir Roger, KCB, CBE
Wheeler, Maj. Gen. TNS, CB, CBE
Wheldon, Maj. Sir Huw, MC
White, Mrs Olivia (Mrs David Thompson)

Y

Z

Zaid, Sheikh
Zerrouck, Mme Angela (Angela Purdon)
"Ziggi". Sqn. Ldr.

DECORATIONS AWARDED TO BRITISH OFFICERS SERVING IN THE SULTAN OF OMAN'S ARMED FORCES, APRIL 1967 – APRIL 1970,
including subsequent Awards and highest known rank

Aber, C. Flt. Lt., Commendation Medal

Affleck-Graves, HE Major, Commendation Medal

Anderson, RGH, Lieut. Col., Distinguished Service Medal

Angus, DD Flt. Lt., Bravery Medal

Barnes, BAS Lieut. Col. Distinguished Service Medal

Beale, KS, MC Lieut. Col. Distinguished Service Medal (Gallantry), Commendation Medal

Bennett, PBC Maj., Commendation Medal

Bentall-Warner, CW Maj., Distinguished Service Medal, Commendation Medal

Best, AG, TD., Lt. Col. Distinguished Service Medal

Brett, J. Flt. Lt. Commendation Medal

Bridges, AG, CBE, Group Capt. Distinguished Service Medal

Brocklehurst, AR, Lieut. Col. Distinguished Service Medal, Commendation Medal

Brook, PMR, MBE, Lieut. Col, Distinguished Service Medal (Twice)

Brown, RVC, Lieut. Col. Bravery Medal, Commendation Medal

Cameron, RN, Maj. Bravery Medal

Clarke, J. Lieut. Col. Distinguished Service Medal

Coates, PM, Capt. Commendation Medal

Cooper, JM, MBE, DCM, Lieut. Col. Commendation Medal

Dachtler, AH. Flt. Lt. Commendation Medal

Dawson, AR Maj. Commendation Medal

Denison, MG Brig. Order of Oman, Distinguished Service Medal, Commendation Medal

Edward Collins, JR Lieut. Col. Distinguished Service Medal, Commendation Medal

Fullarton, BM. Flt. Lt. Commendation Medal (Twice)

Fuller, ABI, Capt. Commendation Medal

Gamblin, RW, Flt. Lt. Commendation Medal

Gerrard, JJ, Maj. BEM, Distinguished Service Medal, Commendation Medal

Goodfellow, W, Flt. Lt., Commendation Medal

Gordon, ACG, Lt. Col., Distinguished Service Medal

Gordon-Smith, P. Maj. Bravery Medal, Distinguished Service Medal

Harvey, MG, Brig. CBE, MC, Order of Oman, Bravery Medal (Immediate), Distinguished Service Medal, Commendation Medal (Twice)

Hepworth, CF, Brig. Capt., Bravery Medal

Hill, JE, Maj. MBE, Distinguished Service Medal

Holdaway, CRS, Maj. Commendation Medal

Hulme, PS, Sqn. Ldr. Gallantry Medal (Immediate), Bravery Medal, Commendation Medal

Hynd, IM, Lieut. Col. Commendation Medal

John, RS, Col., Distinguished Service Medal, Commendation Medal

Jones, RLT, Lieut. Col. Distinguished Service Medal

Kane, RJ, Maj. Bravery Medal

Kelly, M. Flt. Lt. Bravery Medal

Kinsella Bevan, RD. Col., Commendation Medal (Twice)

Lancaster, JAS, Col. Distinguished Service Medal

Landon, GTW, KCVO, Brig., Order of Oman, Commendation Medal (Twice)

Lawrence, NA, Maj., Distinguished Service Medal

Lee, JRCB, Maj., Bravery Medal (Immediate)

Lewis, JC, Maj., Commendation Medal

McFrederick, JJ, Lt. Col. Distinguished Service Medal

MacKain Bremner, A.F. Col., OBE, Distinguished Service Medal (Gallantry) Commendation Medal,

McLean, CPB, Lieut. Col. Distinguished Service Medal, Commendation Medal

Mallett, LA, Lieut. Col. Commendation Medal

Mangin, PE, Maj. Distinguished Service Medal, Commendation Medal

Maxwell, CC, Brig., Order of Oman, Distinguished Service Medal

Milling, JC, Maj. Distinguished Service Medal

Mintowt-Czyz. Sqn. Ldr., Distinguished Service Medal

Moore, HJA, Col. OBE, Distinguished Service Medal

Murphy, JC, Maj. Commendation Medal

Murray, MF Lieut, Col. Commendation Medal
Nason, JH. Maj. Distinguished Service Medal, Commendation Medal
Parsons, SJ, Maj. Distinguished Service Medal, Commendation Medal
Peters, RWL Capt. Commendation Medal
Powell, NA, Maj. MBE, Distinguished Service Medal (Gallantry), Bravery
   Medal, Commendation Medal
Prince, WTT, Maj. Commendation Medal
Purdon, CWB, CBE, MC, CPM, Maj. Gen., Bravery Medal (Immediate),
   Distinguished Service Medal, Commendation Medal
Raven, P.G. Lieut. Col, Bravery Medal
Raybould, JTC, Capt. Bravery Medal, Commendation Medal
Sheridan, JJM, Lieut. Col. Distinguished Service Medal
Sheridan, JMG, Col., OBE, Commendation Medal
Shillinglaw, DC, Maj. Bravery Medal
Sloane, SF, Maj. Bravery Medal, Commendation Medal
Snow, WJ, Capt. Distinguished Service Medal
Southwood-Hayton, PD, Capt. Commendation Medal
Tailyour, SES, Col. OBE, Bravery Medal
Thompson, TD, Capt. Commendation Medal
Thwaites, PT, Brig., Bravery Medal, Distinguished Service Medal,
   Commendation Medal
Turnill, E, Lt. Col. OBE, Bravery Medal
Twisleton-Wykeham-Fiennes, OBE, Capt. Sir Ranulph, Bt., Bravery Medal
Vivian, JEG, Maj. MC and Bar., Commendation Medal
Vutirakis, EGC, Capt. Bravery Medal
Walton, PS, Col. Distinguished Service Medal, Commendation Medal
Warton, KF, Flt. Lt., Commendation Medal
Webb, MFD, Wing Cdr., Commendation Medal
Wilkinson, JN, Flt. Lt., Distinguished Service Medal, Commendation
   Medal
Wray, AED, Col., Bravery Medal

List of Arab names and post-nominal letters (in Oman)
for these decorations

Order of Oman-Wisam Oman	WO
Gallantry Medal-Wisam Shuja'at	W Sh
Bravery Medal-Wisam al Jura'at	WB
Distinguished Service Medal-Wisam Khidmat al Mumtaza	W KhM
Commendation Medal-Wisam at Tawseet	

BUCKINGHAM PALACE

4th February, 1964.

Dear Secretary of State

      The Queen has directed me to write
to you about the visit which the First Battalion,
the Royal Ulster Rifles, made to Australia last
year and on which a special report was made by
the British High Commissioner in Canberra.

      Her Majesty seldom has the opportunity
to commend individual Battalions of the Army in
peace time unless she visits them herself in
training or sees them on some ceremonial parade,
but Sir William Oliver has given such a good
account of their activities that she wishes to
make an exception, and she would be glad if you
would tell Lieutenant-Colonel Purdon for the
information of all ranks of the Battalion under
his command, how much pleased she has been to
learn of the success of their attachment to the
Australian Army and of the good opinions which
they earned during it and which are much to the
credit of their Regiment and of the Army.

Yours sincerely

Michael Adeane

The Right Honourable James Ramsden, M.P.

20th February, 1964

Dear Colonel,

Her Majesty The Queen has seen a despatch submitted by the British High Commissioner in Canberra about the visit of your Battalion to Australia in November and December last year. I have been asked by Her Majesty to tell you, for the information of all ranks of the Battalion under your command, how much pleased she has been to learn of the success of the attachment of your Battalion to the Australian Army and of the good opinions which it has earned during it, and which are much to the credit of your Regiment and of the Army.

May I add my congratulations and those of the Secretary of State for Commonwealth Relations for the excellent way in which you and your whole Battalion acquitted yourselves during this attachment.

Yours sincerely

James Ramsden

Lieutenant-Colonel C.W.B. Purdon, M.C.